First Edition

Great Gay & Lesbian Places to Live

"The Official Guide"

by
Lanie Dills & Lynn West

Lanie Dills—Memphis, Tennessee, Publisher

First Edition, June 1995

ISBN 0-916744-03-5

DEDICATION

To: Tim, Trey, Brandi, Batti, Brinkli, Nicci
and of course, Jim Bob
Our Children

Special Thanks To:
Kathy, Linda, Melody & Linda

Table of Contents

Table of Contents

Table of Contents

Table of Contents

Table of Contents

Table of Contents

INTRODUCTION

Over the years, my precious spouse and I, while walking in the park or out to dinner; would enviously observe straight couples holding hands or sitting close together or kissing. Our comment to each other would inevitably be, wouldn't it be great if we could do that. As time passed on, we became increasingly aware of just how limited and closeted our lives were. So, we were determined to move to a more open and "out" place. But where? The pursuit of answering that question is how this book came to be born. We felt that if we wanted to know what our living place options were, then many other people did as well. We found, through our research, that we did indeed have choices. In fact, we found that we have many, many choices all over the country; and that there were lovely places to live in freedom.

The vast majority of you live in communities that are more than happy to receive your tax dollars, but would rather not even acknowledge your existence. Make no mistake, with the republican sweep, homophobia is rampant in the land. Countless communities still discriminate against us. Gay bashings, murders and suicides are not a thing of the past, and the fear of being publicly outed still abounds. As gay and bisexual men and women you can continue to live in places where you find it necessary to hide your sexual orientation; and where people, if they knew of your true sexual orientation, would ostracize, harass, and discriminate against you. Or, you can choose to relocate to a place where your rights are protected and where your relationships can be nurtured and affirmed.

We believe that lesbians, gay,s and bisexuals look for all the same things in ideal places to live that everyone else does. In addition, we also long to live our lives "out" in the open without fear.

Our research has shown that there truly are "Green Acres" for gays, lesbians, and bisexuals in these United States. There are places to live where you can be free to live the life you only dream about. One thing is for sure, you will live your life somewhere so why not live where you can live without fear, where you can be your true self, where you can be comfortable, where you can enjoy the things you love to do, where you can drop the stifling straight pretense, and where you can concentrate your energies on living your life to the fullest.

This book is not meant to be all encompassing, rather it is intended to show you that you do indeed have choices when you begin your search for the ideal place to live. We have tried to include both the positive and negative aspects of each community. For example, Northampton, Mass. is an absolutely terrific place for Lesbians and Gays to live from every aspect except one. There is a shortage of jobs. You are advised not to move there unless you can independently support yourself or unless you can open a business needed by the community.

"Great Gay and Lesbian Places to Live" details 133 cities across the United States from a gay and lesbian perspective. From each state, we have profiled at least one city or town; however, from some of those states having gay rights protection, you will find several cities or towns profiled. We have interviewed gays, lesbians, and bisexuals who actually live in each town to learn what they think of their town; see section, "What the Locals Say." You will find information on lesbian and gay restaurants, bars, coffeehouses, support groups, political groups, social organizations, community centers, businesses, religious organizations, churches, AIDS projects, health care, best neighborhoods to live in, companies that prohibit discrimination based on sexual orientation, and gay publications. We have even included a contact phone number for each city or town so you can find out from a local gay organization what is actually happening in the community before you move.

Because crime and other demographic information is important when you are considering relocating, we have included that type of information as well. Now you will know before you move about the population size, growth, and make-up; per-capita income; climate; job growth; unemployment rate; educational opportunities; number of hospitals; and average cost of home (renting and owning). Crime statistics vary drastically from place to place. We've given you the number of total crimes for each area; but then we've broken it down into the various categories of violent and property crimes.

With this information you have the resource to help guide you to the most gay positive areas in the country.

Every attempt was made during our research to ensure that the information is correct. However, since some of the information came from talking to people who actually live in each   area; then some of the information is, of course, personal opinion. Be aware that there is a good deal of gay rights and anti-discrimination legislation in the works across the country so the gay rights information changes almost daily. Also, because of harassment and sometimes discontinued funding, the contact number is sometimes subject to change. The contact organization should still be operational though, so call information for the new number or contact the MCC churches or other listed organizations in the area. We did not try to include everything, but we did try to give somewhat of an overview of each area; enough so you could decide if it is an area you would like to pursue further. You should,4 in all cases, do a thorough investigation yourself of any area before moving.

If you are living in an area you would like to see included in the next revision of this book, please write us and tell us about your town at: Relocation Station, 1725 B. Madison Ave., Suite 774, Memphis, Tennessee 38104.

HOW TO USE THIS GUIDE

Turn to the Table Of Contents and find the state or states you're interested in. Each chapter analyzes a different state and included cities and towns within that state. The covered cities and towns will be listed alphabetically.

States and cities vary concerning sodomy laws, gay civil rights, and domestic partnership benefit provisions. The United States Map in the appendices shows the states in gray which have no sodomy laws. These states in gray would be good ones to consider; however, many states having state sodomy laws do have cities or towns within them that have great gay rights protection. For that reason, we have included some cities and towns which have city or county gay rights protection even though they are located in a "Sodomy Law" state. Some "Sodomy Law" states have no city or town with any form of gay rights protection. But, since we wanted to include at least one city or town from every state; we have included a city or town with a large contingency of gays and lesbians forming a visible support base from those states.

Some listed cities and towns are located in states which have no sodomy laws, but that doesn't mean that they have any special form of gay rights protection. Pay special attention to the sections concerning sodomy laws and gay rights protection.

Look in the appendices. There is a wealth of information concerning sodomy laws, domestic partnership benefits, companies that don't discriminate based on sexual orientation, gay BBS's, and so forth.

When you find a town that looks interesting to you, check it out. Call the contact number; get a "feel" for the community yourself. We have found during our research that gay and lesbian men and women are some of the most helpful and understanding people in the world.

SYMBOLS

N/A	=	Not Available
W	=	White
B	=	Black
AI/E/A	=	American Indian/Eskimo/Aleuth
A/PA	=	Asian, Pacific, Islander
C	=	Chinese
F	=	Filipino
H	=	Hispanic
M	=	Mexican
PR	=	Puerto Rican
O	=	Other

▼Denotes city or town which has some degree of gay civil rights protection.

These cities and towns are considered the best places to live. The information from the statistical data is from the 1990 United States Census Bureau. The population information is the total population within that specific city limits. The population information is further broken down by race. The unemployment rate is self-explanatory. The cost of living is based on the ACCRA figures. No figures were available for some cities. The population growth reports if the population has increased or decreased since 1980. The job-growth statistic reports if there has been an increase or decrease in jobs since 1980. The housing cost figures are based on the median cost of a home, and the rental cost is the median cost for rent in that specific city. The number of churches that are open and affirming are listed. The Gay/Lesbian section is broken down into the following categories: Gay and Lesbian friendly businesses, the number of Gay/Lesbian bars and restaurants, the number of Gay/Lesbian organizations (community centers, switchboards, resource centers, task forces, social groups, and recreational groups). Since the number of general bookstores that sell Gay/Lesbian books are increasing, we decided to count those bookstores having a large selection of Gay/Lesbian books, feminist bookstores, and the strictly Gay/Lesbian bookstores. The number of community hospitals are listed along with the number of beds in the total hospital community. The information on the state and city laws and ordinances concerning gay civil rights comes from the individual cities as the laws are passed and also from the National Gay and Lesbian Task Force. The information on the number of businesses comes from talking to Gays and Lesbians in each city and from the *Gay and Lesbian Yellow Pages.*

DEFINITIONS

TOTAL CRIME: The total number of all crimes reported to police in 1993.

VIOLENT CRIME:

MURDER = The unlawful killing of a human being in which the element of malice aforethought was present.

RAPE = The carnal knowledge of a person forcibly and against that person's will.

ROBBERY = The felonious and forcible taking of property from the care, custody or control of a person or persons by violence or putting the person in fear and against his will.

ASSAULT = The unlawful attack or an attempt to attack through force or violence to do physical injury to another.

PROPERTY CRIME:

BURGLARY = An unlawful or attempted forcible entry of a structure to commit a felony or larceny, even though force may not be used to gain entry.

LARCENY THEFT = The unlawful taking of property of another with intent to deprive him of ownership without the use of force, violence, or fraud.

MOTOR VEHICLE THEFT = The unlawful taking or attempted taking of a motor vehicle.

ARSON = Any willful or malicious burning or attempt to burn, with or without intent to defraud.

ALABAMA

STATE LAWS REGARDING HOMOSEXUALITY:

Heterosexual and homosexual sodomy is illegal. The maximum sentence is 20 years. In 1992, the state legislature passed a bill forbidding the use of public funds to "foster or promote a lifestyle or actions" that are illegal under the state sodomy laws. The new law was used to prevent funds from being allocated to gay student groups at state universities.

CITIES: (60,000 AND UP)

BIRMINGHAM:

Gay Civil Rights: None

What the Locals Say . . .

There really hasn't been much change in the gay community in 30 years. Gays and Lesbians aren't really harassed, although they are still afraid to be open. The best areas to live and be around family members are the south side of town in the Highland Avenue area and the north part of the city. Highland Avenue is a hangout area for gays and lesbians. There are various support groups and a few youth groups. Birmingham has a coffee shop called Celestial Realm which draws a young mixed crowd. Sport groups include a softball league, volleyball league, and a bowling league. Easter weekend there is a softball tournament where participants throughout the United States are invited to attend. "22nd Street Jazz Cafe" is mixed and has alternative shows on Wednesday. The bar scene is mostly mixed. Some of the most popular bars are: "Quest" a cruise bar/dance bar on the weekends, "Mikatan" a dance bar and "Buchanan's" a dance bar that draws a younger crowd. One of the best women's bars is "Bill's Club." Rapport between health care providers and gays and lesbians is somewhat supportive or rather nobody's really heard of any problems. The Birmingham AIDS Organization is an active AIDS outreach organization. The Metropolitan Community Church is growing rapidly and includes a children service. There are approximately 100 members and they are trying to build a larger church. *The Alabama Forum* is a monthly gay/lesbian newspaper published in Birmingham.

LOCATION: BIRMINGHAM IS LOCATED IN THE NORTH CENTRAL PART OF THE STATE IN THE APPALACHIAN RIDGE AND VALLEY REGION.

GAY/LESBIAN FRIENDLY BUSINESSES: 12

GAY/LESBIAN BARS AND RESTAURANTS: 5

GAY/LESBIAN ORGANIZATIONS: 8

GAY/LESBIAN RELIGIOUS ORGANIZATIONS, CHURCHES: 2

GAY/LESBIAN BOOKSTORES: 1
GAY/LESBIAN PUBLICATIONS: 1
COMPANIES THAT PROHIBIT DISCRIMINATION: N/A
INFORMATION NUMBER: 205-326-8600 LAMBDA GAY/LESBIAN INFORMATION
TOTAL CRIMES: 31,776
VIOLENT = (MURDER = 121, RAPE = 297, ROBBERY = 1,706, ASSAULT = 4,554)
PROPERTY = (BURGLARY = 6,628, LARCENY = 4,926, MOTOR VEHICLE THEFT = 3,544)

Things to Do!!!

Outdoor activities in Birmingham take advantage of the area's mild climate. There are almost 100 parks in the city and plenty of waterways suitable for water sports. Beaches of the Gulf of Mexico are a 5-hour drive away, and in the winter, skiing is available in Cloudmont which is 2 hours north. Other areas of interest include: (1) The Vulcan, (2) Arlington, (3) Birmingham Museum of Art, (4) The Discovery Place, (5) Birmingham/ Jefferson Civic Center, (6) Alabama Sports Hall of Fame Museum, (7) Sloss Furnaces National Historic Landmark, (8) Birmingham Zoo, (9) Birmingham Botanical Gardens, (10) Ruffner Mountain Nature Center, (11) Red Mountain Museum, (12) Rickwood Caverns State Park, (13) Oak Mountain State Park, (14) De Soto Caverns. ANNUAL EVENTS: (1) Dogwood Festival, (2) International Fair, (3) Plantation Homes Tours, (4) State Fair.

POPULATION: 264,984 PERSONS- W = 95,655, B = 168,277, AI/E/A = 321, C = 493, F = 92, M = 344, PR = 104

POPULATION GROWTH: - 6.8%

AGE OF POPULATION: (21-24) = 6.3%, (25-34) = 17.7%, (35-44) = 14.2%, (45-54) = 8.5%, (55-64) = 8.7%, (65-74) = 8.1%, (75 AND OVER) = 6.8%

HOUSING COST AVERAGES: OWNING = $44,500   RENTAL = $322

COMMUNITY HOSPITALS: 13 = 4,343 BEDS

CLIMATE: JAN—AVG. (41.5 DEGREES), JULY—AVG. (79.8 DEGREES),

ANNUAL PRECIPITATION 54.58 INCHES

PER CAPITA INCOME: $10,127

UNEMPLOYMENT RATE: 7.3%

JOB GROWTH SINCE 1980: -3%

COST OF LIVING: 100.9

EDUCATION: UNIVERSITY OF ALABAMA BIRMINGHAM, UNIVERSITY OF MONTEVALLO, UNIVERSITY OF ALABAMA MEDICAL SCHOOL, STAMFORD COLLEGE

MOBILE

Gay Civil Rights: None

What the Locals Say . . .

The gay community in Mobile has well represented groups on both sides of "OUT." Relatively few people live openly gay; but rainbow flags can be seen flying here and there. Both the mayor and the city government are liberal. A local members only dining club, has recently started letting couples of the same sex join. The police don't seem to harass gays and they appropriately supervise Gay Pride Day. Mobile has no history of gay hate crimes nor overt acts of violence towards gays. The best area to live for gays is Midtown, a historic district of older homes. Four to five hundred people attend the Gay Pride Celebration. There is a big rally with a Day In The Park for volleyball, softball, etc. The Mobile Aids Support Services office is extremely knowledgeable and efficient. There is a PFLAG group in the area, and a Gay, Lesbian, Bisexual Alliance at the University of South Alabama. Many Gay/Lesbian activities in the area are organized through the local MCC. There are no local publications, but the community is represented in the *Alabama Forum* out of Birmingham. "B' Bob's" is a popular mixed bar with dancing and drag shows. "Gabriel's" is mixed. "Trooper's" is a men's bar. There is no specific bar for women although "The Society" has more women. Health care is above average since there are five hospitals in the area. Finding a good doctor is a word of mouth process. Barnes and Noble stocks a good selection of Gay/Lesbian books. There is a very active MCC.

LOCATION: MOBILE IS LOCATED IN SOUTHWESTERN ALABAMA WHERE THE RIVER FLOWS INTO THE MOBILE BAY.

GAY/LESBIAN FRIENDLY BUSINESSES: 10

GAY/LESBIAN BARS AND RESTAURANTS: 6

GAY/LESBIAN ORGANIZATIONS: 2

GAY/LESBIAN RELIGIOUS ORGANIZATIONS, CHURCHES, : 1

GAY/LESBIAN BOOKSTORES: 1

COMPANIES THAT PROHIBIT DISCRIMINATION: N/A

INFORMATION NUMBER: 205-425-2286, GAY, LESBIAN, BISEXUAL ALLIANCE.

TOTAL CRIMES: 18,567

VIOLENT = (MURDER = 42, RAPE = 122, ROBBERY = 1,186, ASSAULT = 870)

PROPERTY = (BURGLARY = 4,884, LARCENY = 9,926, MOTOR VEHICLE
THEFT = 1,537)

Things to Do!!!

Recreational activities take full advantage of sitting on Mobile Bay
and the Gulf of Mexico. Swimming, surfing, sailing, and water skiing
are all available at many places in the area. Other areas of interest
include: (1) Oakleigh, (2) Bellingrath Gardens and Home, (3) Fine
Arts Museum of the South, (4) The Exploreum Museum of Discovery,
(5) Phoenix Fire Museum, (6) Carlen House Museum, (7) Museum of
the City of Mobile, (8) Heustis Medical Museum, (9) Alabama State
Docks, (10) Battleship USS Alabama Memorial Park, (11) Malbis
Greek Orthodox Church. ANNUAL EVENTS: (1) Senior Bowl
Football Game, (2) Mardi Gras, (3) Blessing of the Shrimp Fleet, (4)
Greater Gulf State Fair. SEASONAL EVENTS: Azalea Trail Festival.

POPULATION: 201,896 PERSONS= W = 117,022, B = 76,407, AI/E/A =
443, C = 345, F = 201, M = 484, PR = 224

POPULATION GROWTH: +.7%

AGE OF POPULATION: (21-24) = 6.3%, (25-34) = 16.5%, (35-44) =
14%, (45-54) = 9.5%, (55-64) = 8.6%, (65-74) = 7.9%, (75 AND
OVER) = 5.8%

HOUSING COST: OWNING = $55,400 RENTAL = $332

COMMUNITY HOSPITALS: 7 = 1,898 BEDS

CLIMATE: JAN—AVG. (49.9 DEGREES), JULY—AVG. (82.3 DEGREES),
ANNUAL PRECIPITATION (63.96 INCHES)

PER CAPITA INCOME: $12,509

UNEMPLOYMENT RATE: 7.3%

JOB GROWTH SINCE 1980: + 2.6%

COST OF LIVING: 92.0

EDUCATION: UNIVERSITY OF SOUTH ALABAMA, U. S. SPORTS
ACADEMY, MOBILE COLLEGE

TUSCALOOSA

Gay Civil Rights: None

What the Locals Say . . .

The gay and lesbian community in Tuscaloosa is mostly closeted.
There is a good sized lesbian community here, but they are not "out"
to the community as a whole. Tuscaloosa is probably more open than
many places in the state. If you were moving there from Centerville,
AL, it would seem like Heaven; but, if you were moving from anywhere having gay civil rights protection, you would find it very frus-
trating. The state and city governments are anti-gay. The President of

the University has made a statement that the university would not discriminate based on sexual orientation, but that's about as far as it has gone. It is still a very controversial issue in Tuscaloosa. The Lesbian Coalition (TLC) meets monthly in homes. They have social events and work for progress in the area. They publish a newsletter, *The TLC*, which is mailed out monthly. The University of Alabama Gay Lesbian Alliance, the oldest gay/lesbian student group in the state (since 1983), meets once a week. Call or write either one of these groups for information. There is no gay bookstore; however, there is a store called Illusions which sells gay books, t-shirts, buttons, and has Tuscaloosa's only "adult room." Illusions is also a "head shop." Most people go to Lodestar Books in Birmingham. There are some bowling teams, women's softball, and men's softball groups mostly organized out of Birmingham. The only bar is "Michaels," a mixed dance bar. The West Alabama AIDS Outreach has a clinic and is located in Tuscaloosa. There is a HIV support group sponsored by the University Psychology Department. There is a MCC group operating through the Parish Extension Program now meeting in a local motel but planning to have their own building soon.

LOCATION: TUSCALOOSA IS LOCATED ON THE BLACK WARRIOR RIVER IN WESTERN ALABAMA.

GAY/LESBIAN FRIENDLY BUSINESSES: 5

GAY/LESBIAN BARS AND RESTAURANTS: 1

GAY/LESBIAN ORGANIZATIONS: 4

GAY/LESBIAN RELIGIOUS ORGANIZATIONS, CHURCHES, : 0

GAY/LESBIAN BOOKSTORES: 0

GAY/LESBIAN PUBLICATIONS: 0

COMPANIES THAT PROHIBIT DISCRIMINATION: N/A

INFORMATION NUMBER: 205-348-7210 UNIVERSITY OF ALABAMA GAY, LESBIAN BISEXUAL ALLIANCE, OR 205 333-8227 THE LESBIAN COALITION.

TOTAL CRIMES: 8,865

VIOLENT= (MURDER = 8, RAPE = 56, ROBBERY = 382, ASSAULT = 657)

PROPERTY = (BURGLARY = 1,093, LARCENY = 6,421, MOTOR VEHICLE THEFT = 348)

Things to Do!!!

Sights to see and things to do include: (1) Battle-Friedman House, (2) The Strickland House, (3) Old Tavern, (4) National Headquarters of Gulf States Paper Corporation, (5) North River Historical Area, (6) Mound State Monument, (7) Lake Tuscaloosa, (8) Lake Lurleen State Park. ANNUAL EVENTS: Tuscaloosa Heritage Week

POPULATION: 78,732 PERSONS—W = 48,871, B = 27,598, AI/E/A = 106, C = 281, F = 71, M = 163, PR = 76

POPULATION GROWTH: + 4.7%

AGE OF POPULATION: (21-24) = 11.9%, (25-34) = 15.4%, (35-44) = 12.6%, (45-54) = 7.7%, (55-64) = 7.9%, (65-74) = 6.8%, (75 AND OVER) = 4.9%

HOUSING COST: OWNING = $62,900 RENTAL = $342

COMMUNITY HOSPITALS: 2 = 575 BEDS

CLIMATE: JAN—AVG. (42.8 DEGREES), JULY—AVG. (81.1 DEGREES), ANNUAL PRECIPITATION (54.90 INCHES)

PER CAPITA INCOME: $11,469

UNEMPLOYMENT RATE: 6.3%

JOB GROWTH SINCE 1980: + 12.3%

COST OF LIVING: 99.1

EDUCATION: UNIVERSITY OF ALABAMA

ALASKA

STATE LAWS REGARDING HOMOSEXUALITY:

No sodomy law exists in Alaska. The Alaska Supreme Court ruled in 1969 that the term "crime against nature" was unconstitutional.

CITIES: (60,000 AND UP)

▼ANCHORAGE

Gay Civil Rights: Bans discrimination based on sexual orientation for public employment.

What the Locals Say . . .

Anchorage offers a high quality of life from a work standpoint. The job opportunities are like no other place in the United States HB226, which initially would have barred any unmarried spouse from obtaining employment benefits was amended to allow benefits to couples with economic dependence (joint checking accounts, joint property such as home or vehicle, etc.). Voters in Anchorage elected three candidates for assembly (City Council) who support gay/lesbian/bi rights; however, you probably wouldn't move to Anchorage to live a flaming lifestyle since the community at large is fairly conservative. Anywhere in Anchorage is o.k. to live except Fairview. "The Raven" and "The Blue Moon" are bars serving both men and women. "O'Brady's" is a popular gay restaurant. "Bona Dea: the Alaska Women's Bookstore" is much more than a bookstore. It is host to The Women's Coffeehouse, various visiting author appearances, and a myriad of other events. It also acts as a drop-off and pick-up place for individuals and groups in the community. The Anchorage gay and lesbian community seems to be very well organized. Identity is a non-profit, non-political organization which sponsors the Gay/Lesbian Helpline, monthly Potluck Socials, health projects, Human Rights Campaign Fund, and a drive for a gay/lesbian community center. It also publishes the *North View*, a 60 page, monthly gay and lesbian newspaper which is quite impressive. Some other groups and organizations in Anchorage are: PFLAG, several gay and lesbian AA groups, Women's Two-Step Dance, Northern Exposure (gay bowling league), The Family (UAA student association), EQUAL (provides education about political issues concerning the gay/lesbian community), GAY BAR (questions and answers on legal issues of interest to lesbians and gay men), Feminist Sing-A-Long, Anchorage Lesbian Families' Alliance (ALFA), HIV+ Men's Support Group, SLAA (Sex and Love Addicts Anonymous), Alaska Women's Political Caucus, Anchorage Garden Buddies (a social group of gay men looking for an alternative to the bar scene), Imperial Court of All Alaska (social and support group), IMRU (youth group), and The Alaska Women's Cultural Center . *The KLONDYKE*

KONTACT, a terrific bimonthly newsletter which is chock full of information including the area calendar of events, news, poetry, thought provoking essays, etc., is published by The Alaska Women's Cultural Center. Health care in the area is good, and there are some gay friendly doctors. Open and affirming churches and religious groups include the Anchorage Unitarian Universalist Fellowship, Lamb of God MCC, Unity Church of Anchorage and Anchorage Church of Religious Science

LOCATION: ANCHORAGE IS LOCATED IN SOUTH CENTRAL ALASKA.

GAY/LESBIAN FRIENDLY BUSINESSES: 180

GAY/LESBIAN BARS AND RESTAURANTS: 4

GAY/LESBIAN ORGANIZATIONS: 30+

GAY/LESBIAN RELIGIOUS ORGANIZATIONS, CHURCHES, : 4

GAY/LESBIAN BOOKSTORES:1

GAY/LESBIAN PUBLICATIONS: 2

COMPANIES THAT PROHIBIT DISCRIMINATION: SEE GAY CIVIL RIGHTS INFORMATION NUMBER: 907-258-4777 GAY HELPLINE

TOTAL CRIMES: 138

VIOLENT = (MURDER = 2, RAPE = 0, ROBBERY = 6, ASSAULT = 33)

PROPERTY = (BURGLARY = 13, LARCENY = 75, MOTOR VEHICLE THEFT = 9)

Things to Do!!!

Massive and challenging peaks, rivers full of fish, and a diverse cast of animal life can be reached in less than a day from Anchorage. Specific points of interest include: (1) Anchorage Museum of History and Art, (2) Cook Inlet Historical Society, (3) Visual Arts Center of Alaska, (4) Anchorage Symphony Orchestra, (5) Anchorage Opera, (6) Alaska Repertory Theatre, (7) Alaska Experience Theatre, (8) Wolverine Peak, (9) Flattop Mountain, (10) Rabbit Lake, (11) Suicide Peak. ANNUAL EVENTS: (1) Mayors Marathon, (2) Fur Rendezvous. SEASONAL EVENTS: The Anchorage Music Festival

POPULATION: 226,338 PERSONS—W = 182,736, B = 14,544, AI/E/A = 14,569, C = 783, F = 3,199, M = 4,606, PR = 1,134

POPULATION GROWTH: + 41.%

AGE OF POPULATION: (21-24) = 6.2%, (25-34) = 21.5%, (35-44) = 19.2%, (45-54) = 10.3%, (55-64) = 5.3%, (65-74) = 2.7%, (75 AND OVER) = 1.0%

HOUSING COST: OWNING = $109,700   RENTAL = $564

COMMUNITY HOSPITALS: 2 = 579 BEDS

CLIMATE: JAN—AVG. (14.9 DEGREES), JULY—AVG. (58.4 DEGREES), ANNUAL PRECIPITATION (15.91 INCHES)

PER CAPITA INCOME: $19,620
UNEMPLOYMENT RATE: 6.7%
JOB GROWTH SINCE 1980: + 36.2%
COST OF LIVING: 128.5
EDUCATION: UNIVERSITY OF ALASKA ANCHORAGE, ALASKA PACIFIC
UNIVERSITY

ARIZONA

STATE LAWS REGARDING HOMOSEXUALITY:

Heterosexual and homosexual sodomy is illegal and considered a misdemeanor in Arizona. The maximum sentence is 30 days. In 1976, the Arizona Supreme Court upheld the constitutionality of the state's sodomy laws, citing the Bible and stating that "the right to privacy is not unqualified and absolute and must be considered in the light of the circumstances."

CITIES: (60,000 AND UP)

▼PHOENIX

Gay Civil Rights: Bans discrimination based on sexual orientation in public employment, housing and public accommodations.

What the Locals Say . . .

Phoenix started really coming out of the closet a few years ago, and the gay community is still evolving. There doesn't seem to be animosity from the straight community. The best areas to live are in the central area (McDowell to 7th street to 7th avenue to Dunlap). There are 5 historic districts that the gay/lesbian community helped restore and now there are many family members living there. North Phoenix is also a recommended area to live. Phoenix has approximately 200 different gay/lesbian organizations. The organizations include women's and men's groups, softball, bowling, couples, desert adventures, etc. The bar scene runs the gamut. The majority of bars have a mixed crowd. The bars that are primarily for men also draw women and vice versa. Some of the gay bars are: "B.S. West," "Metro," "Winks," "Fosters." The lesbian bars are: "Nobody's Biz, "Nasty Habit," "Desert Rose," "In Cognito." "Charlie's" is a fun bar for everyone-gay/lesbian/straight!! "Johnny Mc's" caters to the older gay and lesbian crowd. The health care providers seem to have a good rapport with HIV + and AIDS patients. *The Echo* and *The Western Express* are the local gay/lesbian publications. The religious organizations of Phoenix are very open to the gay and lesbian community. There are Episcopalian, Catholic, Gentle Shepherd, MCC, and various other supportive churches.

LOCATION: PHOENIX IS LOCATED ON THE RIVER IN THE SALT RIVER VALLEY OF CENTRAL ARIZONA.

GAY/LESBIAN FRIENDLY BUSINESSES: 29

GAY/LESBIAN BARS AND RESTAURANTS: 26

GAY/LESBIAN RELIGIOUS ORGANIZATIONS, CHURCHES, : 17

GAY/LESBIAN BOOKSTORES: 2

GAY/LESBIAN PUBLICATIONS: 4

COMPANIES THAT PROHIBIT DISCRIMINATION: SEE GAY CIVIL RIGHTS INFORMATION NUMBER: 602-234-2752 LESBIAN AND GAY COMMUNITY SWITCHBOARD

TOTAL CRIMES: 96,476

VIOLENT = (MURDER = 158, RAPE = 444, ROBBERY = 3,437, ASSAULT = 7,872)

PROPERTY = (BURGLARY = 20,617, LARCENY = 48,382, MOTOR VEHICLE THEFT = 15,566,

Things to Do!!!

The Phoenix area has all the outdoor activities suitable to its warm climate in addition to skiing in the nearby mountains. Hiking, rock climbing, horseback riding, gliders, sailplanes, fishing, boating and tubing are popular activities in the region's rugged terrain. Other points of interest include: (1) Arizona State Museum, (2) Arizona Historical Society Museum-Phoenix, (3) Arizona Mineral Museum, (4) Arizona State Parks Board, (5) Desert Botanical Garden, (6) Hall of Fame, (7) Phoenix Art Museum, (8) Pioneer Arizona, (9) Pueblo Grande Museum, (10) The Phoenix Zoo, (11) Metro Pops Orchestra, (12) Phoenix Symphony Orchestra, (13) Ballet Arizona, (14) Professional Sports: Football-Cardinals, Basketball- Suns.

POPULATION: 1,012,230 PERSONS—W = 803,332, B = 51,053, AI/E/A = 18,225, C = 4,254, F = 2,519, M = 176,139, PR = 2,478

POPULATION GROWTH: + 28.2%

AGE OF POPULATION: (21-24) = 6.2%, (25-34) = 19.5%, (35-44) = 15.6%, (45-54) = 9.9%, (55-64) = 7.4%, (65-74) = 5.9%, (75 AND OVER) = 3.8%

HOUSING COST: OWNING = $77,100 RENTAL = $442

COMMUNITY HOSPITALS: 13 = 3,452 BEDS

CLIMATE: JAN—AVG. (53.6 DEGREES), JULY—AVG. (93.5 DEGREES), ANNUAL PRECIPITATION (7.66 INCHES)

PER CAPITA INCOME: $14,096

UNEMPLOYMENT RATE: 5.0%

JOB GROWTH SINCE 1980: + 32.4%

COST OF LIVING: 99.8

EDUCATION: ARIZONA STATE UNIVERSITY

TUCSON

Gay Civil Rights: Bans discrimination based on sexual orientation in public employment.

What the Locals Say . . .

Tucson is a very gay friendly town with a tradition of intellectual and artistic interests. The gay community has an open liaison with the police department which deters crimes committed against the gay and lesbian community. The transit system is one of the best in the country. If you want to live around family members, the best areas to live are west and north of the University and in the Downtown area. The Downtown area is going through a renaissance where older homes are getting facelifts. The Downtown area already has numerous galleries, bookstores, coffeehouses, and some bars. Wingspan is a unique organization which acts as a clearinghouse for information concerning gays, lesbians, battered women, youth, etc. Wingspan has a lending library as well as several brochures. Tucson has a very active gay rodeo association, and also offers a gay bowling league and a gay softball league. Hinnel Park and Reed Park are frequented by gays and lesbians although they are not classified as gay parks. The Gay Pride celebration, and National Candlelight Vigil are annual celebrations. The bar scene is mixed including: "Stonewall," a disco bar with a quiet section for talking; "25-20," a country/disco club with a place for conversation as well; "IBT's" college clientele of both gays and lesbians; and "Venture N," predominately a men's bar. "Ain't Nobody's Business" is primarily women, although friendly to men, and "Hours" is mostly women. The Shanti Foundation, PACT, and the Tucson AIDS Project are very helpful AIDS organizations. The Pima County Health Department is also a wonderful health resource. *The Observer* is a weekly publication for the gay and lesbian community. The MCC, Cornerstone Fellowship, and St. Francis in the Foothills are all openly gay and lesbian churches.

LOCATION: TUCSON IS LOCATED IN SOUTH CENTRAL ARIZONA SIXTY FIVE MILES FROM THE BORDER OF MEXICO. THE CITY EXTENDS FROM THE SONORA DESERT TO SEVERAL MOUNTAIN RANGES.

GAY/LESBIAN FRIENDLY BUSINESSES: 16

GAY/LESBIAN BARS AND RESTAURANTS: 8

GAY/LESBIAN ORGANIZATIONS: 12

GAY/LESBIAN RELIGIOUS ORGANIZATIONS, CHURCHES, : 4

GAY/LESBIAN BOOKSTORES: 1

GAY/LESBIAN PUBLICATIONS: 1

COMPANIES THAT PROHIBIT DISCRIMINATION: SEE GAY CIVIL RIGHTS

INFORMATION NUMBER: 520-624-1779 WINGSPAN: TUCSON'S GAY,LESBIAN & BISEXUAL COMMUNITY CENTER

TOTAL CRIMES: 48,945

VIOLENT = (MURDER = 44, RAPE = 314, ROBBERY = 894, ASSAULT = 3,111)

PROPERTY = (BURGLARY = 7,363, LARCENY = 32,076, MOTOR VEHICLE THEFT = 5,143)

Things to Do!!!

Many public facilities and resorts offer golf, tennis and other sports. Skiing is only a short drive away. Hot air balloon and horseback rides are available. Other places of interest are: (1) The Aquary Museum, (2) Arizona-Sonora Desert Museum, (3) DeGrazia Art & Cultural Foundation, (4) Flandrau Planetarium, (5) Old Pueblo Museum, (6) Mission San Xavier Del Bar, (7) Old West Wax Museum, (8) Pima Air Museum, (9) Tucson Museum of Art, (10) Tucson Art Institute, (11) Reid-Park Zoo, (12) Civic Orchestra of Tucson, (13) Tucson Symphony Orchestra, (14) Arizona Opera Companies, (15) Arizona Theatre Company,(16) Biosphere

POPULATION: 415,079 PERSONS—W = 305,055, B = 17,366, AI/E/A = 6,464, C = 2,558, F = 1,061, M = 107,139,PR = 2,478

POPULATION GROWTH: + 25.6%

AGE OF POPULATION: (21-24) = 8.0%, (25-34) = 18.9%, (35-44) = 13.7%, (45-54) = 8.3%, (55-64) = 7.5%, (65-74) = 7.2%, (75 AND OVER) = 5.4%

HOUSING COST: OWNING = $66,800 RENTAL = $377

COMMUNITY HOSPITALS: 8 = 2,016 BEDS

CLIMATE: JAN—AVG. (51.3 DEGREES), JULY—AVG. (86.6 DEGREES), ANNUAL PRECIPITATION (12.00 INCHES)

PER CAPITA INCOME: $11,184

UNEMPLOYMENT RATE: 3.9%

JOB GROWTH SINCE 1980: + 29.8%

COST OF LIVING: 100.6

EDUCATION: UNIVERSITY OF ARIZONA, UNIVERSITY OF PHOENIX AT TUCSON

ARKANSAS

STATE LAWS REGARDING HOMOSEXUALITY:

Homosexual sodomy is illegal and carries a maximum sentence of 1 year if convicted. In 1975, a bill was approved making it a misdemeanor to have sex with someone of the same gender. In 1994, a repeal measure was defeated in the state senate by a 6-1 committee vote.

CITIES: (60,000 AND UP)

LITTLE ROCK

Gay Civil Rights: None

What the Locals Say . . .

Little Rock can be described as a middle-of-the -road community. The gay and lesbian community, for the most part, is not what you would call closeted but not what you would call out either. Most couples would not feel comfortable holding hands or being affectionate in public. The state has a sodomy law applying only to homosexuals. The politicians are mostly anti-gay. Part of the Quapaw area (near downtown), as well as the Hillcrest/Pulaski Heights area, has a gay and lesbian presence. The atmosphere in Hillcrest/Pulaski Heights is more relaxed and has beautiful old homes surrounded by huge maple and oak trees. The Hillcrest/Pulaski area is like a small community within itself. The Arkansas Gay and Lesbian Task Force sponsors the information switchboard and People of Alternative Lifestyles (PALS), a group for gays and lesbians 16-22. Diamond State Rodeo is a gay group that hosts a regional gay rodeo and has a clubhouse with various activities. There is a radio program, "Queer Frontier," carried on the community radio station. The "League to Make a Difference" commonly referred to as "The League" is composed of individuals with a high income. "The League" is a philanthropic organization which gives money to AIDS organizations and the Arkansas Gay and Lesbian Task Force. There is a gay bowling league. The Lesbian Network meets twice a month at the Women's Project. The Women's Project has a small bookstore and lending library with books and items of interest to gay, lesbian, bisexual, and transgendered people, and the Project also sponsors a monthly women's coffeehouse. "Friends," sponsored by Spirit Song MCC, is a group of single people of all ages who are not into the bar scene. "Silver Dollar" is a lesbian bar and is one of the state's oldest bars. "Backstreet 701" is a lesbian dance bar and "Backstreet 501" is a gay men's bar. " Michael's" is mixed with gays and lesbians. "Discovery III" is a gay-friendly straight bar. The Regional AIDS Network is the largest and best organized AIDS group in Arkansas. Dr. Ralph Hyman is a psychotherapist who offers 3 support groups (HIV, gay men's, lesbian). Dr. Hyman is very active in the community; and in fact, won a community service award for his involvement and support of AIDS issues. *Triangle Rising* is a monthly publication put out by the Arkansas Gay and Lesbian Task Force. There is a listing of gay and lesbian businesses as well as gay friendly businesses; although, for complete resource information, contact the Switchboard. The Spirit Song MCC and MCC of the Rock in North Little Rock are predominately gay and lesbian churches. The Unitarian and Pulaski Heights Christian Church Disciples of Christ are very open to gays and lesbians.

LOCATION: LITTLE ROCK IS LOCATED IN THE CENTER OF THE STATE OF ARKANSAS ON THE ARKANSAS RIVER. THE OUACHITA MOUNTAINS ARE APPROXIMATELY FIFTY MILES WEST OF THE METRO AREA.

GAY/LESBIAN FRIENDLY BUSINESSES: 15

GAY/LESBIAN BARS AND RESTAURANTS: 5

GAY/LESBIAN ORGANIZATIONS: 7

GAY/LESBIAN RELIGIOUS ORGANIZATIONS, CHURCHES, : 4

GAY/LESBIAN BOOKSTORES: 1

GAY/LESBIAN PUBLICATIONS: 1

COMPANIES THAT PROHIBIT DISCRIMINATION: N/A

INFORMATION NUMBER: 501-375-5504 ARKANSAS GAY & LESBIAN TASK FORCE

TOTAL CRIMES: 28,244

VIOLENT = (MURDER = 68, RAPE = 215, ROBBERY = 1,136, ASSAULT = 4,468)

PROPERTY = (BURGLARY = 5,796, LARCENY = 14,306, MOTOR VEHICLE THEFT = 2,081, ARSON = 174)

Things to Do!!!

There are numerous parks suitable for all types of outdoor activity. Camp Robinson, home of the Arkansas National Guard, is open to the public for hiking, fishing, and hunting. Pinnacle Mountain State Park has hiking trails. Other places of interest include: (1) Arkansas Arts Center, (2) Arkansas Museum of Science & History, (3) Arkansas Territorial Restoration, (4) The Old State House, (5) Little Rock Zoo, (6) Arkansas Symphony Orchestra, (7) Arkansas Repertory Theatre, (8) Arkansas Opera Theatre.

POPULATION: 176,870 PERSONS = W = 113,707, B = 59,742, AI/E/A = 449, C = 332, F = 300, M = 673, PR = 123

POPULATION GROWTH: + 11.1%

AGE OF POPULATION: (21-24) = 6.3%, (25-34) = 18.7%, (35-44) = 16.0%, (45-54) = 9.6%, (55-64) = 7.8%, (65-74) = 6.9%, (75 AND OVER) = 5.6%

HOUSING COST: OWNING = $64,200 RENTAL = $415

COMMUNITY HOSPITALS: 7 = 2,463 BEDS

CLIMATE: JAN—AVG. (39.1 DEGREES), JULY—AVG. (81.9 DEGREES), ANNUAL PRECIPITATION (50.86 INCHES)

PER CAPITA INCOME: $15,307

UNEMPLOYMENT RATE: 5.8%

JOB GROWTH SINCE 1980: + 17.5%

COST OF LIVING: 101.1

EDUCATION: UNIVERSITY OF ARKANSAS AT LITTLE ROCK, UNIVERSITY OF ARKANSAS GRADUATE INSTITUTE OF TECHNOLOGY, UNIVERSITY OF ARKANSAS AT LITTLE ROCK LAW SCHOOL, UNIVERSITY OF ARKANSAS FOR MEDICAL SCIENCES

FAYETTEVILLE

Gay Civil Rights: None

What the Locals Say . . .

Fayetteville is a small city, although there is a rather large gay and lesbian community. Since the area is so small, there is difficulty in getting on the inside to find out where and what gay and lesbian activities there are. Fayetteville has a larger lesbian community than a gay male one. There are three gay and lesbian groups on the campus of the University of Arkansas. They are: Women's Alliance— a feminist group, Pagan Student Association, and The Gay and Lesbian Association. The Fayetteville community has BGLAAD—Bisexual Gay and Lesbian Action Delegation and PFLAG—Parents of Lesbians and Gays. "Soap and Vic" is a production company that brings in entertainment. "Women's Night Out" is a dance event held at a smokehouse where approximately 400 attend. Spinsterhaven is a retirement community in development. "Ron's Place" is a gay bar with a predominantly male clientele, although, lesbians do go there. *The Ozark Feminist Review* is a monthly publication out of Fayetteville. The MCC and Unitarian Church are open to gays and lesbians. The Unitarian Church sponsors some workshops on gay and lesbian issues and tries hard to be open and supportive.

LOCATION: FAYETTEVILLE IS LOCATED IN THE HILLS OF NORTHWEST ARKANSAS.

GAY/LESBIAN FRIENDLY BUSINESSES: 2

GAY/LESBIAN BARS AND RESTAURANTS: 1

GAY/LESBIAN ORGANIZATIONS: 5

GAY/LESBIAN RELIGIOUS ORGANIZATIONS, CHURCHES, : 1

GAY/LESBIAN BOOKSTORES: 0

GAY/LESBIAN PUBLICATIONS: 0

COMPANIES THAT PROHIBIT DISCRIMINATION: N/A

INFORMATION NUMBER: 501-521-4509

TOTAL CRIMES: 2,140
VIOLENT = (MURDER = 1, RAPE = 29, ROBBERY = 14, ASSAULT = 83)
PROPERTY = (BURGLARY = 305, LARCENY = 1,542, MOTOR VEHICLE = 165, ARSON = 1)

Things to Do!!!

This beautiful area offers a variety of activities for the outdoors. There are fishing, hunting, swimming, boating, golfing, tennis, camping, hiking and various other outdoor activities. Many activities are centered around the Arkansas Razorbacks, whose home is in Fayetteville. The Razorbacks enjoy state-wide fan support which brings in numerous visitors on a regular basis. Other activities include: (1) Headquarters House, (2) Prairie Grove Battlefield State Park, (3) Devil's Den State Park, (4) Walton Fine Arts Center, (5) Washington County Fair. ANNUAL EVENTS: Fall and Winter Arts and Crafts Festivals.

POPULATION: 46,071 PERSONS—W = 39,206, B = 1,580, AI/E/A = 481, C = 201, F = 31, M = 344, PR = 52

POPULATION GROWTH: + 25.8%

AGE OF POPULATION: (21-24) = 13.7%, (25-34) = 18.4%, (35-44) = 13.1%, (45-54) = 7.3%, (55-64) = 5.6%, (65-74) = 5.1%, (75 AND OVER) = 4.6%

HOUSING COST: OWNING = $66,200 RENTAL = $351

COMMUNITY HOSPITALS: 3 = 441 BEDS

CLIMATE: JAN—AVG. (34.0 DEGREES), JULY—AVG. (78.7 DEGREES), ANNUAL PRECIPITATION (44.04 INCHES)

PER CAPITA INCOME: $12,184

UNEMPLOYMENT RATE: 3.9%

JOB GROWTH SINCE 1980: + 27.6%

COST OF LIVING: 91.6

EDUCATION: UNIVERSITY OF ARKANSAS

RURAL AREAS (UNDER 5,000)

EUREKA SPRINGS

Gay Civil Rights:None

What the Locals Say . . .

Eureka Springs is composed of a variety of residents. The townspeople are very liberal. 99% of the businesses here are related to tourism. Forty minutes away in Bentonville, Arkansas, is the national headquarters for the nation's largest discount chain, Wal-Mart. Eureka

Springs has become a gay and lesbian vacationer's mecca in recent years. It is estimated that 1/3 of the population is gay or lesbian. If statistics are correct, there are more bed and breakfasts that cater to gays and lesbians in Eureka Springs than in any other place in middle-America. The City Manager is gay as are various other prominent residents. Gays and Lesbians can hold hands in public and or dance together in public if they desire. If someone has a problem with that, then the person having the problem is asked to leave the establishment. There is not really any harassment. The town is so small that there aren't areas divided into depressed areas or rich areas or gay areas. There are various gay activities throughout the year. There is an Annual Fine Arts Festival and Women Vision that runs through the month of May. The Basin Park Hotel is one of the most famous hotels in Eureka Springs, and they host a SocHop in the Grand Ballroom for gays and lesbians. The townspeople tend to think of gays and lesbians as just another group (kids, adults). There wouldn't be people outside bothering you as you go in. They just wouldn't go. There aren't any specific gay and lesbian bars because once again the town is so small. However, the "Center Street Bar and Grill" is owned and operated by lesbians. Some nights are real gay and others are real straight. "Chelsea's" is another place that is sometimes gay and sometimes straight. "Ermilio's" is an excellent Italian restaurant.

LOCATION: EUREKA SPRINGS IS LOCATED IN THE NORTHWESTERN SECTION OF ARKANSAS AND SITS ON THE SIDES OF THE OZARK MOUNTAINS.

GAY/LESBIAN FRIENDLY BUSINESSES: ALL

GAY/LESBIAN BARS AND RESTAURANTS: 1

GAY/LESBIAN ORGANIZATIONS: 0

GAY/LESBIAN RELIGIOUS ORGANIZATIONS, CHURCHES, : 1

GAY/LESBIAN BOOKSTORES: 0

GAY/LESBIAN PUBLICATIONS: 0

COMPANIES THAT PROHIBIT DISCRIMINATION: N/A

INFORMATION NUMBER: 501-253-5283 GREENWOOD HOLLOW RIDGE BED & BREAKFAST

TOTAL CRIMES: 99

VIOLENT = (MURDER = 1, RAPE = 0 ROBBERY = 1, ASSAULT = 24)

PROPERTY = (BURGLARY = 19, LARCENY = 73, MOTOR VEHICLE = 1, ARSON = 0)

Things to Do!!!

This is a small Victorian resort area which has beautiful scenery and excellent fishing. Specific areas of interest include: (1) Shopping on Spring and Main streets, (2) Hammond Museum of Bells, (3) Eureka Springs Historical Museum, (4) The Rosalie House, (5) Pivot Rock and Natural Bridge, (6) Sacred Arts Center, (7) Thorncrown Chapel,

(8) Blue Spring, (9) The Castle and Museum at Inspiration Point, (10) Onyx Cave Park. ANNUAL EVENTS: (1) Spring tour of Historic Homes, (2) Ozark Folk Festival, (3) Jazz Festival, (4) Art Festival, (5) Christmas Time in Eureka Springs. SEASONAL EVENTS: (1) Country Music Shows, (2) The Great Passion Play.

POPULATION: 1,900 PERSONS—W = 1,840, B = 0, AI/E/A = 53, O = 4

POPULATION GROWTH: COUNTY HAS DOUBLED IN SIZE IN LAST 10 YEARS.

AGE OF POPULATION: (21-24) = 46, (25-34) = 535 (35-44) = 271, (45-54) = 78, (55-64) = 105, (65-74) = 466, (75 AND OVER) = 4.6%

PER CAPITA INCOME: $10,849

UNEMPLOYMENT RATE: 5.5%

JOB GROWTH SINCE 1980: N/A

COST OF LIVING: N/A

EDUCATION: NONE

CALIFORNIA

STATE LAWS REGARDING HOMOSEXUALITY:

There are no sodomy laws in the great state of California as of May 1st, 1975. In April 1980, Governor Jerry Brown signed an executive order prohibiting anti-gay discrimination in state hiring. In January 1993, a law prohibiting job discrimination in public or private employment based on sexual orientation went into effect. In March of 1993, a Los Angeles appeals court ruled that the statewide law effectively nullified local anti-discrimination laws, which were often stronger. California does include crimes based on sexual orientation as hate crimes. The state of California does provide protection from discrimination based on sexual orientation in the following areas-public employment, public accommodations, private employment, and education.

CITIES: (60,000 AND UP)

▼BERKELEY

Gay Civil Rights: Bans discrimination based on sexual orientation in public employment, private employment, education, housing, credit, and union practices.

What the Locals Say . . .

The city of Berkeley is fairly open, although not as much as nearby San Francisco. There is a strong lesbian community which is very well organized. The town is often thought to be extremely liberal. In reality, it is half conservative and half liberal. There isn't a distinct location in town for gays and lesbians to live, everyone lives everywhere. Political groups in Berkeley include the East Bay Queer Nation, ACT-UP, Lesbian Avengers, and the East Bay Lesbian/Gay Democratic Club. The Pacific Center for Human Growth focuses on services for mental health through peer and support groups. Some of the support groups are social with games and cards nights and some are 12-step recovery groups. The discussion groups are peer run, not therapist run. The "White Horse" bar is located on the border with Oakland. It is a dance bar and is gay friendly. "Thunder Bay/The Mix" has a youth night. The "Teaspot" is a lesbian cafe. "Mama Bears" is a women's bookstore and cafe. Berkeley has a plethora of health organizations for gays and lesbians including the Berkeley Free Clinic which also sponsors a HIV Clinic, and the Berkeley Women's Clinic. The Center for AIDS services and East Bay Shanti are very well organized and very good organizations for AIDS patients. Open Hands is an organization for practical and emotional support. New Life Metropolitan Community Church is open to gays and lesbians.

LOCATION: THE CITY OF BERKELEY IS LOCATED ON THE EAST SIDE OF SAN FRANCISCO BAY AND NORTH OF OAKLAND.

GAY/LESBIAN FRIENDLY BUSINESSES: 8
GAY/LESBIAN BARS AND RESTAURANTS: 3
GAY/LESBIAN ORGANIZATIONS: 8
GAY/LESBIAN RELIGIOUS ORGANIZATIONS, CHURCHES, : 1
GAY/LESBIAN BOOKSTORES: 1
GAY/LESBIAN PUBLICATIONS: 3
COMPANIES THAT PROHIBIT DISCRIMINATION: SEE STATE LAWS & GAY CIVIL RIGHTS
INFORMATION NUMBER: 510-548-8283 PACIFIC CENTER FOR HUMAN GROWTH
TOTAL CRIMES: 13,154
VIOLENT = (MURDER = 8, RAPE = 35, ROBBERY = 815, ASSAULT = 773)
PROPERTY = (BURGLARY = 2,383, LARCENY = 7,915, MOTOR VEHICLE THEFT = 1,161, ARSON = 64)

Things to Do!!!

(1) The Berkeley Art Center, (2) Botanical Garden, (3) Lawrence Hall of Science, (4) Museum of Paleontology, (5) Berkeley Repertory Theatre, (6) Berkeley Shakespeare Festival, (7) Berkeley Ballet Theatre, (8) Berkeley Conservatory Ballet, (9) Bade Institute of Biblical Archaeology, (10) Judah L. Magnes Museum, (11) Municipal Rose Garden, (12) Grizzly Peak Blvd., (13) Charles Lee Tilden Regional Park, (14) Wildcat Regional Park, (15) Berkeley Marina.

POPULATION: 101,122 PERSONS—W = 63,833, B = 19,281, AI/E/A = 653, C = 6,674, F = 1,408, M = 5,297, PR = 370
POPULATION GROWTH: -2.1%
AGE OF POPULATION: (21-24) = 12.1%, (25-34) = 18.9%, (35-44) = 17.1%, (45-54) = 10.2%, (55-64) = 6.1%, (65-74) = 5.9%, (75 AND OVER) = 5.0%
HOUSING COST: OWNING: = $261,000   RENTAL = $426
COMMUNITY HOSPITALS: 1 = 459 BEDS
CLIMATE: JAN—AVG. (49.9 DEGREES), JULY—AVG. (62.1 DEGREES), ANNUAL PRECIPITATION (24.30 INCHES)
PER CAPITA INCOME: $18,720
UNEMPLOYMENT RATE: 5.2%
JOB GROWTH SINCE 1980: + 8.0%
COST OF LIVING: N/A
EDUCATION: UNIVERSITY OF CALIFORNIA AT BERKELEY

▼LAGUNA BEACH

Gay Civil Rights: Bans discrimination based on sexual orientation in public and private employment, public accommodations, housing, education, credit, and union practices.

What the Locals Say . . .

The Laguna Beach gay and lesbian community is very open. There is not a particular neighborhood where gays and lesbian live. "Different Drummer" is a bookstore that has speakers, poetry nights, as well as a variety of gay and lesbian books. The Southern California Physicians for Human Rights is out of Laguna Beach as well as the Log Cabin Republicans Club of Orange County. "Leap of Faith" is a gay coffeehouse, and "Little Shrimp" is a bar/restaurant where gays and straights hang out. "Mainstreet" is a primarily a men's bar, "Boom Boom Room" is for dining and dancing for gays and lesbians. Laguna Beach Community Beach Clinic, Laguna Outreach, and Laguna Shanti are all superb health care clinics and organizations. Different Drummer puts out a monthly newsletter and *The Blade* is a monthly publication out of Laguna Beach. The group,Integrity,offers open services for gays and lesbians.

LOCATION: LAGUNA BEACH IS LOCATED ON THE PACIFIC OCEAN, SOUTH OF LOS ANGELES.

GAY/LESBIAN FRIENDLY BUSINESSES: 20

GAY/LESBIAN BARS AND RESTAURANTS: 3

GAY/LESBIAN ORGANIZATIONS: 3

GAY/LESBIAN RELIGIOUS ORGANIZATIONS, CHURCHES, ETC.: 1

GAY/LESBIAN BOOKSTORES: 1

GAY/LESBIAN PUBLICATIONS: 2

COMPANIES THAT PROHIBIT DISCRIMINATION: SEE STATE LAW AND GAY CIVIL RIGHTS

INFORMATION NUMBER: 714-534-3261 ORANGE COUNTY HOTLINE

TOTAL CRIMES: 1,616

VIOLENT = (MURDER = 0, RAPE = 5, ROBBERY = 22, ASSAULT = 164)

PROPERTY = (BURGLARY = 412, LARCENY = 874, MOTOR VEHICLE THEFT = 139, ARSON = 3)

Things to Do!!!

Laguna Beach is an artist haven filled with arts, crafts, antique shops, as well as beautiful beaches. ANNUAL EVENTS: Winterfest. SEASONAL EVENTS: (1) Festival of Arts and Pageant of the Masters, (2) Sawdust Festival.

POPULATION: 23,170 PERSONS—W = 22,191, B = 163, AI/E/A = 71, A/PI = 404, H = 1,590

POPULATION GROWTH: N/A

AGE OF POPULATION: (21-24) = 1,070, (25-34) = 9,233, (35-44) = 3,723, (45-54) = 1,143 (55-64) = 1,023 (65-74) = 3,226 (75 AND OVER) = 1,773

HOUSING COST: OWNING = $311,800   RENTAL = $859
COMMUNITY HOSPITALS: 0
CLIMATE: JAN—AVG. (N/A DEGREES), JULY—AVG. (N/A DEGREES), ANNUAL PRECIPITATION (N/A INCHES)
PER CAPITA INCOME: $ N/A
UNEMPLOYMENT RATE: N/A
JOB GROWTH SINCE 1980: N/A
COST OF LIVING: N/A
EDUCATION: NONE

▼LONG BEACH

Gay Civil Rights: Bans discrimination based on sexual orientation in public employment and private employment.

What the Locals Say . . .

Long Beach gay and lesbian community is fairly open. In the past 10-12 years the legislature has helped tremendously with anti-discrimination. The approximate gay and lesbian population is 30-40,000 and is considered by many to be the 2nd largest gay population in California. The legislature is still pro-gay, although it is teetering to the conservative side. The majority of gays and lesbians live on the east side. The east side is the downtown area through Bellmont Shores - approximately 60 blocks. There are numerous gay bars, businesses, coffee shops, bookstores, photographers, hair stylists and restaurants in this area. Other areas are Naples and California Heights. The Annual Gay Pride Festival and Parade attracts people from Wyoming, Alaska and Colorado as well as throughout California and is considered the 2nd largest in California. "Pearl Booksellers" is a gay and lesbian bookstore in Long Beach. There are 40 different meetings at the "One Community Center," ranging from bisexual rap, gay fathers, HIV testing, various lesbian groups, significant others group, Hispanic groups, drawing club, etc. Recreational groups include: bowling, softball, hardball, walking, running, cycling, whitewater rafting, trips to Yosemite, trips to museums, bike paths to mountains, and bus trips to Sea World. The AIDS Walk is supported by the gay community and non-gay community. There is a Long Beach Lambda Democratic Club. Some of the most popular bars for gay men include: "Floyd's," a country and western bar, and "Ripples," a large disco bar that is on the ocean drawing a younger crowd of gays and lesbians. There are two leather bars: "Wolf's," the largest, and "Sweetwater Saloon." Some of the most popular lesbian bars are "In Cahoots," "Que Sera Sera," the oldest and the largest, and "Executive Suite," a two story restaurant and dance bar. The State of California and the county provide health care service for those that can't pay. AIDS Project Long Beach has social workers and provides services for HIV + persons. Services include food, housing, personal necessities and a buddy system. *The Center Post* is a once a month publication. The three most popular publications in the Long Beach area are: *Frontier, Edge* and the *Advocate*, all of which are published in Los Angeles. The MCC has a predominately gay and lesbian congregation and has a lesbian minister. The Episcopalian Christ Chapel provides a food bank for HIV + individuals. Affirmations, Evangelical's Concerned, and Integrity Southland are all gay and lesbian groups.

LOCATION: LONG BEACH IS TWENTY TWO MILES SOUTH OF DOWNTOWN LOS ANGELES ON THE SOUTHERN COAST OF LOS ANGELES COUNTY.

GAY/LESBIAN FRIENDLY BUSINESSES: 17

GAY/LESBIAN BARS AND RESTAURANTS: 18

GAY/LESBIAN ORGANIZATIONS: 12

GAY/LESBIAN RELIGIOUS ORGANIZATIONS, CHURCHES, ETC.: 5

GAY/LESBIAN BOOKSTORES: 1

GAY/LESBIAN PUBLICATIONS: 4

COMPANIES THAT PROHIBIT DISCRIMINATION: SEE STATE LAW & GAY CIVIL RIGHTS

INFORMATION NUMBER: 310-434-4455 ONE COMMUNITY CENTER

TOTAL CRIMES: 35,630

VIOLENT = (MURDER = 126, RAPE = 200, ROBBERY = 3,717, ASSAULT = 3,073)

PROPERTY = (BURGLARY = 6,780, LARCENY = 14,108, MOTOR VEHICLE THEFT = 7,626, ARSON = 243)

Things to Do!!!

Long Beach is the largest beach city in California. The Metro Blue Line, a 21.5 mile light rail system connects Los Angeles to Long Beach. Other points of interest include: (1) El Dorado Nature Center, (2) Long Beach Museum of Art, (3) Rancho Los Alamitos, (4) Long Beach Community Orchestra, (5) Long Beach Symphony Orchestra, (6) Long Beach Civic Light Opera, (7) Long Beach Opera, (8) Queen Mary Seaport, (9) Shoreline Village, (10) Queen Wharf, (11) Long Beach Convention and Entertainment Center, (12) Alamitos Bay, (13) Rancho Los Cerritos, (14) Catalina Island Cruises.

POPULATION: 438,771 PERSONS—W = 250,716, B = 58,761, AI/E/A = 2,781, C = 3,771, F = 17,329, M = 80,523, PR = 2,063

POPULATION GROWTH: + 21.4%

AGE OF POPULATION: (21-24) = 8.2%, (25-34) = 21.2%, (35-44) = 14.7%, (45-54) = 8.2%, (55-64) = 6.4%, (65-74) = 6.1%, (75 AND OVER) = 6.9%

HOUSING COST: OWNING = $222,900   RENTAL =$605

COMMUNITY HOSPITALS: 6 = 1,853 BEDS

CLIMATE: JAN—AVG. (55.9 DEGREES), JULY—AVG. (73.1 DEGREES), ANNUAL PRECIPITATION (11.80 INCHES)

PER CAPITA INCOME: $15,639

UNEMPLOYMENT RATE: 7.7%

JOB GROWTH SINCE 1980: + 24.7%

COST OF LIVING: 121.1

EDUCATION: CALIFORNIA STATE UNIVERSITY AT LONG BEACH

▼LOS ANGELES

Gay Civil Rights: Bans discrimination based on sexual orientation in public and private employment, public accommodations, education, housing, credit, and union practices.

What the Locals Say . . .

The Los Angeles gay and lesbian community is very open with numerous groups, organizations, bars, restaurants and activities. The name Los Angeles brings to mind different areas to different people. For the purpose of this book, Los Angeles is comprised of Silver Lake, North Hollywood and the actual city of Los Angeles. The Silver Lake area has a large gay and lesbian community. The restaurants, "Casita del Campo" and "Cobalt Cantina," a neighborhood leather bar, "Cuffs," and a multicultural bar "Hyperion" are all popular with the gay and lesbian community in Silver Lake. Los Angeles has numerous gay and lesbian groups including: Great Outdoors/L.A., L.A. Tennis Association, Different Spokes, PFLAG. Political groups in Los Angeles include: Gays and Lesbians Alliance Against Defamation (GLAAD), Log Cabin Republican Club, ACT-UP, Project Rainbow/Society for Gay and Lesbian Citizens Inc., L.A. Radical Women and Stonewall Democratic Club. There is a Youth Outreach Program, Passion Fruits/Gay & Lesbian Vegetarians of Los Angeles, and L.A. Nude Guys. "Sisterhood" bookstore has a variety of lesbian books, periodicals, music and mail order items. The Great American Yankee Freedom Band, SAGA Ski Club, California Great Outdoor, and The Gay & Lesbian Sports Alliance offers soccer, badminton, aquatics, volleyball, softball, etc.. Groups for older gays and lesbians include The Coalition of Older Lesbians, Project Rainbow, and the Society for Senior Gay & Lesbian Citizens Group. Some popular bars in Los Angles are: "Jewel's Catch One," a lesbian bar; "Tempo," "Incognito Valley," "Mag Lounge," "Rawhide," and "Circus Disco" are all men's bars; and "In Touch East," a mixed bar. The "Venture Inn" is a popular place to eat in Los Angeles. Some of North Hollywood's most popular bars include: "Apache Territory," a mixed dance bar, and "Oxwood Inn," a lesbian neighborhood bar. Some of the most popular bars in West Los Angeles are: "Klub Banshee" for women and "Connection" a women's dance bar. The "Golden Bull" is a popular restaurant in West Los Angeles. The Center in Hollywood handles the legal, mental and health services for those with AIDS. The AIDS Project Los Angeles (APLA) is an educational organization. *The Southern California Yellow Pages* is published in Los Angeles, *Edge Magazine,* and *Frontiers* are published twice a month, *Lesbian News, Alternative,* and *SBC* are all published monthly. The Los Angeles Gay and Lesbian Religious Coalition, Dignity of L.A., Evangelical's Together, Seventh Day Adventist International, Gay/Lesbian Buddhist Group, United Lesbian & Gays Christian Scientists, Integrity/Gay & Lesbian Episcopalians, Ministry with Lesbian & Gay Catholics meet regularly. The Free Spirit MCC, Holy Trinity Community Church, First Unitarian Church of Los Angeles, Freedom Tree, Universal Fellowship of MCC, New Directions Church, St. John Episcopalian Church and United Methodist Church are open to gays and lesbians. Lutherans Concerned meets in North Hollywood and In The Valley MCC is in North Hollywood.

LOCATION: LOS ANGELES IS LOCATED IN SOUTHERN CALIFORNIA.

GAY/LESBIAN FRIENDLY BUSINESSES: 500 +

GAY/LESBIAN BARS AND RESTAURANTS: 23 +

GAY/LESBIAN ORGANIZATIONS: 100+

GAY/LESBIAN RELIGIOUS ORGANIZATIONS, CHURCHES, ETC.: 25

GAY/LESBIAN BOOKSTORES: 3

GAY/LESBIAN PUBLICATIONS: 18

COMPANIES THAT PROHIBIT DISCRIMINATION: LOS ANGELES TIMES, LOS ANGELES WEEKLY, SEE STATE LAW & GAY CIVIL RIGHTS

INFORMATION NUMBER: 213-993-7400 LOS ANGELES COMMUNITY CENTER

TOTAL CRIMES: 312,789

VIOLENT = (MURDER = 1,076, RAPE = 1,773, ROBBERY = 38,415, ASSAULT = 42,437)

PROPERTY = (BURGLARY = 50,232, LARCENY = 119,092, MOTOR VEHICLE THEFT = 59,764, ARSON = 5,119)

Things to Do!!!

Griffith Park is a 4,000 acre area that has numerous recreational opportunities that include the L. A. Zoo, horseback riding, scenic drives and hikes, and various sports. Beaches for surfing, scuba diving, fishing and swimming are also available. Other places of interest include: (1) Downtown Area, (2) El Pueblo de Los Angeles Historic Monument, (3) Los Angeles State and County Arboretum, (4) Mulholland Drive, (5) Farmers Market, (6) Southwest Museum, (7) Paramount Film & Television Studios, (8) Television Production Studios, (9) Universal Studios-Hollywood, (10) Los Angeles County Museum of Art, (11) Beit Hashoah, Museum of Tolerance, (12) Watts Towers, (13) Professional Sports: Baseball-Dodgers & Angels, Basketball-Clippers & Lakers, Football- Raiders & Rams, Hockey -

Kings. CLOSE BY—Hollywood, Disneyland, Knotts Berry Farm. ANNUAL EVENTS: (1) Chinese New Year, (2) Hanamatsuri, (3) Cinco de Mayo Celebration, (4) Asian Cultural Festival, (5) Nisei Week, (6) Los Angeles County Fair.

POPULATION: 3,489,779 PERSONS—W = 1,841,182, B = 487,674, AI/E/A = 16,379, C = 67,196, F = 87,625, M = 936,507, PR = 14,367

POPULATION GROWTH: + 17.6%

AGE OF POPULATION: (21-24) = 7.9%, (25-34) = 20.7%, (35-44) = 15.0%, (45-54) = 9.2%, (55-64) = 7.2%, (65-74) = 5.8%, (75 AND OVER) = 4.2%

HOUSING COST: OWNING = $244,500   RENTAL = $600

COMMUNITY HOSPITALS: 28 = 7,656 BEDS

CLIMATE: JAN—AVG. (58.3 DEGREES), JULY—AVG. (74.3 DEGREES), ANNUAL PRECIPITATION (14.77 INCHES)

PER CAPITA INCOME: $16,188

UNEMPLOYMENT RATE: 9.0%

JOB GROWTH SINCE 1980:+ 21%

COST OF LIVING: 121.1

EDUCATION: UNIVERSITY OF CALIFORNIA AT LOS ANGELES, CLEVELAND CHIROPRACTIC COLLEGE, UNIVERSITY OF SOUTHERN CALIFORNIA, LOYOLA MARYMOUNT UNIVERSITY, CALIFORNIA STATE UNIVERSITY LOS ANGELES

▼PALM SPRINGS

Gay Civil Rights: Bans discrimination based on sexual orientation in the following areas-public employment, public accommodations, private employment, and education. (State Law)

What the Locals Say . . .

Palm Springs has a very large gay and lesbian population. More gay than lesbian, though lesbians are locating here at a brisk rate. It is estimated that 30% of the population is gay/lesbian. The city government and the police make no difference between straights and gays. Being gay in Palm Springs is a non-issue. There is a Gay Pride Celebration, Palm Springs Lesbian/Gay Pride, Desert Aids Project, Aids Walk, Bicycle Ride to San Francisco to benefit AIDS, HIV Support Groups, PFlag, Lesbian Rap Groups, Gay Bible Groups, A.A. Groups, Vet. Groups, Gay Youth Groups, Gay Men's Social Club, High Desert Social Club, and on and on. Anywhere is o.k. to live. Most of the bars and clubs are located in Cathedral City just three miles away. There is a multitude of bars, restaurants, and accommodations in the Palm Springs area since this is a resort area. Three of the more popular bars are "C.C. Construction Co," "Choices," and "Streetbar." "Deliah's" is the women's bar. Health care for gays in the Palm Springs area is excellent. People move here from the East to take advantage of the quality health care. Some local publications are: *The Bottom Line* and *The Palm Springs Directory*, published annually. It's a directory of gay supportive businesses. *The Advocate*, published in L.A. but with a Palm Springs issue is also available. Some churches in the area are: MCC of the Desert, Christ Chapel of the Desert, Joshua's House, and the 7th Day Adventist.

LOCATION: PALM SPRINGS IS SOUTHEAST OF LOS ANGELES.

GAY/LESBIAN FRIENDLY BUSINESSES: 38

GAY/LESBIAN BARS AND RESTAURANTS: 19

GAY/LESBIAN ORGANIZATIONS: 20+

GAY/LESBIAN RELIGIOUS ORGANIZATIONS, CHURCHES, ETC.: 5

GAY/LESBIAN BOOKSTORES: 3

GAY/LESBIAN PUBLICATIONS: 3

COMPANIES THAT PROHIBIT DISCRIMINATION: SEE GAY CIVIL RIGHTS

INFORMATION NUMBER: 619-322-8769, PALM SPRINGS LESBIAN GAY PRIDE.

TOTAL CRIMES: 4,070

VIOLENT = (MURDER = 7, RAPE = 18, ROBBERY = 155, ASSAULT = 324)

PROPERTY = (BURGLARY = 1,189, LARCENY = 1,875, MOTOR VEHICLE THEFT= 502, ARSON = 82)

Things to Do!!!

(1) Palm Springs Desert Museum, (2) Palm Springs Golf Course, (3) Palm Springs Aerial Tramway, (4) Moorten's Botanical Garden, (5) Oasis Waterpark, (6) Palm Canyon, (7) Village Green Heritage Center.

POPULATION: 40,623 PERSONS—W = 33,411, B = 1,814, AI/E/A = 297, C = 117, F = 793, M = 5,939, PR = 98

POPULATION GROWTH: + 25.5%

AGE OF POPULATION: (21-24) = 4.8%, (25-34) = 14.4%, (35-44) = 13.0%, (45-54) = 10.8%, (55-64) = 11.8%, (65-74) = 13.8%, (75 AND OVER) = 12.0%

HOUSING COST: OWNING = $141,200   RENTAL = $563

COMMUNITY HOSPITALS: 1 = 348 BEDS

CLIMATE: JAN—AVG. (56.4 DEGREES), JULY—AVG. (92.0 DEGREES), ANNUAL PRECIPITATION (5.31 INCHES)

PER CAPITA INCOME: $19,725

UNEMPLOYMENT RATE: 9.2%

JOB GROWTH SINCE 1980: + 23.9%

COST OF LIVING: 117.8
EDUCATION: NONE

▼PALO ALTO

Gay Civil Rights: Bans discrimination based on sexual orientation in education.

What the Locals Say . . .

Palo Alto has a good sized gay/lesbian community. It is home to Stanford University and also the first Gay Liberation Sculpture in the country. Stanford Lesbian, Gay, Bisexual Community Center organizes and sponsors many activities including Monday night movies, seminars, speakers, dances, and workshops. They have "BE IN" nights at the Stanford Coffeehouse. Palo Alto just passed a domestic partnership law for the city which is now just a registry, but they are moving toward health benefits and other benefits in the future. PLACE is the political and social organization for the community. They are a networking organization which helps with a gay/lesbian youth group, holds monthly socials, and works for political change. PLACE publishes a monthly newsletter. There are no gay bars in Palo Alto and most people go to San Francisco for night life. Gay friendly coffeehouses in the area are: Printer's Ink., which is also a bookstore, and St. Michaels Cafe. There is an ARIS Project for Santa Clara Co. Health care is excellent. Stanford is one of the leading research hospitals in the country. *The Fire Truck House Flame* is the local monthly publication put out by the Stanford Lesbian, Gay, Bisexual Community Center and the *Place Newsletter* is put out by the PLACE organization. There is a Lutheran Church and a Sanford Memorial Church in the area which are gay friendly. The Stanford Memorial Church has performed several gay commitment services. There is also a Unitarian Church in the area.

LOCATION: PALO ALTO IS LOCATED AT THE SOUTHWESTERN END OF SAN FRANCISCO BAY.

GAY/LESBIAN FRIENDLY BUSINESSES: 5

GAY/LESBIAN BARS AND RESTAURANTS: 3

GAY/LESBIAN ORGANIZATIONS: 4

GAY/LESBIAN RELIGIOUS ORGANIZATIONS, CHURCHES, ETC.: 2

GAY/LESBIAN BOOKSTORES: 1

GAY/LESBIAN PUBLICATIONS: 2

COMPANIES THAT PROHIBIT DISCRIMINATION: HEWLETT-PACKARD COMPANY, STANFORD UNIVERSITY, APPLE, SEE STATE LAW AND GAY CIVIL RIGHTS

INFORMATION NUMBER: 415-725-4222, STANFORD LESBIAN, GAY, BISEXUAL COMMUNITY CENTER.

TOTAL CRIMES: 3,409
VIOLENT = (MURDER = 0, RAPE = 11, ROBBERY = 61, ASSAULT = 66)
PROPERTY = (BURGLARY = 487, LARCENY = 2,596, MOTOR VEHICLE
THEFT = 188, ARSON = 15)

Things to Do!!!

Points of interest include: (1) Ancient Redwood trees for which the city is named, (2) Palo Alto Junior Museum, (3) Winter Lodge.

POPULATION: 56,189 PERSONS—W = 47,458, B = 1,612, AI/E/A =
150,C = 2,897, F = 430, M= 1,519, PR = 95
POPULATION GROWTH: + 1.7%
AGE OF POPULATION: (21-24) = 5.2%, (25-34) = 18.8%, (35-44) =
17.8%, (45-54) = 13.0%, (55-64) = 9.1%, (65-74) = 8.8%, (75 AND
OVER) = 6.7%
HOUSING COST: OWNING = $457,800   RENTAL = $851
COMMUNITY HOSPITALS: 0
CLIMATE: JAN—AVG. (47.5 DEGREES), JULY—AVG. (66.4 DEGREES),
ANNUAL PRECIPITATION (14.96 INCHES)
PER CAPITA INCOME: $32,489
UNEMPLOYMENT RATE: 3.3%
JOB GROWTH SINCE 1980: + 5.2%
COST OF LIVING: N/A
EDUCATION: STANFORD

▼RIVERSIDE

Gay Civil Rights: Bans discrimination based on sexual orientation in
public employment.

What the Locals Say . . .

The gay community is very quiet; they are there, but subtle. There is not a strong well organized group in Riverside. The best place to live would be Canyon Crest (CUR area). It is not safe to live in Casa Blanca, the East Side, and Rubidoux. The Gay Pride Fair held on the 4th of July is located at the Humane Society. There is an AIDS Dance-A-Thon for the Inland Empire. There is a Great Outdoors group in the Inland Empire. The bar scene is limited. "The Menagerie" and the "VIP Club" are both mixed. A coffeehouse, The Green Carnation, also houses the Gay and Lesbian Center. The center offers snacks, a specialty gift shop, a coffeeshop, a TV room, and a wide variety of support groups. It is known as a safe, comfortable place to socialize. Publications such as the *Gay and Lesbian Times,* published weekly out of San Diego, include listings for the

Riverside/San Bernardino/Inland Empire area. Riverside is home to the Inland Aids Project. There is Affirmations United Methodist for Lesbian, Gay and Bisexual concerns.

LOCATION: RIVERSIDE IS IN SOUTHERN CALIFORNIA, EAST OF LOS ANGELES.

GAY/LESBIAN FRIENDLY BUSINESSES: 3

GAY/LESBIAN BARS AND RESTAURANTS: 3

GAY/LESBIAN ORGANIZATIONS: 2

GAY/LESBIAN RELIGIOUS ORGANIZATIONS, CHURCHES, ETC.: 1

GAY/LESBIAN BOOKSTORES: 1

GAY/LESBIAN PUBLICATIONS: 0

COMPANIES THAT PROHIBIT DISCRIMINATION: SEE STATE LAW AND GAY CIVIL RIGHTS

INFORMATION NUMBER: 909-884-5447 COMMUNITY CENTER

TOTAL CRIMES: 22,147

VIOLENT = (MURDER = 33, RAPE = 131, ROBBERY = 1,287, ASSAULT = 2,524)

PROPERTY = (BURGLARY = 4,975, LARCENY = 9,635, MOTOR VEHICLE THEFT = 3,562, ARSON = 338)

Things to Do!!!

(1) Book of Life Building and Museum, (2) California Museum of Photography, (3) Jurupa Mountains Cultural Center, (4) Riverside Art Museum, (5) Riverside Municipal Museum, (6) Riverside Symphony Orchestra, (7) Riverside Ballet Theatre, (8) Parent Washington Navel Orange Tree, (9) Castle Amusement Park. ANNUAL EVENTS: Easter Sunrise Pilgrimage.

POPULATION: 238,601 PERSONS—W = 160,344, B = 16,740, AI/E/A = 1,910, C = 1,792, F = 2,293, M = 50,152, PR = 1,320

POPULATION GROWTH: + 39.9%

AGE OF POPULATION: (21-24) = 7.2%, (25-34) = 19.4%, (35-44) = 14.5%, (45-54) = 8.4%, (55-64) = 6.4%, (65-74) = 5.3%, (75 AND OVER) = 3.6%

HOUSING COST: OWNING = $134,800   RENTAL = $575

COMMUNITY HOSPITALS: 4 = 955 BEDS

CLIMATE: JAN—AVG. (53.9 DEGREES), JULY—AVG. (77.9 DEGREES), ANNUAL PRECIPITATION (9.58 INCHES)

PER CAPITA INCOME: $14,235

UNEMPLOYMENT RATE: 10.4%

JOB GROWTH SINCE 1980: + 35.2%

COST OF LIVING: 114.5

EDUCATION: UNIVERSITY OF CALIFORNIA AT RIVERSIDE

▼SACRAMENTO

Gay Civil Rights: Bans discrimination based on sexual orientation in public and private employment, public accommodations, education, housing, credit, and union practices.

What the Locals Say . . .

The gay and lesbian community is large in Sacramento, although they do not know how to work together to get things done. There is a large concentration of gays and lesbians in Mid-Town, sometimes referred to as "Lavender Heights," where there are coffeehouses, restaurants, shops and bars although, gays and lesbians live throughout the town. The Gay Pride Celebration is held in June and is marked with 10 days of events. There is an entertainment stage, comedians, dancers, vendors, and people and organizations that support the community. Life Lobby is a civil rights group for AIDS. There is also the Lambda Letters Project and the River City Democratic Club, and the Log Cabin Club. Sacramento has a Bears Group, a men's' focus group, which is an alternative to the bar. "Cafe Lambda" is a gay coffeehouse that serves desserts and is an alternative to the bar scene. Sacramento has a couples group and the Gay Men's Chorus group. There are professional men's and women's groups, African American groups, Hispanic groups, Asian groups, coming out groups for men, women and youth of all ages. The Community Center has a Senior Group that has social activities including bicycling, pot lucks, game nights, etc.. Sacramento has a gay fathers group, several AA groups, codependent groups, Outdoor Adventures group, a women's camping group, and a women's center. "Lioness Books" is the gay and lesbian bookstore. The Sacramento Rainbow Festival is held in September where a few blocks are closed off and vendors and entertainment are available. "Faces" is a popular men's dance bar although some nights many women are there. "Mirage" is mixed with gays and lesbians. "Jammin Joe's Sports Bars" is a lesbian bar. *The Latest Issue* is published once a month and is very news oriented. *Mom, Guess What!* focuses on the the news, while *Dad, Guess What!* focuses on social events. The Guess What newspapers are published one on alternating weeks. Although not an exclusively gay and lesbian newspaper, *News N Review* is extremely gay-friendly. Dignity of Sacramento is available for gay and lesbian Catholics to attend. The River City Metropolitan Community Church is open to gays and lesbians.

LOCATION: SACRAMENTO IS LOCATED IN A LARGE VALLEY IN NORTH CENTRAL CALIFORNIA WITH THE SIERRA NEVADAS TO THE EAST AND THE PACIFIC COAST TO THE WEST.

GAY/LESBIAN FRIENDLY BUSINESSES: 12

GAY/LESBIAN BARS AND RESTAURANTS: 10

GAY/LESBIAN ORGANIZATIONS: 14

GAY/LESBIAN RELIGIOUS ORGANIZATIONS, CHURCHES, ETC.: 2

GAY/LESBIAN BOOKSTORES: 1

GAY/LESBIAN PUBLICATIONS: 2

COMPANIES THAT PROHIBIT DISCRIMINATION: SEE STATE LAW AND GAY CIVIL RIGHTS

INFORMATION NUMBER: 916-442-0185 LAMBDA COMMUNITY CENTER

TOTAL CRIMES: 39,485

VIOLENT = (MURDER = 85, RAPE = 167, ROBBERY = 2,310, ASSAULT = 2,288)

PROPERTY = (BURGLARY = 8,080, LARCENY = 18,670, MOTOR VEHICLE THEFT = 7,885, ARSON = N/A)

Things to Do!!!

Recreation in the area centers on the Sacramento River and the American River. Boat launches as well as white water rafting are available. The American River Parkway is a twenty-three mile long system that runs adjacent to the river with trails for biking, walking, jogging, horseback riding, picnics, fishing, etc. Other places of interest include: (1) California State Capital, (2) California State Indian Museum, (3) California State Railroad Museum, (4) Camelia Symphony Orchestra, (5) Sacramento Symphony Orchestra, (6) Sacramento Opera, (7) Sacramento Theatre Company, (8) Capital City Ballet, (9) Theatre Ballet of Sacramento, (10) William Land Park, (11) Sacramento History Museum, (12) Crocker Arts Museum, (13) Sacramento Science Center, (14) Professional Sports: Basketball-Kings. SEASONAL EVENTS: (1) Sacramento Jazz Festival, (2) California State Fair.

POPULATION: 382,816 PERSONS—W = 221,963, B = 56,521, AI/E/A = 4,561, C = 18,904, F = 7,195, M = 48,673, PR = 1,607

POPULATION GROWTH: + 38.8%

AGE OF POPULATION: (21-24) = 6.3%, (25-34) = 19.3%, (35-44) = 15.6%, (45-54) = 8.9%, (55-64) = 7.4%, (65-74) = 6.9%, (75 AND OVER) = 5.2%

HOUSING COST: OWNING = $115,800   RENTAL = $495

COMMUNITY HOSPITALS: 7 = 2,408 BEDS

CLIMATE: JAN—AVG. (45.2 DEGREES), JULY—AVG. (75.7 DEGREES), ANNUAL PRECIPITATION (17.52 INCHES)

PER CAPITA INCOME: $14,087

UNEMPLOYMENT RATE: 7.2%

JOB GROWTH SINCE 1980: + 38.4%

COST OF LIVING: N/A

▼SAN DIEGO

Gay Civil Rights: Bans discrimination based on sexual orientation in public and private employment, public accommodations, housing, education, credit and union practices.

What the Locals Say . . .

San Diego seems to be more conservative than some of its sister cities to the north. However, more and more individuals are coming out of the closet. San Diego is a military town and the site for the best military hospital for the treatment of AIDS. Hillcrest is a gay community in the downtown area. The north county area is very conservative and therefore more closeted. In some areas you would be comfortable holding your lover's hand while in others this would not be wise. There is a wide variety of activities to be involved in including: lesbian theater group, lesbian and gay theater group, Democratic and Republican clubs, numerous religious groups, outdoor clubs—running, boating, cycling, tennis, softball, soccer, teachers' groups, rodeo, leather groups, recovery and support groups, bingo, youth groups, rap groups. The Imperial Court is a social organization for gays and lesbians that donates gay and lesbian scholarships and other needed items to the community. The bar scene is very mixed. If you want a specific country, leather, or dance bar contact the Lesbian and Gay Men's Community Center and ask for more information. "The Flame" is a women's bar with different themes on different nights. Later on Sundays, "The Flame" has an older lesbian clientele. "Club Bombay" is another women's bar. Later on Sundays, There are several organizations for older gays and lesbians including: FOG (Fellowship of Older Gays), SAG (Seniors Active in a Gay Environment), Slightly Older Lesbians, and Old Dykes. These organizations have speakers and various activities for members. There is also a Lesbian Community Cultural Event Arts and Crafts Expo. *The Gay and Lesbian Times* is a weekly publication.

LOCATION: SAN DIEGO IS LOCATED ON THE SAN DIEGO BAY IN THE SOUTHERN MOST MAJOR METRO AREA IN CALIFORNIA. IT EXTENDS FROM THE SIERRA NEVADAS TO THE PACIFIC OCEAN AND SOUTH TO THE BORDER WITH MEXICO.

GAY/LESBIAN FRIENDLY BUSINESSES: 63

GAY/LESBIAN BARS AND RESTAURANTS: 28

GAY/LESBIAN ORGANIZATIONS: 24

GAY/LESBIAN RELIGIOUS ORGANIZATIONS, CHURCHES, ETC.: 7

GAY/LESBIAN BOOKSTORES: 2

GAY/LESBIAN PUBLICATIONS: 7

COMPANIES THAT PROHIBIT DISCRIMINATION: SEE STATE LAW AND GAY CIVIL RIGHTS

INFORMATION NUMBER: 619-692-4297 LESBIAN & GAY COMMUNITY CENTER

TOTAL CRIMES: 85,227

VIOLENT = (MURDER = 133, RAPE = 396, ROBBERY = 4,651, ASSAULT = 8,283)

PROPERTY = (BURGLARY = 14,583, LARCENY = 37,862, MOTOR VEHICLE THEFT = 19,319, ARSON = 245)

Things to Do!!!

The San Diego area has a wide variety of terrain and waterways for recreational use. The world famous San Diego Zoo is one of the most famous zoos in the country. Balboa Park includes craft centers, botanical gardens, theater and nine museums. Boating, deep sea fishing, swimming activities, and scuba diving are also available in many areas. Specific points of interest include: (1) Old Town, (2) Cabrillo National Monument, (3) Gaslamp Quarter, (4) Whale Watching Trips, (5) Museum of Contemporary Art, (6) Naval Ship Tour, (7) Seaport Village, (8) San Diego Bay and The Embarcadero, (9) Mission Bay Park, (10) Maritime Museum Association, (11) San Diego Wild Animal Park, (12) Professional Sports: Baseball - Padres, Football - Chargers, Soccer - Sockers, Hockey - Gulls. ANNUAL EVENTS: (1) Corpus Christi Fiesta, (2) Festival of Bells, (3) Admission Day, (4) Cabrillo Festival, (5) Christmas Light Boat Parade.

POPULATION: 1,148,851 PERSONS—W = 745,406, B = 104,261, AI/E/A = 6,800, C = 14,076, F = 63,381, M = 194,400, PR = 5,337

POPULATION GROWTH: + 31.2%

AGE OF POPULATION: (21-24) = 8.6%, (25-34) = 21.1%, (35-44) = 15.3%, (45-54) = 8.7%, (55-64) = 6.9%, (65-74) = 6.1%, (75 AND OVER) = 4.1%

HOUSING COST: OWNING = $189,400   RENTAL = $603

COMMUNITY HOSPITALS: 12 = 2,943 BEDS

CLIMATE: JAN—AVG. (57.4 DEGREES), JULY—AVG. (71.0 DEGREES), ANNUAL PRECIPITATION (9.90 INCHES)

PER CAPITA INCOME: $16,401

UNEMPLOYMENT RATE: 6.2%

JOB GROWTH SINCE 1980: + 33.3%

COST OF LIVING: 124.8

EDUCATION: SAN DIEGO STATE UNIVERSITY, UNIVERSITY OF CALIFORNIA AT SAN DIEGO, UNIVERSITY OF SAN DIEGO

▼SAN FRANCISCO

Gay Civil Rights: Bans discrimination based on sexual orientation in public and private employment, public accommodations, housing, education, credit, and union practices.

What the Locals Say . . .

Where do you begin with San Francisco? First, it is probably the most open gay and lesbian community in the United States. Secondly, it probably has one of the largest gay and lesbian populations in the United States. Thirdly, there is something gay everywhere you look. San Francisco has changed in that gays and lesbians are more scattered throughout the city than before. There are still neighborhoods that are very heavily populated with family members. The Castro is predominately gay men, Mission is predominately Latino men, Noe Valley is very mixed with gays and straights, Potrero Hill has a greater number of lesbians. Nob Hill is probably the most expensive, although none of these areas are slums. Polk Street is a non-residential area that is kind of a cruise area. Market Street is the main street the gay and lesbian parade route takes as well as the location for many bars and restaurants. There are hundreds of gay and lesbian groups in San Francisco. The following are just a few: Golden Gate Performing Arts, S. F. Gay Men's Chorus, S.F. Lesbian/Gay Freedom Band, The Sisters of Perpetual Indulgence, Theatre Rhinoceros—producer and presenter of gay and lesbian theater. Political groups in San Francisco include the Harvey Milk Lesbian & Gay Democratic Club, Log Cabin Republicans Club of S. F., and Alice B. Toklas Democratic club. A social organization for older gay and lesbians is the G Forty Plus Club. Sport and recreational groups include: S.F. Hiking Club, Different Spokes, Foggy City Dancers, Gay Tennis Federation, S.F. Frontrunner/Walkers Club, Homosexuals in the Martial Arts, Golden State Rodeo Association, Community Bowling League and the Northern California Rainbow Divers and Scuba club. The San Francisco Gay Pride Festival attracts approximately 400,000 people. There is a big parade, street dancing, and wall to wall people. The Folsum Street Fair is a leather festival. The bookstore, "Different Light," is a popular bookstore in the Castro. Some of the most popular men's bars in the Castro are: "Detours," "End Up," "Midnight Sun," "Elephant Walk," and the "Phoenix," although the list seems endless. "The Cafe," "The Club," and "Girl Bar" are some of the more popular lesbian bars. Some of the most popular restaurants in the Castro are: the "Baghdad Cafe," "Cafe Flone," "Hot N Hunky," "M and L Market" and "Zuni Cafe." Some of the most popular bars on Polk Street are "Giraffe Lounge," "Kimos," and "The Swallow." The downtown areas has "China Moon Cafe" and "Laxcaux Bar and Rotisserie" restaurants. Some of the most popular restaurants on Polk Street are "Grubstake II," and "Stars Cafe." Some of the most popular bars in the Mission/Potrero Hill area are the lesbian bars, "Faster Pussycat/Snatch," and "Girl Bar;" and the male bar, "Pleasuredome."

Popular restaurants in the Mission/Potrero Hill area include: "Eichelberger's," "Just For You," "Hamburger Mary's," "Red Dora's Bearded Lady." "Shanti" is the largest whole network AIDS organization, it provides a variety of HIV testing sites, support, advocacy, transportation, and recreational activities. There is also the Asian Health Services, Center for AIDS Services, Project Open Hand is expanding but primarily provides food for those infected with AIDS. Operation Concern is a counseling organization for those HIV +. *Ten Percent* and *The Gay Book* are published in San Francisco. The *San Francisco Bay Times* is a gay and lesbian newspaper that is published every two weeks. *The Sentinel* is a weekly publication that focuses more on gay males. *The Bay Area Reporter* is a weekly publication. The Golden Gate Metropolitan Community Church, Trinity Episcopal Church, Congregation Sha'ar Zahav, The MCC of San Francisco are open and supportive to gays and lesbians. Dignity of San Francisco, Unitarian Universalist Gay Lesbian and Bisexual Caucus, The Parsonage, and Lutherans Concerned welcome gays and lesbians.

LOCATION: SAN FRANCISCO IS LOCATED IN NORTHERN CALIFORNIA SURROUNDING THE SAN FRANCISCO BAY.

GAY/LESBIAN FRIENDLY BUSINESSES: 500 +

GAY/LESBIAN BARS AND RESTAURANTS: 500 +

GAY/LESBIAN ORGANIZATIONS: 72

GAY/LESBIAN RELIGIOUS ORGANIZATIONS, CHURCHES, ETC.: 9

GAY/LESBIAN BOOKSTORES: 3

GAY/LESBIAN PUBLICATIONS: 28

COMPANIES THAT PROHIBIT DISCRIMINATION: BANK OF AMERICA, MORRISON & FOERESTER, WORKING ASSETS FUNDING SERVICE, GENETECH INC., LEVI STRAUSS & CO., ORRICK, HERRINGTON & SUTCLIFFE, PACIFIC GAS & ELECTRIC COMPANY, CHARLES SCHWAB & COMPANY, INC., WELLS FARGO & COMPANY

INFORMATION NUMBERS: 510-548-8283 PACIFIC CENTER FOR HUMAN GROWTH

TOTAL CRIMES: 70,132

VIOLENT = (MURDER = 129, RAPE = 361, ROBBERY = 8,454, ASSAULT = 4,421)

PROPERTY = (BURGLARY = 11,153, LARCENY = 34,558, MOTOR VEHICLE THEFT = 11,056, ARSON = 488)

Things to Do!!!

San Francisco Bay is an excellent site for all types of boating, sailing, wind surfing, canoeing, fishing and whale watching. Specific points of interest include: (1) U.S.S. Pampanito, (2) S. S. Jeremiah, (3) Pacific Heritage Museum, (4) National Maritime Museum, (5) Old Mint, (6) Monterey Bay Aquarium, (7) San Francisco Zoo, (8) Chinese Historical Society of America, (9) Alcatraz, (10) Civic Center, (11)

Cow Palace, (12) Twin Peaks, (13) Golden Gate Bridge, (14) San Francisco Museum of Art, (15) Treasure Island Museum, (16) Randall Museum, (17) Exploratorium, (18) California Academy of Sciences, Natural History Museum and Aquarium, (19) The Mexican Museum, (20) San Francisco Zoo, (21) Pier 39, (22) China Town, (23) Nob Hill, (24) Fisherman's Wharf, (25) Professional Sports: Football - 49ers, Baseball - Giants. Annual Events: (1) Harvest Festival, (2) Fleet Week, (3) Carnival, (4) Cherry Blossom Festival.

POPULATION: 728,921 PERSONS= W = 387,783, B = 79,039, AI/E/A =3,456, C=127,140,

F = 42,652, H = 40,744, PR = 4,701

POPULATION GROWTH: + 7.4%

AGE OF POPULATION: (21-24) = 6.8%, (25-34) = 21.9%, (35-44) = 17.9%, (45-54) = 10.3%, (55-64) = 8.8%, (65-74) = 7.9%, (75 AND OVER) = 6.6%

HOUSING COST: OWNING = $298,900   RENTAL = $653

COMMUNITY HOSPITALS: 12 = 3,640 BEDS

CLIMATE: JAN—AVG. (51.1 DEGREES), JULY—AVG. (59.1 DEGREES), ANNUAL PRECIPITATION (19.71 INCHES)

PER CAPITA INCOME: $19,695

UNEMPLOYMENT RATE: 5.6%

JOB GROWTH SINCE 1980: + 12.6%

COST OF LIVING: N/A

EDUCATION: MERRITT COLLEGE, SAN FRANCISCO STATE UNIVERSITY, UNIVERSITY OF CALIFORNIA, UNIVERSITY OF SAN FRANCISCO

▼SAN JOSE

Gay Civil Rights: Bans discrimination based on sexual orientation in public employment.

What the Locals Say . . .

The San Jose gay and lesbian community is open in some places and very closeted in others. If there were some big gay/lesbian event in town, some would feel comfortable holding hands there. There is not really an area that gays and lesbians congregate to live. There is a group of High Tech Gays and Bay Area Network of Gay/Lesbian Education. The Community Center offers various classes from car tune-up to dog obedience. The Community Center has a lounge area that serves gourmet coffee, offers card games, bingo in a non alcohol and smoke free environment, bicycle service and many other activities. "Levitco" is a popular coffeeshop. Sister Spirit is a gay and lesbian bookstore and is housed in the Community Center. San Jose has 3 youth groups and 1 group for women 40 and older. There are various sports to choose from including volleyball, bowling, softball, hiking, kayaking, and cycling. There is a Gay Pride Celebration that includes a parade. "Selections" and "Savoy" are lesbian bars. "Club St. John" is predominantly men, although there are women's days. "Greg's" and "Renegades" are gay men's bars. There is an adult and child guidance center for gays and lesbians to utilize. ARIS is an AIDS organization. *Out Now* is the main gay and lesbian publication out of San Jose and it comes out every other week. There is a Dignity group and a MCC and Prince of Peace Church that welcomes gays and lesbians.

LOCATION: SAN JOSE IS LOCATED IN THE SOUTH END OF THE SAN FRANCISCO BAY, 50 MILES FROM SAN FRANCISCO.

GAY/LESBIAN FRIENDLY BUSINESSES: 11

GAY/LESBIAN BARS AND RESTAURANTS: 8

GAY/LESBIAN ORGANIZATIONS: 22

GAY/LESBIAN RELIGIOUS ORGANIZATIONS, CHURCHES, ETC.: 4

GAY/LESBIAN BOOKSTORES: 1

GAY/LESBIAN PUBLICATIONS: 3

COMPANIES THAT PROHIBIT DISCRIMINATION: FRAME TECHNOLOGY, SEE STATE LAW AND GAY CIVIL RIGHTS

INFORMATION NUMBER: 408-293-2429 BILLY DEFRANK LESBIAN & GAY COMMUNITY CENTER

TOTAL CRIMES: 36,743

VIOLENT = (MURDER = 41, RAPE = 391, ROBBERY = 1,186, ASSAULT = 3,699)

PROPERTY = (BURGLARY = 6,014, LARCENY = 21,398, MOTOR VEHICLE THEFT = 4,014, ARSON = 318)

Things to Do!!!

(1) Kelley Park, (2) Rosicrucian Park, (3) Alum Rock Park, (4) Municipal Rose Gardens, (5) Lick Observatory, (6) San Jose Museum of Art, (7) Winchester Mystery House, (8) American Museum of Quilts & Textiles. ANNUAL EVENTS: (1) San Jose American Festival, (2) Obon Festival, (3) Santa Clara County Fair, (4) Firefighters Rodeo.

POPULATION: 801,331 PERSONS—W = 491,280, B = 36,790, AI/E/A = 5,416, C = 31,112, F = 38,169, M = 173,803, PR = 4,472

POPULATION GROWTH: + 27.3%

AGE OF POPULATION: (21-24) = 7.0%, (25-34) = 21.3%, (35-44) = 16.1%, (45-54) = 10.2%, (55-64) = 6.7%, (65-74) = 4.4%, (75 AND OVER) = 2.8%

HOUSING COST: OWNING = $259,100   RENTAL = $755

COMMUNITY HOSPITALS: 6 = 1,692 BEDS

CLIMATE: JAN—AVG. (49.4 DEGREES), JULY—AVG. (69.5 DEGREES), ANNUAL PRECIPITATION (14.42 INCHES)

PER CAPITA INCOME: $16,905
UNEMPLOYMENT RATE: 6.4%
JOB GROWTH SINCE 1980: + 32.4%
COST OF LIVING: N/A
EDUCATION: SAN JOSE STATE UNIVERSITY

▼SANTA BARBARA

Gay Civil Rights: Bans discrimination based on sexual orientation in public employment and education.

What the Locals Say . . .

Part of the gay and lesbian community in Santa Barbara is definitely out and about, but there are some that are still in the closet. Santa Barbara does enjoy having an openly out city council member which provides the gay and lesbian community with a voice. The very existence of the community center is a positive sign. The Santa Barbara press is generally responsive and positive to the gay community. The architecture of the city is Victorian and Spanish style throughout. Although unofficial, there are 2 apartment complexes who solicit gay and lesbian business. The Merhoho Apartments and the Arlington Apartments rent to numerous family members. To the south of Santa Barbara is a community called Montecito. Montecito is a very upscale neighborhood where some gay celebrities live. Great Outdoors is an organization for men and women and offers a non-bar alternative via various outdoor activities. Nature oriented, the activities include: fishing, whale watching, camping, hiking, and pot lucks, etc. Choices Books/Coffeeshop is a gay and lesbian bookstore. The Greater Santa Barbara Business Association is a group of businesses and entrepreneurs that encourage gays and lesbians to choose gay and lesbian businesses to meet their needs. The Community Center offers counseling and recovery programs, youth services, gay and lesbian support groups, HIV support groups. The AIDS organization is a sub-group of the community center. The AIDS organization is the largest organization between Los Angeles and San Francisco. Service is offered throughout the county. Services include a food pantry for low income individuals with AIDS, meals on wheels, transportation, internships, nurse care management, outreach and education. Local Response is a political group that endorses candidates. Queer Nation is a militant queer rights group and Stonewall Democratic Club endorses Democrats. ACT-UP is the AIDS Coalition to Unleash Power. "Queer Radio" is the name of the radio station out of the University of California Santa Barbara. The local access television station runs gay and lesbian programs from time to time. There is a Santa Barbara Gay and Lesbian Film Festival. The Gay Pride Celebration is a weekend of events on the beach and has dance floors, various gay friendly organizations, volleyball tournaments, sky divers, boats and yachts displaying pride flags. "Cafe Sienna" is a gay coffeehouse that draws a young gay crowd and "The Green Dragon" is mixed with straight and gays. "Club Oasis" is the oldest bar and caters to men and women, as does the "Gold Coast." "Elsie's"s attracts more lesbians. The "Pub" is predominantly a men's bar. *The Bulletin* is a monthly Santa Barbara publication. The MCC, Unitarian Community Church and St. Mark's Catholic are gay friendly.

LOCATION: SANTA BARBARA FACES EAST AND WEST ON THE PACIFIC OCEAN, ALONG THE CALMEST STRETCH OF THE PACIFIC, AND LIES NORTH OF LOS ANGELES.

GAY/LESBIAN FRIENDLY BUSINESSES: 10

GAY/LESBIAN BARS AND RESTAURANTS: 6

GAY/LESBIAN ORGANIZATIONS: 9

GAY/LESBIAN RELIGIOUS ORGANIZATIONS, CHURCHES, ETC.: 3

GAY/LESBIAN BOOKSTORES: 1

GAY/LESBIAN PUBLICATIONS: 1

COMPANIES THAT PROHIBIT DISCRIMINATION: SEE STATE LAW AND GAY CIVIL RIGHTS

INFORMATION NUMBER: 805-963-3636 THE GAY & LESBIAN RESOURCE CENTER

TOTAL CRIMES: 5,152

VIOLENT = (MURDER = 5, RAPE = 44, ROBBERY = 159, ASSAULT = 463)

PROPERTY = (BURGLARY = 938, LARCENY = 3,317, MOTOR VEHICLE THEFT = 226, ARSON = 18)

Things to Do!!!

(1) Santa Barbara Historical Museum, (2) Santa Barbara Museum of Natural History, (3) Santa Barbara County Courthouse, (4) Mission Santa Barbara, (5) El Paseo, (6) Santa Barbara Museum of Art, (7) Los Padres National Forest, (8) Santa Barbara Zoo, (9) Santa Barbara Botanic Garden, (10) Stearns Wharf. ANNUAL EVENTS: (1) Santa Barbara International Orchid Show, (2) Summer Sports Festival, (3) Santa Barbara National Horse Show, (4) Old Spanish Days Fiesta.

POPULATION: 85,119 PERSONS—W = 66,529, B = 1,920, AI/E/A = 758, C = 421, F = 425, M = 23,798, PR = 183

POPULATION GROWTH: + 14.4%

AGE OF POPULATION: (21-24) = 8.4%, (25-34) = 20.6%, (35-44) = 16.0%, (45-54) = 8.5%, (55-64) = 7.2%, (65-74) = 7.5%, (75 AND OVER) = 8.7%

HOUSING COST: OWNING = $346,900   RENTAL = $715

COMMUNITY HOSPITALS: 4 = 538 BEDS

CLIMATE: JAN—AVG. (52.0 DEGREES), JULY—AVG. (65.4 DEGREES), ANNUAL PRECIPITATION (16.25 INCHES)
PER CAPITA INCOME: $18,934
UNEMPLOYMENT RATE: 4.7%
JOB GROWTH SINCE 1980: + 25.2%
COST OF LIVING: N/A
EDUCATION: UNIVERSITY OF CALIFORNIA AT SANTA BARBARA

▼SANTA CRUZ

Gay Civil Rights: Bans discrimination based on sexual orientation in public employment.

What the Locals Say . . .

Santa Cruz is predominately a lesbian community, with a breakdown of about 60% lesbian and 40% gay males. The Lesbian community is very strong and very out. The atmosphere throughout Santa Cruz is come as you are. It is not uncommon to see gay or lesbian couples holding hands on main street. There is no specific area where gays and lesbians live, they are scattered throughout. "Her Land" is a book shop/cafe which is a clearinghouse for lesbian information in the city. It plays host to several lesbian popular artists when they come to town, and sponsors a variety of activities that go on in the lesbian community. There is a gay volleyball beach organization, a lesbian chorus, and a gay youth group. Annual Gay Pride Parade and Day has booths and activities throughout the day. Santa Cruz has a gay evening in May and it is quite a gala. The Lesbian Avengers is a new group formed in Santa Cruz. "Nickelodeon" is a cinema that plays lesbian and gay films as well as straight newly released films. There is a spa that has a women's only night. Santa Cruz has a closet free radio slot on the college radio station. There are several support groups for AIDS/HIV. "The Blue Lagoon" is a gay dance bar, although the proprietor is thinking of turning it into an alternative dance bar for the college crowd. Rumor has it that there is a new gay bar opening-but no details. There is a bagel brunch at the community center. The Santa Cruz AIDS Project (SCAP) is very large and offers many services. The gay and lesbian newsletters are *News and Views*, published once a month by the Community Center, and a quarterly newsletter called *Lavender Reader*.

LOCATION: SANTA CRUZ IS LOCATED ON THE PACIFIC OCEAN IN THE SOUTHWESTERN PART OF THE METRO AREA.
GAY/LESBIAN FRIENDLY BUSINESSES: 5
GAY/LESBIAN BARS AND RESTAURANTS: 1
GAY/LESBIAN ORGANIZATIONS: 3
GAY/LESBIAN RELIGIOUS ORGANIZATIONS, CHURCHES, ETC.: 8

GAY/LESBIAN BOOKSTORES: 1

GAY/LESBIAN PUBLICATIONS: 2

COMPANIES THAT PROHIBIT DISCRIMINATION: SEE STATE LAW AND GAY CIVIL RIGHTS

INFORMATION NUMBER: 408-425-5422 LESBIAN GAY & BISEXUAL COMMUNITY CENTER

TOTAL CRIMES: 4,211

VIOLENT = (MURDER = 3, RAPE = 8, ROBBERY = 109, ASSAULT = 354)

PROPERTY = (BURGLARY = 724, LARCENY = 2,793, MOTOR VEHICLE THEFT = 220, ARSON = 33)

Things to Do!!!

Santa Cruz is a busy seaside resort with an arts and crafts center and 29 miles of public beaches. Specific points of interest include: (1) Santa Cruz Mission State Historical Park, (2) Santa Cruz Museum of Natural History, (3) Mystery Spot, (4) Felton Covered Bridge, (5) West Cliff Drive, (6) Santa Cruz Beach Boardwalk, (7) Bargetto Winery, (8) Wilder Ranch, (9) Big Basin Redwoods, (10) Henry Cowell Redwoods, (11) Natural Bridge Beach, (12) Sea cliff Beach. ANNUAL: (1) Cabrillo Music Festival, (2) National Begonia Festival, (3) Santa Cruz County Fair, (4) Mountain Man Rendezvous. SEASONAL EVENTS: Shakespeare/ Santa Cruz Festival.

POPULATION: 48,835 PERSONS = W = 42,115, B = 1,129, AI/E/A = 425, C = 646, F = 499, M = 5,204, PR = 125

POPULATION GROWTH: + 17.7%

AGE OF POPULATION: (21-24) = 11.0%, (25-34) = 19.0%, (35-44) = 18.1%, (45-54) = 8.0%, (55-64) = 5.3%, (65-74) = 5.3%, (75 AND OVER) = 4.8%

HOUSING COST: OWNING = $263,200   RENTAL = $707

COMMUNITY HOSPITALS: 1 = 265 BEDS

CLIMATE: JAN—AVG. (49.9 DEGREES), JULY—AVG. (63.5 DEGREES), ANNUAL PRECIPITATION (28.99 INCHES)

PER CAPITA INCOME: $15,538

UNEMPLOYMENT RATE: 8.3%

JOB GROWTH SINCE 1980: + 34.0%

COST OF LIVING: N/A

EDUCATION: UNIVERSITY OF SANTA CRUZ, UNIVERSITY OF CALIFORNIA AT SANTA CRUZ

▼SANTA MONICA

Gay Civil Rights: Bans discrimination based on sexual orientation in public and private employment, public accommodations, housing, education, credit, and union practices.

What the Locals Say . . .

Gays are everywhere here but not necessarily out. They "blend in" with the rest of the community. They are in Santa Monica living, not to be around other gays. Many family members can be found on the 3rd Promenade and Main Streets. Any neighborhood is safe, with the Venice area, Santa Monica near Ocean Park, and the area around Santa Monica College being more gay/lesbian prevalent. Groups located in the area are: Front Runners, a running group for gays and lesbians, The Santa Monica Lesbian Network, Asian Pacific Lesbian and Gay Club, Webb Lesbian and Gay Advisory Council and Aids Project. There is also a job hot line. Companies known not to discriminate against gays and lesbians are the Gay and Lesbian Community Center and Aunt Bea's Laundry. Events include the West Hollywood Pride Parade and the West Long Beach Festival held in May. There are a couple of bars. "The Friendship," a mixed neighborhood bar and the "Palms," mostly women. There is a great coffeehouse called "Vango"s Ear." There are lots of other bars in West Hollywood, not very far away. There are many publications which can be obtained at any bar or coffeehouse. Churches friendly to us are: Christ Chapel Of The Valley, Unitarian Community Church, and United Methodist Church.

LOCATION: SANTA MONICA IS LOCATED AT THE END OF WILSHIRE BOULEVARD, WEST OF LOS ANGELES.

GAY/LESBIAN FRIENDLY BUSINESSES: 10

GAY/LESBIAN BARS AND RESTAURANTS: 1

GAY/LESBIAN ORGANIZATIONS: 5

GAY/LESBIAN RELIGIOUS ORGANIZATIONS, CHURCHES, ETC.: 6

GAY/LESBIAN BOOKSTORES: 1

GAY/LESBIAN PUBLICATIONS: 0

COMPANIES THAT PROHIBIT DISCRIMINATION: SEE STATE LAW AND GAY CIVIL RIGHTS

INFORMATION NUMBER: 213-993-7400 LOS ANGELES COMMUNITY CENTER

TOTAL CRIMES: 10,891

VIOLENT = (MURDER = 9, RAPE = 49, ROBBERY = 716, ASSAULT = 671)

PROPERTY = (BURGLARY = 1,511, LARCENY = 6,181, MOTOR VEHICLE THEFT = 1,754, ARSON = 137)

Things to Do!!!

(1) Santa Monica Pier, (2) Promenade, (3) Santa Monica Heritage Museum, (4) Palisades Park, (5) Museum of Flying, (6) Santa Monica State Beach.

POPULATION: 87,064 PERSONS—W = 71,961, B = 3,920, AI/E/A = 384, C = 1,760, F = 494, M = 8,583, PR = 195

POPULATION GROWTH: - 1.4%

AGE OF POPULATION: (21-24) = 4.7%, (25-34) = 22.6%, (35-44) = 20.1%, (45-54) = 11.2%, (55-64) = 8.5%, (65-74) = 8.2%, (75 AND OVER) = 8.3%

HOUSING COST: OWNING = $500,001   RENTAL = $532

COMMUNITY HOSPITALS: 2 = 647 BEDS

CLIMATE: JAN—AVG. (57.2 DEGREES), JULY—AVG. (65.5 DEGREES), ANNUAL PRECIPITATION (13.21 INCHES)

PER CAPITA INCOME: $29,134

UNEMPLOYMENT RATE: 5.8%

JOB GROWTH SINCE 1980: + 4.8%

COST OF LIVING: N/A

EDUCATION: VIDAL SASSOON ACADEMY, SANTA MONICA COMMUNITY COLLEGE

SANTA ROSA

Gay Civil Rights: Bans discrimination based on sexual orientation in public and private employment, public accommodations, housing, education, credit and union practices. (State Law)

What the Locals Say . . .

The Santa Rosa community including the Russian River Resort area is mostly open and has a large gay/lesbian population. Police make no difference between gays and straights. Santa Rosa is referred to as "God's Country" by the locals. Within an hour's drive are the California Redwoods. The political atmosphere is mixed but mostly accepting. Renting is reasonable, but owning is very expensive. Almost anywhere in Santa Rosa is good to live. The Russian River Resort area is within 15-20 minutes away. Approximately 30% of its population is gay. Activities in the area are Gay Pride Picnic held on the Santa Rosa Jr College campus, Gay/Lesbian Comedy Night, Talent No Talent. There is a Project 10 which provides AIDS support in the way of a food bank, education, speakers. Face To Face , GALAP In Motion, RAM of Men, Bay Area Career Women, and Theatre Co. are also in the area. There is a weekly radio show called "Straight Talk," for the gay community. "The Santa Rosa Inn" is a mixed dance bar with pool tables. "The Rainbow Cattle Co." is for men. "The Blue Moon" and "Lolita's" are for women. "The Molly Brown's Saloon" is a mixed bar/restaurant. "Ziggurat" is a mixed bar. A couple of gay friendly coffeehouses are Cafe Uropa and Aroma Roaster. The Breeze Inn Barb-Q has take out and is mixed. North Light Books is owned by two women. Health care is good. The local publication, *We The People*, can be found at the bookstores and coffeehouses. New Hope MCC is in Santa Rosa. There is also the Russian River MCC.

LOCATION: SANTA ROSA IS LOCATED IN SONOMA COUNTY SURROUNDED BY MOUNTAINS AND VINEYARDS IN THE NORTHWESTERN PART OF THE SAN FRANCISCO METRO AREA.

GAY/LESBIAN FRIENDLY BUSINESSES: 36

GAY/LESBIAN BARS AND RESTAURANTS: 11

GAY/LESBIAN ORGANIZATIONS: 10

GAY/LESBIAN RELIGIOUS ORGANIZATIONS, CHURCHES, ETC.: 1

GAY/LESBIAN BOOKSTORES: 2

GAY/LESBIAN PUBLICATIONS: 1

COMPANIES THAT PROHIBIT DISCRIMINATION: SANTA ROSA JR. COLLEGE, SEE STATE LAW AND GAY CIVIL RIGHTS

INFORMATION NUMBER: 510-548-8283

TOTAL CRIMES: 7,696

VIOLENT = (MURDER = 7 RAPE = 102, ROBBERY = 197, ASSAULT = 326)

PROPERTY = (BURGLARY = 1,545, LARCENY = 5,011, MOTOR VEHICLE THEFT = 508, ARSON = 58)

Things to Do!!!

(1) Snoopy's Gallery, (2) Sonoma County Museum, (3) Luther Burbank Home and Graves. ANNUAL: Sonoma County Fair

POPULATION: 116,554 PERSONS—W = 101,270, B = 2,031, AI/E/A = 1,382, C = 771, F = 516, M = 8,170, PR = 257

POPULATION GROWTH: + 41%

AGE OF POPULATION: (21-24) = 5.4%, (25-34) = 16.5%, (35-44) = 17.1%, (45-54) = 9.4%, (55-64) = 7.2%, (65-74) = 8.6%, (75 AND OVER) = 7.7%

HOUSING COST: OWNING = $193,88 RENTAL = $638

COMMUNITY HOSPITALS: 4 = 510 BEDS

CLIMATE: JAN—AVG. (47.4 DEGREES), JULY—AVG. (67.6 DEGREES), ANNUAL PRECIPITATION (30.30 INCHES)

PER CAPITA INCOME: $17,259

UNEMPLOYMENT RATE: 5.1%

JOB GROWTH SINCE 1980: + 49.2%

COST OF LIVING: 131.0

EDUCATION: NONE

▼WEST HOLLYWOOD

Gay Civil Rights: Bans discrimination based on sexual orientation in public and private employment, public accommodations, housing, education, credit, and union practices.

What the Locals Say . . .

West Hollywood is very close to Los Angeles, in fact when you ask about gay and lesbian activities in Los Angeles, more often than not the answer will be, "it is in West Hollywood." West Hollywood is unique in that the main drag (Santa Monica Boulevard) is lined with gay pride flags. The city of West Hollywood was founded approximately 10 years ago for two basic reasons. The Los Angeles Police Department tended to harass gays and lesbians in Los Angeles so many family members would go to West Hollywood to be out of their jurisdiction. The other reason was for renter rights or rent stabilization. Two of the the city council members are openly gay. West Hollywood has its own "Frontrunners Track Club," "Women's Chorus of Los Angeles," "West Coast Singers," and "Gay Men's Chorus of Los Angeles." There is a gay fathers group, the "Gay & Lesbian Media Coalition," the "Butch Femme Network," a couples group, the "Golden State Gay Rodeo Association," "Tinseltown Squares" and the "West Hollywood Democratic Club." "Maverick Productions" produces lesbian and gay comedy at The Comedy Store. "The Los Angeles International Gay and Lesbian Film Festival" is held in West Hollywood. "The Los Angeles Business and Professionals Association" is located in West Hollywood. The "French Quarter Market Place," "Little Frida's Coffee Bar," "The Six Gallery Cafe" and "Yukon Mining Co." are popular places to eat. The Gay Pride Celebration is huge because Los Angeles and West Hollywood's are together and attract around 500,000. There are big city block parties for Mardi Gras and Halloween. The famous "Don't Panic Store" is located in West Hollywood as well as the "Different Light Bookstore." "Circus of Books" is a lesbian/gay feminist bookstore. There are several men's bars in West Hollywood including "Hunters," "The Gold Coast," and "Mother Lode;" are all neighborhood bars. "The Palms" is a lesbian neighborhood bar, and "Girl Bar" is a lesbian dance bar. "Arena," "Rage," and "Rafters" are gay men's dance bars. The Lesbian Health Project is in West Hollywood. *Frontiers* and *Planet Homo* are published in West Hollywood. There is a group of Dignity and Affirmations that meet regularly. The congregation Kolami, Evangelical's Together, St. Ambrose Roman Catholic Church, United Methodist, and West Hollywood Presbyterian Church are open to gays and lesbians.

LOCATION: WEST HOLLYWOOD IS LOCATED NORTHWEST OF LOS ANGELES.

GAY/LESBIAN FRIENDLY BUSINESSES: MAJORITY

GAY/LESBIAN BARS AND RESTAURANTS: 9

GAY/LESBIAN ORGANIZATIONS: 40

GAY/LESBIAN RELIGIOUS ORGANIZATIONS, CHURCHES, ETC.: 6

GAY/LESBIAN BOOKSTORES: 3

GAY/LESBIAN PUBLICATIONS: 3

COMPANIES THAT PROHIBIT DISCRIMINATION: SEE STATE LAW AND GAY CIVIL RIGHTS

INFORMATION NUMBER: 213-993-7400 LOS ANGELES COMMUNITY CENTER

TOTAL CRIMES: 4,250

VIOLENT = (MURDER = 5, RAPE = 26, ROBBERY = 485, ASSAULT = 352)

PROPERTY = (BURGLARY = 675, LARCENY = 1,838, MOTOR VEHICLE THEFT = 869, ARSON = 20)

Things to Do!!!

There are many speciality shops in West Hollywood. The Pacific Design Center is an interior design mall.

POPULATION: 35,209 PERSONS—W = 32,571, B = 1,235, AI/E/A = 130, C = 191, F = 246, M = 1,425, PR = 132

POPULATION GROWTH: N/A

AGE OF POPULATION: (21-24) = 5.3%, (25-34) = 28.7%, (35-44) = 20.6%, (45-54) = 9.8%, (55-64) = 8.5%, (65-74) = 8.5%, (75 AND OVER) = 9.8%

HOUSING COST: OWNING = $351,700   RENTAL = $608

COMMUNITY HOSPITALS: 0

CLIMATE: JAN—AVG. (58.3 DEGREES), JULY—AVG. (74.3 DEGREES), ANNUAL PRECIPITATION (14.77 INCHES)

PER CAPITA INCOME: $ $24,386

UNEMPLOYMENT RATE: 10.6%

JOB GROWTH SINCE 1980: N/A

COST OF LIVING: N/A

EDUCATION: NONE

COUNTIES:

ALAMEDA COUNTY

Gay Civil Rights:

Cities and Towns included within Alameda County:

Alameda
Albany
Albrae
Altamont
Alvarado Hall
Ashland

Berkeley
Baumberg
Castro Valley
Cherryland
Dublin
El Cerrito
Elmhurst
Emeryville
Estudillio
Fairview
Fremont
Fruitvale
Hayward
Hayward Highlands
Irvington
Livermore
Melrose
Mountain View
Mulford
Newark
Oakland
Piedmont
Pleasanton
Radum
Redmont Cut
Richmond
San Leandro
San Lorenzo
Sunol
Trevarno
Ulmar
Union City

SAN MATEO COUNTY

Gay Civil Rights: Bans discrimination based on sexual orientation in public and private employment and housing.

Cities and Towns included within San Mateo County:

Atherton
Belmont
Brisbane
Broadmoor
Burlingame
Colma
Daly City
East Palo Alto
ElGranada
Emerald Lake Hills
Foster City
Half Moon Bay
Highland
Hillsboroush
Millbrae
Menlo
Montara Moss Beach
North Fair Oaks
Pacifica
Portola Valley
Redwood City
San Bruno
San Carlos
San Francisco
South San Francisco
San Mateo
West Menlo Park
Woodside

SANTA BARBARA COUNTY

Gay Civil Rights: Bans discrimination based on sexual orientation in public employment.

Cities and Towns included within Santa Barbara County:

Buellton
Carpinteria
Cuyama
Guadalupe

Isla Vista
Lompoc
Mission Hills
Santa Barbara
Santa Maria
Santa Ynez
Solvang
Vanderberg
Vanderberg Village

SANTA CRUZ COUNTY

Gay Civil Rights: Bans discrimination based on sexual orientation in public employment.

Cities and Towns included within Santa Cruz County:

Aptos
Boulder Creek
Ben Lomond
Capitola
Corralitos
Day Village
Fellow
Felton
Freedom
Interlaken
Live Oak
Opal Cliffs
Rio de Mar
Santa Cruz
Scotts Valley
Soquel Capitola
Twin Lakes
Watsonville

COLORADO

STATE LAWS REGARDING HOMOSEXUALITY:

In 1971, Governor John A. Love signed a new penal code that legalized homosexual acts between consenting adults. In 1992, Amendment 2, a constitutional amendment that barred lesbian and gay men from receiving any civil rights protection nullified civil rights laws in Denver, Boulder, and Aspen. Colorado, therefore, was nicknamed the 'HATE STATE." However, the initiative was declared unconstitutional in December 1993 by the State Supreme Court. The case is currently pending in the United States Supreme Court. There is statewide protection in public employment covering sexual orientation.

CITIES: (60,000 AND UP)

▼BOULDER

Gay Civil Rights: Bans discrimination based on sexual orientation in public and private employment and public accommodations.

What the Locals Say . . .

Gays and Lesbians are safer in Boulder than in any other city in Colorado. The city has gay civil rights protection voted in by the populace. The right wing is not strong in Boulder. It is a very liberal city; however, most of the towns around Boulder are very closed. Gays living in Boulder say it is five square miles surrounded by reality. Boulder is "white" and "wealthy." Gays and lesbians are plentiful in the city but are hard to find. They blend in with the rest of the community. Good areas to live are central and downtown. The bar scene is limited since Denver is only 45 minutes away; however, there is one called "The Yard" which has a mixed crowd on Fridays and a Lesbian crowd on Saturdays. Boulder is described as the coffeehouse capital of the world and most of them are gay friendly. Two are thought to be particularly gay friendly; the "Java Hut" and the "Walnut Cafe." There is a city sponsored project called Valuing and Celebrating Diversity which aims to help educate the community concerning gay and lesbian issues. For lesbians there is The Lesbian Connection; it's an activities and social group. For gays there is a group called Man 2 Man. For people 20 and under, there is Coming Out Boulder. There is also a Colorado Aids Project and GLB Resource Center and a Lesbian, Bisexual and Gay Alliance. The First Methodist and The First Congregational Churches are both gay friendly. Also, there is a Gay and Concerned Catholics group. Because of the city ordinance, the city of Boulder does not discriminate against its gay and lesbian employees.

LOCATION: BOULDER IS LOCATED AT THE HEAD OF A RICH AGRICULTURAL VALLEY AND THE BASE OF THE ROCKY MOUNTAINS.

GAY/LESBIAN FRIENDLY BUSINESSES: 5

GAY/LESBIAN BARS AND RESTAURANTS: 3

GAY/LESBIAN ORGANIZATIONS: 10

GAY/LESBIAN RELIGIOUS ORGANIZATIONS, CHURCHES, ETC.: 3

GAY/LESBIAN BOOKSTORES: 0

GAY/LESBIAN PUBLICATIONS: 0

COMPANIES THAT PROHIBIT DISCRIMINATION: CELESTIAL SEASONING, INC., SEE STATE LAW AND GAY CIVIL RIGHTS

INFORMATION NUMBER: 303-441-1244 COMING OUT BOULDER

TOTAL CRIMES: 5,817

VIOLENT = (MURDER = 1, RAPE = 20, ROBBERY = 40, ASSAULT = 122)

PROPERTY = (BURGLARY = 947, LARCENY = 4,398, MOTOR VEHICLE THEFT = 289, ARSON = 18)

Things to Do!!!

Boulder is unique in that it is the only city in the world that obtains part of its water supply from a city-owned glacier. Because of its mild climate, the outdoor enthusiasts can choose from a variety of activities. Other places of interest include: (1) Boulder Center of the Visual Arts, (2) Downtown Mall, (3) Boulder Laboratories of the National Institute of Standards and Technology, National Oceanic and Atmospheric Administration, and National Telecommunications and Information Administration, (4) National Center for Atmospheric Research, (5) Boulder Historical Society, (6) Boulder Reservoir. ANNUAL EVENTS: (1) Kinetic Conveyance Challenge, (2) Bolder Boulder. SEASONAL EVENTS: (1) Colorado Music Festival, (2) Colorado Shakespeare Festival.

POPULATION: 85,616 PERSONS—W = 77,090, B = 1,048, AI/E/A = 414, C = 949, F = 125, M = 2,517, PR = 138

POPULATION GROWTH: + 11.6%

AGE OF POPULATION: (21-24) = 12.4%, (25-34) = 20.4%, (35-44) = 16.6%, (45-54) = 8.4%, (55-64) = 5.3%, (65-74) = 4.0%, (75 AND OVER) = 3.8%

HOUSING COST: OWNING = $122,700   RENTAL = $521

COMMUNITY HOSPITALS: 1 = 209 BEDS

CLIMATE: JAN—AVG. (32.6 DEGREES), JULY—AVG. (73.0 DEGREES), ANNUAL PRECIPITATION (18.58 INCHES)

PER CAPITA INCOME: $17,268

UNEMPLOYMENT RATE: 3.7%

POPULATION GROWTH: + 11.6%

COST OF LIVING: 113.2

▼DENVER

Gay Civil Rights: Bans discrimination based on sexual orientation in public and private employment, public accommodations, education, housing and union practices.

What the Locals Say . . .

Denver is pretty open and there is a lot more acceptance than Amendment 2 would portray. In some areas you can be openly affectionate with your partner. The best area to live around family is the Capital Hill area. Pride Fest is the biggest gay and lesbian celebration in Denver. There is a softball and bowling league, a Colorado Outdoor and Ski Association, a Women's Outdoor Club, a Bicycle Boys From Hell Club, and various support groups. The Community Center provides services for lesbigay youth up to 21 years of age, a gay men's group 25 years and under, young lesbian support group for women 25 and under. There are several social groups in Denver, Coming Out/Being Out Group, a men's group, Every Woman's Coming Out Group, Capital Hill United Neighborhood Group, Prime Timers, Slightly Older Lesbians Group, Girth & Mirth of the Rockies and numerous others. The Denver Women's Chorus, The Denver Men's Chorus, Mile High Freedom Band are very popular. "Category Six Books" is the gay and lesbian bookstore. The Colorado Business Guild, Lesbian, Gay & Bisexual People in Medicine, and The Teachers Group are gay and lesbian business organizations in Denver. Coffeehouses are very popular, such as the "Blue Note Cafe," and other restaurants. The bar scene is for the most part mixed. Some of the best gay bars include: (1) Country-Western - "Charlie's," (2) Drag Bar - "Outlet," (3) Dancing - "Metro." Some of the best lesbian bars include: (1) Top 40 - "Bobcat," (2) Variety - "Elle," (3) "3 Sisters." Denver has its own gay and lesbian television show. The rapport between health care professionals and family members varies from person to person and facility to facility. The Community Center has a resource book of gay or gay friendly sources of medical treatment. There are 5 newspapers including; (1) *Outfront,* (2) *FagMag,* (3) *Lesbians in Colorado,* (4) *Homo,* (5) *Quest.* The following churches are open to gays and lesbians MCC of the Rockies, St. Paul's United Methodist Church. The groups Axios/Eastern Orthodox Christians, Evangelical's Reconciled, Lutherans Concerned and Tikvat Shalom welcome gays and lesbians.

LOCATION: DENVER IS LOCATED IN NORTH CENTRAL COLORADO EAST OF THE ROCKY MOUNTAINS.

GAY/LESBIAN FRIENDLY BUSINESSES: 55

GAY/LESBIAN BARS AND RESTAURANTS: 27

GAY/LESBIAN ORGANIZATIONS: 41

GAY/LESBIAN RELIGIOUS ORGANIZATIONS, CHURCHES, ETC.: 6

GAY/LESBIAN BOOKSTORES: 11

GAY/LESBIAN PUBLICATIONS: 5

COMPANIES THAT PROHIBIT DISCRIMINATION: SEE STATE LAW AND GAY CIVIL RIGHTS

INFORMATION NUMBER: 303-831-6268 GAY & LESBIAN COMMUNITY CENTER OF COLORADO

TOTAL CRIMES: 39,796

VIOLENT = (MURDER = 74, RAPE = 393, ROBBERY = 1,863, ASSAULT = 2,922)

PROPERTY = (BURGLARY = 9,128, LARCENY = 17,858, MOTOR VEHICLE THEFT = 7,558, ARSON = 440)

Things to Do!!!

The Denver Mountain Park System is located in the foothills of the Rocky Mountains. It includes 13,488 acres, with 201 parks. Boating, fishing, golfing and numerous other activities are available. River rafting on the Colorado and Utah Rivers offers exciting trips of varying lengths. Other points of interest include: (1) State Capital Complex, (2) United States Mint, (3) The Denver Center For The Performing Arts, (4) Sakura Square, (5) Larimer Square, (6) Molly Brown House Museum, (7) Denver Firefighters Museum, (8) Pearce-McAllister Cottage, (9) Museum of Western Art, (10) Forney Transportation Museum, (11) Denver Museum of Natural History, (12) Denver Botanic Gardens, (13) Elitch Gardens, (14) Cherry Creek State Recreational Area, (15) Comanche Crossing Museum, (16) Arvada Center for the Arts and Humanities. ANNUAL EVENTS: (1) Cherry Blossom Festival, (2) National Western Livestock Show, Horse Show and Rodeo. SEASONAL EVENTS: (1) Greyhound racing, (2) Denver Symphony Orchestra Concerts, (3) Professional Sports: Football - Broncos, Basketball - Nuggets.

POPULATION: 483,852 PERSONS—W = 337,198, B = 60,046, AI/E/A = 5,381, C = 1,553, F = 759, M = 74,629, PR = 1,131

POPULATION GROWTH: - 1.8%

AGE OF POPULATION: (21-24) = 5.9%, (25-34) = 20.5%, (35-44) = 16.5%, (45-54) = 9.1%, (55-64) = 8.2%, (65-74) = 7.6%, (75 AND OVER) = 6.2%

HOUSING COST: OWNING = $79,000 RENTAL = $386

COMMUNITY HOSPITALS: 11 = 3,487 BEDS

CLIMATE: JAN—AVG. (29.7 DEGREES), JULY—AVG. (73.5 DEGREES), ANNUAL PRECIPITATION (15.40 INCHES)

PER CAPITA INCOME: $15,590

UNEMPLOYMENT RATE: 5.4%

JOB GROWTH SINCE 1980: - 3.6%

COST OF LIVING: 106.5

EDUCATION: UNIVERSITY OF DENVER, UNIVERSITY OF COLORADO AT DENVER

TOWNS: (5,000—60,000)

▼ASPEN

Gay Civil Rights: Bans discrimination based on sexual orientation in public and private employment, public accommodations, and housing.

What the Locals Say . . .

Aspen was the 2nd or 3rd city in the nation to have a non-discrimination gay rights ordinance. The residents of Aspen did not support Amendment 2. The resort areas in general seem to be more tolerant of gays and lesbians than other areas. Being gay in Aspen seems to be a non-issue. Gays and lesbians are not afraid to be openly affectionate in public. There is not a specific gay or lesbian bar in Aspen because there is not enough population to support it. Although, there are certain bars and restaurants that have certain nights where gays and lesbians are in greater numbers. The best way to meet people is through the Aspen Gay and Lesbian Community. Gay Ski Week is the gay communities biggest event. Depending on the year, participants range from 1,500-2,500. There is a monthly potluck dinner with 20-80 people attending, depending on the time of the year. Mid April until mid May the town is almost like a ghost town. The health care community and the gay and lesbian community get along very well. There is a resource list that has names of pro-gay physicians and other health care professionals. The Aspen Gay and Lesbian Community puts out a newsletter monthly, except in the off-season. The following churches are relatively open and take a positive position on gays and lesbians; Community Church (United Methodist) and Prince of Peace Chapel (non-denominational).

LOCATION: ASPEN IS LOCATED APPROXIMATELY 100 MILES SOUTHWEST OF DENVER COLORADO.

GAY/LESBIAN FRIENDLY BUSINESSES: MAJORITY

GAY/LESBIAN BARS AND RESTAURANTS: 0

GAY/LESBIAN ORGANIZATIONS: 1

GAY/LESBIAN RELIGIOUS ORGANIZATIONS, CHURCHES, ETC.: 2

GAY/LESBIAN BOOKSTORES: 0

GAY/LESBIAN PUBLICATIONS: 1

COMPANIES THAT PROHIBIT DISCRIMINATION: SEE STATE LAW AND GAY CIVIL RIGHTS

INFORMATION NUMBER: 303-925-9249, ASPEN GAY AND LESBIAN COMMUNITY

TOTAL CRIMES: 630

VIOLENT = (MURDER = 0 , RAPE = 0 ROBBERY = 0, ASSAULT = 48)

PROPERTY = (BURGLARY = 81, LARCENY THEFT = 468, MOTOR VEHICLE THEFT = 33, ARSON = N/A)

Things to Do!!!

Skiing is the focal point in the Aspen area. Aspen Mountain, Buttermilk, Snowmass, and Aspen Highlands are the main ski areas. River rafting includes whitewater and extended wilderness trips as well as fishing expeditions on the Roaring Fork, Arkansas, Colorado, Dolores, Gunnison and Green rivers. Hiking, climbing, horseback riding, ice skating, hunting, kayaking, hang gliding, sail planing, ballooning, golf and tennis are some additional activities to enjoy in Aspen. Other places of interest include: (1) Aspen Highland Society Museum, (2) Ashcroft Mining Camp. ANNUAL EVENTS: (1) Winterskol Carnival, (2) Banana Season. SEASONAL EVENTS: (1) Aspen Music-Festival, (2) Ballet/Aspen.

POPULATION: 5,049 PERSONS—W = 4,883, B = 15, AI/E/A = 24, A/PI = 73

POPULATION GROWTH: N/A

AGE OF POPULATION: (21-24) = 6.3%, (25-34) = 19.3%, (35-44) = 15.6%, (45-54) = 8.9%, (55-64) = 7.4%, (65-74) = 6.9%, (75 AND OVER) = 5.2%

HOUSING COST: OWNING = $500,000   RENTAL = $717

COMMUNITY HOSPITALS: 1

CLIMATE: N/A

PER CAPITA INCOME: N/A

UNEMPLOYMENT RATE: N/A

JOB GROWTH SINCE 1980: N/A

COST OF LIVING: N/A

EDUCATION: NONE

COUNTIES:

BOULDER COUNTY

Gay Civil Rights: Bans discrimination based on sexual orientation in public employment.

Towns or cities included:

Boulder

Broomfield
Lafayette
Longmont
Louisville

MORGAN COUNTY

Gay Civil Rights: Bans discrimination based on sexual orientation in public employment.

Towns or cities included:

Brush
Ft. Morgan
Wiggins
Log Lane Village

CONNECTICUT

STATE LAWS REGARDING HOMOSEXUALITY:

In 1969, the Connecticut state senate approved a new penal code legalizing homosexuality. In 1991, Connecticut passed a gay civil rights law, banishing anti-gay discrimination in public and private employment, housing, public accommodations, education, credit and union practices. Hate crimes include crimes based on sexual orientation.

CITIES: (60,000 AND UP)

▼HARTFORD

Gay Civil Rights: Bans discrimination based on sexual orientation in public and private employment, public accommodations, education, housing, credit, and union practices.

What the Locals Say . . .

The gay community in Hartford is kind of split and is not as unified or open as some would like it to be. Some feel the split is between those who want to flaunt their homosexuality and others who want to hide it. Hartford would not be a good place to be openly affectionate to your lover. The west end of Hartford is gay friendly and has gay businesses. The Evergreen Avenue area might be making a comeback as a gay and lesbian place to live. Couples can register for Domestic Partnerships in Hartford. The yearly pride celebration, rally, and parade is the biggest gay and lesbian event of the year. There is a gay bowling and softball league. Support groups, aerobics and variety shows are other ongoing activities to participate in. The bar scene is mostly mixed but with some bars that are specifically male. Although, once or twice a month those bars will have a women's night. The older crowd frequents "Nick's," while the younger crowd and those wanting to dance, go to the "Sanctuary." "Chexest" is mostly male. The Gay and Lesbian Health Collective is an organization which conducts anonymous AIDS testing. The medical community has come a long way as far as being more accepting and supportive of gays and lesbians. GEMS is a social service outreach organization that is not limited to, but does focus on seniors. GEMS is sponsored by Capital Region of Churches. The Metropolitan Community Church and the group Dignity is very popular in Hartford. *Metroline* is a gay and lesbian newspaper which is published every 2 weeks.

LOCATION: HARTFORD IS LOCATED ON THE CONNECTICUT RIVER IN NORTH CENTRAL CONNECTICUT.

GAY/LESBIAN FRIENDLY BUSINESSES: 9

GAY/LESBIAN BARS AND RESTAURANTS: 6

GAY/LESBIAN ORGANIZATIONS: 12

GAY/LESBIAN RELIGIOUS ORGANIZATIONS, CHURCHES, ETC.: 3

GAY/LESBIAN BOOKSTORES: 1

GAY/LESBIAN PUBLICATIONS:1

COMPANIES THAT PROHIBIT DISCRIMINATION: SEE STATE LAW AND GAY CIVIL RIGHTS

INFORMATION NUMBER: 203-724-5542 COMMUNITY CENTER

TOTAL CRIMES: 17,927

VIOLENT = (MURDER = 30, RAPE = 99, ROBBERY = 1,243, ASSAULT = 1,470)

PROPERTY = (BURGLARY = 3,628, LARCENY = 8,824, MOTOR VEHICLE THEFT = 2,633, ARSON = 277)

Things to Do!!!

(1) Raymond E. Baldwin Museum of Connecticut History, (2) Wadsworth Museum, (3) Science Museum of Connecticut, (4) State Capital, (5) Old State House, (6) Mark Twain House, (7) Noah Webster Foundation and Historical Society, (8) Professional Sports: Hockey-Whalers, (9) Travelers Tower, (10) Elizabeth Park, (11) Bushnell Park, (12) Talcott Mountain State Park, (13) Connecticut Audubon Society, (14) Holland Brook Nature Center. ANNUAL EVENTS: (1) Taste of Hartford, (2) Riverfest, (3) Christmas Crafts Expo I & II.

POPULATION: 131,995 PERSONS—W = 55,869, B = 54,338, AI/E/A = 450, C = 312, F = 106, M = 409, PR = 38,176

POPULATION GROWTH: - 3.2%

AGE OF POPULATION: (21-24) = 8.7%, (25-34) = 19.7%, (35-44) = 13.0%, (45-54) = 8.1%,

(55-64) = 6.6%, (65-74) = 5.4%, (75 AND OVER) = 4.5%

HOUSING COST: OWNING = $133,800   RENTAL = $504

COMMUNITY HOSPITALS: 3 = 1,759 BEDS

CLIMATE: JAN—AVG. (24.6 DEGREES), JULY—AVG. (73.7 DEGREES), ANNUAL PRECIPITATION (44.14 INCHES)

PER CAPITA INCOME: $11,081

UNEMPLOYMENT RATE: 10.5%

JOB GROWTH SINCE 1980: + 3.4%

COST OF LIVING: 125.0

EDUCATION: UNIVERSITY OF HARTFORD, TRINITY COLLEGE

▼NEW HAVEN

Gay Civil Rights: Bans discrimination based on sexual orientation in public and private employment, public accommodations, education, housing, credit, and union practices.

What the Locals Say . . .

The gay and lesbian community of New Haven is fairly large and relatively open. The areas of town that have the highest concentration of gays and lesbians are Fairhaven Heights and Westville. Some of the big meeting places are antique shows, which are numerous throughout the state. New Haven has many gay and lesbian groups including; a veterans group, African American group, Gay Fathers of Greater New Haven, Lesbian Mother's Group, Gay Men's Chorus, Another Octave which is a women's chorus, and a group for lesbians in long term relationships. "Cafe 1150" is a popular cafe and bar, and there are several that are gay friendly such as "Koffee" and "LuLu's." New Haven has two radio programs "Amazon Radio" and "Wild Women Radio." New Haven also has representative "Team Connecticut Pride" for the Gay Games Team. "Stephanie's Living Room Production" holds dances once a month. Another active group in New Haven is the Gay Activity Graduates of Yale. The Golden Thread Booksellers is a gay friendly bookstore and is aware of many of the activities going on in New Haven. "Choices" is a big dance bar which draws a mixed crowd and is located in Wallingford. "D.V. 8" is a popular bar that draws gays and straights. There is a Women and AIDS Awareness Group. *The Lesbian Position* is the local gay and lesbian publication. The Catholic group Dignity and the Metropolitan Community Church welcomes gays and lesbians.

LOCATION: NEW HAVEN IS LOCATED AT THE HEAD OF THE NEW HAVEN HARBOR IN THE SOUTHERN REGION OF CONNECTICUT.

GAY/LESBIAN FRIENDLY BUSINESSES: 9

GAY/LESBIAN BARS AND RESTAURANTS: 4

GAY/LESBIAN ORGANIZATIONS: 9

GAY/LESBIAN RELIGIOUS ORGANIZATIONS, CHURCHES, ETC.: 2

GAY/LESBIAN BOOKSTORES: 1

GAY/LESBIAN PUBLICATIONS: 1

COMPANIES THAT PROHIBIT DISCRIMINATION: SEE STATE LAW AND GAY CIVIL RIGHTS

INFORMATION NUMBER: 203-777-7807 GOLDEN THREAD BOOKSELLERS

TOTAL CRIMES: 15,553

VIOLENT = (MURDER = 22, RAPE = 130, ROBBERY = 1,238, ASSAULT = 1,154)

PROPERTY = (BURGLARY = 3,417, LARCENY = 7,719, MOTOR VEHICLE THEFT = 1,873, ARSON = 134)

Things to Do!!!

(1) Yale University, (2) New Haven Colony Historical Society Museum, (3) The Green, (4) Ft. Hale Park and Restoration, (5) East Rock Park, (6) West Rock Nature Center, (7) Historic New Haven Harbor, (8) Long Island Sound Cruises. ANNUAL EVENTS: (1) Powder House Day, (2) Volvo International Tennis Tournament, (3) Downtown Summertime Street Festival. SEASONAL EVENTS: (1) Long Wharf Theatre, (2) New Haven Symphony Orchestra.

POPULATION: 123,966 PERSONS—W = 70,263, B = 47,157, AI/E/A = 402, C = 1,077, F = 217, M = 611, PR = 13,866

POPULATION GROWTH: - 1.7%

AGE OF POPULATION: (21-24) = 9.3%, (25-34) = 20.2%, (35-44) = 12.8%, (45-54) = 7.7%, (55-64) = 6.3%, (65-74) = 6.4%, (75 AND OVER) = 5.9%

HOUSING COST: OWNING = $133,800   RENTAL = $504

COMMUNITY HOSPITALS: 2 = 1,261 BEDS

CLIMATE: JAN—AVG. (28.9 DEGREES), JULY—AVG. (73.7 DEGREES), ANNUAL PRECIPITATION (41.66 INCHES)

PER CAPITA INCOME: $12,968

UNEMPLOYMENT RATE: 7.6%

JOB GROWTH SINCE 1980: + 15.8%

COST OF LIVING: N/A

EDUCATION: YALE UNIVERSITY, SOUTHWEST CONNECTICUT STATE UNIVERSITY

NORWALK

Gay Civil Rights: Bans discrimination based on sexual orientation in public and private employment, public accommodations, education, housing, credit, and union practices.

What the Locals Say . . .

Norwalk's gay and lesbian community is more closeted than it has reason to be. The two overriding community values are property rights and propriety - that a man (or woman) is entitled to own property and that people are expected to behave. There is a sense that if one works within the system the system will respond. Direct action as a political tactic does not go over too well. Norwalk can best be characterized as a place where it is possible for an openly gay or lesbian to grow up and live openly. The community is visible, although the individual people are not. Most gays and lesbians seem to be in the closet at work, while they may be out to their families and friends. Long term couples are the norm -10 years or more is not out of the ordinary. They buy houses in middle class neighborhoods in Norwalk, where the housing costs are lower but the taxes are higher than nearby towns. Stratford is popular among women, possibly due to its proximity to New Haven, a long-time center of women's activism. Stratford and Bridgeport are nearby and have significant lesbian populations. There really isn't a specific neighborhood where gays and lesbians congregate; you will see a couple on this block and on that block. The Community Center in East Norwalk serves gays and lesbians in Fairfield County. Racism runs deep and may be intractable. Housing costs are high and unemployment (especially among gays and lesbians) is high. There is a train line running into New York City and a number of residents commute, although fewer than in days gone by. This train is also a great way to get into "the City" for all its cultural activities, etc.. The Community Center has a number of rap groups including lesbians, gay men, bisexuals and youth groups. PFLAG is one of the strongest and best organized groups in Fairfield County. There is a women's social group for women 35 and older. There are approximately 8-10 groups that meet at the community center once a month. Other times there are fund raisers, dinner events and other social activities. One of the most popular bars is "The Brook" located in Westport and it is mixed. The "Triangle" in Danbery is mixed. Bridgeport has a feminist gay and lesbian bookstore that serves the Norwalk area. The Community Center has an AIDS liaison that helps persons infected with AIDS. The Health Department in Norwalk provides primary care service. *News and Views* is a monthly newsletter. The Westport United Church of Christ is an affirming congregation.

LOCATION: NORWALK IS LOCATED IN FAIRFIELD COUNTY IN THE SOUTHWESTERN PART OF CONNECTICUT.

GAY/LESBIAN FRIENDLY BUSINESSES: 5

GAY/LESBIAN BARS AND RESTAURANTS: 3

GAY/LESBIAN ORGANIZATIONS: 10

GAY/LESBIAN RELIGIOUS ORGANIZATIONS, CHURCHES, ETC.: 1

GAY/LESBIAN BOOKSTORES: 1

GAY/LESBIAN PUBLICATIONS: 1

COMPANIES THAT PROHIBIT DISCRIMINATION: SEE STATE LAW

INFORMATION NUMBER: 203-853-0600 TRIANGLE COMMUNITY CENTER

TOTAL CRIMES: 4,233

VIOLENT = (MURDER = 9, RAPE = 10, ROBBERY = 188 ASSAULT = 118)

PROPERTY = (BURGLARY = 840, LARCENY = 2,516, MOTOR VEHICLE THEFT = 552, ARSON = 13)

Things to Do!!!

(1) Historic South Norwalk, (2) St. Paul's on the Green, (3) Mill

Hill Historic Park, (4) WPA Murals, (5) Maritime Center at Norwalk, (6) Lockwood-Mathews Mansion Museum. ANNUAL EVENTS: (1) Round Hill Scottish Games, (2) SoNo Arts Celebration, (3) Oyster Festival, (4) International In-Water Boat Show.

Population: 78,528 persons—W = 62,106, B= 12,123, AI/E/A = 100, C = 353, F = 187, M = 306, PR = 2,874

Population Growth: + 1.0%

Age of Population: (21-24) = 6.1%, (25-34) = 21.5%, (35-44) = 15.5%, (45-54) = 11.1%, (55-64) = 9.7%, (65-74) = 7.3%, (75 and over) = 5.3%

Housing Cost: Owning = $241,300   Rental = $738

Community Hospitals: 1 = 316 beds

Climate: JAN-avg. (27.5 degrees), July- avg. (72.9 degrees), Annual Precipitation (46.80 inches)

Per Capita Income: $23,075

Unemployment Rate: 5.6%

Job Growth Since 1980: + 10.0%

Cost of Living: N/A

Education: None

▼STAMFORD

Gay Civil Rights: Bans discrimination based on sexual orientation in public and private employment, public accommodations, education, housing, credit, and union practices.

What the Locals Say . . .

Stamford has a very closeted gay and lesbian community.However, you are only a 1/2 hour train ride away from the resources and anonymity in New York. A number of single men live in apartments around downtown Stamford. If residents of Stamford want to have closer access to organizations they utilize the Norwalk community. Stamford does have an AIDS project called Stamford Cares.

LOCATION: STAMFORD IS LOCATED IN THE CENTER OF FAIRFIELD COUNTY IN THE SOUTHWESTERN PART OF THE STATE.

GAY/LESBIAN FRIENDLY BUSINESSES: 1

GAY/LESBIAN BARS AND RESTAURANTS: 1

GAY/LESBIAN ORGANIZATIONS: 4

GAY/LESBIAN RELIGIOUS ORGANIZATIONS, CHURCHES, ETC.:

GAY/LESBIAN BOOKSTORES: 0

GAY/LESBIAN PUBLICATIONS: 0

COMPANIES THAT PROHIBIT DISCRIMINATION: SEE STATE LAW AND GAY CIVIL RIGHTS

INFORMATION NUMBER: 203-327-0767 GAY & LESBIAN GUIDELINE

TOTAL CRIMES: 5,872

VIOLENT = (MURDER = 2, RAPE = 22, ROBBERY = 270, ASSAULT = 237)

PROPERTY = (BURGLARY = 1,105, LARCENY = 3,503, MOTOR VEHICLE THEFT = 727, ARSON = 31)

Things to Do!!!

Stamford has an assortment of beaches and marinas that provide recreational opportunities on Long Island Sound. Specific points of interest include: (1) Festival of Arts, (2) Headquarters of 20 Fortune 500 Companies.

POPULATION: 107,590 PERSONS—W = 82,421, B = 19,217, AI/E/A = 135, C = 834, F = 379, M = 561, PR = 3,461

POPULATION GROWTH: + 5.0%

AGE OF POPULATION: (21-24) = 6.2%, (25-34) = 20.6%, (35-44) = 15.3%, (45-54) = 11.1%, (55-64) = 10.1%, (65-74) = 7.7%, (75 AND OVER) = 5.5%

HOUSING COST: OWNING = $295,700   RENTAL = $794

COMMUNITY HOSPITALS: 2 = 463 BEDS

CLIMATE: JAN-AVG. (27.4 DEGREES), JULY—AVG. (72.6 DEGREES), ANNUAL PRECIPITATION (49.43 INCHES)

PER CAPITA INCOME: $27,092

UNEMPLOYMENT RATE: 5.6%

JOB GROWTH SINCE 1980: + 15.2%

COST OF LIVING: N/A

EDUCATION: UNIVERSITY OF CONNECTICUT

DELAWARE

STATE LAWS REGARDING HOMOSEXUALITY:

There are no sodomy laws in Delaware. In 1972, Governor Russell W. Peterson signed a new criminal code, dropping penalties for consenting homosexual acts. The age of consent was 16. The new law redefined sodomy as "deviant sexual intercourse with another person without that person's consent."

CITIES: (60,000 AND UP)

WILMINGTON

Gay Civil Rights: None

What the Locals Say . . .

Wilmington is just thirty minutes from Philadelphia, just a quick scoot up I-95. The gay community is conservative as is the community at large. Gays and straights alike pretty much do their own thing. Wilmington is a nice town home; a great place to live. As a gay person, you would feel very safe and comfortable living in Wilmington. You probably would not want to move here to "flame out" though; it's just a small conservative town. There is a large network of people who get together, but not a lot of organized activities. The "Renaissance" is a mixed bar with dancing, disco, country and western music sometimes, pool tables, and drag shows. There is also a women's bar in the area called "Sisters." People go to Philadelphia for a more varied bar scene. Organizations include: The Delaware Gay and Lesbian Health Advocate (DLGHA), Friends That Care, Wilmington AIDS Clinic, A Men's Support Group, and a Black Women's Support Group. Since there are three colleges in the area there are gay campus organizations all over the place. *PGN*, a weekly paper out of Philadelphia, covers the area. The Westminster Presbyterian is gay supportive.

LOCATION: WILMINGTON IS LOCATED IN NEW CASTLE COUNTY IN NORTHEASTERN DELAWARE.

GAY/LESBIAN FRIENDLY BUSINESSES: 4

GAY/LESBIAN BARS AND RESTAURANTS: 4

GAY/LESBIAN ORGANIZATIONS: 6

GAY/LESBIAN RELIGIOUS ORGANIZATIONS, CHURCHES, ETC.: 3

GAY/LESBIAN BOOKSTORES: 0

GAY/LESBIAN PUBLICATIONS: 2

INFORMATION NUMBER: 302-652-6776 , DLGHA

TOTAL CRIMES: N/A

VIOLENT = N/A

PROPERTY = N/A

COMPANIES THAT PROHIBIT DISCRIMINATION: DUPONT, MBA, BAND OF NY,

Things to Do!!!

(1) Grand Opera House, (2) Old Town Hall Museum, (3) Delaware Art Museum, (4) Hagley Museum, (5) Delaware Museum of Natural History, (6) Brandywine Zoo Park, (7) Brandywine Springs Park, (8) Banning Park, (8) Brandywine Creek State Park, (9) Bellevue State Park. ANNUAL EVENTS: (1) Hagley's Irish Festival, (2) Wilmington Garden Day, (3) Victorian Ice Cream Festival, (4) Delaware Nature Society, (5) Harvest Moon Festival. SEASONAL EVENTS: Horse racing: Delaware Park

POPULATION: 72,411 PERSONS—W = 30,124, B = 37,446, AI/E/A = 156, C = 59, F = 69, M = 481, PR = 3,945

POPULATION GROWTH: + 3.2%

AGE OF POPULATION: (21-24) = 6.1%, (25-34) = 19.1%, (35-44) = 14.3%, (45-54) = 9.0%, (55-64) = 7.8%, (65-74) = 8.0%, (75 AND OVER) = 6.7%

HOUSING COST: OWNING = $77,800 RENTAL = $450

COMMUNITY HOSPITALS: 4 = 1,488 BEDS

CLIMATE: JAN—AVG. (30.6 DEGREES), JULY—AVG. (76.4 DEGREES), ANNUAL PRECIPITATION (40.84 INCHES)

PER CAPITA INCOME: $14,256

UNEMPLOYMENT RATE: 7.5%

JOB GROWTH SINCE 1980: + 20.4%

COST OF LIVING: 112%

EDUCATION: UNIVERSITY OF DELAWARE, GOLDEY- BEACOM COLLEGE

DISTRICT OF COLUMBIA

STATE LAWS REGARDING HOMOSEXUALITY:

In 1993, the District of Columbia repealed its sodomy laws.

▼WASHINGTON D.C.

Gay Civil Rights: Bans discrimination based on sexual orientation in public and private employment, public accommodations, education, housing, credit and union practices.

What the Locals Say . . .

The gay and lesbian community is generally an open community. There are several areas where a large number of gays and lesbians live including Dupont Circle, Capital Hill, Takoma Park, Maryland, and Alexandria, Virginia. Dupont Circle draws both gays and lesbians. Capital Hill has a large population of gay and lesbians. Takoma Park has a large lesbian population and it is not uncommon to see lesbians walking down the street holding hands. There are several popular gay friendly cafes including "17th Street," "Pop Stop Cafe" and "HIV+ Coffeehouse." Some gay friendly restaurants are: "Trumpets," "Annie's Paramount Steaks," "Howard's Grill," "Two Quail," and "Roxanne." Lambda Rising and Lammas Women's Books and More offer a wide variety of gay and lesbian literature in the D.C. metro area. There are numerous clubs, organizations and groups in the D.C. metro area, the following are only a sampling. Social groups include the Academy Awards (drag group), Deaf Gays, D.C. Different Drummer, Four Seasons Garden Club, Capital Region GLBVA (Gay, Lesbian & Bisexual Veterans), D.C. Coalition of Black Lesbians and Gay Men, Gay Fathers Coalition, Gay Married Men's Association, Metropolitan Retirees and National Latino Lesbian and Gay Organization. Thousands attend the Black Lesbian and Gays Pride Day. The Gay and Lesbian Pride Festival is a week long festival. The Gay and Lesbian Film Festival is very popular. The Gay and Lesbian Theatre Group is called Freedom SL. There are numerous sports groups in the D.C. metro area including: Adventuring (canoeing and hiking), Atlantic State Gay Rodeo Association, D.C. Aquatic Group, D.C. Ice Hockey Group, D.C. Rowing Club, D.C. Golfers Association, D.C. Capital Punishment Club, D.C. Sports Association, Federal Triangle Soccer Club, Lesbian Table Tennis, Wander Women, Water polo group, Frontrunners, Lambda Scuba Divers, Women's Rugby, Cycling, and International Gay Bowling. Since Washington D.C. is the nations capital, there are many national groups headquartered out of D.C. The following are a partial list of them: AIDS National Interfaith Network, Community Real Estate, Gay and Lesbian Americans Gay and Lesbian Victory Fund, International Gay Travel Association,

Lambda Legal Defense and Education, Lesbian Mothers National Defense Fund, National Gay Pilots Association and the National Federation of Parents and Friends of Gays. Some lesbian and gay political groups in D.C. are: the Human Rights Campaign Fund, Capital Area Log Cabin, Gay and Lesbian Alliance Against Defamation, and Gay and Lesbian Activists Alliance. Professional groups in Washington D.C. are the Bell Atlantic GLOBE (Gay, Lesbian Bisexual Employees), Gay Restaurant Owners, Capitol Area Physicians For Human Rights, Gay and Lesbian Postal Employees Network, National Lawyers Guild, Federal GLOBE (Gay,Lesbian Bisexual Employees), Gannett-USA Today Gay and Lesbian Network, Gays and Lesbians in Foreign Affairs Agencies (GLIFAA), Lesbian, Gay and Bisexual in Medicine D.C., Library of Congress GLOBE, National Gay Pilots Association, Gay and Lesbian Teachers Networks and the Gay and Lesbian International Relations group. "Trumpets" is a mixed upscale bar, "Friends Restaurant and Piano Bar" has a mixed crowd, "JR's" draws a young men's yuppie crowd, "Hung Jury" and "Phase I" are lesbian bars. "Fraternity House" and "Badlands" are men's dance bars. The Whitman Walker Clinic offers services for gays and lesbians, those with AIDS, HIV+, mental health and substance abuse. *The Washington Blade* is a weekly gay and lesbian publication, *LLEGO* is a Latino lesbigay newsletter and *Woman's Monthly* is a men's and women's weekly metro guide to arts, entertainment and social events. Churches in the D.C. metro area that are open and affirming to gays and lesbians are MCC of Washington D.C., All Souls Unitarian, Faith Temple (Pentecostal gay/lesbian church), First Congregational Church, Immanual Church on the Hill, Free Catholic Church, Inner Light Unity Fellowship Church and Westminster Presbyterian Church.

LOCATION: WASHINGTON D.C. IS LOCATED IN SOUTHERN MARYLAND AND NORTHERN VIRGINIA. THE POTOMAC RIVER DIVIDES THE METRO AREA.

GAY/LESBIAN FRIENDLY BUSINESSES: 100+

GAY/LESBIAN BARS, RESTAURANTS: 46

GAY/LESBIAN ORGANIZATIONS: 85

GAY/LESBIAN RELIGIOUS ORGANIZATIONS, CHURCHES, ETC.: 22

GAY/LESBIAN BOOKSTORES: 3

GAY/LESBIAN PUBLICATIONS: 9

COMPANIES THAT PROHIBIT DISCRIMINATION: BUREAU OF NATIONAL AFFAIRS, FEDERAL NATIONAL MORTGAGE ASSOCIATION (FANNIE MAE), GREENPEACE INTERNATIONAL, NATIONAL ORGANIZATION FOR WOMEN (NOW), NATIONAL PUBLIC RADIO (NPR), PUBLIC BROADCASTING SYSTEM (PBS), SEE GAY CIVIL RIGHTS

INFORMATION NUMBER: 202-833-3234 GAY & LESBIAN HOTLINE, WHITMAN WALKER CLINIC

TOTAL CRIMES: 67,946

VIOLENT = (MURDER = 454, RAPE = 324, ROBBERY = 7,107, ASSAULT = 9,003)

PROPERTY = (BURGLARY = 11,532, LARCENY = 31,466, MOTOR VEHICLE THEFT = 8,060, ARSON = 200)

Things to Do!!!

(1) Capitol Area—Library of Congress, Supreme Court of the U.S, Senate Office Building, Government Printing Office, walking and jogging trails. Boating, golf and tennis, U.S. Botanic Garden, Union Station, (2) Federal Triangle Area—The National Archives, U.S. Navy Memorial, Federal Trade Commission Building, Labor Departments, Department of Justice, Department of Energy, Department of Commerce Building, Pavilion at the Old Post Office, (3) The Mall and Tidal Basin- National Gallery of Art, Freer Gallery, National Museum of African Art, National Air and Space Museum, Smithsonian Institution, Washington Monument, Department of the Treasury, Department of the Interior, John F. Kennedy Center for Performing Arts, National Museum of American Art, National Museum of Women in the Arts, Ford's Theatre, Walter Reed Army Medical Center, Rock Creek Park, The White House, Bureau of Engraving and Printing, Lafayette Square, American Red Cross, National Academy of Sciences, Vietnam Veterans Memorial, Lincoln Memorial, Potomac Park, Thomas Jefferson Park, Theodore Roosevelt Memorial,

POPULATION: 585,221 PERSONS—W = 179,667, B = 399,604, AI/E/A = 1,466, C = 3,144, F = 2,082, M = 2,981, PR = 2,204

POPULATION GROWTH: - 8.3%

AGE OF POPULATION: (21-24) = 7.8%, (25-34) = 20.0%, (35-44) = 15.7%, (45-54) = 10.2%, (55-64) = 8.4%, (65-74) = 7.3%, (75 AND OVER) = 5.5%

HOUSING COST: OWNING = $123,900 RENTAL = $479

COMMUNITY HOSPITALS: 11 = 4,262 BEDS

CLIMATE: JAN—AVG. (34.6 DEGREES), JULY—AVG. (80.0 DEGREES), ANNUAL PRECIPITATION (38.63 INCHES)

PER CAPITA INCOME: $18,881

UNEMPLOYMENT RATE: 7.7%

JOB GROWTH SINCE 1980: + 2.5%

COST OF LIVING: 134.2

EDUCATION: GEORGETOWN, UNIVERSITY OF DISTRICT OF COLUMBIA, GEORGE WASHINGTON UNIVERSITY, HOWARD UNIVERSITY

FLORIDA

STATE LAWS REGARDING HOMOSEXUALITY:

Heterosexual and homosexual sodomy is considered a misdemeanor. In 1977, the state of Florida passed laws banning same sex marriages. Adopting children by same sex couples is also banned, although this law has been ruled unconstitutional by judges in Sarasota and Monroe counties. In 1991, hate crimes started including anti-gay attacks.

CITIES: (60,000 AND UP)

Ft. LAUDERDALE

Gay Civil Rights: Bans discrimination based on sexual orientation in public employment, public accommodations and housing. (County Ordinance)

What the Locals Say . . .

Ft. Lauderdale has a very open gay and lesbian community. Victoria Park is a very old neighborhood that has a high concentration of gays and lesbians. Wilton Manors also has older homes and attracts many gays and lesbians. There are gay bars and restaurants in both of these neighborhoods. "The Cabaret" is an upscale theatrical supper club. "Legends Cafe" and "Galeria G'Vannis: The Boulevard Dining Gallery" are popular dining spots as well. The Gay Pride Festival includes a parade and booths and entertainment at Holiday Park. "Outbooks" is a gay and lesbian bookstore. Ft. Lauderdale has several political organizations including: Dolphin Democratic Club, Broward Unites Against Discrimination (BUYD) and Log Cabin Club/Broward County. The Sunshine Athletic Association has numerous sport and recreational activities. There are volleyball, softball and bowling leagues as well as a gay boating and scuba diving club. The "Gold Coast Roller Rink" has a gay night for skating. The Lesbian and Gay Community Center in Ft. Lauderdale has many support groups and activities that offer a non-bar alternative. Social/support groups in Ft. Lauderdale are numerous. Some of the more popular ones include: gay AA meetings, PFLAG, Gay Men's Chorus of South Florida, Asians & Friends of Florida, Black Men Couples, Under 25 Youth Group, Sons and Daughters of Gays and Lesbians, SAGE of Broward County (Senior Action In A Gay Environment) and a lesbian rap group. There is also a very good women's networking organization called Broward Women in Network (BWIN) which has approximately 500 members. The group has monthly meetings which feature guest speakers and networking activities as well as lots of social events. "Copa" and "Chardees" are popular gay and lesbian bars. "Cathode Ray" and "Male Box 825" are popular men's bars. "Club 21" and "Other Side" are popular lesbian bars. Center One is an AIDS organization that provides education and support. *The Scoop* is a weekly publication for gays and lesbians. There is group of Dignity and All Saints Catholic Mission in Ft. Lauderdale. The Sunshine Cathedral MCC is a predominately gay church, and the Unitarian Church is gay friendly.

LOCATION: FT. LAUDERDALE IS LOCATED IN THE SOUTHEASTERN REGION OF FLORIDA. IT IS NORTH OF MIAMI AND SOUTH OF PALM BEACH. IT STRETCHES ACROSS SEVEN MILES OF ATLANTIC BEACH.

GAY/LESBIAN FRIENDLY BUSINESSES: 26

GAY/LESBIAN BARS AND RESTAURANTS: 22

GAY/LESBIAN ORGANIZATIONS: 16

GAY/LESBIAN RELIGIOUS ORGANIZATIONS, CHURCHES, ETC.: 3

GAY/LESBIAN BOOKSTORES: 1

GAY/LESBIAN PUBLICATIONS: 5

COMPANIES THAT PROHIBIT DISCRIMINATION:

INFORMATION NUMBER: 305-563-9500 COMMUNITY CENTER

TOTAL CRIMES: 25,775

VIOLENT = (MURDER = 31, RAPE = 76, ROBBERY = 1,270, ASSAULT = 973)

PROPERTY = (BURGLARY = 5,822, LARCENY = 14,477, MOTOR VEHICLE THEFT = 3,126, ARSON= 63)

Things to Do!!!

All the different water areas are the main attraction in Ft. Lauderdale. Besides the Atlantic Ocean, there are many rivers, inlets, and man made canals. Port Everglades is here, which is the deepest harbor in the state. Other points of interest include: (1) Discovery Center Museum, (2) Museum of Art, (3) Ocean World, (4) Everglades Holiday Park, (5) International Swimming Hall of Fame and Pool Complex, (6) Hugh Taylor Birch State Recreation Area, (7) Lawrence Artificial Reef, (8) Mercedes I Artificial Reef, (8) Cruises. ANNUAL EVENTS: Winterfest. SEASONAL EVENTS: (1) Horse racing, (2) Symphony concerts, (3) Civic Music Concerts, (4) Parker Playhouse, (5) Professional Sports: (Baseball- Spring Training for New York Yankees).

POPULATION: 148,524 PERSONS—W = 103,980, B = 41,995, AI/E/A = 321, C = 226, F = 182, M = 732, PR = 2,209

POPULATION GROWTH:- 3.1%

AGE OF POPULATION: (21-24) = 6.9%, (25-34) = 18.7%, (35-44) = 16.1%, (45-54) = 10.6%, (55-64) = 9.5%, (65-74) = 9.1%, (75 AND OVER) = 8.6%

HOUSING COST: OWNING = $99,200 RENTAL = $486

COMMUNITY HOSPITALS: 8 = 2,194 BEDS

CLIMATE: JAN—AVG. (67.2 DEGREES), JULY—AVG. (82.6 DEGREES), ANNUAL PRECIPITATION (60.64 INCHES)

PER CAPITA INCOME: $19,814

UNEMPLOYMENT RATE: 7.4%

JOB GROWTH SINCE 1980: + 3.3%

COST OF LIVING: N/A

EDUCATION: NOVA SOUTHEASTERN UNIVERSITY

▼MIAMI BEACH

Gay Civil Rights: Bans discrimination based on sexual orientation in public and private employment, public accommodations and housing.

What the Locals Say . . .

The gay and lesbian community is very open in Miami Beach. It is estimated that the gay and lesbian population is 25% of the population (40% on the weekends). The gay population is larger than the lesbian population. The politicians are considered tolerant of homosexuality. The climate is great year-round and the atmosphere is very laid back. Miami Beach has many organizations, but if you can't find what you're looking for, go to nearby Miami. The South Beach area between 1st and 20th street is filled with many gay and lesbian residents, bars, and restaurants. The closer you get to the 50's and 60's block the more older/retired people you will find. In the area between Ocean and Washington, you can walk and hold hands. The architecture is very art deco and very tropical. The gay and lesbian community is just starting to develop. There are two gay and lesbian bookstores "GW Miami Beach" and "Lambda Passages." The Lesbian Gay & Bisexual Community Center offers a variety of services and alternative activities including: GYNA, a lesbian health action group, brunches, coffeehouses, movie nights, reading group, gardening club, game nights, youth programming, library and archives. Allard Lowenstein Democratic Club is a political group in Miami Beach. There are numerous support groups. There is a Gay Fathers Group, several Coming Out groups, Black & White Men Together Group, Friday Night Womyn's Group, N.L.A.: South Florida (a leather group). The South Beach Business Guild is a group of gay and lesbian businesses. *Conmocion* is an international Latino Lesbian network and publication. The Community Pride Organization Roundtable is a meeting of leaders of different gay and lesbian organizations. The Panzies is a horticulture club. There is a volleyball game on the beach almost all the time. The group Southeastern Great Outdoors is located in Miami Beach. There are numerous gay and gay-friendly restaurants. One of the most popular is "The Palace," although any restaurant located between Ocean and Washington and 12th Street is considered very gay-friendly. Rainbow Adventures is a sailing charter business. Some of the most popular men's bars are "Risk," "La Muscle," "Icon" and "Hombre." "Twist" is the local watering hole for gays, lesbians and straights. The "Kremlin" and "West End" tend to draw a mixed crowd of gays and lesbians. "821" draws more women. The South Shore Hospital and Stratogen are very accepting of the gay and lesbian community. The Miami Beach HIV/AIDS Project is an educational and outreach program which provides a variety of direct services to all residents of Miami Beach. *Newzette, Hot Spots, Wire, Shout* and *Planet Homo* are gay and lesbian publications in Miami Beach. The MCC South Beach, Grace Metropolitan Church, Christ Metropolitan Church and the Congregation Etz Chaim/MCC Synagogue of Greater Miami are open and affirming to gays and lesbians.

LOCATION: MIAMI BEACH IS LOCATED IN SOUTHEASTERN MIAMI. THE ISLAND IS 10 MILES LONG AND 1-3 MILES WIDE.

GAY/LESBIAN FRIENDLY BUSINESSES: 34

GAY/LESBIAN BARS AND RESTAURANTS: 32

GAY/LESBIAN ORGANIZATIONS: 18

GAY/LESBIAN RELIGIOUS ORGANIZATIONS, CHURCHES, ETC.: 4

GAY/LESBIAN BOOKSTORES: 2

GAY/LESBIAN PUBLICATIONS: 5

COMPANIES THAT PROHIBIT DISCRIMINATION: SEE GAY CIVIL RIGHTS

INFORMATION NUMBER: 305-531-3666, LESBIAN GAY & BISEXUAL COMMUNITY CENTER

TOTAL CRIMES: 16,517

VIOLENT = (MURDER = 13, RAPE = 64, ROBBERY = 744, ASSAULT = 993)

PROPERTY = (BURGLARY = 2,975, LARCENY = 9,317, MOTOR VEHICLE THEFT = 2,411, ARSON = 26)

Things to Do!!!

This area is filled with outdoor recreational activities. There is everything from the sun, beach, shopping, concerts, to world class dining. Miami Beach has: (1) Art Deco District, (2) Bass Museum of Art, (3) Barnacle State Historic Site, (4) Sightseeing cruises, (5) Miami Beach Garden Center and Conservatory. ANNUAL EVENTS: (1) Art Deco Weekend, (2) Festival of the Arts. SEASONAL EVENTS: Theatre.

POPULATION: 90,896 PERSONS—W = 81,800, B = 4,798, AI/E/A = 142, C = 228, F = 351, M = 760, PR = 4,517

POPULATION GROWTH:- 5.6%

AGE OF POPULATION: (21-24) = 4.9%, (25-34) = 16.2%, (35-44) = 12.7%, (45-54) = 9.5%, (55-64) = 9.8%, (65-74) = 11.5%, (75 AND OVER) = 18.6%

HOUSING COST: OWNING = $191,300   RENTAL = $427

COMMUNITY HOSPITALS: 4 = 1,139 BEDS

CLIMATE: JAN—AVG. (68.1 DEGREES), JULY—AVG. (86.9 DEGREES), ANNUAL PRECIPITATION (45.35 INCHES)

PER CAPITA INCOME: $16,504

UNEMPLOYMENT RATE: 10.2%

JOB GROWTH SINCE 1980: + 39.4%

COST OF LIVING: 106.8

EDUCATION: NONE

ORLANDO

Gay Civil Rights: None

What the Locals Say . . .

Within the last three years Orlando has become a very close-knit community for gays and lesbians. Though the area is very transient, those that have been there a while have developed a strong infrastructure. Gays and lesbians typically don't worry about being out in Orlando. The community is becoming more visible everyday, although there are still many in the closet. The historic downtown area is emerging as the gay and lesbian neighborhood. There is a residential area and several gay friendly restaurants and businesses. The Gay Triangle, the area that falls between College Park, is very gay and very yuppie. The area is evenly populated with heterosexuals and homosexuals. The homes in this area are older and are going through a renaissance period. There are other pockets of neighborhoods throughout Orlando where gays and lesbians live. Lake Davis attracts a lot of gays. Gay Pride Month starts off with Gay Day at Disney. Disney has a large gay and lesbian work force. The annual Pride Parade goes through the middle of downtown across from City Hall. The rally is held at the state fairgrounds. There are numerous activities in Orlando during the Pride Celebration. The Rainbow Democratic Club is a political group that focuses on local gay and lesbian issues. Social groups include a theater group, a coming out group for men and women, a singles group, a youth group, a Committed Couples group, men's discussion, and a Prime Timers group. The Metropolitan Business Association is the business guild for the Orlando Gay and Lesbian Community. They provide a buyers guide to direct you to family members who are in business. Spectrum is an awards ceremony that honors gay and lesbians in the community. The Gay Chorus puts on three concerts a year. Orlando has a gay volleyball league, a large bowling league and women's softball league. "Out N About" is a popular bookstore and coffee shop. "Moorefields" is a popular restaurant that could be considered gay. The coffeehouse "Yab Yum" in downtown is popular as well as "Chapters" which serves coffee and lunch. "The Cactus Club" and "Southern Nights" are popular men's bars. The Parliament House Motor Inn is a complex consisting of five bars, a hotel, a diner, a pool and a lake area. The "Complex" houses "City Lights" and "The Eagle" bars, a leather store "Absolute Leather," "Video Express" and a fitness center. "Faces" is a popular women's dance bar. AIDS Resource Alliance is a government run organization. Hope & Help is a group that provides support groups, education, prevention, food bank, and case workers who assist with government regulations. *The Triangle* is published monthly by the Gay and Lesbian Community Center of Central Florida. *Watermark* is published twice a month. Joy MCC has a congregation that is mostly gay and lesbian. The 1st Unitarian Church is very gay friendly. A chapter of Dignity, a gay and lesbian Catholic group, is also located in Orlando.

LOCATION: ORLANDO IS LOCATED IN CENTRAL FLORIDA.

GAY/LESBIAN FRIENDLY BUSINESSES: 20

GAY/LESBIAN BARS AND RESTAURANTS: 12

GAY/LESBIAN ORGANIZATIONS: 9

GAY/LESBIAN RELIGIOUS ORGANIZATIONS, CHURCHES, ETC.: 2

GAY/LESBIAN BOOKSTORES: 2

GAY/LESBIAN PUBLICATIONS: 1

COMPANIES THAT PROHIBIT DISCRIMINATION: N/A

INFORMATION NUMBER: 407-843-4297, GAY & LESBIAN COMMUNITY CENTER OF CENTRAL FLORIDA

TOTAL CRIMES: 21,953

VIOLENT = (MURDER = 15, RAPE = 209, ROBBERY = 1,107, ASSAULT = 2,809)

PROPERTY = (BURGLARY = 4,352, LARCENY = 11,655, MOTOR VEHICLE THEFT = 1,806, ARSON = 73)

Things to Do!!!

Orlando has 54 lakes within the city limits. Walt Disney World & Epcot Center, one of the most famous attractions in the world, is located in Orlando. Other points of interest: (1) The Kennedy Space Center, (2) Sea World of Florida, (3) Leu Botanical Gardens, (4) Loch Haven Park, (5) Municipal Recreation Areas- (Eola Park, Turkey Lake Park, Lake Fairview Park, Church Street Station, Universal Studios Florida), (6) Wet 'N Wild, (7) Mystery Fun House, (8) Ben White Raceway. ANNUAL EVENTS: (1) Orlando Scottish Highland Games, (2) Florida Citrus Sports Holiday, (3) The Nestle Invitational, (4) Pioneer Days Folk Festival. SEASONAL EVENTS: (1) Florida Symphony Orchestra, (2) Professional Sports: Baseball-Spring Training- Minnesota Twins; Basketball - Magic.

POPULATION: 174,215 PERSONS—W = 113,243, B = 44,303, AI/E/A = 506, C = 342, F = 581, M = 1,535, PR = 7,035

POPULATION GROWTH: + 35.8%

AGE OF POPULATION: (21-24) = 8.4%, (25-34) = 22.6%, (35-44) = 13.8%, (45-54) = 8.0%, (55-64) = 7.0%, (65-74) = 6.3%, (75 AND OVER) = 5.0%

HOUSING COST: OWNING = $74,300   RENTAL = $506

COMMUNITY HOSPITALS: 4 = 2,536

CLIMATE: JAN—AVG. (59.7 DEGREES), JULY—AVG. (82.3 DEGREES), ANNUAL PRECIPITATION (48.11 INCHES)

PER CAPITA INCOME: $13,879

UNEMPLOYMENT RATE: 6.9%

JOB GROWTH SINCE 1980: + 42%

COST OF LIVING: 98.2

EDUCATION: UNIVERSITY OF CENTRAL FLORIDA

PENSACOLA

Gay Civil Rights: None

What the Locals Say . . .

The gay and lesbian community in Pensacola is fairly open. One of the most successful gay businesses is located on the main drag of town. Approximately $65 million a year is pumped into Pensacola via the gay and lesbian community. The city council is very gay-friendly with the exception of one radical homophobe. Government Street/Alcaniz and Alcaniz/Intendencia is a four block area where there are gay bars, restaurants and a residential section. "North Hill" is a neighborhood that has many old Victorian style homes that have been refurbished and are very popular with gays and lesbians. "East Hill" is an area with older smaller homes that attracts a lot of gays and lesbians. Memorial Day Weekend attracts 60,000 gays and lesbians to the 13 mile gay beach, sometimes referred to as the Gay Riviera. "Just For Us" is the unofficial tourist information center for gays and lesbians. "Just For Us" carries T-shirts, books, periodicals, and gifts. "Sanger" is a gay friendly theater that many in the community enjoy. Some of the most popular gay restaurants are "Scotto's" and "Badenheimers." The University of West Florida has a gay and lesbian group. There is a PFLAG organization, Everybody's Brother, and Southern Nights. The Women's Social Organization has both straight and lesbian women. There are three political groups in Pensacola including "Log Cabin Republican," "Human Rights Campaign," and "Queer Caucus." The "Park Pub" is a popular bar for young preppy gays and lesbians. "Numbers" is a male bar. "JJ's" and "Chapters" draw a mixed crowd, while "Red Carpet" is a lesbian bar. Locals say that the

"Office on Wright Street" is a bar that doesn't allow gays except over Memorial Day Weekend when they can make more money. Escambia AIDS Services & Education (EASE) provides AIDS education and testing, medical assistance, and a food pantry to those with HIV and AIDS. There are three gay and lesbian publications in Pensacola. *Christopher Street South* is a quarterly publication, *Et. Cetera* is a weekly publication and *Community News* is a monthly publication. The Holy Cross Metropolitan Community Church is open and affirming to gays and lesbians and performs commitment ceremonies.

LOCATION: PENSACOLA IS LOCATED ON THE GULF OF MEXICO IN WESTERN FLORIDA.

GAY/LESBIAN FRIENDLY BUSINESSES: 20 +

GAY/LESBIAN BARS AND RESTAURANTS: 11

GAY/LESBIAN ORGANIZATIONS: 17

GAY/LESBIAN RELIGIOUS ORGANIZATIONS, CHURCHES, ETC.: 1

GAY/LESBIAN BOOKSTORES: 1

GAY/LESBIAN PUBLICATIONS: 3

COMPANIES THAT PROHIBIT DISCRIMINATION: N/A

TOTAL CRIMES: N/A

VIOLENT = N/A

PROPERTY = N/A

Things to Do!!!

Most of the activities in Pensacola revolve around the Gulf of Mexico. There is skin diving and scuba diving, swimming, fishing, as well as many events held on the beaches. (1) Pensacola Museum of Art, (2) Historic Pensacola Village, (3) Naval Air Station, (4) Gulf Islands National Seashore; ANNUAL EVENTS: Fiesta of the Five Flags, Great Gulfcoast Arts Festival, Mardi Gras and the Pensacola Interstate Fair.

POPULATION: 59,773 PERSONS—W= 38,198, B = 18,557, AI/E/A = 302, C = 132, F = 149, M = 239, PR = 155

POPULATION GROWTH: 3.7%

AGE OF POPULATION: (21-24) = 5.9%, (25-34) = 15.4%, (35-44) = 14.6%, (45-54) = 10.1%, (55-64) = 10.1%, (65-74) = 9.5%, (75 AND OVER) = 6.9 %

HOUSING COST: OWNING = $63,600   RENTAL = $388

COMMUNITY HOSPITALS: 4 = 1,584 BEDS

CLIMATE: JAN—AVG. (50.6 DEGREES), JULY—AVG. (89.9 DEGREES), ANNUAL PRECIPITATION (62.25 INCHES)

PER CAPITA INCOME: $14,795

UNEMPLOYMENT RATE: 5.4%

JOB GROWTH SINCE 1980: +8.6%
COST OF LIVING: N/A
EDUCATION: UNIVERSITY OF WEST FLORIDA

▼TAMPA

Gay Civil Rights: Bans discrimination based on sexual orientation in public employment, housing and public accommodations.

What the Locals Say . . .

The Tampa gay and lesbian community is very open. The six year long battle over the city/county human rights ordinance that includes sexual orientation has brought the gay and lesbian community out and together. The growth in the gay and lesbian community in the last 7-8 years has been phenomenal. The community has come from the point where police used to take license tag numbers off cars at gay bars to where the city council meets and hears concerns from the the gay and lesbian community. The neighborhoods with the highest concentration of lesbians and gays are: Hyde Park, Palma Ceia, and Seminole Heights. Hyde Park is the most established area and it is getting expensive to live there. Palma Ceia is an established area as well. Seminole Heights is the up and coming area where older homes are being refurbished. Seminole Heights is the fastest growing area for gays and lesbians in Tampa. Fine arts groups include: Gays Men's Chorus, Creshindo (a lesbian chorus), "One in 10 Players" (a gay and lesbian theater group), and a gay and lesbian band. Some of the most popular coffeehouses in Tampa are "Rascals," "Joffreys" and "Wired" which are not primarily gay, but very gay-friendly. The Human Rights Task Force is the largest and most organized political group in Tampa. They are a very strong, very organized group that focuses on the Tampa gay community, although they also network with other organizations in other cities to achieve a statewide effect as well. Digital Queers is a computer club that assists other gays and lesbians with computer help. Sport groups include softball leagues, bowling leagues, sailing groups, volleyball leagues, Frontrunners groups, camping group, and a scuba/diving group. There are numerous social groups to meet everyone's needs. The "Women's Energy Bank" is a group of women that meet monthly. The "Tampa Pharo's" is a philanthropic organization of gays and lesbians that sponsors dinners and dances to raise money. Once a year they make donations to gay/ lesbian/AIDS organizations. "Prime Timers" is a group for older gays and lesbians and their admirers. The Gay and Lesbian Business Guild has 200 members and has a resource directory of gay and lesbian friendly businesses. "Tomes and Treasures" is a big bookstore that has gay and lesbian books and gifts and is located in the Hyde Park area. The "M C Film Festival" is a video store that carries a large variety of gay and lesbian films, as well as gifts. The Greater Tampa Bay Pride Committee organizes pride events such as the Summer Gay Pride which includes a rally, march, entertainment, and candlelight vigil. Winter Gay Pride, which is held indoors, has dancing, booths, and entertainment. The Film Festival is a 10-day event in September and attracts 12,000 or more individuals. The Film Festival is held in historic Tampa Theatre. "Tracks" is a mega complex in Ybor City (art district) and attracts men and women. "The Cherokee Club" is a block away from "Tracks" and is primarily a lesbian bar. The bar scene is mixed. "2606" is a leather/levi club with a predominately male clientele. The Tampa AIDS Network is a very strong and very large organization with a multi-million dollar budget. This organization is powerful and enjoys community wide support. The mayor is on the board of the Tampa AIDS Network. Services include case management, food bank, and financial/legal assistance. The PWA Coalition is also very big. *The Gazette* and *Stonewall* are monthly gay and lesbian news publications. *Encounter* is more of a bar magazine and comes out twice a month. There is a MCC, 1st United Church of Tampa and Beth Rachameem are very affirming and open to gays and lesbians.

LOCATION: THE CITY OF TAMPA IS LOCATED ON THE WESTERN PENINSULA OF FLORIDA AND SPRAWLS AROUND THE MOUTH OF THE HILLSBOROUGH RIVER AT THE HEAD OF TAMPA BAY.

GAY/LESBIAN FRIENDLY BUSINESSES: 150

GAY/LESBIAN BARS AND RESTAURANTS: 27

GAY/LESBIAN ORGANIZATIONS: 40

GAY/LESBIAN RELIGIOUS ORGANIZATIONS, CHURCHES, ETC.: 3

GAY/LESBIAN BOOKSTORES: 1

GAY/LESBIAN PUBLICATIONS: 3

COMPANIES THAT PROHIBIT DISCRIMINATION: SEE GAY RIGHTS

INFORMATION NUMBER: 813-837-4485 GAY AND LESBIAN COMMUNITY CENTER

TOTAL CRIMES: 45,373

VIOLENT = (MURDER = 43, RAPE = 247, ROBBERY = 2,965, ASSAULT = 6,124)

PROPERTY = (BURGLARY = 8,987, LARCENY = 18,534, MOTOR VEHICLE THEFT = 8,473, ARSON = 216)

Things to Do!!!

Tampa is considered the business and vacation hub of Florida's west coast. Specific areas of interest include: (1) Adventure Island, (2) Busch Gardens—"The Dark Continent," (3) Hillsborough County Historical Commission Museum, (4) Tampa Bay Performing Arts Center, (5) Tampa Museum of Art, (6) Museum of Science and Industry, Lowry Park, (7) Ybor City, (8) Waterfront. ANNUAL EVENTS: (1) Hall Of Fame Bowl, (2) Florida State Fair, (3) Gasparilla Pirate Invasion, (4) Florida Strawberry Festival/Hillsborough County Fair. SEASONAL EVENTS: (1) Jai-

Alai, (2) Greyhound Racing, (3) Concerts, (4) Horse racing, (5) Professional Sports: Football - Buccaneers, Soccer - Rowdies, Baseball - Spring Training for Cincinnati Reds.

POPULATION: 284,737 PERSONS—W = 198,542, B = 70,131, AI/E/A = 834, C = 456, F = 702, M = 2,556, FR = 9,863

POPULATION GROWTH: + 4.8%

AGE OF POPULATION: (21-24) = 6.4%, (25-34) = 18%.9, (35-44) = 14.1%, (45-54) = 9.4%, (55-64) = 8.8%, (65-74) = 8.3%, (75 AND OVER) = 6.3%

HOUSING COST: OWNING = $59,000   RENTAL = $408

COMMUNITY HOSPITALS: 10 = 2,575 BEDS

CLIMATE: JAN—AVG. (59.9 DEGREES), JULY—AVG. (82.1 DEGREES), ANNUAL PRECIPITATION (43.92 INCHES)

PER CAPITA INCOME: $13,277

UNEMPLOYMENT RATE: 6.7%

JOB GROWTH SINCE 1980: +14.1%

COST OF LIVING: 97.0

EDUCATION: UNIVERSITY OF TAMPA, UNIVERSITY OF SOUTH FLORIDA

▼WEST PALM BEACH

Gay Civil Rights: Bans discrimination based on sexual orientation in public employment. The city also passed a resolution that the city will not conduct business with, nor appropriate any funds to, any organization which discriminates based on sexual orientation.

What the Locals Say . . .

West Palm Beach is pretty open. Approximately 75% of the community is out, although some are still afraid. The local politicians are split but are leaning to the right. West Palm Beach is a beautiful place. Northeast of West Palm Beach there is a neighborhood called Northwood. Northwood is a historic district where homes are being refurbished. This area is relaxed enough that many would feel comfortable holding their partner's hand. It is estimated that 40-60% of the population is gay in this area. Lake Worth is an area of older homes and is experiencing a large influx of gays and lesbians. Compass is the Gay/Lesbian/Bisexual Community Center for Palm Beach County. Compass supports the social and physical, emotional and mental health of gay men, lesbians and bisexuals. Compass has HIV support groups, teen programs, new alternatives for ages 18-30, a bisexual, lesbian and gay men's group, a synagogue group, aerobics, PFLAG, Palm Beach County Women In Network (WYM) and Broward County Women In Network (WYM). There is also an Older Lesbian Connection (50+) group, and a Single Lesbians Over 50. The Human Rights Council and the Atlantic Coast Democratic Club, The Lesbian & Gay Task Force for Social Justice, The Lesbian Task Force of the Treasure Coast Women's Political Caucus are in West Palm Beach. The "Rhythm Cafe" is a popular gay and lesbian restaurant. "The Underground Coffee Works" is a popular coffee shop. There is a small lesbigay bookstore in Compass, and also a lesbigay bookstore called "Changing Times. There is a gay bowling league, gay volleyball and Sunshine Athletic Association. The "Whimsey" is a safe haven for women traveling in overnight campers, RV's, tents, vans and campers. "Heartbrakers" is a mixed dance club, "Inn Exile" is a mixed video alternative club, "H.G. Roosters" is a men's neighborhood bar, and "K & E's" is a women's neighborhood bar. The Comprehensive AIDS Program provides direct services, nutritional support and volunteer/buddy support. *The Community Voice* is the monthly gay and lesbian publication in West Palm Beach. Our Lady of Wisdom, an independent Catholic Church, Church of Today, Congregation Yeladim Shel Yisrael and MCC of The Palm Beaches are open and affirming to gays and lesbians. There is also a group of Integrity and Dignity.

LOCATION: WEST PALM BEACH IS LOCATED AT THE SOUTHERN END OF FLORIDA ON THE EAST COAST OF THE ATLANTIC OCEAN.

GAY/LESBIAN FRIENDLY BUSINESSES: 7

GAY/LESBIAN BARS AND RESTAURANTS: 12

GAY/LESBIAN ORGANIZATIONS: 10

GAY/LESBIAN RELIGIOUS ORGANIZATIONS, CHURCHES, ETC.: 6

GAY/LESBIAN BOOKSTORES: 2

GAY/LESBIAN PUBLICATIONS: 1

COMPANIES THAT PROHIBIT DISCRIMINATION: SEE GAY CIVIL RIGHTS

INFORMATION NUMBER: 407-966-3777 COMPASS OF WEST PALM BEACH

TOTAL CRIMES: N/A

VIOLENT = N/A

PROPERTY = N/A

Things to Do!!!

West Palm Beach has evolved into a resort city because of its accessibility to nearby beaches and to the West Palm Beach canal that leads to the sporting attractions of the Everglades. Golfing enjoys great popularity on the 112 area courses. Specific points of interest include: (1) Dreher Park Zoo, (2) Norton Gallery and School of Art, (3) Union Congregational Church, (4) Lion Country Safari, Inc., (5) Riverboat

Cruises, (6) Boating. ANNUAL EVENTS: (1) South Florida Fair & Exposition, (2) SunFest. SEASONAL EVENTS: (1) Palm Beach Polo, (2) Professional sports: baseball- Spring Training for Atlanta Braves, Montreal Expos, (3) Gulfstream Polo Field, (4) Palm Beach Jai Alai, (5) Greyhound racing.

POPULATION: 67,723 PERSONS—W = 42,889, B = 22,063, AI/E/A = 94, C = 56, F = 106, M = 836, PR = 1,472

POPULATION GROWTH: + 7.0%

AGE OF POPULATION: (21-24) = 5.9%, (25-34) = 19.0%, (35-44) = 13.9%, (45-54) = 9.2%, (55-64) = 8.8%, (65-74) = 9.2%, (75 AND OVER) = 9.0%

HOUSING COST: OWNING = $72,000 RENTAL = $517

COMMUNITY HOSPITALS: 5 = 975 BEDS

CLIMATE: JAN—AVG. (65.1 DEGREES), JULY—AVG. (82.2 DEGREES), ANNUAL PRECIPITATION (60.75 INCHES)

PER CAPITA INCOME: $15,712

UNEMPLOYMENT RATE: 7.4%

JOB GROWTH SINCE 1980: + 16.6%

COST OF LIVING: 104.7

EDUCATION: PALM BEACH ATLANTIC COLLEGE, NORTHWOOD UNIVERSITY

TOWNS: (5,000—60,000)

▼KEY WEST

Gay Civil Rights: Bans discrimination based on sexual orientation in public and private employment, public accommodations and credit.

What the Locals Say . . .

Key West is described as "Paradise" by the local gays. In fact, if you love the ocean, the sun, great food and a laid back kind of life; you will love Key West. It has a very open gay community and most straights are very accepting. The gay community is progressive and politically active. There is only one drawback to moving to Key West. You must be able to support yourself before moving here. The best ways are to own your own business or to be independently wealthy. The cost of living is disproportionately high compared to the service industry job scale in the area. Key West is not the place to move if you are pinching your pennies. For example, a studio apartment goes for $450 and up. A one-bedroom goes for $550 to $600 and up. There's also first and last month and a security deposit, so you could easily need from $1500 to $2000 just to get into your living space. The island is only five square miles, but does offer everything imaginable for gays/lesbians. Fantasy Fest, held in October, is a Mardi Gras for the island; it culminates in the crowning of the Queen and King of Fantasy Fest. The Queen and King are selected based on who has raised the most money for AIDS. There are Art Festivals, Film Festivals, Home Tours; and, of course, all the water and beach activities, fishing, boating, etc.. Key West sent the largest contingent of contestants per capita to the Gay Games of any city in the country. You will see both men and women at all the bars; however, "Copa-Key West" is more for men, "Club International" is mixed but you will see more women, "Saloon One" is a men's levi and leather bar, "Atlantic Shores" is mixed and has a tea dance in the afternoons, "Numbers" is for men, and the "801 Bar" is more for men. Call The Key West Business Guild (gay/lesbian) for the complete scoop on anything that's happening on the island. The community is very supportive of AIDS projects. Immune Care offers the finest outpatient service in the country for HIV. AIDS Help Inc. of Monroe Co. offers absolutely the most comprehensive health care available with case management, food, housing, referrals, and a housing complex for PWA's. Old Town Medical Center provides excellent care also. There's even a weekly T.V. talk show called "Open Closet." *The Key West Citizen* is very gay positive. *The Pride Connection* is published weekly and the *Fountain*, a Lesbian paper, comes out monthly. Good bookstores are Caroline St. Books and Blue Heron Books. There is, of course, a MCC Key West.

LOCATION: KEY WEST IS THE SOUTHERNMOST CITY OF THE CONTINENTAL UNITED STATES, LOCATED ON THE STRING OF ISLANDS SOUTH OF FLORIDA.

GAY/LESBIAN FRIENDLY BUSINESSES: 44

GAY/LESBIAN BARS AND RESTAURANTS:12

GAY/LESBIAN ORGANIZATIONS: 3

GAY/LESBIAN RELIGIOUS ORGANIZATIONS, CHURCHES, ETC.: 1

GAY/LESBIAN BOOKSTORES: 2

GAY/LESBIAN PUBLICATIONS: 3

COMPANIES THAT PROHIBIT DISCRIMINATION: SEE GAY CIVIL RIGHTS

INFORMATION NUMBER: 305-294-4603 OR 1-800-535-7797, KEY WEST BUSINESS GUILD

TOTAL CRIMES:3,826

VIOLENT = (MURDER = 3, RAPE = 20, ROBBERY = 135, ASSAULT = 224)

PROPERTY = (BURGLARY = 742, LARCENY = 2,356, MOTOR VEHICLE THEFT = 346, ARSON = 3)

Things to Do!!!

Diving for sunken treasures, shopping, arts and crafts, deep sea fishing, and gourmet dining are among the most popular attractions in the area. Other areas of interest include: (1) Audubon House and

Gardens, (2) Key West Lighthouse Museum, (3) East Martello Gallery and Museum, (4) The Wreckers Museum, (5) Ernest Hemingway Home and Museum, (6) Key West Aquarium. SEASONAL EVENTS: (1) Old Island Days, (2) Hemingway Days.

POPULATION: 24,832 PERSONS = W = 21,368, B = 2,579, AI/E/A = 84, A/P/I = 349, H = 4,097

POPULATION GROWTH: N/A

AGE OF POPULATION: (21-24) = 1,673, (25-34) = 10,252, (35-44) = 2,370, (45-54) = 908 (55-64) = 988, (65-74) = 2,898, (75 AND OVER) = 1428

HOUSING COST: OWNING = $147,000 RENTAL = $559

COMMUNITY HOSPITALS: N/A

CLIMATE: N/A

PER CAPITA INCOME: N/A

UNEMPLOYMENT RATE:N/A

JOB GROWTH SINCE 1980: N/A

COST OF LIVING: N/A

EDUCATION: NONE

COUNTIES:

BROWARD COUNTY

Gay Civil Rights: Bans discrimination based on sexual orientation in public employment, public accommodations and housing.

Towns and Cities included in Broward County:

Coral Springs
Dania
Deerfield Beach
Ft. Lauderdale
Hillsboro Beach
Lauderdale-by-the-Sea
Lighthouse Point
Margate
Plantation
Pompano Beach
Oakland Park
Tamarac

PALM BEACH COUNTY

Gay Civil Rights: Bans discrimination based on sexual orientation in public employment, public accommodations and housing.

Towns and Cities included in Palm Beach County:

Atlantis
Belle Glade
Boca Raton
Boca Del Mar
Boca Point West
Boca West
Boynton Beach
Briny Breezes
Canal Point
Century Village
Cloud Lake
Country Club Trail
Cypress Lakes
Del Ray Beach
Glen Ridge
Golden Lakes
Golfview
Greenacres City
Gulf Stream
Havenhill
High Point
Highland Beach
Hypolux
Juno Beach
Jupiter
Lakeside Green
Lake Clarke Shores
Lake Park
Lake Worth
Lantana
Ocean Ridge
Manalapan
Mangonia Park
North Palm Beach Shores
Palm Beach
Palm Beach Gardens

Palm Beach Shores
Rainbow Lakes
Riviera Beach
Tequesta
Village of Oriole
West Palm Beach
Westgate

GEORGIA

STATE LAWS REGARDING HOMOSEXUALITY:

Heterosexual and homosexual sodomy is illegal with a maximum sentence of 20 years imprisonment. In 1993, a law was passed stating that same-sex couples will be recognized for the purpose of refusing alimony payments.

CITIES: (60,000 AND UP)

▼ATLANTA

Gay Civil Rights: Bans discrimination based on sexual orientation in city employment and companies doing business with the city.

What the Locals Say . . .

There is a large gay and lesbian community in Atlanta and a substantial part of it is open. In fact, some people refer to Atlanta as the gay mecca of the south. Gays and lesbians from small towns in Georgia, Alabama, the Carolinas, and Tennessee come to Atlanta so they can be out. The City of Atlanta did have a domestic partnership ordinance, but it was overturned by the state Supreme Court. There was a positive note to this ruling, the judge stated that the city of Atlanta has the authority to pass anti-discrimination laws, and that these laws were not special rights. Couples can still register as domestic partners. Although they cannot receive any other benefits, they can document their relationship legally. The gay and lesbian population is spread throughout suburbia. "Midtown" has a substantial gay and lesbian population. "Ansley Park" is another neighborhood with a high number of gays and lesbians. There is a small breezeway mall and strip mall that contains many gay-friendly shops and bars. Candler Park and Inman Park are also highly concentrated gay and lesbian areas. Grant Park, where many homes have been restored, is an area where family members are moving. The Atlanta Gay Center, which offers a variety of programs and resources, is a non-profit community organization that has been around 19 years. "Out Write" is a gay and lesbian bookstore. "Brushstrokes" is a lesbian and gay variety store. Social/support groups include the following: Bereavement support group, Caregiver Night Out, HIV Group, Prime Timers, Outsiders, The Men of Little Five Points, Women's Outdoor Network, Atlanta Couples Together, Different Voice Chorus, Coming Out Group, Lesbian Support Group, African American Lesbian Gay Alliance, and PFLAG. ACT-UP, Atlanta Green Part, Georgia Political Awareness Coalition (GAPAC), Republicans For Individual Freedoms and The Lesbian Avengers are some of the more popular political groups. Atlanta has a strong broadcast media for the gay and lesbian community. There is one radio show, "Gay Graphite" on 89.9 FM, which plays music and talks about Atlanta's Gay and Lesbian Community. There are four gay and lesbian television programs: "Dyke TV," "Out In Atlanta" and "Gay USA Television" on channel 12, "Gay Entertainment TV" on channel 32. Sport groups are numerous. There is a chapter of Frontrunners, AVS bowling, AVS walking and bicycling, Women's Social Tennis, Atlanta Team Tennis, Hotlanta Soccer, Basketball and Volleyball. Atlanta also has a group called "Atlanta Venture Sports." The Greater Atlanta Business Coalition dedicates itself to the development and growth of businesses that support the gay and lesbian community. Feminist Women's Health Center has gynecological services especially for lesbians. The Atlanta Gay Center Clinic has support available as well as anonymous HIV testing. Contact Atlanta Gay Center for numerous AIDS support and treatment organizations throughout Atlanta. Publications incude: *Atlanta's Community Yellow Pages* (one of the best in the country), *Aurora Rising, Etc., Southern Voice*, and *The News* (provocative commentaries, timely up-dates, excellent news coverage). The religious groups in Atlanta are the Gay Catholics of Georgia and Friends, Integrity/Atlanta, Presbyterians For Lesbian and Gay Concerned. There are numerous churches that are open and affirming to gays and lesbians including: All Saints MCC, First MCC, Grant Park/Aldersgate Methodist Church, Congregation Bet Haverim.

LOCATION: ATLANTA IS LOCATED IN THE NORTHWESTERN SECTION OF GEORGIA.

GAY LESBIAN FRIENDLY BUSINESSES: 500 +

GAY/LESBIAN BARS AND RESTAURANTS: 80

GAY/LESBIAN ORGANIZATIONS: 107

GAY/LESBIAN RELIGIOUS ORGANIZATIONS, CHURCHES, ETC.: 25

GAY/LESBIAN BOOKSTORES: 2

GAY/LESBIAN PUBLICATIONS: 8

COMPANIES THAT PROHIBIT DISCRIMINATION:

INFORMATION NUMBER: 404-876-5372 ATLANTA GAY CENTER

TOTAL CRIMES: 69,914

VIOLENT = (MURDER = 203, RAPE = 492, ROBBERY = 6,045, ASSAULT = 9,541)

PROPERTY = (BURGLARY = 13,168, LARCENY = 31,249, MOTOR VEHICLE THEFT = 9,216, ARSON = 248)

Things to Do!!!

(1) State Capitol, (2) Georgia Department of Archives and History, (3) A. G. Rhodes Memorial Hall, (4) Robert W. Woodruff Arts Center, (5) Martin Luther King, Jr. National Historic Site, (6) Atlanta Historical Society, (7) Fox Theatre, (8) Museum of the Jimmy Carter

Library, (9) SciTrek-The Science and Technology Museum of Atlanta, (10) Wren's Nest, (11) Atlanta Botanical Garden, (12) Atlanta State Farmers' Market, (13) Six Flags Over Georgia, (14) Atlanta Botanical Garden, (15) Stone Mountain Park, (16) Kennesaw Mountain National Battlefield Park, (17) Yellow River Game Ranch, (18) Fort McPherson, (19) Peachtree Street. ANNUAL EVENTS: (1) Atlanta Hunt and Steeplechase, (2) Atlanta Dogwood Festival, (3) Georgia Renaissance Festival, (4) Atlanta Golf Classic, (5) Jazz Festivals. SEASONAL EVENTS: (1) Atlanta Symphony Orchestra, (2) Theatre of the Stars, (3) Auto Racing, (4) Alliance Theatre Company, (5) Professional Sports: Baseball - Braves, Basketball - Hawks, Football - Falcons.

POPULATION: 394,848 PERSONS—W = 122,327, B = 264,262, AI/E/A = 563, C = 932, F = 153, M = 3,715, PR = 782

POPULATION GROWTH: - 7.1%

AGE OF POPULATION: (21-24) = 7.3%, (25-34) = 19.3%, (35-44) = 15.4%, (45-54) = 9.4%, (55-64) = 7.2%, (65-74) = 6.0%, (75 AND OVER) = 5.3%

HOUSING COST: OWNING = $71,200   RENTAL = $422

COMMUNITY HOSPITALS: 16 = 5,529

CLIMATE: JAN—AVG. (41.0 DEGREES), JULY—AVG. (78.8 DEGREES), ANNUAL PRECIPITATION (50.77 INCHES)

PER CAPITA INCOME: $15,279

UNEMPLOYMENT RATE: 6.5%

JOB GROWTH SINCE 1980: +1.4%

COST OF LIVING: 97.0

EDUCATION: GEORGIA TECH, GEORGIA INSTITUTE OF TECHNOLOGY

HAWAII

STATE LAWS REGARDING HOMOSEXUALITY:

No sodomy laws exist in Hawaii. In 1973, private homosexual acts between consenting adults became law. In 1991, a bill was signed forbidding job discrimination on the basis of sexual orientation in private and public employment.

CITIES: (60,000 AND UP)

▼HONOLULU

Gay Civil Rights: Bans discrimination based on sexual orientation in public employment.

What the Locals Say . . .

Honolulu is a beautiful safe place to live. The gay and lesbian population is very visible, although not openly affectionate towards their partners. There is not really a gay and lesbian residential neighborhood, although there is a gay and lesbian business district. Starting at the intersection of Kalakaua and Kuhio, there are many gay & lesbian restaurants, bars, cafes and other businesses. Cafe Valentini is a very popular cafe. Waikiki has a large number of gays and lesbians mixed with a large number of straight people. Queens Surf Beach is a predominately gay men's beach. Mountain hiking, dances, talks, forums, support groups, swimming, snorkeling, mopeds are just a few of the activities available in this paradise setting. Honolulu Men's Chorus, running groups and volleyball are other popular activities. The Pride festival is a month long event in June. There are numerous cookouts, film festivals, a gay parade and rally. The bar scene is mixed although most are mainly mens bars. Some of the more popular gay men's bars are: "Hamburger Mary's," "Hulas," "Fusion," and "Windows"—has a piano bar and ladies nights. The most popular bar for women is "Metropolis." Honolulu has a large AIDS support network. Life Foundation offers education, care, and support for HIV+ and AIDS patients, families and friends. There are also a number of clinics and physicians who specialize in treatment of HIV and AIDS. Blazing Saddles is a social organization for gays and lesbians who want to dance in a nonalcoholic, non-smoking environment. *Island Lifestyles* is the gay and lesbian newspaper and is published once a month. MCC and Dignity churches are completely open to gay and lesbian churchgoers.

LOCATION: HONOLULU IS LOCATED ON THE ISLAND OF OAHU IN THE HAWAIIAN ISLANDS.

GAY/LESBIAN FRIENDLY BUSINESSES: 100

GAY/LESBIAN BARS AND RESTAURANTS:20

GAY/LESBIAN ORGANIZATIONS: 30

GAY/LESBIAN RELIGIOUS ORGANIZATIONS, CHURCHES, ETC.: 4

GAY/LESBIAN BOOKSTORES: 0

GAY/LESBIAN PUBLICATIONS: 3

COMPANIES THAT PROHIBIT DISCRIMINATION: SEE STATE LAWS AND GAY CIVIL RIGHTS

INFORMATION NUMBER: 808-951-7000 GAY AND LESBIAN COMMUNITY CENTER

TOTAL CRIMES: 56,405

VIOLENT = (MURDER = 31, RAPE = 286, ROBBERY = 1,085, ASSAULT = 1,099)

PROPERTY = (BURGLARY = 9,296, LARCENY = 40,148, MOTOR VEHICLE THEFT = 4,460, ARSON = 276)

Things to Do!!!

Honolulu is famous as a world wide tourist destination. The Pacific Ocean surrounds the Island of Oahu and offers a variety of water activities. Deep sea fishing, dinner cruises, luaus, scuba, snorkeling, surfing as well as many other activities are available. Other points of interest include: (1) Mission House Museum, (2) U.S. Army Museum, (3) Honolulu Zoo, (4) Honolulu Aquarium, (5) Lunalilo Tomb, (6) Iolani Palace, (7) Kawaiahao Church, (8) Honolulu Symphony Arts, (9) Honolulu Community Theatre, (10) Chamber Music Hawaii, (11) Manda Valley Theatre, (12) Hawaiian Opera Theatre, (13) Hanauma Bay, (14) Diamond Head, (15) Waikiki Beach, (16) Pearl Harbor Memorial. Annual Events: (1) Hawaiian Open Golf Tournament, (2) Triple Crown of Surfing, (3) Hula Bowl, (4) Waikiki Beach

POPULATION: 371,320 PERSONS—W = 97,527, B = 1,126, AI/E/A = 1,126, C = 44,841, F = 44,932, M = 3,039, PR = 4,435

POPULATION GROWTH: + 1.7%

AGE OF POPULATION: (21-24) = 6.1%, (25-34) = 17.6%, (35-44) = 16.2%, (45-54) = 10.8%, (55-64) = 10.3%, (65-74) = 9.8%, (75 AND OVER) = 6.2%

HOUSING COST: OWNING = $353,900 RENTAL =$623

COMMUNITY HOSPITALS: 7 = 1,828 BEDS

CLIMATE: JAN—AVG. (71.4 DEGREES), JULY—AVG. (78.9 DEGREES), ANNUAL PRECIPITATION (21.53 INCHES)

PER CAPITA INCOME: $18,554

UNEMPLOYMENT RATE: 2.3%

JOB GROWTH SINCE 1980: + 3.3%

COST OF LIVING: N/A

EDUCATION: UNIVERSITY OF HAWAII

IDAHO

STATE LAWS REGARDING HOMOSEXUALITY:

Heterosexual and homosexual sodomy is illegal, carrying a life sentence if convicted. In 1971, a new penal code was signed eliminating all penalties for private homosexual acts between consenting adults.

CITIES: (60,000 AND UP)

BOISE

Gay Civil Rights: None

What the Locals Say . . .

The Boise gay and lesbian community is in the middle of the road—not too closeted, not too open. In November of 1994, an anti-gay initiative was defeated, but it forced more of the community to come out and help fight. The best place to live if you are gay or lesbian in Idaho is Boise. There is a men's Triangle Group, and a Triangle Connection social group. The Triangle Connection group decides what activities they want to do and then they plan them for different dates. Bowling, hiking trips, desert trips, volleyball, bike riding, are all some of the activities available through the Triangle Connection. Boise has a Log Cabin Republican group and Womyn's Community Production. Gay Pride Week includes a parade, and booths set up by organizations. There are entertainers and other events that lead up to the parade. The "Oly" is the oldest gay bar and is a leather Levi establishment. "Emerald City Club" is the largest bar, although it is being taken over by straights on Thursday nights and weekends. "Partners" draws a gay and lesbian crowd; it is the newest bar and it has a Disc Jockey one night, live entertainment one night, as well as other activities. The Central District Health Department has open and closed HIV support groups. It provides HIV testing, although if you are positive the results are given out. If you go to Oregon, the information is not divulged. *Diversity* is a gay and lesbian monthly newspaper that is published statewide. MCC, Affirmation (Mormon affiliate), Dignity and Integrity are open to gays and lesbians.

LOCATION: BOISE IS LOCATED IN SOUTHWEST IDAHO.

GAY /LESBIAN FRIENDLY BUSINESSES: 5

GAY/LESBIAN BARS AND RESTAURANTS: 2

GAY/LESBIAN ORGANIZATIONS: 3

GAY/LESBIAN RELIGIOUS ORGANIZATIONS, CHURCHES, ETC.: 1

GAY/LESBIAN BOOKSTORES: 0

GAY/LESBIAN PUBLICATIONS: 1
COMPANIES THAT PROHIBIT DISCRIMINATION: N/A
INFORMATION NUMBER: 208-336-3870 THE COMMUNITY CENTER
TOTAL CRIMES: 7,722
VIOLENT = (MURDER = 3, RAPE = 72, ROBBERY = 48, ASSAULT = 494)
PROPERTY = (BURGLARY = 1,204, LARCENY = 5,538, MOTOR VEHICLE THEFT = 324, ARSON = 39)

Things to Do!!!

Jogging, hiking, walking, and biking trails alongside the Boise River are popular. The Boise River Trail, a twenty two mile long trail, connects Eagle Island Park to Lucky Peak State Park. Other points include: (1) Bogus Basin Ski Park, (2) Boise National Forest, (3) Table Rock, (4) Wild Water, (5) Julia Davis Park,(6) Platt Garden & Union Pacific Depot, (7) M-K Nature Center, (8) Idaho Botanical Garden, (9) Discovery Center of Idaho, (10) Basque Museum and Cultural Center. ANNUAL EVENTS: (1) Boise River Festival, (2) River Super Float, (3) Western Idaho Fair. SEASONAL EVENTS: (1) Thoroughbred Racing, (2) Idaho Shakespeare Festival.

POPULATION: 135,506 PERSONS—W = 121,262, B = 730, AI/E/A = 808, C = 341, F = 180, M = 2,052, PR = 99

POPULATION GROWTH: + 32.5%

AGE OF POPULATION: (21-24) = 6.5%, (25-34) = 18.5%, (35-44) = 16.5%, (45-54) = 9.5%, (55-64) = 7.0%, (65-74) = 6.6%, (75 AND OVER) = 5.3%

HOUSING COST: OWNING = $67,700   RENTAL = $404

COMMUNITY HOSPITALS: 3 = 557 BEDS

CLIMATE: JAN—AVG. (29.0 DEGREES), JULY—AVG. (74.0 DEGREES), ANNUAL PRECIPITATION (12.11 INCHES)

PER CAPITA INCOME: $15,208

UNEMPLOYMENT RATE: 4.0%

JOB GROWTH SINCE 1980: + 26.9%

COST OF LIVING: 102.2

EDUCATION: BOISE STATE UNIVERSITY

ILLINOIS

STATE LAWS REGARDING HOMOSEXUALITY:

In 1961, Illinois became the first state to repeal its sodomy law. Anti-gay discrimination in public employment is banned. In 1990, a bill was signed to include anti-gay violence as a hate crime.

CITIES: (60,000 AND UP)

▼CHAMPAIGN

Gay Civil Rights: Bans discrimination based on sexual orientation in public and private employment, public accommodations, housing, and union practices.

What the Locals Say . . .

Champaign is more business oriented than its sister city, Urbana. The University of Illinois campus is located in Urbana and Champaign. Champaign and Urbana are often combined as one city. The best area for gays and lesbians to live in is Old Towne. There are several organizations in Champaign including The Alternate Current, (a men's discussion group), Champaign/Urbana men's chorus, Lavender Prairie Collective (a social group for women), and GAMMA (a Gay and Married Men's Association). Champaign also has a men's coffeehouse, Sister Insider—a women's only space discussion group, Spectrum—a U. of Illinois gay, lesbian, bisexual and transgender group, Amasung—a women's chorus, women's coffeehouse, and GALES—Gay and Lesbian youth group. "Jane Adams" is a feminist bookstore in Champaign. "La Fiesta" is a Mexican restaurant that is gay owned and managed. "Chester Street" is a straight/gay bar. The Gay Community AIDS Project helps and assists those with HIV or AIDS. There is also a house for people living with AIDS. For the most part, health care providers give information the stereotypical way. *The Lavender Prairie News* is a monthly publication, and *Lesbian and Gay Concerns* is a University of Illinois gay and lesbian publication, *G Capsule* is a once a month publication put out by the Gay Community AIDS Project. The United Church of Christ, McKinley Presbyterian Church, and the Unitarian Universalist are churches that perform commitment ceremonies as well as open their doors to gays and lesbians.

LOCATION: CHAMPAIGN IS LOCATED IN EASTERN ILLINOIS, NORTH OF URBANA.
GAY/LESBIAN FRIENDLY BUSINESSES: 15
GAY/LESBIAN BARS AND RESTAURANTS: 2
GAY/LESBIAN ORGANIZATIONS: 11

GAY/LESBIAN RELIGIOUS ORGANIZATIONS, CHURCHES, ETC.: 3

GAY/LESBIAN BOOKSTORES: 1

GAY/LESBIAN PUBLICATIONS: 2

COMPANIES THAT PROHIBIT DISCRIMINATION: SEE STATE LAWS AND GAY CIVIL RIGHTS

INFORMATION NUMBER: 217-384-8040 LESBIAN GAY & BISEXUAL SWITCHBOARD

TOTAL CRIMES: 5,836

VIOLENT = (MURDER = 3, RAPE = 58 ROBBERY = 211, ASSAULT = 409)

PROPERTY = (BURGLARY = 1,343, LARCENY = 3,593, MOTOR VEHICLE THEFT = 199, ARSON = 20)

Things to Do!!!

(1) Champaign County Historical Museum, (2) William M. Staerkel Planetarium,

POPULATION: 64,350 PERSONS—W = 51,254, B = 9,006, AI/E/A = 113, C = 799, F = 231, M = 550, PR = 98

POPULATION GROWTH: + 10.4%

AGE OF POPULATION: (21-24) = 16.1%, (25-34) = 17.7%, (35-44) = 12.3%, (45-54) = 6.5%, (55-64) = 5.6%, (65-74) = 4.7%, (75 AND OVER) = 3.5%

HOUSING COST: OWNING = $66,500 RENTAL = $422

COMMUNITY HOSPITALS: 0

CLIMATE: JAN—AVG. (23.8 DEGREES), JULY—AVG. (75.0 DEGREES), ANNUAL PRECIPITATION (39.71 INCHES)

PER CAPITA INCOME: $13,025

JOB GROWTH SINCE 1980: + 12%

UNEMPLOYMENT RATE: 2.3%

COST OF LIVING: 101.7

EDUCATION: UNIVERSITY OF ILLINOIS-URBANA/CHAMPAIGN

▼CHICAGO:

Gay Civil Rights: Bans discrimination based on sexual orientation in public and private employment, public accommodations, education and credit.

What the Locals Say . . .

Chicago is open in certain areas and is not as mid-western conservative as some would think. There are approximately 100,000-200,000 gays and lesbians in the area. Within the city itself, the politicians seem to be pro-gay which helps foster more gay civil rights. The North side of Chicago (New Town/Lakeview area) has several bars and organizations and for the most part is relatively safe. The 44th Ward next to Wrigley Field is thought to be 40% gay and lesbian. The Broadway, Hallstead, and Clark Streets are areas with a high number of gays and lesbians. There are several sports clubs and leagues including: baseball, bowling, volleyball, swimming, and softball in Lincoln Park. The Horizons Community Center is the focal point of the gay community for the psychological side and Howard Brown takes care of the physical/medical side. Mountain Moving Coffeehouse is a women's and children's-only, substance free organization that has numerous entertainment activities throughout the year. The Gay Pride Parade goes through the North side of the city and ends up at Lincoln Park where speeches are given. Most of the bars in Chicago are gay men's, although women are welcome. Some of the most popular are: "A A Meatmarket," "Foxy's," "LA Connection," "Loading Dock." The "Closet" is a neighborhood lesbian bar, and "Paris Dance" is the largest lesbian bar. The relationship between the health care community and the gay and lesbian community is excellent. Horizons maintains a list of physicians and psychotherapists that cater to gays and lesbians. *The Windy City Times* is a weekly publication and is the largest in Chicago. *Gay Chicago Magazine* is also a weekly publication. *Nightlines/Outlines* is a monthly publication which focuses on nighttime activities. There are several religious organizations that are very gay and lesbian-friendly including: Chicago Interfaith Congress, MCC, Lutheran, Dignity, Gay Christian Scientists, Unitarian, United Church of Christ Coalition and several others.

LOCATION: CHICAGO IS LOCATED ON LAKE MICHIGAN IN THE NORTHEASTERN REGION OF ILLINOIS.

GAY/LESBIAN FRIENDLY BUSINESSES: 44

GAY/LESBIAN BARS AND RESTAURANTS: 56

GAY/LESBIAN ORGANIZATIONS: 58

GAY/LESBIAN RELIGIOUS ORGANIZATIONS, CHURCHES, ETC.: 16

GAY/LESBIAN BOOKSTORES: 3

GAY/LESBIAN PUBLICATIONS: 7

COMPANIES THAT PROHIBIT DISCRIMINATION: ANDERSEN CONSULTING, ARTHUR ANDERSEN CONSULTING & CO., SEE STATE LAWS AND GAY CIVIL RIGHTS

INFORMATION NUMBER: 312-929-4357 HORIZONS COMMUNITY CENTER HELPLINE

TOTAL CRIMES: 287,805

VIOLENT = (MURDER = 845, RAPE = 2,920, ROBBERY = 35,189, ASSAULT = 39,753)

PROPERTY = (BURGLARY = 45,670, LARCENY = 121,314, MOTOR VEHICLE THEFT = 40,438, ARSON = 1,676)

Things to Do!!!

There are 21 beaches on Lake Michigan within the city of Chicago. Boating, canoeing and fishing are very popular. Morton Arboretum features trees and plants from around the world that shade a 1,500 acre outdoor museum. Other points of interest include: (1) The Art Institute of Chicago, (2) The Museum of Contemporary Art, (3) Chicago Symphony Orchestra, (4) Lyric Opera of Chicago, (6) Chicago Sinfonietta, (7) The Field Museum of Natural History, (8) Museum of Science and History, (9) John G. Shedd Aquarium, (10) Adler Planetarium, (11) Lincoln Park Zoo, (12) John Hancock Center Observatory, (13) Professional Sports: Football - Bears, Basketball-Bulls, Baseball- White Sox & Cubs, Hockey - Blackhawks.

POPULATION: 2,768,483 PERSONS—W = 1,263,524, B = 1,087,711, AI/E/A =7,064, C = 22,295, F = 27,443, M = 352,560, PR = 119,866

POPULATION GROWTH: - 7.9%

AGE OF POPULATION: (21-24) = 6.8%, (25-34) = 19.3%, (35-44) = 13.9%, (45-54) = 9.3%, (55-64) = 8.1%, (65-74) = 6.9%, (75 AND OVER) = 5.0%

HOUSING COST: OWNING = $78,700 RENTAL = $445

COMMUNITY HOSPITALS: 42 = 12,896 BEDS

CLIMATE: JAN—AVG. (22.4 DEGREES), JULY—AVG. (75.1 DEGREES), ANNUAL PRECIPITATION (37.38 INCHES)

PER CAPITA INCOME: $12,899

UNEMPLOYMENT RATE: 8.4%

JOB GROWTH SINCE 1980: - .6%

COST OF LIVING: 112.4

EDUCATION: CHICAGO STATE UNIVERSITY, UNIVERSITY OF ILLINOIS AT CHICAGO, NORTHEASTERN UNIVERSITY OF CHICAGO

TOWNS: (5,000-60,000)

▼OAK PARK

Gay Civil Rights: Bans discrimination based on sexual orientation in public accommodations and housing.

What the Locals Say . . .

Oak Park is considered to be very liberal and pretty open. Most gays are very discreet about showing affection in public. The Oak Park Housing Center on South Boulevard is an excellent place to start looking for a place to rent. They ask you what you want, then give you 2-3 choices, and you go and look; then, you can come back and say what you liked or didn't like, etc.. Oak Park is a relatively small town. There isn't a distinct area that is gay and lesbian. There are major cost differences in homes in Oak Park ranging from $500,000-$100,000. Typically, north Oak Park is more upper class and south Oak Park has lower cost. Oak Park has a gay and lesbian organization that hosts potlucks and meetings. There is a mom's group and a youth group in Oak Park. The Gay and Lesbian Festival is a big event in May. "Pride Agenda" is a gay owned bookstore that is a good source for local happenings. There are not any gay or lesbian bars in Oak Park, but there are numerous private dinner parties. *The Oak Park Newsletter* is a bi-monthly publication. *The 708* is a newsletter of poetry and short fiction published in Oak Park. The MCC and the Unitarian Church are open to gays and lesbians. The Methodist and Lutheran Churches allow gay and lesbian organizations to meet in their facilities.

LOCATION: OAK PARK IS A SUBURB WEST OF CHICAGO.

GAY/LESBIAN FRIENDLY BUSINESSES: 3

GAY/LESBIAN BARS AND RESTAURANTS: 0

GAY/LESBIAN ORGANIZATIONS: 3

GAY/LESBIAN RELIGIOUS ORGANIZATIONS, CHURCHES, ETC.: 2

GAY/LESBIAN BOOKSTORES: 1

GAY/LESBIAN PUBLICATIONS: 2

COMPANIES THAT PROHIBIT DISCRIMINATION: SEE STATE LAWS AND GAY CIVIL RIGHTS

INFORMATION NUMBER: 708-289-2346 WOMEN OF THE WESTERN SUBURB

TOTAL CRIMES: 3,675

VIOLENT = (MURDER = 2, RAPE = 13, ROBBERY = 209, ASSAULT = 32)

PROPERTY = (BURGLARY = 749, LARCENY = 2,352, MOTOR VEHICLE THEFT = 305, ARSON = 13)

Things to Do!!!

(1) Ernest Hemingway Museum, (2) Frank Lloyd Wright Home Studio, (3) Oak Park Visitors Center.

POPULATION: 54,217 PERSONS—W = 41,313, B = 9,804, AI/E/A = 73, C = 338, F = 397, M = 923, PR = 275

AGE OF POPULATION: (21-24) = 5.6%, (25-34) = 20.7%, (35-44) = 19.1%, (45-54) = 10.2%, (55-64) = 6.7%, (65-74) = 5.6%, (75 AND OVER) = 5.9%

POPULATION GROWTH: - 1.2%

HOUSING COST: OWNING = $138,700 RENTAL = $535

COMMUNITY HOSPITALS: 2 = 585 BEDS

CLIMATE: JAN—AVG. (22.4 DEGREES), JULY—AVG. (75.1 DEGREES), ANNUAL PRECIPITATION (37.38 INCHES)

PER CAPITA INCOME: $21,269
UNEMPLOYMENT RATE: 4.9%
JOB GROWTH SINCE 1980: + 8.0%
COST OF LIVING: N/A
EDUCATION: WEST SUBURBAN COLLEGE OF NURSING

▼URBANA

Gay Civil Rights: Bans discrimination in public and private employment, public accommodations, education and housing.

What the Locals Say . . .

Urbana is the sister city to Champaign. The two cities share the University of Illinois campus. Urbana is primarily a bedroom community with a major University in its city. The city of Urbana is kind of middle-of-the-road as far as lesbian and gay issues go since it is a university town. The neighborhoods in Urbana are typically referred to as University Ghetto since many students live in Urbana. The majority of gay and lesbian activities are in Champaign.

LOCATION: URBANA IS LOCATED IN EASTERN ILLINOIS, SOUTH OF CHAMPAIGN.

GAY/LESBIAN FRIENDLY BUSINESSES: SEE CHAMPAIGN

GAY/LESBIAN BARS AND RESTAURANTS: SEE CHAMPAIGN

GAY/LESBIAN ORGANIZATIONS: SEE CHAMPAIGN

GAY/LESBIAN RELIGIOUS ORGANIZATIONS, CHURCHES, ETC.: SEE CHAMPAIGN

GAY/LESBIAN BOOKSTORES: SEE CHAMPAIGN

GAY/LESBIAN PUBLICATIONS: SEE CHAMPAIGN

COMPANIES THAT PROHIBIT DISCRIMINATION: SEE STATE LAWS AND GAY CIVIL RIGHTS

INFORMATION NUMBERS: 217-384-8040 LESBIAN GAY & BISEXUAL SWITCHBOARD

TOTAL CRIMES: 1,168

VIOLENT = (MURDER = 1, RAPE = 17, ROBBERY = 36, ASSAULT = 54)

PROPERTY = (BURGLARY = 262, LARCENY = 755, MOTOR VEHICLE THEFT = 37, ARSON = 6)

Things to Do!!!

University of Illinois-Krannert Art Museum, World Heritage Museum of Natural History.

POPULATION: 36,081 PERSONS—W = 27,527,B = 4,159, AI/E/A = 55, C = 161, F = 202, M = 344, PR = 86

POPULATION GROWTH: + .3%

AGE OF POPULATION: (21-24) = 14.3%, (25-34) = 20.5%, (35-44) = 10.9%, (45-54) = 5.8%, (55-64) = 5.1%, (65-74) = 4.5%, (75 AND OVER) = 4.5%

HOUSING COST: OWNING = $69,000 RENTAL = $413

COMMUNITY HOSPITALS: 2 = 805 BEDS

CLIMATE: JAN—AVG. (23.8 DEGREES), JULY—AVG. (75.0 DEGREES), ANNUAL PRECIPITATION (39.71 INCHES)

PER CAPITA INCOME: $11,439

UNEMPLOYMENT RATE: 4.5%

JOB GROWTH SINCE 1980: + 2.0%

HOUSING COST: OWNING = $69,000 RENTAL = $413

COMMUNITY HOSPITALS: 2 = 805 BEDS

COST OF LIVING: 101.7

EDUCATION: UNIVERSITY OF ILLINOIS AT URBANA/CHAMPAIGN

COUNTIES:
COOK COUNTY

Gay Civil Rights: Bans discrimination based on sexual orientation in public and private employment, public accommodations, education and credit.

Cites and Towns Within Cook County:

Alsip
Arlington Heights
Barrington Bacog
Barrington Hills
Bartlett
Bedford Park
Bellwood
Berkeley
Berwyn
Blue Island
Bridgeview
Broadview
Buffalo Grove
Burbank
Burnham

Calumet City
Calumet Park
Chicago
Chicago Heights
Chicago Ridge
Cicero
Country Club Hills
Countryside
Crestwood
Des Plains
Dolton
East Hazel Crest
Elk Grove Village
Elmwood Park
Evanston
Evergreen Park
Flossmoor
Ford Heights
Forest Park
Forest View
Franklin Park
Glencoe
Glenview
Glenwood
Golf
Hanover Park
Harvey
Harwood Heights
Hazel Crest
Hickory Hills
Hillside
Hodgkins
Hoffman Estates
Hometown
Homewood
Indian Head Park
Kenilworth
Justice

La Grange
La Grange Park
Lansing
Lemont
Lincolnwood
Lynwood
Lyons
Maywood
McCook
Maton Grove
Melrose Park
Merrionette Park
Midlothian
Morton Grove
Mt. Prospect
Niles
Norridge
North Riverside
Northbrook
Northlake
OakForest
OakLawn
Oak Park
Olympia Fields
Orland Hills
Orland Park
Palatine
Palos Heights
Palos Park
Park Forest
Park Ridge
Phoenix
Posen
Prospect Heights
Righton Park
River Forest
River Grove
Riverdale

Riverside
Robbins
Rolling Meadows
Rosemont
Sauk Village
Schaumburg
Schiller Park
Skokie
South Chicago Heights
South Holland
Steger
Stone Park
Streamwood
Summit
Thornton
Tinley Park
Westchester
Western Springs
Wheeling
Willow Springs
Wilmette
Winnetka

INDIANA

STATE LAWS REGARDING HOMOSEXUALITY:

In 1976, as part of a general law reform, sodomy laws were repealed.

CITIES: (60,000 AND UP)

▼BLOOMINGTON

Gay Civil Rights: Bans discrimination based on sexual orientation in public and private employment, public accommodations, education, housing,

What the Locals Say . . .

Bloomington is fairly open and has a very active gay and lesbian community. Indiana University is located in Bloomington, therefore there's a large young population, away from home and not afraid to be out. Gays and lesbians are evenly distributed throughout town. The feminist bookstore, "Aquarius Books," has lesbian, gay and feminists titles. "Aquarius Books" also sponsors poetry readings, potlucks, and "Sparks"—a women's group that sponsors a softball team. The University Campus has a group called "Out" which is a gay/lesbian/bisexual group that sponsors dances, and a music festival called "Queerstock." The National Music Festival is held in June. The four day event is recognized in the women's community as a major national festival attracting over 3,000 women from across the country. There are workshops, dramatic presentations, art fairs, and sporting competitions. "Men In The Process" is a men's social group, "Outreach" is a women's social group. Bloomington has a "Gay Men's Fellowship," an "Over 40 Lesbian Discussion Group," and Gay and Lesbian AA groups. The only gay and lesbian political groups, Bloomington Coalition and QUEST (Queers United for Equal Social Treatment), disbanded; but now are getting back together. During the 1st week of November, there are several gay and lesbian events. The PFLAG has 40-50 members. Indiana Youth Gay (IYG) is a youth group of gays under 21. "Bullwinkle's" is a dance bar with a mixed clientele of lesbian/gay/straight. "The Other Bar" is a neighborhood tavern which caters to an older gay male crowd. A brand new feminist/lesbian bar is "Labyris." Health care in Bloomington is very good. The South Central Community Center has several counseling and support groups for HIV, AA, and numerous others. They also fund Project Find, an AIDS organization. Project Find has a buddy program that teams people up with someone who can help shop and run errands. Public Health Nursing fees are based on income. *The Word* is the gay and lesbian publication read by residents of Bloomington, although it is published in Indianapolis. The group Integrity-Lesbians and Gay Episcopalians and their friends, Lutherans For Gay, Lesbian, and Bisexual Concerns, Catholic Mass for Gay, Lesbian and Bisexual People, Affinity - Unitarian Universalist for Lesbian, Gay and Bisexual Concerns meet regularly.

LOCATION: BLOOMINGTON IS LOCATED 70 MILES SOUTH WEST OF INDIANAPOLIS, INDIANA.

GAY/LESBIAN FRIENDLY BUSINESSES: 15

GAY/LESBIAN BARS AND RESTAURANTS: 3

GAY/LESBIAN ORGANIZATIONS: 10

GAY/LESBIAN RELIGIOUS ORGANIZATIONS, CHURCHES, ETC.: 5

GAY/LESBIAN BOOKSTORES: 1

GAY/LESBIAN PUBLICATIONS: 1

COMPANIES THAT PROHIBIT DISCRIMINATION: SEE GAY CIVIL RIGHTS

INFORMATION NUMBER: 812-855-5OUT, GAY & LESBIAN SWITCHBOARD

TOTAL CRIMES: 2,826

VIOLENT = (MURDER = 0, RAPE = 10, ROBBERY = 10, ASSAULT = 485)

PROPERTY = (BURGLARY = 354, LARCENY = 1,797, MOTOR VEHICLE THEFT = 160, ARSON = 5)

Things to Do!!!

(1) Monroe County Historical Society Museum, (2) Oliver Winery, (3) Butler Winery, (4) Lake Monroe, (5) McCormick's Creek State park, (6) Brown County State Park. ANNUAL EVENTS: (1) Little 500 Bicycle Race, (2) Monroe County Fair, (3) Madrigal Feast.

POPULATION: 61,503 PERSONS—W = 55,271, B = 2,441, AI/E/A = 122, C = 848, F = 120, M = 368, PR = 126

POPULATION GROWTH: + 16.8%

AGE OF POPULATION: (21-24) = 20.8%, (25-34) = 16.4%, (35-44) = 9.3%, (45-54) = 5.3%, (55-64) = 4.4%, (65-74) = 3.8%, (75 AND OVER) = 3.1%

HOUSING COST: OWNING = $76,300 RENTAL = $403

COMMUNITY HOSPITALS: 1 = 285 BEDS

CLIMATE: JAN—AVG. (27.3 DEGREES), JULY—AVG. (75.8 DEGREES), ANNUAL PRECIPITATION (43.14 INCHES)

PER CAPITA INCOME: $10,616

UNEMPLOYMENT RATE: 3.5%

JOB GROWTH SINCE 1980: +24.6%

COST OF LIVING: N/A

INDIANAPOLIS
Gay Civil Rights: None

What the Locals Say . . .

The gay and lesbian community is not very unified, but it is becoming more so. Part of the community is open, part is not. There are several neighborhoods that have a large number of gays and lesbians. Watson Park/Meridian Park is an older neighborhood and is very transitional. Most of the homes here are large and established, and there is a park and many winding roads throughout. Herron Morton is in the downtown area. Chatham Arch has smaller homes in the downtown area built at the turn of the century. Several bars are in the area. Real estate prices are going sky high. Irvington is on the east side of town. This area is more quiet, more middle class and has more white Irish Catholic. Woodruff Place is one of the first planned neighborhoods in the United States. Fountains line the boulevard. There are huge older homes, but most are divided into apartments. Lockerbie Square is in the heart of downtown. The streets are cobblestone and the homes are not less than $100,000 each. Lockerbie Square is a friendly neighborhood with several committees that meet regularly to discuss continued improvements of the neighborhood. Broad Ripple is more bohemian and laid back, and the bungalow homes are in northside (north of downtown). If you are out and actively looking for something, you will find many things to do. Indianapolis Business Outreach is a networking association for gay, lesbian and gay friendly professionals. "Out N About" is a social/recreational association consisting of a bowling league, poker group, Sunday Sandlot Volleyball, writers club, and a spirituality group. Other recreational groups include a beach volleyball group, Frontrunners/Frontwalkers, No Nonsense Bowling League, and a Bridge group. Indianapolis has a Lambda Car Club, Indianapolis Youth Groups, Indianapolis Couples Together, PFLAG, Sweet Misery, Men Of All Colors Together, and Gay and Lesbian Bisexual Veterans Association. There is a lesbian and gay rollerskating and dance party once a month at "USA Skate East." "Goddess of The Rock" is a big women's social event and fundraising event for the Women's Music Festival in Bloomington. Political groups in Indianapolis are: "Gays and Lesbian Working Against Violence," and the "Gay and Lesbian Rights Task Force," a branch of the Indiana Civil Rights Union. The Lavendula Society is a horticulture Club, The Country Club is a gay and lesbian country and western dance group. Some of the most popular bars are the "501 Tavern" which is a men's dance bar. "Jimmy's Bar and Restaurant" and "Our Place" all draw a gay male crowd. "NY Connections" is a mixed dance bar. "The Ten" is a women's dance bar. "Coffee Zon" is a popular restaurant. "Dreams and Swords" is a feminist bookstore. The Damien Center is an educational and support facility for AIDS patients, families and significant others. The Indiana Cares Annual "Garage Party" is a major fundraiser for HIV/AIDS. *The Indiana Word* is a monthly gay and lesbian publication. The religious groups: Dignity, Gays and Lesbians in Unity, Gays and Lesbians Affirming Disciples From the Christian Church Disciples of Christ (GLAD), Presbyterians for Lesbian & Gay Concerns and the Indianapolis Gay and Lesbian Jewish Group. The Jesus Metropolitan Church, Broadway United Christian Church, Unitarian Universalist Church of Indianapolis and the First Congregational Church of the United Church of Christ all welcome gays and lesbians.

LOCATION: INDIANAPOLIS IS LOCATED IN CENTRAL INDIANA WITH LAKE MICHIGAN AND THE OHIO RIVER BEING EQUAL DISTANCE FROM THE CITY NORTH AND SOUTH.

GAY/LESBIAN FRIENDLY BUSINESSES: 30+

GAY/LESBIAN BARS AND RESTAURANTS: 11

GAY/LESBIAN ORGANIZATIONS: 27

GAY/LESBIAN RELIGIOUS ORGANIZATIONS, CHURCHES, ETC.: 10

GAY/LESBIAN BOOKSTORES: 2

GAY/LESBIAN PUBLICATIONS: 1

COMPANIES THAT PROHIBIT DISCRIMINATION: N/A

INFORMATION NUMBER: 317-253-4297 GAY AND LESBIAN HOTLINE

TOTAL CRIMES: 33,530

VIOLENT = (MURDER = 68, RAPE = 517, ROBBERY = 2,050, ASSAULT = 3,657)

PROPERTY = (BURGLARY = 7,629, LARCENY 14,383, MOTOR VEHICLE THEFT = 5,226, ARSON = 246)

Things to Do!!!

Eagles Creek is in Indianapolis and is one of the largest municipal parks in the country. Fishing, swimming, hiking, biking, cross country skiing, tennis and golf are some of the activities to choose from. Other points of interest include: (1) Indianapolis Museum of Art, (2) Eli Lilly Collection of Oriental Art, (3) The Herron Gallery, (4) Indianapolis Symphony, (5) Indianapolis Opera, (6) Indiana Opera Theatre, (7) The Indiana Repertory Theatre, (8) Indianapolis Motor Speedway Hall of Fame, (9) President Benjamin Harrison Home,(10) Professional Sports: Basketball - Pacers. ANNUAL EVENTS: (1) Shakespeare Festival, (2) Indianapolis 500.

POPULATION: 746,538 PERSONS—W = 554,423, B = 165,570, AI/E/A = 1,574, C = 1,198, F = 1,057, M = 4,113, PR = 936

POPULATION GROWTH: + 6.5%

AGE OF POPULATION:(21-24) = 6.4%, (25-34) = 20.1%, (35-44) = 14.6%, (45-54) = 9.3%, (55-64) = 8.3%, (65-74) = 6.7%, (75 AND OVER) = 4.8%

HOUSING COST: OWNING = $60,800 RENTAL = $410

COMMUNITY HOSPITALS: 8 = 4,220 BEDS

CLIMATE: JAN—AVG. (25.5 DEGREES), JULY—AVG. (75.4 DEGREES), ANNUAL PRECIPITATION (39.94 INCHES)

PER CAPITA INCOME: $14,478

UNEMPLOYMENT RATE: 5.1%

JOB GROWTH SINCE 1980: + 12.1%

COST OF LIVING: 96.3

EDUCATION: INDIANA UNIVERSITY-PURDUE, UNIVERSITY OF INDIANAPOLIS, BUTLER UNIVERSITY

IOWA

STATE LAWS REGARDING HOMOSEXUALITY:

In 1977, Iowa repealed its sodomy laws. Iowa hate crimes includes crimes based on sexual orientation.

TOWNS: (5,000—60,000)

▼AMES

Gay Civil Rights: Bans discrimination based on sexual orientation in public and private employment, public accommodations, education, housing, credit, and union practices.

What the Locals Say . . .

There's a good sized Lesbian and Gay community in Ames, but the community is mostly closed. Iowa State University is located in Ames. The University Department of Public Safety does a great job protecting everyone. Due to the Midwest mentality, you probably wouldn't walk down the street holding your lover's hand. It's not that you would be openly harassed, you would just receive some "shocked looks." Anywhere in Ames is o.k. to live. There's a National Coming Out celebration with concerts, socials, speakers, etc. Some groups in the area are: The Lesbian, Gay, Bisexual Alliance, The GLB Ames, The Gay, Lesbian, Bisexual Teen Support Group, The Story County AIDS Coalition. Socializing in Ames is mostly through private circles of friends. The closest gay bar is in DesMoines about forty minutes away. Some gay friendly restaurants in the area are: Cafe Beaudelaire, Cyclone Cafe, Cafe Lovish, Pizza Kitchen, and Lucullans. The Medical community does a good job relating to gays and lesbians. Your lover would more than likely be treated as any other family member in a hospital visitation situation. Iowa State University has a non-discrimination provision and a domestic partnership provision. GLB Ames puts out a newsletter. LGBA puts out the *ALLOY* once a month, but not in the summer. The Unitarian Fellowship is gay friendly.

LOCATION: AMES IS LOCATED IN CENTRAL IOWA, NORTH OF DES MOINES

GAY/LESBIAN FRIENDLY BUSINESSES: 6

GAY/LESBIAN BARS AND RESTAURANTS: 5

GAY/LESBIAN ORGANIZATIONS: 8

GAY/LESBIAN RELIGIOUS ORGANIZATIONS, CHURCHES, ETC.: 1

GAY/LESBIAN BOOKSTORES: 0

GAY/LESBIAN PUBLICATIONS: 2

COMPANIES THAT PROHIBIT DISCRIMINATION: IOWA STATE UNIVERSITY, SEE GAY CIVIL RIGHTS

INFORMATION NUMBER: 515-294-2104 GAY/LESBIAN/BISEXUAL ALLIANCE

TOTAL CRIMES: 1,645

VIOLENT = (MURDER = 1 RAPE = 16, ROBBERY = 5, ASSAULT = 21)

PROPERTY = (BURGLARY = 144, LARCENY = 1,389, MOTOR VEHICLE THEFT = 69, ARSON = N/A)

Things to Do!!!

Ames might best be described as a college town, with most of the activities focused on Iowa State University. The Special Olympics are held in Ames each May.

POPULATION: 46,672 PERSONS—W = 42,421, B = 1,155, AI/E/A = 66, C = 1,134, F = 85, M = 238, PR = 129

POPULATION GROWTH: + 2.0%

AGE OF POPULATION: (21-24) = 22.1%, (25-34) = 16.1%, (35-44) = 10.0%, (45-54) = 6.1%, (55-64) = 4.8%, (65-74) = 3.6%, (75 AND OVER) = 3.2%

HOUSING COST: OWNING = $72,500 RENTAL = $404

COMMUNITY HOSPITALS: 1 = 216 BEDS

CLIMATE: JAN—AVG. (18.2 DEGREES), JULY—AVG. (74.2 DEGREES), ANNUAL PRECIPITATION (32.94 INCHES)

PER CAPITA INCOME: $11,347

UNEMPLOYMENT RATE: 2.3%

JOB GROWTH SINCE 1980: + 17.2%

COST OF LIVING: 103.2

EDUCATION: IOWA STATE UNIVERSITY

DES MOINES

Gay Civil Rights: None

What the Locals Say . . .

Des Moines has a very mixed community. The ones that are open are really open; however, most folks are still pretty closed. The attitude of the local government runs from tolerant to middle-of-the-road to anti-gay. Des Moines has been a fairly liberal city; but since the 1994 elections and the Republican sweep, there has been an attempt on the state level to legislate funds away from any state supported school which has anything to do with gays or lesbians. The measure did fail, but the pot is starting to boil. There are no problems with police protection. The Sherman Hill area is home to many gays and lesbians. The Gay and Lesbian Resource Center provides office space, gay and lesbian publications, a library, and a safe comfortable place to talk, meet, and read. The Out Reach Center of Central Iowa sponsors socials, picnics, road trips, forums, speakers, and coming out groups. They have a mixed Coming Out Group and also a Coming Out Group for women only. They also sponsor a Tuesday Night Men's Group. The Women's Cultural Collective has been active for ten years. They have a social on the 4th Saturday of each month. They also have a literary group and a singles rap group on Sunday. Onyx is a black lesbian group which is organized for socials. Des Moines has a Pride Week in June which includes a parade. "The Garden" is a nice large mixed bar with a good dance area and a patio for doing barbecues. "Blazing Saddles" which is also mixed but has more men is popular. "Our Place" is a small mixed bar which has country/western music on Friday nights. "Shooters" is a small pub-like bar for men. A very gay-friendly and popular coffeehouse is "Java Joe's." Java Joe's is connected to "The Book Store" which has gay and lesbian magazines. "Zanzabar's" is also a popular, gay-friendly coffeehouse. DV8 is a gay friendly retail store which sells T-shirts, jewelry, etc. and also supports the gay community in a big way. Borders and Barnes and Noble both carry a good selection of gay/lesbian books. There is The AIDS Project of Central Iowa and also the Hospice of Central Iowa. *Out-Ward* is a local publication which comes out every two months. It keeps everyone informed of what's happening in the community. There are two smaller publications: *The Pen Magazine* which covers the bar scene and *Visions* which also has bar information but in addition has editorials. Churches in the area include an MCC, The Word of Truth United Church of Christ, Plymouth Congregational, Trinity Lutheran, Trinity United Methodist, and the Unitarian.

LOCATION: DES MOINES IS SOUTH OF THE GEOGRAPHICAL CENTER OF IOWA.

GAY/LESBIAN FRIENDLY BUSINESSES: 10

GAY/LESBIAN BARS AND RESTAURANTS: 8

GAY/LESBIAN ORGANIZATIONS: 14

GAY/LESBIAN RELIGIOUS ORGANIZATIONS, CHURCHES, ETC.: 6

GAY/LESBIAN BOOKSTORES: 2

GAY/LESBIAN PUBLICATIONS: 3

COMPANIES THAT PROHIBIT DISCRIMINATION: U.S. WEST, NORTHWEST, AND PRINCIPLE FINANCIAL.

INFORMATION NUMBER: 515-284-0245, GAY AND LESBIAN RESOURCE CENTER.

TOTAL CRIMES: 15,549

VIOLENT = (MURDER = 10, RAPE = 89, ROBBERY = 276, ASSAULT = 551)

PROPERTY = (BURGLARY = 1,945, LARCENY = 11,822, MOTOR VEHICLE THEFT = 856, ARSON = N/A)

Things to Do!!!

(1) Des Moines Art Center, (2) Civic Center, (3) State Capital, (4) Science Center, (5) Polk County Heritage Gallery, (6) Living History Farms, (7) Aquarium Center and Botanical Garden; ANNUAL EVENTS: (1) Two Rivers Festival and (2) Iowa State Fair.

POPULATION: 194,540 PERSONS—W = 172,417 , B = 13,741 , AI/E/A = 699 , C = 297 , F = 193 , M = 3,651 , PR = 156

POPULATION GROWTH: + 1.9%

AGE OF POPULATION: (21-24) = 6.8%, (25-34) = 19.0%, (35-44) = 14.4%, (45-54) = 9.0%, (55-64) = 8.2%, (65-74) = 7.3%, (75 AND OVER) = 6.1%

HOUSING COST: OWNING = $49,500   RENTAL = $408

COMMUNITY HOSPITALS: 6 = 2,045 BEDS

CLIMATE: JAN—AVG. (76.6 DEGREES), JULY—AVG. (10.7 DEGREES), ANNUAL PRECIPITATION (33.12 INCHES)

PER CAPITA INCOME: $13,710

UNEMPLOYMENT RATE: 4.5%

JOB GROWTH SINCE 1980: + 6..3%

COST OF LIVING: N/A

EDUCATION: DRAKE UNIVERSITY

▼IOWA CITY

Gay Civil Rights: Bans discrimination based on sexual orientation in public and private employment, public accommodations, credit and union practices.

What the Locals Say . . .

Iowa City is home to a good number of gays and lesbians. The gay community is mostly open and generally positive. The political atmosphere towards gays is fairly favorable. There are no known gay bashings. Even though Iowa City is a university town, it would not be common to see gays holding hands in public; but it would depend on the people. If at all, maybe in the downtown area. More gays and lesbians live in the downtown area near the east end. The University of Iowa student organization (GLBPU) operates a telephone service, sponsors various outreach and support groups, a speakers bureau, and coffeeshops, dances, and other social events. The Women's Resource and Action Center organizes discussion groups. Other area groups are: University of Iowa Gay, Lesbian, and Bisexual Staff and Faculty, Lesbian

Alliance, Iowa Center AIDS Resources and Education (ICARE), and the AIDS Project. The only bar is "6:20," a mixed dance bar. Wednesdays are more or less Lesbian nights. The Java House is a popular coffeehouse, but there are several more springing up. "The Prairie Lights Bookstore" is gay friendly. *Common Lives/Lesbian Lives* is a national quarterly publication out of Iowa City. *The Iowa Women's Magazine*, a national, is also published in Iowa City. There are Presbyterians for Lesbian/Gay Concerns and also a United Campus Ministry supporting gays, lesbians, and bisexuals in the area.

LOCATION: IOWA CITY IS LOCATED IN EASTERN IOWA.

GAY/LESBIAN FRIENDLY BUSINESSES: 5

GAY/LESBIAN BARS AND RESTAURANTS: 1

GAY/LESBIAN ORGANIZATIONS: 8

GAY/LESBIAN RELIGIOUS ORGANIZATIONS, CHURCHES, ETC.: 2

GAY/LESBIAN BOOKSTORES: 3

GAY/LESBIAN PUBLICATIONS: 2

COMPANIES THAT PROHIBIT DISCRIMINATION: UNIVERSITY OF IOWA AND IOWA CITY

INFORMATION NUMBER: 319-335-3251 (LES BI GAYLINE) AND 319-335-1486 (WOMEN'S RESOURCE AND ACTION CENTER).

TOTAL CRIMES: N/A

VIOLENT = N/A

PROPERTY = N/A

Things to Do!!!

The University of Iowa is the major focal point in Iowa City. Other things to do and sights to see include: (1) Plum Grove, (2) Kalona Historical Village, (3) Herbert Hoover National Historic Site, (4) Lake Macbride State Park. ANNUAL EVENTS: (1) Old Capital Criterium Bike Race, (2) Iowa Festival, (3) Kalona Fall Festival, (4) Coralville Lake.

POPULATION: 59,313 PERSONS—W = 54,410, B = 1,516, AI/E/A = 116, C = 1,363, F = 118, M = 440, PR = 100

POPULATION GROWTH: + 17.4%

AGE OF POPULATION: (21-24) = 18.1%, (25-34) = 19.6%, (35-44) = 12.8%, (45-54) = 6.2%, (55-64) = 4.4%, (65-74) = 3.5%, (75 AND OVER) = 3.0%

HOUSING COST: OWNING = $79,000 RENTAL = $414

COMMUNITY HOSPITALS: 2 = 1,108 BEDS

CLIMATE: JAN—AVG. (20.6 DEGREES), JULY—AVG. (76.3 DEGREES), ANNUAL PRECIPITATION (36.31 INCHES)

PER CAPITA INCOME: $ 13,277

UNEMPLOYMENT RATE: 1.9%
JOB GROWTH SINCE 1980: + 23.2%
COST OF LIVING: 114.8
EDUCATION: UNIVERSITY OF IOWA

KANSAS

STATE LAWS REGARDING HOMOSEXUALITY:

Homosexual sodomy is illegal and carries a 6 month maximum sentence. The state of Kansas defines sodomy as "oral or anal copulation" between persons of the same sex.

CITIES: (60,000 AND UP)

WICHITA

Gay Civil Rights: None

What the Locals Say . . .

The gay and lesbian population is estimated at being 2/3 closeted and 1/3 very open. There are still many individuals afraid to come out of the closet. In the last 2 years, Wichita has been on the verge of transition towards becoming more open. The politicians for the most part are anti-gay. The major concentration of gay and lesbian residences is in the Riverside area and the College Hill area. The Riverside area, composed of older houses, has a river that runs through the middle of the neighborhood. There is a park, zoo, and botanical garden. The College Hill area is a neighborhood of homes built in the 1900's to 1950's. "Vision and Dreams" is the only lesbian bookstore in the state of Kansas. The owners have expanded it into a cafe/coffeeshop called, "The Freedom Cafe." There are many services at the community center including news, information and referrals. Wichita has the Kansas Gay Rodeo Association, several A.A. groups, a women's group called "Women's Celebration" that attracts 60-120 per meeting. There are two political groups, the Wichita Gay and Lesbian Alliance (once a month potluck), and Kansas for Human Dignity which is a social activist group which oversees the community center. The Wichita Pride committee organizes the Pride Celebration, which includes 10 days of celebration leading up to the march or parade. The community center and bars do different activities on different nights. The "Wichita Business Professionals League" raises and donates money to the gay and lesbian community. This group of individuals are people who feel they can't come out of the closet professionally, so they make up for it financially from behind the scenes. "Lawrence and Company" is a gay travel Company. The PFLAG group is in the process of putting together a book for the community. Oak Park, Herman Hill Park, and North Riverside Park are all heavily populated with gays and lesbians. "Our Fantasy Complex" is lesbian owned and is one of the largest in the Midwest. It contains a country western bar, a disco/dance bar, a video bar, a restaurant - "Harrison," and in the back a volleyball sand pit, pool, and a lake. Some fundraisers are held here. "B.S.A." is a gay owned bar that draws a mixed crowd, although you will find a few more men there than women. "Dreamers" is a lesbian owned bar that draws a mixed crowd, although you will find a few more lesbians there than gay men. The Wichita Community Clinical AIDS Project is the largest AIDS clinic in Wichita. A.R.S. is the AIDS referral service. In addition, Wichita has an AIDS house for persons with AIDS. *The Liberty Press* is a monthly publication. There are several churches in Wichita that welcome gays and lesbians including: MCC, Wichita Praise and Worship (Pentecostal), Cathedral of the Plains, Unitarian, College Hill United Methodist.

LOCATION: WICHITA IS LOCATED ON THE ARKANSAS RIVER IN CENTRAL KANSAS.

GAY/LESBIAN FRIENDLY BUSINESSES: 10

GAY/LESBIAN BARS AND RESTAURANTS: 3

GAY/LESBIAN ORGANIZATIONS: 12

GAY/LESBIAN RELIGIOUS ORGANIZATIONS, CHURCHES, ETC.: 5

GAY/LESBIAN BOOKSTORES: 1

GAY/LESBIAN PUBLICATIONS: 1

INFORMATION NUMBER: 316-262-3991 WICHITA, KANSAS COMMUNITY CENTER

COMPANIES THAT PROHIBIT DISCRIMINATION: N/A

TOTAL CRIMES: 27,737

VIOLENT = (MURDER = 48, RAPE = 265, ROBBERY = 1,327, ASSAULT = 1,103)

PROPERTY = (BURGLARY = 5,847, LARCENY = 16,264, MOTOR VEHICLE THEFT = 2,883, ARSON = N/A)

Things to Do!!!

There are a variety of things to do in Wichita including: (1) Century II - a civic center, (2) Wichita-Sedgwick County Historical Museum, (3) Indian Center Museum, (4) Wichita Art Museum, (5) Omnisphere and Science Center, (6) Old Cowtown Museum, (7) Wichita Art Association, (8) Sedgwick County Zoo and Botanical Garden, (9) Lake Afton Public Observatory, (10) Cheney State Park, (11) O.J. Watson Park, (12) Professional Sports: Wichita Wings (soccer). ANNUAL EVENTS: (1) Jazz Festival, (2) Wichita River Festival, (3) Indian Pow Wow, (4) National Championship Baseball Tournament, (5) Octoberfest, (6) Old Sedgwick, (7) International Holiday Festival, (8) Christmas Through the Windows at Old Cowtown Museum. SEASONAL EVENTS: (1) Wichita Symphony Orchestra.

POPULATION: 311,746 PERSONS—W = 250,176, B = 34,301, AI/E/A = 3,527, C = 961, F = 415, M = 12,572, PR = 440

POPULATION GROWTH: + 11.4%

AGE OF POPULATION: (21-24) = 6.4%, (25-34) = 19.4%, (35-44) = 14.5%, (45-54) = 8.7%, (55-64) = 8.1%, (65-74) = 7.2%, (75 AND OVER) = 5.2%

HOUSING COST: OWNING = $56,700 RENTAL = $395

COMMUNITY HOSPITALS: 4 = 1,840 BEDS

CLIMATE: JAN—AVG. (29.5 DEGREES), JULY—AVG. (81.4 DEGREES), ANNUAL PRECIPITATION (29.33 INCHES)

PER CAPITA INCOME: $14,516

UNEMPLOYMENT RATE: 4.7%

JOB GROWTH SINCE 1980: + 9.3%

COST OF LIVING: 96.7

EDUCATION: FRIENDS UNIVERSITY, WICHITA STATE UNIVERSITY

TOWNS: (5,000-60,000)

▼LAWRENCE

Gay Civil Rights: Bans discrimination based on sexual orientation in public and private employment, public accommodations and housing.

What the Locals Say . . .

Lawrence is a pretty queer-friendly town. In May of 1995, the city commission passed an anti-discrimination ordinance. The law provides protection for public and private employment, housing and public accommodations. The fundamentalists are fighting for a ballot initiative to try and strike it down. The group, "Simply Equal", was the coalition that worked on getting the ordinance included several churches, businesses and all types of people. "HideAway" is a bar that welcomes gays, lesbians, bisexuals, and straights. The owner is gay friendly. "Barefoot Iguana" is gay-owned and draws lesbians, gays, bisexuals, and straights. "Tellers" Italian restaurant has a "family night" for gays and lesbians on Tuesday nights. The local bookstore, "Tera Nova," carries a large selection of lesbigay publications. "Java Break" is a gay friendly coffeehouse. The Freedom Coalition focuses on lesbian and gay issues. There are several University of Kansas Gay and Lesbian groups. The main group is called "LesBiGay Services of Kansas." Other groups include: Gay and Lesbian Staff Advocate, Lambda Study Group— gay and lesbian graduate students' discussion group, Bionics—a bisexual group, Straight Allies—a straight group that supports gays and lesbians, and a Lesbian & Gay discussion group. There is a Lesbian Avenger group coming soon. In the actual community of Lawrence there is a women's potluck called "1st Fridays" and a men's potluck group called "Network." Douglas County AIDS Project is the AIDS resource organization in the area. The headquarters crisis center refers individuals to whatever group they are needing during a crisis. Freedom Coalition publishes a newsletter. The Unitarian Church and

Ecumenical Christian Ministries as well as Friends Meeting, a Quaker Church, are open to gays and lesbians.

LOCATION: LAWRENCE IS LOCATED IN EASTERN KANSAS.

GAY/LESBIAN FRIENDLY BUSINESSES: 7

GAY/LESBIAN BARS AND RESTAURANTS: 3

GAY/LESBIAN ORGANIZATIONS: 10

GAY/LESBIAN RELIGIOUS ORGANIZATIONS, CHURCHES, ETC.: 3

GAY/LESBIAN BOOKSTORES: 0

GAY/LESBIAN PUBLICATIONS: 1

COMPANIES THAT PROHIBIT DISCRIMINATION: THE UNIVERSITY OF KANSAS

INFORMATION NUMBER: 913-864-3091 LESBIGAY SERVICES OF KANSAS

TOTAL CRIMES: N/A

VIOLENT = N/A

PROPERTY = N/A

Things to Do!!!

(1) Watkins Community Museum, (2) Lawrence Arts Center, (3) Outdoor Sculpture Exhibit, (4) Clinton State Park. ANNUAL EVENTS: (1) Kansas Relays (2) Douglas County Fair.

POPULATION: 67,824 PERSONS - W = 57,149, B = 3,192, AI/E/A = 1,945, C = 987, F = 120, M = 1,163, PR = 110

POPULATION GROWTH: + 28.6%

AGE OF POPULATION: (21-24) = 16.8%, (25-34) = 18.3%, (35-44) = 12.3%, (45-54) = 6.4%, (55-64) = 4.9%, (65-74) = 3.9%, (75 AND OVER) = 3.1%

HOUSING COST: OWNING = $56,700   RENTAL = $395

COMMUNITY HOSPITALS: 1 = 197 BEDS

CLIMATE: JAN—AVG. (29.2 DEGREES), JULY—AVG. (80.3 DEGREES), ANNUAL PRECIPITATION (39.28 INCHES)

PER CAPITA INCOME: $11,760

UNEMPLOYMENT RATE: 3.5%

JOB GROWTH SINCE 1980: + 30.1%

COST OF LIVING: 95.6

EDUCATION: UNIVERSITY OF KANSAS, BAKER UNIVERSITY, HASKELL INDIAN JUNIOR COLLEGE

KENTUCKY

STATE LAWS REGARDING HOMOSEXUALITY:

In 1992 the Kentucky State Supreme Court struck down the state sodomy law.

CITIES:(60,000 AND UP)

LEXINGTON:

Gay Civil Rights: None

What the Locals Say . . .

The most open people in Lexington are not as open as OPEN people are in big cities. However, approximately 40% consider themselves open to friends, fewer to family, and even a smaller percentage are out at work. A current project in Lexington is to get a lesbian and gay community center. There are several gay and lesbian friendly restaurants in Lexington including: Italian Oven, Ed and Fred's Desert Moon, Alfalfa Restaurant, and A La Lucie. Common Grounds is a gay friendly coffeeshop. The University of Kentucky Lambda group is a very strong group of lesbian, bisexual, and gay students and faculty. UK Lambda sponsors Womyn Weave, a group that focuses on social activities for lesbian, bisexual, and straight women. Pride Week in Lexington is three weeks long and includes a picnic, political discussion, church services, and a dance party. The picnic is media free so family members feel comfortable coming without having to risk their pictures being all over the local news. The Rack is a gay and lesbian variety store. Country Dykes, Lexington Men's Chorus, PFLAG, Rainbow Bowling League, Names Project, Tri-State Gay Rodeo/Lexington Chapter, and The Royal Sovereign Court of All Kentucky are groups in Lexington. The Gay and Lesbian Service Organization provides a monthly newsletter, monthly public forums, publishes the *Pink Pages* an annual resource guide and coordinates Pride Week Festivities. The Lexington-Fayette Human Rights Commission offers assistance to those victims subjected to hate/bias related crimes and collects data on these incidents to show there is a need for increased protection. The Fairness Campaign endorses candidates that support gay civil rights and they also work to secure gay civil rights for gays and lesbians. The Central Kentucky Council for Peace and Justice is located in Lexington. "Joe's" and "Alfalfa" are gay and lesbian restaurants. "The Bar Complex" has a disco, cabaret, and a lounge area that draws gays and lesbians. "Crossings", is predominately a men's leather bar, and it also has a leather shop. "Town Square" is a lesbian bar. AIDS Volunteers of Lexington and Hospice of the Bluegrass are in Lexington. *The GSLO News* is a lesbian and gay newspaper in Lexington. Lexington has several open and affirming churches including: The Lexington MCC, Unitarian Universalist Church (has Interweave social group that coordinates potlucks and retreats), Phoenix Institute and The Episcopal Church of the Resurrection. Religious groups in Lexington are Honesty (Southern Baptists), Dignity (Catholic), Gay Lesbian and Affirming Disciples of Christ (GLAD), Lexington Friends Meeting (Quakers).

LOCATION: LEXINGTON IS LOCATED IN NORTH CENTRAL KENTUCKY.

GAY LESBIAN FRIENDLY BUSINESSES: 35

GAY/LESBIAN BARS AND RESTAURANTS: 11

GAY/LESBIAN ORGANIZATIONS: 20

GAY/LESBIAN RELIGIOUS ORGANIZATIONS, CHURCHES, ETC. 8

GAY/LESBIAN BOOKSTORES: 1

GAY/LESBIAN PUBLICATIONS: 1

COMPANIES THAT PROHIBIT DISCRIMINATION: N/A

INFORMATION NUMBER: 606-223-1448 INTERWEAVE

TOTAL CRIMES: 15,641

VIOLENT = (MURDER = 8, RAPE = 139, ROBBERY = 558, ASSAULT = 1,455

PROPERTY = (BURGLARY = 3,187, LARCENY = 9,684, MOTOR VEHICLE THEFT = 610, ARSON = 50)

Things to Do!!!

The steel-blue tint of the grass is legendary and only visible in May's early morning sun. Places of specific interest include: (1) Hut-Morgan House, (2) Mary Todd Lincoln House, (3) Ashland, (4) Guild Gallery, (5) Opera House, (6) Headley-Whitney Museum, (7) Lexington Cemetery, (8) Kentucky Horse Park, (9) Horse farms, (10) Victorian Square. ANNUAL EVENTS: (1) Blue Grass Stakes, (2) High Hope Steeplechase, (3) Rolex-Kentucky Event & Trade Fair, (4) Egyptian Event, (5) Festival of the Bluegrass, Grand Circuit Meet. SEASONAL EVENTS: (1) Thoroughbred racing, (2) Harness racing.

POPULATION: 232,562 PERSONS - W = 190,448, B = 30,143, AI/E/A = 351, C = 1,083, F = 190, M = 888, PR = 325

POPULATION GROWTH: +13.9%

AGE OF POPULATION: (21-24) = 8.3%, (25-34) = 20.3%, (35-44) = 15.9%, (45-54) = 9.5%, (55-64) = 7.4%, (65-74) = 5.8%, (75 AND OVER) = 4.1%

HOUSING COST: OWNING = $73,900 RENTAL = $394

COMMUNITY HOSPITALS: 7 = 1,851 BEDS

CLIMATE: JAN—AVG. (30.8 DEGREES), JULY—AVG. (75.8 DEGREES), ANNUAL PRECIPITATION (44.55 INCHES)

PER CAPITA INCOME: $14,962
UNEMPLOYMENT RATE: 3.8%
JOB GROWTH SINCE 1980: +18.8%
COST OF LIVING: 100.1
EDUCATION: UNIVERSITY OF KENTUCKY, TRANSYLVANIA UNIVERSITY

LOUISVILLE

Gay Civil Rights: None

What the Locals Say . . .

Louisville is a very pleasant, out of the way, city. Louisvillians are not quite as energetic, visionary, or willing to take chances as many people in larger communities. The city has a conservative feel to it—even the gay and lesbian activists tend to be more conservative. Politics tend towards just right or left of center, depending on who is in office. In the last couple of years, gays and lesbians have suffered the defeat of having an anti-discrimination proposal, which included sexual orientation, defeated. The crime rate is lower per capita than other cities its size, and it has some very lovely neighborhoods, such as the Highlands/Bardstown Road area. Crescent Hill and Clifton are charming turn of the century Victorian neighborhoods that house many gay and lesbian businesses and groups. In general the Highlands/Bardstown Road area has more gay men and Crescent Hill and Clifton have more lesbians. Old Louisville is the "gay ghetto," and is another Victorian neighborhood. Carmichael's Bookstore, in the Highland area, allocates approximately 1/3 of its store to gay and lesbian books. Holly Cook is a large bookstore with a large gay and lesbian section. There are several organizations in Louisville including: Gays and Lesbians United for Education (GLUE), Black & White Men Together (BMWT), Pride Committee, PFLAG, bowling league, and a youth group. The University of Louisville has a group called GLOBAL. Political groups include: The Fairness Campaign; The Kentucky Fairness Alliance, a lobbying group; and Just Queers, a direct action group. Louisville has a lively gay and lesbian night life, with eight bars ranging from "The Connection Complex" (which has its own large theatre as well as dance bar and piano bar); "Murphy's" (a good old-fashioned bar with a diverse clientele); "The Annex," (a humpy cruising bar); "Triangles" (a country-western bar); "Teddy Bears" (for the underbelly); "Sparks" (a straight/gay bar for the alternative crowd); the "Mag Bar" (a neighborhood bar in Old Louisville that attracts a lot of straights and is near the University of Louisville); and "Tynkers" (a popular lesbian bar). AIDS Services Center runs a hotline and has workshops etc. AIDS HIV Program is more of a fundraising group. Louisville has one gay / lesbian newspaper called *The Letter* which has a growing reputation for professionalism. *Furies* is a lesbian newspaper that is published once every two months. There are numerous religious organizations for gays and lesbians including:

Affirmations, two groups of ALLEGRO, B'Nai Shalom, Conference for Catholic Lesbians, Lutherans Concerned, Integrity, Phoenix Rising, MCC, Central Presbyterian, Christ Church Cathedral and Third Lutheran Church which are all open to gays and lesbians.

LOCATION: LOUISVILLE IS LOCATED ON THE NORTHERN BORDER WITH INDIANA. IT IS SITUATED AT THE FALLS OF THE OHIO RIVER.

GAY/LESBIAN FRIENDLY BUSINESSES: 20

GAY/LESBIAN BARS AND RESTAURANTS: 8

GAY/LESBIAN ORGANIZATIONS: 9

GAY/LESBIAN RELIGIOUS ORGANIZATIONS, CHURCHES, ETC.: 14

GAY/LESBIAN BOOKSTORES: 0

GAY/LESBIAN PUBLICATIONS: 2

COMPANIES THAT PROHIBIT DISCRIMINATION: N/A

INFORMATION NUMBER: 502-897-2475, GAY & LESBIAN BI ALLIANCE HOTLINE

TOTAL CRIMES: 17,329

VIOLENT = (MURDER = 37, RAPE = 135, ROBBERY = 1,393, ASSAULT = 1,159

PROPERTY = (BURGLARY = 4,204, LARCENY = 8,076, MOTOR VEHICLE THEFT = 2,325, ARSON = 257)

Things to Do!!!

One of the most famous annual events in the world is the Kentucky Derby, which is held in Louisville. The city is also the nation's leading producer of bourbon. Most Louisville residents are focused on the social aspect of the city. Specific points of interest include: (1) Zachary Taylor National Cemetery, (2) Jefferson County Courthouse, (3) Cave Hill Cemetery, (4) Louisville Falls Fountain, (5) Water Tower, (6) Churchill Downs, (7) Kentucky Derby Museum, (8) Kentucky Center for the Arts, (9) Kentucky Fair and Exposition Center, (10) Otter Creek Park, (11) Louisville Zoological Garden, (12) E. P. Tom Sawyer State Park. ANNUAL EVENTS: (1) Oxmoor Steeplechase, (2) Kentucky Derby Festival, (3) Kentucky State Fair, (4) Louisville Bluegrass and American MusicFest, (5) Corn Island Storytelling Festival, (6) Christmas in the City. SEASONAL EVENTS: (1) Heritage Weekends, (2) Performing Arts, (3) Horse Racing.

POPULATION: 271,038 PERSONS—W = 186,208, B = 79,783, AI/E/A = 507, C = 345, F = 227, M = 591, PR = 262

POPULATION GROWTH: - 9.3%

AGE OF POPULATION: (21-24) = 5.8%, (25-34) = 17.6%, (35-44) = 14.0%, (45-54) = 8.8%, (55-64) = 9.5%, (65-74) = 9.1%, (75 AND OVER) = 7.5%

HOUSING COST: OWNING = $44,300   RENTAL = $308

COMMUNITY HOSPITALS: 11= 3,559 BEDS

CLIMATE: JAN—AVG. (31.7 DEGREES), JULY—AVG. (77.2 DEGREES), ANNUAL PRECIPITATION (44.39 INCHES)

PER CAPITA INCOME: $11,527

UNEMPLOYMENT RATE: 7.7%

JOB GROWTH SINCE 1980: - 5.8%

COST OF LIVING: 90.4

EDUCATION: UNIVERSITY OF LOUISVILLE, BELLARMINE COLLEGE

LOUISIANA

STATE LAWS REGARDING HOMOSEXUALITY:

Heterosexual and homosexual sodomy is illegal and punishable with up to a maximum 5 year sentence. In 1967, the Louisiana State Supreme Court ruled that oral sex between women should be considered "unnatural carnal copulation" and was punishable in the same way as sodomy between men. In 1992, Governor Edwin Edwards signed an executive order that banned anti-gay discrimination by state agencies. Private firms doing business with the state may not discriminate either. In May 1993, a New Orleans parish court ruled the sodomy law unconstitutional.

CITIES: (60,000 AND UP)

▼NEW ORLEANS

Gay Civil Rights: Bans discrimination based on sexual orientation in public and private employment, public accommodations and housing.

What the Locals Say . . .

The gay and lesbian community of New Orleans is very open and has a domestic partnership ordinance in place. Homosexuals for the most part are not afraid of living out in New Orleans. One of the most popular places where gays and lesbians live is the "French Quarter," considered to be 60% gay and lesbian. This is the entertainment and restaurant area. Faubourg Maringny is adjacent to the French Quarter and has at least as many gay family members in residence. This area is less expensive than the French Quarter. There are six gay clubs in the area and the houses have a little more space. The Bywater area is adjacent to Faubourg Maringny and is cheaper than Faubourg Maringny. The biggest movement of gays is to the Bywater. The Bywater has turn of the century and Victorian homes which are 1/3 cheaper than Faubourg Maringny. Uptown is a more upscale neighborhood where gays and lesbians are the minority, though many family members still live there especially those in long term relationships. Mid-City and the Lakefront area attract a lot of lesbians. The houses are cheaper and more suburban style with larger yards. There are numerous clubs and organizations in New Orleans. There are numerous gay AA organizations throughout New Orleans. Gay Mardi Gras consists of a public gay costume contest. The Gay Pride Celebration is held late in October since there is so much rain and humidity in June. There is a parade and a 2 day festival in Faubourg Maringny. Expected attendance is approximately 25,000. "Celebration" is the 2nd weekend of June. Celebration is a statewide conference on gay and lesbian issues and approximately 2,000 attend. Prime Timers is a group for 40 and over and their admirers, "Southern

Old Lesbians" is an organization for older lesbians. "Southern Decadence" is a big gay parade of drag queens through the French Quarter. There is a huge Halloween celebration and dance at one of the wharfs and approximately 10,000 gays and lesbians attend. The gay and lesbian bookstore is Faubourg Marigny Bookstore. There are numerous sport groups including: two bowling leagues, volleyball and tennis groups, Frontrunners, and Team New Orleans, who participate in the Gay Games. The Twenty Something Group, having 175 members, is a social alternative to the bars, targets those 18-31, although others can attend. Theatre Maringny is a gay and lesbian theatre. "Third Thursday" is a gay men's and lesbian social group. Lesbian and Gays Politically Active Committee (LAGPAG) works statewide for gay rights. "Forum for Equality" is a more conservative gay and lesbian political group. Both of these groups endorse candidates. The "Cafe La Fite" is the oldest gay bar in the country. The "Bourbon Pub" is predominately male, but women do go. It has a young party disco crowd. The "Mint," "Rawhide," and "Oz" are predominately men's gay bars. "The Clover Grill," "Petunia's," "Bayou Ridge," "Quarter Scene," and "Old Dog New Trick" are all lesbian restaurants. "Wolfendales" is a black bar. "St. Ann's Cafe and Grill" is a lesbian vegetarian establishment. "Charlene's" is a neighborhood lesbian bar, "Ruby Fruit Jungle" is a lesbian disco bar which draws a young crowd. The New Orleans AIDS Task Force is very well organized and in general is a very active organization. There is a gay and lesbian physicians association. *Ambush*, a bar and entertainment newspaper, is published one week. The next week, *Impact*, a more news oriented publication is distributed. *The Southern Forum* comes out monthly.

LOCATION: NEW ORLEANS IS LOCATED IN SOUTHERN LOUISIANA ON LAKE PONCHATRAIN.

GAY/LESBIAN FRIENDLY BUSINESSES: 29

GAY/LESBIAN BARS AND RESTAURANTS: 38

GAY/LESBIAN ORGANIZATIONS: 15

GAY/LESBIAN RELIGIOUS ORGANIZATIONS, CHURCHES, ETC.: 4

GAY/LESBIAN BOOKSTORES: 1

GAY/LESBIAN PUBLICATIONS: 4

COMPANIES THAT PROHIBIT DISCRIMINATION: SEE STATE LAWS AND GAY CIVIL RIGHTS

INFORMATION NUMBER: 504-522-1103 NEW ORLEANS GAY & LESBIAN COMMUNITY CENTER

TOTAL CRIMES: 52,773

VIOLENT = (MURDER = 395, RAPE = 298, ROBBERY = 5,179, ASSAULT = 4,152)

PROPERTY = (BURGLARY = 11,184, LARCENY = 22,019, MOTOR VEHICLE THEFT = 9,546, ARSON = N/A)

Things to Do!!!

(1) Walking Tour in the Vieux Carre'- (Jackson Square, Jackson Brewery, The Cabildo, Pirate's Alley, Pontalba Apartments, French Market, St. Louis Cathedral, The Presbytere, Gallier House Museum, Maison Le Monnier, Beauregard-Keyes House, The Old U.S. Mint, Mid-19th-Century Townhouse, Miro House, Brennan's, Madam John's Legacy, Antoine's, E.H. Southern's Home, Louis Armstrong Park, Hermann-Grima Historic House, Brulatour Courtyard, Historic New Orleans Collection, Adelina Patti's House and Courtyard, (2) Preservation Hall, (3) Levee and Docks, (4) Lafitte National Historic Park, (5) Auto Tour to City Park and Lake Pontchartrain, (6) River, Plantation and Bayou Cruise, (7) Pharmacy Museum, (8) Musee' Conti-Wax Museum of Louisiana Legends, (9) Audubon Park and Zoological Garden, (10) Confederate Museum, (11) World Trade Center of New Orleans, (12) New Orleans Aquarium, (13) Historic New Orleans Custom House, (14) The Superdome, (15) Pilot House, (16) Sternwheeler River Cruises, (17) Longue Vue House and Gardens, (18) Gray Line Bus Tours, (19) San Francisco Plantation, (20) St. Bernard Park, (21) St. Charles Avenue Street Car. ANNUAL EVENTS: (1) Sugar Bowl College Football Classic, (2) Mardi Gras, (3) French Quarter Festival, (4) Spring Fiesta, (5) New Orleans Jazz and Heritage Festival. SEASONAL EVENTS: (1) Horse Racing, (2) Professional Sports: Football-Saints.

POPULATION: 489,595 PERSONS—W = 173,554, B = 307,728, AI/E/A = 759, C = 753, F = 579, M = 2,421, PR = 1,023

POPULATION GROWTH: - 12.2%

AGE OF POPULATION:(21-24) = 6.3%, (25-34) = 16.9%, (35-44) = 14.3%, (45-54) = 8.9%, (55-64) = 8.0%, (65-74) = 7.4%, (75 AND OVER) = 5.6%

HOUSING COST: OWNING = $69,600   RENTAL = $379

COMMUNITY HOSPITALS: 17 = 4,018 BEDS

CLIMATE: JAN—AVG. (51.3 DEGREES), JULY—AVG. (81.9 DEGREES), ANNUAL PRECIPITATION (61.88 INCHES)

PER CAPITA INCOME: $11,372

UNEMPLOYMENT RATE: 6.1%

JOB GROWTH SINCE 1980: - 8.5%

COST OF LIVING: 94.9

EDUCATION: (1) LOYOLA UNIVERSITY, (2) TULANE UNIVERSITY, (3) DILLARD UNIVERSITY, (4) UNIVERSITY OF NEW ORLEANS

MAINE

STATE LAWS REGARDING HOMOSEXUALITY:

In 1976, the state's laws against private sex acts between consenting adults was abandoned. In addition, the age of consent was dropped to 14

CITIES: (60,000 AND UP)

▼PORTLAND

Gay Civil Rights: Bans discrimination based on sexual orientation in public and private employment, public accommodations, education and housing.

What the Locals Say . . .

Presently, Portland is open and gay friendly. The city enjoys a comprehensive anti-discrimination ordinance that protects gay men, lesbians, and bisexuals from discrimination in housing, accommodations, education and employment; however, the state of Maine will face its first anti-gay ballot measure in November, 1995. If the bill passes, it will repeal many laws including the anti-discrimination ordinance in Portland. Both the Governor and the Attorney General are against the anti-gay referendum. Maine Won't Discriminate, a group formed to combat the initiative, has an office in Portland. Most of the police are supportive of the gay community. Being "Out" is still an issue, though. The gays and lesbians in Maine just don't advertise their sexual orientation. The west end of Portland is known to have more gays. There's a Matlovich Society which meets twice monthly; an AIDS Project with an Art Auction and an Aids Walk; an ACT-Up Portland; an A.A. group; P-FLAG; a Gay/Lesbian Alliance at the University of South Maine; an Outright: Portland Alliance of Gay & Lesbian Youth. The "Underground" and "Citi" are both men's bars. "Sisters" is mixed. Woodford's is a gay friendly cafe. *The Community Pride Reporter* (CMR) is the local gay monthly newspaper. The Maine Council of Churches is very supportive of the gay community. There's an MCC, a Dignity group, and a Methodist group which are also supportive.

LOCATION: PORTLAND IS SITUATED ON THE CASCO BAY WITH ITS 365 CALENDAR ISLANDS.

GAY/LESBIAN FRIENDLY BUSINESSES: 10

GAY/LESBIAN BARS AND RESTAURANTS: 4

GAY/LESBIAN ORGANIZATIONS: 12

GAY/LESBIAN RELIGIOUS ORGANIZATIONS, CHURCHES, ETC.: 4

GAY/LESBIAN BOOKSTORES: 1

GAY/LESBIAN PUBLICATIONS: 1

COMPANIES THAT PROHIBIT DISCRIMINATION: SEE GAY CIVIL RIGHTS

INFORMATION NUMBER: 207-874-6956 GAY/LESBIAN ALLIANCE OR 207-879-1342 THE COMMUNITY PRIDE REPORTER

TOTAL CRIMES: 4,808

VIOLENT = (MURDER = 2 RAPE = 61, ROBBERY = 92, ASSAULT = 261)

PROPERTY = (BURGLARY = 1,142, LARCENY = 2,978, MOTOR VEHICLE THEFT = 272, ARSON = 113)

Things to Do!!!

(1) Portland Museum of Art, (2) Children's Museum of Maine, (3) The Museum at Portland Headlight, (4) Wadsworth-Longfellow House, (5) Victoria Mansion, (6) Tate House, (7) Old Port Exchange, (8) Boat Trips, (9) Two Lights, (10) Crescent Beach. ANNUAL EVENTS: (1) Old Port Festival, (2) Deering Oaks Family Festival, (3) Sidewalk Art Show, (4) New Year's Eve Portland. SEASONAL EVENTS: Outdoor Summer Concerts.

POPULATION: 62,756 - W = 62,161, B = 720, AI/E/A = 262, C = 177, F = 107, M = 124, PR = 81

POPULATION GROWTH: + 1.9%

AGE OF POPULATION: (21-24) = 8.4%, (25-34) = 21.6%, (35-44) = 14.9%, (45-54) = 8.1%, (55-64) = 7.8%, (65-74) = 7.5%, (75 AND OVER) = 7.5%

HOUSING COST: OWNING = $112,200   RENTAL = $504

COMMUNITY HOSPITALS: 4 = 1,009 BEDS

CLIMATE: JAN—AVG. (20.8 DEGREES), JULY—AVG. (68.6 DEGREES), ANNUAL PRECIPITATION (44.34 INCHES)

PER CAPITA INCOME: $14,914

UNEMPLOYMENT RATE: 6.4%

JOB GROWTH SINCE 1980: + 18.5%

COST OF LIVING: N/A

EDUCATION: UNIVERSITY OF SOUTHERN MAINE

MARYLAND

STATE LAWS REGARDING HOMOSEXUALITY:

Homosexual sodomy is illegal with a maximum 10 year prison term. Ironically, Maryland does ban anti-gay discrimination in public employment.

CITIES: (60,000 AND UP)

▼BALTIMORE

Gay Civil Rights: Bans discrimination based on sexual orientation in public employment.

What the Locals Say . . .

The Baltimore area is very open, especially in the city of Baltimore. The gay and lesbian community enjoys a good relationship with the mayor, city council, and the media. The Mount Vernon area is an area with many young people. It has several gay bars and clubs where you could feel comfortable holding your lover's hand. The Bolton Hill area is a quieter area with townhouses that have been renovated. Most people own, although some do rent in the Bolton Hill area. The Charles Village area is near Johns Hopkins University and is mixed with college students and gays and lesbians. The Charles Village area probably has the greatest concentration of lesbians. The Gay and Lesbian Pride Weekend attracts 10,000-15,000 participants, and the weekend consists of a parade, block party and festival. There are numerous activities in the Baltimore area including: softball league, volleyball league, two bowling leagues, roller skating, and various support groups. Most of the bars are mixed with a few exceptions. The "Hippo" is mostly a men's large dance club, while "Port in a Storm" is a mostly women's bar. "Central Station" is an upscale bar and restaurant for gays/lesbians and straights, although predominately gay/lesbian. There are several AIDS service providers in the area. Baltimore supports two gay and lesbian publications. *The Baltimore Gay Paper* has perhaps the largest circulation and is published twice a month. The *Alternative* is published once a month. *The City Paper* has been leaning gay/lesbian. There is a gay columnist that writes once a week on some gay or lesbian issue. There are several churches open to family members in the Baltimore area including: MCC, Presbyterian, Lutheran, Unitarian.

LOCATION: BALTIMORE IS LOCATED IN EASTERN MARYLAND ON THE CHESAPEAKE BAY.

GAY/LESBIAN FRIENDLY BUSINESSES: 100

GAY/LESBIAN BARS AND RESTAURANTS: 51

GAY/LESBIAN ORGANIZATIONS: 58

GAY/LESBIAN RELIGIOUS ORGANIZATIONS, CHURCHES, ETC.: 11

GAY/LESBIAN BOOKSTORES: 2

GAY/LESBIAN PUBLICATIONS: 4

COMPANIES THAT PROHIBIT DISCRIMINATION: SEE STATE LAWS AND GAY CIVIL RIGHTS

INFORMATION NUMBER: 410-837-8888, GAY & LESBIAN SWITCHBOARD

TOTAL CRIMES: 91,920

VIOLENT = (MURDER = 353, RAPE = 668, ROBBERY = 12,376, ASSAULT = 8,548)

PROPERTY = (BURGLARY = 17,901, LARCENY = 41,451, MOTOR VEHICLE THEFT = 10,623, ARSON = 545)

Things to Do!!!

(1) Walters Art Gallery, (2) Museum and Library of Maryland History, (3) Maryland Historical Society, (4) Washington Monument, (5) Inner Harbor-National Aquarium, Harborplace, (6) Downtown area, (7) Baltimore Museum of Art, (8) Baltimore Zoo, (9) Sherwood Gardens, (10) Cylburn Arboretum, (11) Gun Powder Falls State Park, (12) Harbor Cruises, (13) Babe Ruth Birthplace/Baseball Center (14) Edgar Allen Poe Home & Grave, (15) Professional Sports: Soccer-Blasts, Hockey-Skipjacks, Baseball-Orioles, Box Lacrosse-Thunder. ANNUAL EVENTS: (1) ACC Crafts Fair, (2) Flower Mart, (3) Harbor Expo, (4) Artscape, (5) Maryland Preakness Celebration, (6) New Year's Eve Extravaganza. SEASONAL EVENTS: (1) Pimlico Race Course, (2) Pier 6.

POPULATION: 726,096 PERSONS—W = 287,753, B = 435,768, AI/E/A = 2,555, C = 2,002, F = 1,251, M = 1,166, PR = 1,857

POPULATION GROWTH: - 7.7%

AGE OF POPULATION: (21-24) = 6.6%, (25-34) = 18.7%, (35-44) = 14.3%, (45-54) = 9.1%, (55-64) = 8.5%, (65-74) = 7.9%, (75 AND OVER) = 5.8%

HOUSING COST: OWNING = $54,700   RENTAL = $413

COMMUNITY HOSPITALS: 18 = 6,203 BEDS

CLIMATE: JAN—AVG. (31.8 DEGREES), JULY—AVG. (77.0 DEGREES), ANNUAL PRECIPITATION (40.76 INCHES)

PER CAPITA INCOME: $11,994

UNEMPLOYMENT RATE: 9.4%

JOB GROWTH SINCE 1980: + .8%

COST OF LIVING: 105.0

EDUCATION: JOHNS HOPKINS UNIVERSITY, UNIVERSITY OF MARYLAND AT BALTIMORE

COUNTIES:
HOWARD COUNTY

Gay Civil Rights: Bans discrimination based on sexual orientation in public and private employment, public accommodations, education, housing, credit and union practices.

Cities and Towns included within Howard County:

Alpha
Ammendale
Beltsville
Columbia
Contee
Cookesville
Elk Ridge
Glenwood
Laurel
Long Corner
Montpelior
Oak Crest
Popular Springs
Savage P.O.
South Laurel
West Friendship
White Oak

MONTGOMERY COUNTY

Gay Civil Rights: Bans discrimination based on sexual orientation in public and private employment, housing and union practices.

Cities and Towns included within Montgomery County:

Aspen Hill
Autrey Park
Barnesville
Beallsville
Brinklow

Brookeville
Burtonsville
Cantonsville
Cedar Grove
Clarksburg
Colesville
Columbia
Comus
Cooksville
Damascus
Dayton
Ednon
Ellicott City
Fairland
Fox Chapel
Germantown
Guilford
Goshen
Hyattstown
Highland
Jonestown
Layhill
Luxmanor
Montrose
Montgomery Village
Norbeck
Norwood
Olney
Potomac
Sandy Spring
Spencerville
Washington Grove
West Friendship
Westmore
Wheaton

MASSACHUSETTS

STATE LAWS REGARDING HOMOSEXUALITY:

Heterosexual and homosexual sodomy is illegal and punishable by up to 20 years in prison, although the Massachusetts Supreme Court has ruled it unconstitutional except in cases involving violence, public sex, or minors. Oral and anal sex by either sex is considered a felony, with a maximum penalty of five years in prison. However, a 1974 ruling decriminalized consensual sexual conduct between adults who had a "reasonable expectation of privacy." In 1989, Governor Michael Dukakis signed a state-wide gay civil rights law.

CITIES: (60,000 AND UP)

▼BOSTON

Gay Civil Rights: Bans discrimination based on sexual orientation in public and private employment, public accommodations, education, credit and union practices.

What the Locals Say . . .

Boston has long been considered a "friendly" place for gays and lesbians to live. The South End of Boston has a large gay male population; lesbians often cluster in Jamaica Plain or west Somerville. Some feel there are more open gays and lesbians living in and around the Boston area than in any other place in the country. Politicians are pretty supportive and tend to lean to the left. The current mayor is considered gay-friendly. The South End is mostly Brownstones, apartments, and townhomes that are being renovated. Jamaica Plain is outside of Boston proper. Many gays and lesbians live here in this residential area. Central Street has a couple of coffeehouses and two bookstores. "Glad Day Bookstore" is the oldest gay and lesbian bookstore. "We Think The World of You" is a gay and lesbian bookstore located at the south end. "The Blue Wave" is a popular gay friendly restaurant as are "Francheska's" and "Mildred's." The annual pride celebration attracts over 200,000 individuals. There is a parade or march, that ends with a rally and lots of partying afterward. There are numerous social groups in Boston including: "30 Something Lesbians," "40+ Lesbians," "Out and About" (a social and support group), lesbian writers group, "Older Lesbian Energy," "Prime Timers" and "Boston Men's Chorus." Professional and business gay and lesbian groups include: Massachusetts Association's Gay Bar (MLGBA), Boston Gay & Lesbian Architects & Designers (BLGLAD), Boston Professional Alliance, Greater Boston Business Council. Political groups in Boston are Lesbian Rights Taskforce, Lesbian Avengers (a grassroots political group focused on lesbian visibility). Support groups in Boston include: PFLAG, Gay Fathers of Boston, Boston Gay and Lesbian

Adolescent Social Services (GLASS), Men of Color Against AIDS, Single Lesbian Menopausal Group, lesbians in mid-life career transition and Latinas Unidas (a group for Latino Lesbians). Sport groups include: "Tennis Four All," Children Mountain Club-hikers, skiers, bicyclists, Frontrunners, and a motorcyclists' group. "Pride Time" is a cable TV program for the area gay, lesbian and bisexual community. "One in Ten" is a radio program for the gay and lesbian community. "Out There" is a gay fan club, "Speaking Out" is a live call in cable TV, "Pride" is an hour of closet free radio for the greater Boston area. "Avalon" is a men's dance bar and "Boston Ramrod" is a men's leather bar, "Club Cafe" is a bar and restaurant that draws a mixed crowd. "Quest" has a women's night, and "Venue de Milo" is a lesbian dance bar. Fenway Community Health is a clinic that serves the gay and lesbian community and does great work in gay and lesbian parenting. Fenway has a gay and lesbian parents monthly meeting, women currently inseminating group, lesbians considering alternative insemination group, Children of Lesbians and Gays Everywhere (COLAGE), HIV testing and education. The local gay and lesbian newspapers are *Bay Windows*, and *In News Weekly*, both are published weekly. A well-regarded feminist monthly is *Sojourner*. The Greater Boston Lesbian/Gay/Bisexual Interfaith Coalition, Dignity/Boston, Integrity Gay and Lesbian Support Group, and Church of The Covenantare religious groups in Boston. MCC/Boston is open to all gays and lesbians.

LOCATION: BOSTON IS SITUATED AROUND BOSTON HARBOR IN EASTERN MASSACHUSETTS.

GAY/LESBIAN FRIENDLY BUSINESSES: 42

GAY/LESBIAN BARS AND RESTAURANTS: 16

GAY/LESBIAN ORGANIZATIONS: 40

GAY/LESBIAN RELIGIOUS ORGANIZATIONS, CHURCHES, ETC.: 7

GAY/LESBIAN BOOKSTORES: 3

GAY/LESBIAN PUBLICATIONS: 7

COMPANIES THAT PROHIBIT DISCRIMINATION: BLUE CROSS BLUE SHIELD OF MASSACHUSETTS, WGBH, CHILDREN'S HOSPITAL OF BOSTON, THE BOSTON GLOBE, STRIDE RITE, SEE STATE LAWS AND GAY CIVIL RIGHTS

INFORMATION NUMBER: 617-267-9001 BOSTON GAY & LESBIAN HELPLINE

TOTAL CRIMES: 55,555

VIOLENT = (MURDER = 98, RAPE = 480, ROBBERY = 4,081, ASSAULT = 6,184)

PROPERTY = (BURGLARY = 7,982, LARCENY = 24,798, MOTOR VEHICLE THEFT = 11,932, ARSON = N/A)

Things to Do!!!

Recreational areas take advantage of the regions location on the Atlantic Ocean. Specific points of interest include: (1) Institute of Contemporary Art, (2) Fogg Art Museum, (3) Boston Ballet, (4) Opera Company of Boston, (5) Boston Symphony Orchestra, (6) Concord Orchestra, (7) New England Philharmonic Orchestra, (8) New England Aquarium, (9) Franklin Park Zoo, (10) Freedom Train, (11) Harbor Walk, (12) Kings Chapel, (13) Paul Revere House, (14) Professional Sports: Baseball-Red Sox, Basketball - Celtics, Hockey - Bruins, Running. ANNUAL EVENTS: (1) Patriots Day Celebration, (2) Boston Marathon, (3) Bunker Hill Day, (4) Harborfest, (5) Charles River Regatta, (6) First Night Celebration. SEASONAL EVENTS: Horse Racing at Suffolk Downs.

POPULATION: 551,675 PERSONS—W 360,875, B = 146,945, AI/E/A = 1,884, C = 16,701, F = 1,025, M = 2,179, PR = 25,767

POPULATION GROWTH: - 2.0%

AGE OF POPULATION: (21-24) = 10.6%, (25-34) = 23.0%, (35-44) = 13.6%, (45-54) = 8.2%, (55-64) = 7.1%, (65-74) = 6.2%, (75 AND OVER) = 5.2%

HOUSING COST: OWNING = $161,400 RENTAL = $625

COMMUNITY HOSPITALS: 19 = 5,903 BEDS

CLIMATE: JAN—AVG. (28.6 DEGREES), JULY—AVG. (73.5 DEGREES), ANNUAL PRECIPITATION (41.51 INCHES)

PER CAPITA INCOME: $15,581

UNEMPLOYMENT RATE: 8.4%

JOB GROWTH SINCE 1980: + 14.7%

COST OF LIVING: 138.6

EDUCATION: BOSTON UNIVERSITY, BOSTON COLLEGE, UNIVERSITY OF MASSACHUSETTS BOSTON, NORTHEASTERN UNIVERSITY

▼CAMBRIDGE

Gay Civil Rights: Bans discrimination based on sexual orientation in public and private employment, public accommodations, education, housing, credit, and union practices.

What the Locals Say . . .

The Cambridge gay and lesbian community is perhaps more liberal than its next door neighbor, Boston's. The community is very visible and open. Boston has an enormous number of gay and lesbian groups and activities so there aren't many in Cambridge. Many people live in Cambridge but run over to Boston to participate in social, political, and other groups. A lot of gays and lesbians tend to congregate at Harvard Square and Inman Square. There are numerous coffeehouses, many gay-friendly, though none specifically gay. "Sportsters" is a popular men's dance bar, and "Paradise" draws lesbians and gay men. There is a support group for pregnant lesbians or new lesbian mothers located in Cambridge. Integrity and Quakers-Friends For Lesbian/Gay Concern are religious groups located in Cambridge. Am Tikva, Church of The Covenant and MCC welcome gays and lesbians to their congregations.

LOCATION: CAMBRIDGE IS LOCATED IN EASTERN MASSACHUSETTS ACROSS THE CHARLES RIVER FROM BOSTON.

GAY/LESBIAN FRIENDLY BUSINESSES: 25

GAY/LESBIAN BARS AND RESTAURANTS:10

GAY/LESBIAN ORGANIZATIONS: SEE BOSTON

GAY/LESBIAN RELIGIOUS ORGANIZATIONS, CHURCHES, ETC.: 4

GAY/LESBIAN BOOKSTORES: SEE BOSTON

GAY/LESBIAN PUBLICATIONS: 0

COMPANIES THAT PROHIBIT DISCRIMINATION: MASSACHUSETTS INSTITUTE OF TECHNOLOGY (MIT), HARVARD UNIVERSITY, LOTUS DEVELOPMENT CORPORATION, SEE STATE LAWS AND GAY CIVIL RIGHTS

INFORMATION LINE: 617-267-9001 BOSTON GAY & LESBIAN HELPLINE

TOTAL CRIMES: 6,388

VIOLENT = (MURDER = 2, RAPE = 27, ROBBERY = 253, ASSAULT = 643)

PROPERTY = (BURGLARY = 929, LARCENY = 3,566, MOTOR VEHICLE THEFT = 968, ARSON = 21)

Things to Do!!!

Cambridge is a very academic community centering around Harvard and Massachusetts Institute of Technology (M.I.T). (1) Harvard University - (Fogg Art Museum, Harvard Museum of Cultural and Natural History, John F. Kennedy School of Government), (2) M.I.T—(M.I.T. Museum, Hart Nautical Galleries, List Visual Arts Center at M.I.T.).

POPULATION: 93,554 PERSONS—W = 72,122, B = 12,930, AI/E/A = 288, C = 3,616, F = 250, M = 801, PR = 1,875

POPULATION GROWTH: - 1.9%

AGE OF POPULATION: (21-24) = 10.8%, (25-34) = 24.9%, (35-44) = 16.1%, (45-54) = 8.2%, (55-64) = 6.2%, (65-74) = 5.6%, (75 AND OVER) = 4.9%

HOUSING COST: OWNING = $263,800   RENTAL = $538

COMMUNITY HOSPITALS: 2 = 459 BEDS

CLIMATE: JAN—AVG. (28.6 DEGREES), JULY—AVG. (73.5 DEGREES), ANNUAL PRECIPITATION (41.51 INCHES)

PER CAPITA INCOME: $19,879

UNEMPLOYMENT RATE: 6.0%

JOB GROWTH SINCE 1980: + 9.8%

COST OF LIVING: N/A

EDUCATION: RADCLIFFE COLLEGE, HARVARD UNIVERSITY, MASSACHUSETTS INSTITUTE OF TECHNOLOGY

TOWNS: (5,000-60,000)

▼WORCESTER

Gay Civil Rights: Bans discrimination based on sexual orientation in public and private employment, public accommodations, education, housing and credit.

What the Locals Say . . .

The gay/lesbian community in Worcester can be open or closed depending on which group you socialize with. The city government is also mixed. Some are supportive of the gay community and some are not so supportive. The local police chief has marched in the Pride March the last three or four years. Rainbow flags can be seen in a few windows throughout the town. You would, for the most part, feel safe living in Worcester. It's one hour from Boston, Hartford, and Northampton. There's a yearly Pride March and Rally in June and a yearly Film Festival. There's a large Gay and Lesbian Community Coalition of Central Mass. which is divided into a political arm and a social arm. The social group has potlucks once a month and sponsors hiking trips and other field trips. The political side does fund raisers and helps with AIDS Project Worcester. There's also a Supporters of Worcester Gay and Lesbian Youth Group. There's a Worcester Area Gay Men's group and a "One in Ten" group. "Club 241" is a mixed dance club and the "Male Box" is a bar with pool tables. They are the only two bars in the town; people go to Boston etc. for a more varied night life. Health care is good in the area. The University of Mass. Medical Center has Clinic Seven for HIV and AIDS. There is also the Worcester Foundation for Experimental Biology, which does a lot of AIDS research. There's a HMO called Fallon Clinic which has good health care and has some gay and lesbian therapists. Worcester has no local gay publications but relies on the big city papers. "Out In New England," a weekly lesbian and gay news and information television program is produced out of Worcester. There's a MCC, an open and affirming United Congregational Church where a PFLAG group meets; a welcoming Baptist Church; two Unitarian Universalists Churches, and another United Church of Christ called The Pakachoag Church.

LOCATION: WORCESTER IS LOCATED IN EAST CENTRAL MASSACHUSETTS.

GAY/LESBIAN FRIENDLY BUSINESSES: 2

GAY/LESBIAN BARS AND RESTAURANTS: 2

GAY/LESBIAN ORGANIZATIONS: 4

GAY/LESBIAN RELIGIOUS ORGANIZATIONS, CHURCHES, ETC.: 2

GAY/LESBIAN BOOKSTORES: 0

GAY/LESBIAN PUBLICATIONS: 0

COMPANIES THAT PROHIBIT DISCRIMINATION: CLARK UNIVERSITY, HEALTH AWARENESS SERVICES, AIDS PROJECT, DIGITAL EQUIPMENT, SEE STATE LAWS AND GAY CIVIL RIGHTS

INFORMATION NUMBER: 508-757-8010 GLCCCM

TOTAL CRIMES: 11,034

VIOLENT = (MURDER = 12, RAPE = 77, ROBBERY = 628, ASSAULT = N/A)

PROPERTY = (BURGLARY = 3,404, LARCENY = 5,221, MOTOR VEHICLE THEFT = 1,692, ARSON = N/A)

Things to Do!!!

(1) Salisbury Mansion, (2) Higgins Armory Museum, (3) Worcester Art Museum, (4) Americas Antiquarian Society, (5) New England Science Center. ANNUAL EVENTS: (1) Worcester Music Festival.

POPULATION: 163,414 PERSONS—W = 147,827, B = 7,669, AI/E/A = 540, C = 694, F = 122, M = 397, PR = 12,166

POPULATION GROWTH: + 1.0%

AGE OF POPULATION: (21-24) = 7.8%, (25-34) = 18.5%, (35-44) = 12.3%, (45-54) = 8.0%, (55-64) = 8.0%, (65-74) = 8.6%, (75 AND OVER) = 7.5%

HOUSING COST: OWNING = $128,900 RENTAL = $527

COMMUNITY HOSPITALS: 4 = 1,311 BEDS

CLIMATE: JAN—AVG. (22.8 DEGREES), JULY—AVG. (69.7 DEGREES), ANNUAL PRECIPITATION (47.75 INCHES)

PER CAPITA INCOME: $13,393

UNEMPLOYMENT RATE: 10.4%

JOB GROWTH SINCE 1980: + 10%

COST OF LIVING: N/A

EDUCATION: WORCESTER STATE COLLEGE, ASSUMPTION COLLEGE, CLARK UNIVERSITY

▼AMHERST

Gay Civil Rights: Bans discrimination based on sexual orientation in public and private employment, public accommodations, education, housing, credit, and union practices.

What the Locals Say . . .

Amherst and Northampton often get lumped together by many outsiders as well as many residents. If one community doesn't have it, the other one will. Amherst tends to have higher housing costs and is more of a higher income bedroom town. "Food For Thought" is a progressive bookstore that carries all kinds of books including gay and lesbian books. There is a FLAG group in Amherst as well as a Gay and Lesbian Educators Groups (GALE), "Face to Face" a gay/lesbian/bisexual speakers bureau, Older Lesbian Discussion Group, Kaleidoscope and a Men's Resource Center of Western Massachusetts. The Lesbian, Bisexual & Gay Men's Counseling Collective is out of UMASS-Amherst. "Queer Fest" is an outdoor festival of pride and power that includes booths, food, games, speakers, ice cream social and a dance. "Queer Fest" is sponsored by UMASS Program for Gay/Lesbian & Bisexual Concerns. "Cyclone" is a bar that has a gay night one night a week. The AIDS Information Collective is the AIDS organization for Amherst. There is a radio program on 91.1 F.M. "Dykes On The Radio." The group Integrity meets in Amherst. Hope Community Church is open and affirming to gays and lesbians.

LOCATION: AMHERST IS LOCATED IN NORTH CENTRAL MASSACHUSETTS.

GAY/LESBIAN FRIENDLY BUSINESSES: 12

GAY/LESBIAN BARS AND RESTAURANTS: 2

GAY/LESBIAN ORGANIZATIONS: 6

GAY/LESBIAN RELIGIOUS ORGANIZATIONS, CHURCHES, ETC.: 2

GAY/LESBIAN BOOKSTORES: 2

GAY/LESBIAN PUBLICATIONS: 3

COMPANIES THAT PROHIBIT DISCRIMINATION: SEE STATE LAW AND GAY CIVIL RIGHTS

INFORMATION NUMBER: 413-731-5403 GAY/LESBIAN INFO SERVICES

TOTAL CRIMES: N/A

VIOLENT = N/A

PROPERTY = N/A

Things to Do!!!

(1) Emily Dickinson Homestead, (2) Jones Library, (3) Amherst History Museum, (4) Hadley Farm Museum. ANNUAL EVENTS: Maple Sugaring.

POPULATION: 35,228 PERSONS—W = 29,930, B = 1,626, AI/E/A = 89, A/P/I = 2,773, H = 3,887

POPULATION GROWTH: N/A

AGE OF POPULATION: (21-24) = 7,523, (25-34) = 7,306, (35-44) = 1,890, (45-54) = 691, (55-64) = 589, (65-74) = 1,796, (75 AND OVER) = 8,769

HOUSING COST: OWNING = $168,400   RENTAL = $519

COMMUNITY HOSPITALS: N/A

CLIMATE: JAN—AVG. (23.6 DEGREES), JULY—AVG. (71.8 DEGREES), ANNUAL PRECIPITATION (42.50 INCHES)

PER CAPITA INCOME: N/A

UNEMPLOYMENT RATE: N/A

JOB GROWTH SINCE 1980: N/A

COST OF LIVING: N/A

EDUCATION: AMHERST COLLEGE, UNIVERSITY OF MASSACHUSETTS, HAMPSHIRE COLLEGE

NORTHAMPTON

Gay Civil Rights: None

What the Locals Say . . .

Northampton is referred to as "Lesbianville, or so says ABC's top rated news show "20/20." Northampton has a small town atmosphere with low crime and good schools. There are two openly gay cops on the police force, three openly gay city officials, and a woman mayor who strongly supports the gay community. It is not uncommon to see two men or two women walking down the street holding hands or kissing. The gay and lesbian community in Northampton is very out and very diverse. One strong word of caution is do not move to Northampton unless you are retired and financially secure or unless you have a business to bring to the area. Jobs are very scarce and difficult to compete for. So, one more time, don't move to Northampton until you look for and secure a job. There are several annual festivals in Northampton including: In May, Pride Day which includes a march and a rally; In late May, the Northampton Area Lesbian and Gay Business Guild (NALGBG) hosts a business fair; In July, The Northampton Lesbian Festival which is held in downtown Northampton and attracts approximately 30,000 spectators; In October, the Northampton Lesbian and Gay Business Guild hosts a Coming Out Ball. There are approximately sixty businesses in the (NALGBG). Northampton has two gay and lesbian radio programs on 1430 A.M., "An Open View" is the newest, which follows the International Gay and Lesbian Radio Newsmagazine, "This Way Out." "Dyke TV" is available on NCTV in Northampton. Some of the most popular restaurants are the "Green Street Cafe," "Spoleto and the "Bela." The Lesbian, Gay & Bisexual Political Alliance of Western Massachusetts is an active political group. There are numerous occupational lesbian and gay groups including: "Lesbians in Science and Technology Group," "G.A.L.E," and "The Lesbian Empowerment Project." "Single Older Ubiquinone Lesbian" (SOUL), and "EastHampton Dykes" have regular potlucks. There are several support groups in Northampton including: Gay/Bi Men discussion group, Valley Gay Men's Support Group, Men With Men Social Group, and PFLAG. "Venture Out" is a sports social and activities group, in nearby Springfield "Women Outdoors" offers a wide range of activities including hiking, birding, backpacking, weekend trips and various social events. *Golden Threads* is a publication for lesbians over 50 and younger. The Lesbian Calendar (TLC) group publishes the "*Valley Gay Men's Calendar*" and the "*The Lesbian Calendar.*" If you want to know what is going on, when and where, TLC is your source of information. "The Northstar Bar", "Pearl Street Nightclub" and "Katinas" all have gay and lesbian nights. LEAH is the Lesbian Education and Health Project. Lambda Resources for Men and Women provides psychotherapy to gay and lesbian individuals, couples, and groups. The Family Planning Council conducts HIV screenings. The Unitarian Universalists are open to gays and lesbians.

LOCATION: NORTHAMPTON IS LOCATED IN NORTH CENTRAL MASSACHUSETTS.

GAY/LESBIAN FRIENDLY BUSINESSES: 40 +

GAY/LESBIAN BARS AND RESTAURANTS: 10 +

GAY/LESBIAN ORGANIZATIONS: 25

GAY/LESBIAN RELIGIOUS ORGANIZATIONS, CHURCHES, ETC.: 1

GAY/LESBIAN BOOKSTORES: 1

GAY/LESBIAN PUBLICATIONS: 2

COMPANIES THAT PROHIBIT DISCRIMINATION: SEE STATE LAW

INFORMATION NUMBER: 413-586-5514 THE LESBIAN CALENDAR

TOTAL CRIMES: 1,186

VIOLENT = (MURDER = 2 , RAPE = 24 , ROBBERY = 18 , ASSAULT = 113)

PROPERTY = (BURGLARY = 182, LARCENY = 717, MOTOR VEHICLE THEFT = 130, ARSON = 3)

Things to Do!!!

(1) Words & Pictures Museum of Fine Sequential Art, (2) Museum Houses-Shepherd, Damon, Parsons, (3) Look Park, (4) Arcadia Nature Center and Wildlife Sanctuary, (5) Massachusetts Audubon Society, (6) Calvin Coolidge Memorial Room. ANNUAL EVENTS: (1) Eastern National Morgan Horse Show, (2) Three County Fair, (3) Maple Sugaring.

POPULATION: 29,028 PERSONS—W = 27,231, B = 522, AI/E/A = 55, C = 175, F = 30, M = 80, PR = 879

POPULATION GROWTH: - .9%

AGE OF POPULATION: (21-24) = 9.1%, (25-34) = 17.6%, (35-44) = 17.0%, (45-54) = 8.7%, (55-64) = 7.3%, (65-74) = 7.5%, (75 AND OVER) = 7.1%

HOUSING COST: OWNING = $132,900 RENTAL = $530

COMMUNITY HOSPITALS: 1 = 186 BEDS

CLIMATE: JAN—AVG. (23.6 DEGREES), JULY—AVG. (71.8 DEGREES), ANNUAL PRECIPITATION (42.50 INCHES)

PER CAPITA INCOME: $14,263

UNEMPLOYMENT RATE: 7.5%

JOB GROWTH SINCE 1980: + 15.3%

COST OF LIVING: N/A

EDUCATION: SMITH COLLEGE

PROVINCETOWN

Gay Civil Rights: None

What the Locals Say . . .

Provincetown is a seasonal community for the most part, although there is a year round gay/lesbian population. There is a sizable lesbian presence with more women's guest houses than any other place in the United States. The job prospects year round are slim, although the summer months tend to make up for it. The population during the winter is around 3000 swelling to 40,000 during the season (May 15th to Sept. 15th). The town is extremely quiet during the off season. P'town is a wide open gay/lesbian community. Gays and Lesbians come to Provincetown to relax and be themselves. You will see people everywhere holding hands, hugging, and kissing. The mayoral equivalent is a lesbian and the Harbormaster is a gay man. Anywhere is o.k. to live; being gay in Provincetown is absolutely a non issue. Recreational opportunities abound during the season with tea-dances, volleyball, softball, clubs, birding, bars, reading, writing, beaches, restaurants, biking, shopping, and water activities. Sirens Workshop Center at Gabriel's offers a myriad of workshops including: Tarot Card Reading, Yoga, Drumming, Holotropic Breathwork and many more. The Provincetown Business Guild actively promotes gay and lesbian tourism. There are several really good bookstores and gay gift shops in P'Town. "The Boat Slip Beach Club" has a tea-dance every afternoon in season and then everyone heads to the bars. The "Atlantic House," a men's bar, actually has three bars (Big Room, Little Room, and Macho Bar). The "Back Street Bar" and the "Crown and Anchor" are also men's bars. "Town House," "Rooster Bar," and "Love Shack" are all mixed bars. The "Pied Piper" is a renowned lesbian bar. Several doctors in the area are gay. The Outer Cape Health Service provides health care. *The Provincetown Magazine* is published weekly, spring through Christmas. *Bay Windows* out of Boston also covers P'town. The Unitarian Church is gay friendly.

LOCATION: PROVINCETOWN IS LOCATED ON THE NORTH END OF CAPE COD.

GAY LESBIAN FRIENDLY BUSINESSES: 83

GAY/LESBIAN BARS AND RESTAURANTS: 23

GAY/LESBIAN ORGANIZATIONS: 3

GAY/LESBIAN RELIGIOUS ORGANIZATIONS, CHURCHES, ETC.: 1

GAY/LESBIAN BOOKSTORES: 7

GAY/LESBIAN PUBLICATIONS: 2

COMPANIES THAT PROHIBIT DISCRIMINATION: ALL BUSINESSES THRIVE ON GAY/LESBIAN BUSINESS AND COULD NOT SURVIVE WITHOUT GAY AND LESBIAN EMPLOYEES. SEE STATE LAW

INFORMATION NUMBER: 1-800-637-8696 PROVINCETOWN BUSINESS GUILD

TOTAL CRIMES: N/A

VIOLENT = N/A

PROPERTY = N/A

Things to Do!!!

Provincetown has wonderful restaurants with great seafood, bird watching, and many guest houses. It is a gay and lesbian mecca during the summer months. Other points of interest include: (1) Town Wharf, (2) Pilgrim Monument and Museum, (3) Provincetown Art Association and Museum, (4) Whale Watching, (5) Various recreational activities- swimming, tennis, shopping, fishing, and beautiful beaches.

POPULATION: 3,561 PERSONS—W = 3,475, B = 56, AI/E/A = 9, A/P/I = 17, H = 42

POPULATION GROWTH: N/A

AGE OF POPULATION: (21-24) = 121, (25-34) = 1,458, (35-44) = 441, (45-54) = 181, (55-64) = 191, (65-74) = 642 , (75 AND OVER) = 420

HOUSING COST: OWNING = N/A   RENTAL = N/A

COMMUNITY HOSPITALS: N/A

CLIMATE: N/A

PER CAPITA INCOME: N/A

UNEMPLOYMENT RATE: N/A

JOB GROWTH SINCE 1980: N/A

COST OF LIVING: N/A

EDUCATION: NONE

MICHIGAN

STATE LAWS REGARDING HOMOSEXUALITY:

In 1990, a Michigan trial court declared unconstitutional the sodomy law prohibiting heterosexual and homosexual sodomy and carrying a 15-year maximum prison sentence. The state bans anti-gay discrimination in public employment.

CITIES: (60,000 AND UP)

▼ANN ARBOR

Gay Civil Rights: **Bans discrimination based on sexual orientation in public and private employment, public accommodations, housing, credit and union practices. Ann Arbor also has a domestic partnership ordinance.**

What the Locals Say . . .

Ann Arbor has a comfortable climate for gays and lesbians. Some are open and some are not. There isn't a gay ghetto to speak of in Ann Arbor. Westside and Northside of Ann Arbor are the most popular areas for gays and lesbians to live; although, lesbians and gays are spread throughout town depending on individual desire in architecture, economic factors, etc.. "Common Language" is a gay and lesbian bookstore in Ann Arbor. "La Casita De Lupe" is a gay owned and gay friendly restaurant. Other gay friendly restaurants are: "The Lord Fox," "Seva," and "Zingerman's Delicatessen Cafe." "Espresso Royale" and "Gratzz" are gay-friendly coffeehouses. Throughout the month of October there are speakers, a dance, a reception, counseling services, seminars, video nights, and potlucks focusing on gay and lesbian issues. Queer Unity Project is an activist group that establishes queer referrals and is based out of U. of Michigan. Washtenaw County Rainbow Action Project is a community political group. There are numerous organizations on the University of Michigan Campus including: International Gay and Lesbian Group, Men's Support Group, Women's Support Group, Dyke Discussion Group, East Quad Social Group, Bisexual Women's Group" and an Asian Pacific Islander Lesbian Gay & Bisexual Group. There are also several academic gay and lesbian groups: Business, Law, Library, Engineering, Social Workers, etc.. Once a month, "Club Fabulous Dances" are held which are chemical and smoke free. Canterbury House is a social group for gays and lesbians. Lesbian Movie/Video Night is also very popular. Community based gay and lesbian organizations include: a Support Group for Gay/Lesbian Adoptees or Birth Parents, Gay Men's Therapy Group, Gay, Lesbian, and Bisexual Women of Color Collective, Lesbian Youth Support Group, Older Lesbian Organization (OLO)—a discussion and potluck group, and Our Little Group (OLG)—a professional men's group. "Nectarine Dance Bar" has queer night two nights a week, "Flame" and "Flicks" are both bars that draw predominately men. Mid-West AIDS Prevention provides education and a variety of other services to those with HIV/AIDS. *Between The Lines* is a statewide gay and lesbian publication. "Closets R 4 Close" is a gay radio program on 88.3 FM. Tree of Life Metropolitan Community Church, Church of the Good Shepherd, Church of the Incarnate, Memorial Christian Church, St. Aidens Episcopal Church, Unitarian Church and the Huron Valley Community Church are open and affirming to gays and lesbians.

LOCATION: ANN ARBOR IS LOCATED IN SOUTHEASTERN MICHIGAN, WEST OF DETROIT.

GAY/LESBIAN FRIENDLY BUSINESSES: 25 +

GAY/LESBIAN BARS AND RESTAURANTS: 9

GAY/LESBIAN ORGANIZATIONS: 20

GAY/LESBIAN RELIGIOUS ORGANIZATIONS, CHURCHES, ETC.: 2

GAY/LESBIAN BOOKSTORES: 1

GAY/LESBIAN PUBLICATIONS: 1

COMPANIES THAT PROHIBIT DISCRIMINATION: UNIVERSITY OF MICHIGAN OFFERS SAME SEX PARTNER BENEFITS, SEE STATE LAW AND GAY CIVIL RIGHTS

INFORMATION NUMBER: 313-763-4186 LESBIAN GAY BISEXUAL PROGRAM OFFICE

TOTAL CRIMES: 5,895

VIOLENT = (MURDER = 2, RAPE = N/A , ROBBERY = 129, ASSAULT = 336)

PROPERTY = (BURGLARY = 1,101, LARCENY = 4,032, MOTOR VEHICLE THEFT = 260, ARSON = 35)

Things to Do!!!

Ann Arbor has a college town atmosphere. The University of Michigan has numerous points of interest including: Power Center for the Performing Arts, Natural Sciences Museum, Museum of Art, Law Quadrangle. Other things to see and do include: (1) Nichols Arboretum, (2) Matthaei Botanical Gardens, (3) Gerald R. Ford Presidential Library, (4) Ann Arbor Symphony, (5) Kempf House, (6) Huron-Clinton Metro park. ANNUAL EVENTS: (1) May Festival, (2) Ann Arbor Summer Festival, (3) Street Art Fair.

POPULATION: 109,766 PERSONS—W = 89,841, B = 9,905, AI/E/A = 386, C = 3,036, F = 397, M = 935, PR = 397

POPULATION GROWTH: + 1.7%

AGE OF POPULATION: (21-24) = 14.2%, (25-34) = 20.7%, (35-44) = 14.5%, (45-54) = 7.6%, (55-64) = 5.3%, (65-74) = 4.0%, (75 AND OVER) = 3.2%

HOUSING COST: OWNING = $116,400 RENTAL = $568

COMMUNITY HOSPITALS: 2 = 1,486 BEDS

CLIMATE: JAN—AVG. (23.2 DEGREES), JULY—AVG. (73.0 DEGREES), ANNUAL PRECIPITATION (32.81 INCHES)

PER CAPITA INCOME: $17,786

UNEMPLOYMENT RATE: 3.6%

JOB GROWTH SINCE 1980: + 8.0%

COST OF LIVING: N/A

EDUCATION: UNIVERSITY OF MICHIGAN AT ANN ARBOR

▼DETROIT

Gay Civil Rights: Bans discrimination based on sexual orientation in public and private employment, public accommodations, education, housing, credit, and union practices.

What the Locals Say . . .

There are areas of Detroit where the gay and lesbian community is out and visible, and there are other areas where almost everyone is closeted. Ferndale is a suburb north of Detroit that houses Affirmations, the Lesbian and Gay Community Center. Affirmations serves the Detroit metropolitan area. Services include a full menu of alternative activities. There are rap groups for gay men, lesbians, age 18-21 gay and lesbian groups, teen groups under 21, teen groups under 18, several coming out groups, bisexual groups, couple groups, Silver Foxes—a Senior group for women, Women In Touch and Men In Touch. Ferndale also has a feminist bookstore, "Women's Prerogative." Ferndale is home to "Doug's Bodyshop" a unique bar and restaurant where customers sit in cars while they dine. The Fans of Ferndale is a neighborhood civic organization for lesbians and gays. Birmingham is a suburb to the northeast that is wealthy and gay friendly. Royal Oak is an area that is very open, relaxed, and trendy. Gays, lesbians, punkers, rockers, etc. live in this area. The area is pretty diverse. There are numerous gay and lesbian bars and restaurants and lots of homes that have gay and lesbian residents. There are new and old houses, condos, apartments and townhomes to choose from. "Chosen Books of Michigan" is a gay and lesbian bookstore in Royal Oak. "Lavender Moon Cafe" is a coffeehouse that many gays and lesbians enjoy. There are different events every night. There are several organizations in Detroit including: Gay & Lesbian Educators of Michigan (GLEAM), Gay and Lesbian Resource Network of the American Red Cross (GALERN), Black & White Men Together (BWMT), PFLAG, Detroit Men's Chorus, Great Lakes Men's Chorus, Girth & Mirth of Detroit and Cadillac Squares. There are several African American Gay and Lesbian groups including BBC, Friends Group, and a group called Family. The Community Referral and

Information Book (CHRIS Book) is a listing of gay, lesbian, or gay-friendly businesses in the Detroit area. Detroit has numerous sport groups and leagues. Some of the most popular ones include a swim team, golf, joggers, cross country, skiing, aerobics, tennis, ice skating, wally ball, racket ball and a softball league. The Michigan International Gay Rodeo and the group Frontrunners are in Detroit. Queer Nation and Michigan Human Rights Campaign Council are political groups in Detroit. There is a Detroit Area Gay & Lesbian Artists Association and a Lesbian Gay Foundation of Michigan. "1515 Broadway" is a gay theatre, "Magic Bag Theatre" has some nights where there are gay comics or films. "Detroit Women's Coffeehouse" and Detroit Gay Men's Coffeehouse are popular. Predominately gay male bars in Detroit are "Menjo's" - a yuppie bar with dancing, "Tiffany's" - a leather bar, and "Gold Coast" has Go Go Dancing. "Sugar Bakers Sports Bar and Grill" is a mixed bar, but more women go there than men. The "Railroad Crossing" is a lesbian dance bar. "Como's Restaurant" is a popular restaurant for gays and lesbians. The Detroit Area Lesbian Women's Health Care Project is a wonderful organization. The Midwest AIDS Prevention Program focuses on preventative education. The Wellness Network, Inc. is located in Ferndale. Ford Motors and General Motors each have gay and lesbian employee groups. Two gay and lesbian publications out of Detroit are *Cruise Magazine* published weekly and *Metra* published every other week and distributed throughout Ohio, Michigan and Illinois. The religious groups Dignity, Integrity, Simch a Jewish group and Affirmations are in Detroit. The MCC, various Lutheran, various Episcopalian, a Church of Latter Day Saints, Full Truth Fellowship of Christ Church, a Jehovah Witness and a Unitarian Universalist welcome gays and lesbians to their congregations.

LOCATION: DETROIT IS LOCATED IN SOUTHEASTERN MICHIGAN, EAST OF ANN ARBOR.

GAY/LESBIAN FRIENDLY BUSINESSES: 50+

GAY/LESBIAN BARS AND RESTAURANTS: 32

GAY/LESBIAN ORGANIZATIONS: 31

GAY/LESBIAN RELIGIOUS ORGANIZATIONS, CHURCHES, ETC.: 12

GAY/LESBIAN BOOKSTORES: 4

GAY/LESBIAN PUBLICATIONS: 3

COMPANIES THAT PROHIBIT DISCRIMINATION: SEE STATE LAW AND GAY CIVIL RIGHTS

INFORMATION NUMBER: 810-398-4297 AFFIRMATIONS

TOTAL CRIMES: 121,837

VIOLENT = (MURDER = 57, RAPE = N/A , ROBBERY = 13,591, ASSAULT = 12,999)

PROPERTY = (BURGLARY = 23,092, LARCENY = 42,818, MOTOR VEHICLE THEFT = 28,061, ARSON = 1,219)

Things to Do!!!

The Detroit Parks and Recreation system controls over 6,000 acres. One park contains a greenhouse, conservatory with tropical and desert plants, as well as the nation's oldest freshwater aquarium. The Detroit Institute of Arts displays the largest collection of Italian art outside of Italy. Other points of interest include: (1) Detroit Artist Market in Harmony Park, (2) Detroit Symphony Orchestra, (3) Detroit Repertory Theatre, (4) Detroit Historical Museum, (5) Fort Wayne, (6) Detroit Zoological Park, (7) Henry Ford Estate, (8) Professional Sports: Football- Lions, Hockey - Red Wings, Basketball - Pistons, Baseball - Tigers.

POPULATION: 1,012,110 PERSONS—W = 222,316, B = 777,316, AI/E/A = 3,655, C = 1,024, F = 1,612, M = 573, PR = 134

POPULATION GROWTH: - 15.9%

AGE OF POPULATION:(21-24) = 6.2%, (25-34) = 16.5 %, (35-44) = 14.2%, (45-54) = 8.6%, (55-64) = 7.9%, (65-74) = 7.2%, (75 AND OVER) = 5.0%

HOUSING COST: OWNING = $25,600   RENTAL = $372

COMMUNITY HOSPITALS: 18 = 6,245 BEDS

CLIMATE: JAN—AVG. (24.7 DEGREES), JULY—AVG. (74.2 DEGREES), ANNUAL PRECIPITATION (32.09 INCHES)

PER CAPITA INCOME: $9,443

UNEMPLOYMENT RATE: 13.1%

JOB GROWTH SINCE 1980: - 13.7%

COST OF LIVING: N/A

EDUCATION: WAYNE STATE UNIVERSITY, UNIVERSITY OF DETROIT MERCY

▼FLINT

Gay Civil Rights: Bans discrimination based on sexual orientation in public and private employment, public accommodations, education, housing and union practices.

What the Locals Say . . .

The gay and lesbian community in Flint is still fairly closeted. Locally, the politicians tend to support the gay and lesbian community; but statewide support is mixed. The Carriage Town area is one of the oldest areas in town. The neighborhood kind of went to the wayside until the city offered these huge dilapidated homes at a reduced rate with little or no interest. A large group of gays and lesbians fixed them up, so now the neighborhood is filled with gays and lesbians. The Pride Community Center offers a non-bar alternative and has a membership of about 200. The coffeeshop "Daily Grind" is gay-friendly and draws a number of gays and lesbians. "Young and Welshan Books" offers a large selection of gay and lesbian literature. "Face The Music" is a feminist music radio show on 95.1 FM. "In The Life", a gay television show is on Station WFUM. Flint has a murder mystery dinner theatre. "Just Friends" is an all female social group, "Over & Under 50 a Few Years" group, PFLAG, Men and Women Coming Out Groups and Survivors of Domestic Violence group are all in Flint. Some of the most popular summer recreational activities are blading, walking, jogging and cycling. Some of the most popular recreational activities in the winter are cross country skiing, and downhill skiing. University of Michigan at Flint has a Gay Lesbian Association of Students, (GLASS). The Human Rights Campaign is a grass roots campaign. "The Club Triangle," "The Merry Inn" and the oldest bar, "The State Bar," cater to gays and lesbians. "The Copa" is straight bar that has two gay nights a week. The Wellness HIV Services is a major provider for HIV/AIDS. The Pride Community Center puts out a monthly newsletter. The Redeemer MCC of Flint, and the Unity Church offer same sex unions; the Unitarian Universalist Church offers commitment ceremonies; and the Life Enrichment Center is a non denominational religious group. All of these churches are open and affirming to gays and lesbians.

LOCATION: FLINT IS LOCATED IN SOUTHEASTERN PART OF MICHIGAN'S LOWER PENINSULA.

GAY/LESBIAN FRIENDLY BUSINESSES: 5

GAY/LESBIAN BARS AND RESTAURANTS: 4

GAY/LESBIAN ORGANIZATIONS: 10

GAY/LESBIAN RELIGIOUS ORGANIZATIONS, CHURCHES, ETC.: 4

GAY/LESBIAN BOOKSTORES: 0

GAY/LESBIAN PUBLICATIONS: 0

COMPANIES THAT PROHIBIT DISCRIMINATION: UNIVERSITY OF MICHIGAN OFFERS SAME SEX PARTNER BENEFITS, TELEVISION CHANNEL 12

INFORMATION NUMBER: 810-238-9854 PRIDE COMMUNITY CENTER

TOTAL CRIMES: 17,964

VIOLENT = (MURDER = 48, RAPE = N/A , ROBBERY = 1,039, ASSAULT = 2,507)

PROPERTY = (BURGLARY = 4,024, LARCENY THEFT = 7,701, MOTOR VEHICLE THEFT = 2,307, ARSON = 338)

Things to Do!!!

Fenton's Silver Lake Park is suitable for many water sports plus a 300 feet sandy beach. Flushing Park includes two miles of woodlands, softball fields and tennis courts. In the winter the area is used for cross country skiing and sledding. Other points of interest include: (1) Cultural Center- (Bower Center, Whiting Auditorium, Flint Institute of Art, Left Bank Gallery), (2) Flint Institute of Music, (3) Flint Symphony Orchestra, (4) Ballet Michigan, (5) Flint School of Performing Arts, (6) Professional Sports: Hockey- Spirits. ANNUAL EVENTS: Buick Open.

POPULATION: 139,311 PERSONS—W = 69,788, B = 67,485, AI/E/A = 1,045, C = 132, F = 128, M = 3,053, PR = 262

POPULATION GROWTH: = 12.7%

AGE OF POPULATION: (21-24) = 6.3%, (25-34) = 17.6%, (35-44) = 13.5%, (45-54) = 8.6%, (55-64) = 7.8%, (65-74) = 6.2%, (75 AND OVER) = 4.5%

HOUSING COST: OWNING = $33,900   RENTAL = $ 375

COMMUNITY HOSPITALS: 5 = 1,799 BEDS

CLIMATE: JAN—AVG. (21.5 DEGREES), JULY—AVG. (70.6 DEGREES), ANNUAL PRECIPITATION (30.28 INCHES)

PER CAPITA INCOME: $10,415

UNEMPLOYMENT RATE: 16.7%

JOB GROWTH SINCE 1980: - 13.0%

COST OF LIVING: N/A

EDUCATION: UNIVERSITY OF MICHIGAN AT FLINT

▼GRAND RAPIDS

Gay Civil Rights: The City Charter bans discrimination based on sexual orientation in public employment.

What the Locals Say . . .

Grand Rapids is very gay friendly. Probably 60% of gays and lesbians are out to friends and family, but not at work. The areas that have the highest concentration of gays and lesbians are the Heritage Hill area, East Town area and the Cherry Hill area. The Cherry Hill area is a four block area that was mostly run down Victorian homes. In the last four years, people have come in and refurbished them; and many of these renovating individuals were gay. The Lesbian & Gay Community Network of Western Michigan is located near the Cherry Hill area and offers many gay and lesbian groups and activities. Political groups in Grand Rapids consist of Lesbian Gay Political Action Network, National Organization for Women, and the Democratic Caucus. There are several support groups in Grand Rapids including: PFLAG, Windfire - a lesbian, gay and bisexual support group, AA groups for gays and lesbians, a Men's Rap group, and a Newly Coming Out group. The Male Tent and Trailer Campers is a men's only social group. There is a square dance club and a Women's Night/Social/Discussion/Potluck group. Frontrunners/Frontwalkers has a group in Grand Rapids. The Gay Pride Day is held at a park in downtown with speakers, entertainment and booths. Mini Pride is held in the winter where participants go ice skating and then to a bar for munchies. "Martini's" is an alternative bar in the East Town area. "Diversions" is a bar that draws a mixed crowd and is very supportive of the gay and lesbian community. The AIDS Resource Center has a referral service, food bank, a buddy program, emergency financial aid help, and transportation. Grand Rapids also has the HIV/AIDS Housing Coalition and the PWA Coalition. *Network News* is published by the Community Center. Aware, with roots in Christian Reformed; Evangelical Concerned, and Dignity are religious groups that welcome gays and lesbians. Bethel Christian Assembly and Reconciliation MCC are open and affirming to gays and lesbians.

LOCATION: GRAND RAPIDS IS LOCATED IN WESTERN MICHIGAN.

GAY/LESBIAN FRIENDLY BUSINESSES: 4

GAY/LESBIAN BARS AND RESTAURANTS: 2

GAY/LESBIAN ORGANIZATIONS: 15

GAY/LESBIAN RELIGIOUS ORGANIZATIONS, CHURCHES, ETC.: 5

GAY/LESBIAN BOOKSTORES: 1

GAY/LESBIAN PUBLICATIONS: 1

COMPANIES THAT PROHIBIT DISCRIMINATION: SEE STATE LAW AND GAY CIVIL RIGHTS

INFORMATION NUMBER: 616-458-3511 LESBIAN AND GAY COMMUNITY NETWORK OF WESTERN MICHIGAN

TOTAL CRIMES: 15,797

VIOLENT = (MURDER = 33, RAPE = N/A , ROBBERY = 829, ASSAULT = 1,793)

PROPERTY = (BURGLARY = 3,161, LARCENY = 8,827, MOTOR VEHICLE THEFT = 1,075, ARSON = 79)

Things to Do!!!

High school football and basketball teams attract a big following in Grand Rapids. There are approximately 1,000 recreational softball teams. Grand Rapids has 21 lakes in and around the city used for boating, swimming and water skiing. The area is known for great salmon fishing. Ten minutes north of the city is a ski resort. Other things to do include: (1) Grand Rapids Art Museum, (2) Race Street Gallery, (3) De Vos Hall, (4) Opera Grand Rapids, (5) Civic Ballet, (6) Grand Rapids Symphony Orchestra. ANNUAL EVENTS: (1) Festival Celebration, (2) Greater Grand Rapids Open Golf Tournament.

POPULATION: 191,230 PERSONS—W = 144,464, B = 35,073, AI/E/A = 1,573, C = 255, F = 120, M = 5,819, PR = 1,845

POPULATION GROWTH: + 5.2%

AGE OF POPULATION: (21-24) = 7.2%, (25-34) = 19.5%, (35-44) = 13.1%, (45-54) = 7.2%, (55-64) = 6.9%, (65-74) = 6.7%, (75 AND OVER) = 6.4%

HOUSING COST: OWNING = $58,300   RENTAL = $414

COMMUNITY HOSPITALS: 5 = 1,460 BEDS

CLIMATE: JAN—AVG. (21.8 DEGREES), JULY—AVG. (71.6 DEGREES), ANNUAL PRECIPITATION (36.04 INCHES)

PER CAPITA INCOME: $12,070

UNEMPLOYMENT RATE: 9.2%

JOB GROWTH SINCE 1980: + 8.1%

COST OF LIVING: N/A

EDUCATION: GRAND VALLEY STATE UNIVERSITY

KALAMAZOO

Gay Civil Rights: None

What the Locals Say . . .

Kalamazoo is a very conservative area. Approximately 50% of the gay and lesbian community is out and 50% is closeted. The politicians are neutral, not pro-gay, not anti-gay. "Pandora Books" is a feminist bookstore that carries lesbian and gay books. "Our Kids" is a social organization for lesbigay parents and their children. PFLAG is very active. Kalamazoo also has a lesbian and gay AA group. Windfire is a support group for lesbian, gay, and bisexual youth. The Western Michigan University Alliance for Lesbians and Gays has a support group, men's social group that has potlucks and a women's group called Lavender Mornings which sponsors dances and potlucks. The "Zoo Bar" is mixed, usually with more men than women, except for ladies night. "Brothers Club" is a mixed bar. Community AIDS Resource & Education Service (CARES) provides professional support, buddy program, case management workers, and transportation. The Resource Center and the group Lavender Mornings each puts out a newsletter every 3-4 months. There is a group of Integrity and a Catholic group for gays and lesbians in Kalamazoo. The Phoenix Community Church is affirming and very supportive to gays and lesbians.

LOCATION: KALAMAZOO IS LOCATED IN SOUTHWESTERN MICHIGAN.

GAY LESBIAN FRIENDLY BUSINESSES: 5

GAY/LESBIAN BARS AND RESTAURANTS: 2

GAY/LESBIAN ORGANIZATIONS: 8

GAY/LESBIAN RELIGIOUS ORGANIZATIONS, CHURCHES, ETC.: 3

GAY/LESBIAN BOOKSTORES: 1

GAY/LESBIAN PUBLICATIONS: 1

COMPANIES THAT PROHIBIT DISCRIMINATION: SEE STATE LAW

INFORMATION NUMBER: 616-345-7878 KALAMAZOO GAY & LESBIAN RESOURCE CENTER

TOTAL CRIMES: 7,336

VIOLENT = (MURDER = 8, RAPE = N/A, ROBBERY = 248, ASSAULT = 1,112)

PROPERTY = (BURGLARY = 1,308, LARCENY = 4,082, MOTOR VEHICLE THEFT = 493, ARSON = 85)

Things to Do!!!

(1) Kalamazoo Nature Center, (2) Institute of Arts, (3) Public Museum, (4) Gilmore-CCCA Museum, (5) Parks- Scotts Mill Park, Echo Valley, Bronson Park, Crane Park, (6) Skiing—Timber Ridge & Bittersweet, (7) Kalamazoo Kitefest, (8) Kalamazoo Air Zoo. ANNUAL EVENTS: (1) Maple Sugaring Festival, (2) Kalamazoo County Flowerfest, (3) Kalamazoo County Fair, (4) Wine & Harvest Festival.

POPULATION: 81,253 PERSONS—W = 62,039, B = 15,053, AI/E/A = 450, C = 298, F = 75, M = 1,490, PR = 99

POPULATION GROWTH: + 1.9%

AGE OF POPULATION: (21-24) = 12.1%, (25-34) = 17.6%, (35-44) = 12.1%, (45-54) = 6.9%, (55-64) = 5.9%, (65-74) = 5.5%, (75 AND OVER) = 5.3%

HOUSING COST: OWNING = $48,600   RENTAL = $403

COMMUNITY HOSPITALS: 5 = 1,460 BEDS

CLIMATE: JAN—AVG. (23.7 DEGREES), JULY—AVG. (73.5 DEGREES), ANNUAL PRECIPITATION (37.03 INCHES)

PER CAPITA INCOME: $ 11,956

UNEMPLOYMENT RATE: 11.1%

JOB GROWTH SINCE 1980: - 4.7%

COST OF LIVING: N/A

EDUCATION: WESTERN MICHIGAN UNIVERSITY, KALAMAZOO COLLEGE

▼LANSING

Gay Civil Rights: Bans discrimination based on sexual orientation in public and private employment, public accommodations, housing, credit and union practices.

What the Locals Say . . .

The gay and lesbian community in Lansing and East Lansing is somewhat mixed. There are some gays and lesbians who are in the closet and are happy to be there, while there are other family members who are out and open and happy to be that way. There is a county law that protects gays and lesbians who are county workers and a state law that protects gays and lesbians who are state workers from sexual orientation discrimination. Currently, the Lansing Equal Rights Task Force is trying to get a comprehensive gay rights anti-discrimination law on the books for private employment, housing and accommodations. Lansing is, for the most part, a middle-class community. Lansing has the worlds longest boardwalk which runs six miles along the Grand River, where people can cycle, walk, jog or run. Approximately 50% of homes in Lansing are rented. The Eastside of Lansing or rather zip code "48912" is a popular place for lesbians to live. Eastside has a lot of bungalows and brownstones. In the last 2-3 years, the westside has also seen a surge of gays and lesbians moving in. This area is a little more upscale than the Eastside and has newer homes. Old Town is the old downtown of Lansing. It is being brought back to life by several members of the gay and lesbian community. There are currently several gay and lesbian owned businesses in the Old town area. The Real World Emporium is a lesbian and gay bookstore and full service cafe which has a full service menu. Real World is a focal point of the lesbigay community serving as a clearinghouse for information, events, exhibitions, etc. There are several cappuccino shops in Lansing, some of the most popular are: "Dancing Goat," "Cafe Venezia" and "Cappuccino Cafe." "El Azteco" is a popular gay friendly restaurant. "Hershee's" is a mainstream restaurant, however they have helped celebrate a lesbian couples anniversary. There are several gay and lesbian events in Lansing. There is a one day Outdoor Music Festival (ChickenStock) that focuses on women's music. Pride Weekend consists of concerts, dancing in the streets of Old Town, a march, a rally, and a festival with numerous activities. Lansing is also the home of Goldenrod Distributors, the premiere distributor of women's music. Lansing has two music production companies,"Our Living Room Concerts" and "Circe Productions." The Prism Awards is a community wide event that honors lesbian and gay individuals who have helped better the quality of life for other family members. The Lansing Association for Human Rights is a lesbian gay political group. Lansing has a bowling league, a women's softball team, Frontrunners group, and a cycling group. The Lesbian Alliance is a social organization that sponsors a film festival and a variety of workshops. Sol Rising is a business that puts on workshops throughout the state and focuses on gay and lesbian issues. Lansing has a Lesbian Moms Group, First Fridays (group of professional women), Capitols Men Club, Lesbian Avengers and PFLAG. There are three bars in Lansing that cater to the gay and lesbian crowd. "Club Paradise" is somewhat mixed with gays and lesbians and attracts a younger crowd, "Club 505" is 70% women and "Esquire Club" is 70% men. The

Lesbian and Gay Health and Wellness Center is located in Lansing. The Lansing Area AIDS Network is a model AIDS program. There are many services offered, including: a buddy program, a barter system, full time staff, and numerous support groups. There are several gay and lesbian publications in Lansing: *The Lesbian Alliance, The Lesbian Connection,* and *Gay and Lesbian News.* The local mainstream newspaper has a section for minority groups to write opinion pieces. The groups rotate and approximately every six weeks, there is a gay and lesbian piece written. The Unitarian Universalist is a gay friendly church. Ecclesia is a multi-denominational religious group, Quakers, Dignity, and a gay Presbyterian Organization are open and affirming religious groups.

LOCATION: LANSING IS NORTHWEST OF DETROIT, IN MICHIGAN. THE GRAND RIVER RUNS THROUGH TOWN.

GAY/LESBIAN FRIENDLY BUSINESSES: 30

GAY/LESBIAN BARS AND RESTAURANTS: 8

GAY/LESBIAN ORGANIZATIONS: 20

GAY/LESBIAN RELIGIOUS ORGANIZATIONS, CHURCHES, ETC.: 5

GAY/LESBIAN BOOKSTORES: 1

GAY/LESBIAN PUBLICATIONS: 3

COMPANIES THAT PROHIBIT DISCRIMINATION: SEE STATE LAW, CITY ORDINANCE, COUNTY LAW, GENERAL MOTORS, AT&T, SPARROW HOSPITAL

TOTAL CRIMES: = 8,835

VIOLENT = (MURDER = 14 , RAPE = N/A, ROBBERY = 302, ASSAULT = 1,066)

PROPERTY = (BURGLARY = 1,372, LARCENY = 5,295, MOTOR VEHICLE THEFT = 700, ARSON = 86)

Things to Do!!!

(1) Fenner Arboretum, (2) Potter Park Zoo, (3) Boars Head: Michigan Public Theater, (4) Michigan Historical Museum, (5) Impression 5 Science Museum, (6) R.E. Olds Transportation Museum, (7) State Capital

POPULATION: 126,722 PERSONS—W = 94,135, B = 23,626, AI/E/A = 1,295, C = 201, F = 171, M = 8,299, PR = 348

POPULATION GROWTH: -2.8%

AGE OF POPULATION: (21-24) = 7.8%, (25-34) = 20.9%, (35-44) = 14.8%, (45-54) = 8.2%, (55-64) = 6.8%, (65-74) = 5.6%, (75 AND OVER) = 4.0%

HOUSING COST: OWNING = $48,400 RENTAL = $399

COMMUNITY HOSPITALS: 4 = 1,438 BEDS

CLIMATE: JAN—AVG. (20.9 DEGREES), JULY—AVG. (70.8 DEGREES), ANNUAL PRECIPITATION (30.62 INCHES)

PER CAPITA INCOME: $12,232

UNEMPLOYMENT RATE: 8.2%

JOB GROWTH SINCE 1980: +2.2%

COST OF LIVING: N/A

EDUCATION: UNIVERSITY OF MICHIGAN, LANSING COMMUNITY COLLEGE

RURAL AREAS (UNDER 5,000)

SAUGATUCK

Gay Civil Rights: None

What the Locals Say . . .

Saugatuck is a very small resort town. Memorial Day until Labor Day the town is filled with gay and lesbian tourists. There are numerous shops, bed and breakfasts, restaurants, and a beautiful beach. The majority of gays and lesbians are open. In the winter, the majority of the population switches to straight people; however, most of the shops are owned by gays and lesbians. The towns next to Saugatuck are very conservative. There is a specific part of the beach where you can pay to go to, and some consider that part the gay beach. There are not a lot of organized activities in Saugatuck. The Douglas Dunes is a resort that includes five bars (Patio Bar, Pool Bar, Cabaret Bar, Bistro Bar and Disco Bar), rooms, suites, cottages, and a restaurant. Though most of the clientele is gay, some are straight. In nearby Holland there is an AIDS Hospice group. Most people go to Grand Rapids for health care.

LOCATION: SAUGATUCK IS LOCATED ON THE WESTERN SIDE OF MICHIGAN ON LAKE MICHIGAN.

GAY/LESBIAN FRIENDLY BUSINESSES: 25+

GAY/LESBIAN BARS AND RESTAURANTS: 1

GAY/LESBIAN ORGANIZATIONS: 0

GAY/LESBIAN RELIGIOUS ORGANIZATIONS, CHURCHES, ETC.: 1

GAY/LESBIAN BOOKSTORES: 0

GAY/LESBIAN PUBLICATIONS: 0

COMPANIES THAT PROHIBIT DISCRIMINATION: SEE STATE LAW

INFORMATION NUMBER: 616-857-4249 DOUGLAS DUNES RESORT

TOTAL CRIMES: 2

VIOLENT = (MURDER = 0 RAPE = 1 , ROBBERY = 0, ASSAULT = 0)

PROPERTY = (BURGLARY = 0 , LARCENY = 0 , MOTOR VEHICLE = 1 ARSON = N/A)

Things to Do!!!

Saugatuck offers beautiful beaches for surfing and swimming on Lake Michigan, hiking and cross country skiing in the dunes, boating and canoeing on the Kalamazoo River, yachting from Marina and a charming shopping area. (1) Major Art Colony, (2) Sightseeing Cruises, (3) S.S. Keewatin Marine Museum, (4) Fenn Valley Vineyards and Wine Cellars.

POPULATION: 2,916 PERSONS—W = 2,810, B = 4, AI/E/A = 15, A/P/I = 8, H = 110

POPULATION GROWTH: N/A

AGE OF POPULATION: (21-24) = 126, (25-34) = 896, (35-44) = 330, (45-54) = 156, (55-64) = 162, (65-74) = 569, (75 AND OVER) = 351

HOUSING COST: OWNING = $73,000   RENTAL = $326

COMMUNITY HOSPITALS: N/A

CLIMATE: N/A

PER CAPITA INCOME: N/A

UNEMPLOYMENT RATE: N/A

POPULATION GROWTH: N/A

COST OF LIVING: N/A

EDUCATION: NONE

COUNTIES:

INGHAM COUNTY:

Gay Civil Rights: Bans discrimination based on sexual orientation in public employment.

Cities and Towns Included Within Ingham County:

East Lansing

Lansing

Leslie

Mason

Meridian

Weberville

Williamston

MINNESOTA

STATE LAWS REGARDING HOMOSEXUALITY:

Heterosexual and homosexual sodomy is illegal with a maximum sentence of 1 year. In 1993, Governor Arne Carlson signed a bill banning anti-gay discrimination in housing, employment, public accommodations, credit, education, and public services. Crimes based on sexual orientation are included in the states hate crime laws.

CITIES: (60,000 AND UP)

▼MINNEAPOLIS

Gay Civil Rights: Bans discrimination based on sexual orientation in public and private employment, public accommodations, education, housing, credit, and union practices.

What the Locals Say . . .

Minneapolis enjoys a fairly open community. It is generally believed that if a politician wants to win he/she will support gay rights. The mayor of Minneapolis is pro-gay and appoints individuals to the council that are gay and lesbian. The Uptown area (Hennepin Lake Area) is a heavily gay area with a lot of foot traffic and coffee shops. The Downtown area is filled with pink triangles and black triangles and gay Pride flags. Loring Park is very heavily gay and has numerous coffeehouses and businesses. Powder Horn Park, often referred to as, "Dyke Heights," is a very lesbian area which is located approximately 30 blocks southeast of downtown. The Pride Festival in 1994 attracted approximately 80,000 participants. There are numerous annual fundraising events (dinners, walks, proms) for gay rights, AIDS, and other gay and lesbian issues. There is an adult prom and a youth prom. Approximately 500 are expected to attend the 1995 adult prom, while 200 are expected to attend the youth gay and lesbian prom. The bar scene is mostly mixed with gay men and lesbians. The "Gay Nineties" is perhaps the largest gay complex in the Midwest and consists of 10 different bars and restaurants. Minnesota Comprehensive Health is a state program which protects you if your health insurance doesn't cover you. There are two gay and lesbian publications available in Minneapolis. *Focus Point* is published every week, while *Gaze* is published twice a month. Carenet publishes a directory of gay and lesbian businesses. There are two churches, Spirit of the Lakes and MCC, that are predominately gay and lesbian. One temple has a lesbian rabbi synagogue. There are many other churches that are open and affirming.

LOCATION: MINNEAPOLIS IS IN EASTERN MINNESOTA AT THE MOUTH OF THE MISSISSIPPI AND THE MINNESOTA RIVERS.

GAY LESBIAN FRIENDLY BUSINESSES: 27

GAY/LESBIAN BARS AND RESTAURANTS: 6

GAY/LESBIAN ORGANIZATIONS: 51

GAY/LESBIAN RELIGIOUS ORGANIZATIONS, CHURCHES, ETC.: 8

GAY/LESBIAN BOOKSTORES: 2

GAY/LESBIAN PUBLICATIONS: 2

COMPANIES THAT PROHIBIT DISCRIMINATION: SEE STATE LAW AND GAY CIVIL RIGHTS

INFORMATION NUMBER: 612-871-5559 GAY AND LESBIAN HOTLINE

TOTAL CRIMES: 40,463

VIOLENT = (MURDER = 58, RAPE = 518, ROBBERY = 3,178, ASSAULT = 2,727)

PROPERTY = (BURGLARY = 9,358, LARCENY = 19,952, MOTOR VEHICLE THEFT = 4,676, ARSON = N/A)

Things to Do!!!

The Minneapolis Park system has been judged one of the best in the country and has over one hundred parks. Specific points of interest include: (1) Queen of the Lakes Cruises, (2) Lyndale Park, (3) Minnehaha Park, (4) Eloise Butler Wildflower Garden and Bird Sanctuary, (5) Minneapolis Planetarium, (6) Hubert Humphrey Metrodome, (7) Skiing-Buck Hill, Hyland Hills, (8) Walker Art Center, (9) Minneapolis Institute of Art, (10) Guthrie Theatre, (11) Hennepin History Museum, (12) Minnesota Transportation Museum, (13) Professional Sports: Basketball - Twins, Football - Vikings, Basketball - Timber Wolves. ANNUAL EVENTS: Minneapolis Aquatennial. SEASONAL EVENTS: (1) Showboat, (2) Somerfest, (3) Minnesota Orchestra, (4) University Theatre.

POPULATION: 362,696 PERSONS—W = 288,967, B = 47,948, AI/E/A = 12,335, C = 157,F = 79, M = 4,295, F = 729

POPULATION GROWTH: -2.2%

AGE OF POPULATION: (21-24) = 8.4%, (25-34) = 23.3%, (35-44) = 15.8%, (45-54) = 7.7%, (55-64) = 6.2%, (65-74) = 6.3%, (75 AND OVER) = 6.6%

HOUSING COST: OWNING = $71,700   RENTAL = $424

COMMUNITY HOSPITALS: 8 = 4,461 BEDS

CLIMATE: JAN—AVG. (11.8 DEGREES), JULY—AVG. (73.6 DEGREES), ANNUAL PRECIPITATION (28.32 INCHES)

PER CAPITA INCOME: $14,830

UNEMPLOYMENT RATE: 4.8%

JOB GROWTH SINCE 1980: + 2.9%

COST OF LIVING: 102.3

EDUCATION: UNIVERSITY OF MINNESOTA-TWIN CITIES, MINNEAPOLIS COLLEGE OF ART AND DESIGN

▼ST. PAUL

Gay Civil Rights: Bans discrimination based on sexual orientation in public and private employment, public accommodations, education, housing, credit, and union practices.

What the Locals Say . . .

St. Paul is not as open as its sister city Minneapolis. Although they share the University of Minnesota, there are some differences in the city. Politicians are more conservative in St. Paul. The best places to live are Cathedral Hill and Crocus Hill. There are numerous rainbow flags and bumper stickers, as well as gay and lesbian couples visible in these areas. Grand Avenue is a yuppie liberal area and has many shops that are gay friendly with some being gay owned. St. Paul has some activities of its own that are different from Minneapolis. The Quatrae Foil is a gay and lesbian library. The Rainbow Forum is a political group dedicated to get more gay rights for St. Paul. One of the most popular bars in St. Paul is the "Townhouse" which is a mixed bar. The "Club Metro" is predominately a women's bar.

LOCATION: ST. PAUL IS LOCATED IN EASTERN MINNESOTA WHERE THE WATERS OF THE MISSISSIPPI AND MINNESOTA RIVERS MEET.

GAY/LESBIAN FRIENDLY BUSINESSES: SEE MINNEAPOLIS

GAY/LESBIAN BARS AND RESTAURANTS: 4

GAY/LESBIAN ORGANIZATIONS: SEE MINNEAPOLIS

GAY/LESBIAN RELIGIOUS ORGANIZATIONS, CHURCHES, ETC.: SEE MINNEAPOLIS

GAY/LESBIAN BOOKSTORES: SEE MINNEAPOLIS

GAY/LESBIAN PUBLICATIONS: SEE MINNEAPOLIS

COMPANIES THAT PROHIBIT DISCRIMINATION: SEE GAY CIVIL RIGHTS

INFORMATION NUMBER: 612-871-5559 GAY & LESBIAN HOTLINE

TOTAL CRIMES: 20,382

VIOLENT = (MURDER = 22, RAPE = 242, ROBBERY = 954, ASSAULT = 1,486)

PROPERTY = (BURGLARY = 4,023, LARCENY = 11,329, MOTOR VEHICLE THEFT = 2,326, ARSON = 324)

Things to Do!!!

(1) Landmark Center, (2) Minnesota History Center, (3) The

Science Museum of Minnesota, (4) Minnesota Museum of American Art, (5) Parks- Indian Mounds Park, Town Square Park, Como Park, Ft. Snelling Park. ANNUAL EVENTS: (1) Winter Carnival, (2) Macalester College Scottish County Fair, (3) Minnesota State Fair.

POPULATION: 268,266 PERSONS—W = 223,947, B = 20,083, AI/E/A = 3,697, C = 765, F = 581, M = 8,542, PR = 572

POPULATION GROWTH: - .7%

AGE OF POPULATION: (21-24) = 7.5%, (25-34) = 20.2%, (35-44) = 14.4%, (45-54) = 7.8%, (55-64) = 6.9%, (65-74) = 6.9%, (75 AND OVER) = 6.8%

HOUSING COST: OWNING = $70,900 RENTAL = $424

COMMUNITY HOSPITALS: 5 = 997 BEDS

CLIMATE: JAN—AVG. (11.8 DEGREES), JULY—AVG. (73.6 DEGREES), ANNUAL PRECIPITATION (28.32 INCHES)

PER CAPITA INCOME: $ 13,727

UNEMPLOYMENT RATE: 5.1%

JOB GROWTH SINCE 1980: + 4.4%

COST OF LIVING: N/A

EDUCATION: UNIVERSITY OF MINNESOTA AT TWIN CITY, UNIVERSITY OF ST. THOMAS, COLLEGE OF ST. CATHERINE.

COUNTIES:
HENNEPIN COUNTY

Gay Civil Rights: Bans discrimination based on sexual orientation in public employment.

Cities and Towns Included in Hennepin County:

Bloomington
Brooklyn Center
Brooklyn Park
Crystal
Deephaven/Woodland Edina
South Lake Minnetonka
Golden Valley
Hopkins
Minneapolis
Minnetonka
Mound
New Hope

Orono
Osseo
Plymouth
Richfield
Robbinsdale
St. Anthony
St. Louis Park
Wayzata
Eden Prairie
Maple Grove
St. Bonifacious/Minnetriste
Champlin
Medina
Corcoran
Dayton
Minnetonka Beach
West Hennepin
Long Lake
Spring Lake

MISSISSIPPI

STATE LAWS REGARDING HOMOSEXUALITY:

Heterosexual and homosexual sodomy is illegal and carries a maximum 10 year prison sentence.

CITIES: (60,000 AND UP)

JACKSON

Gay Civil Rights: None

What the Locals Say . . .

Jackson is described as mainly a low key closeted community. It is not uncommon for elected officials to be gay, but be practicing a heterosexual life in public. Gays and lesbians tend to live throughout Jackson. The Mississippi Phoenix Coalition has adopt a friend programs as well as other HIV and AIDS outreach programs. Prime Timers is a group for men over 35. The women's space group is not functioning at this time. The Mississippi Gay and Lesbian Task Force is a political organization that works towards getting pro-gay legislation passed. There is a local PFLAG organization in Jackson. Bars in Jackson are segregated by race. The black bars are "Club Colors," and "Sugar Bakers." The white bars are "Jaded" and "Jacks Construction Site." There are many healthcare workers who are gay and lesbian, so prejudice is at a minimum. The *Mississippi Voice* is a monthly publication. The MCC Rainbow and St. Stevens Community Church are primarily gay and lesbian congregations.

LOCATION: JACKSON IS LOCATED IN CENTRAL MISSISSIPPI ALONG THE BLUFFS WITH THE PEARL RIVER TO THE EAST.

GAY/LESBIAN FRIENDLY BUSINESSES: 3

GAY/LESBIAN BARS AND RESTAURANTS: 4

GAY/LESBIAN ORGANIZATIONS: 10

GAY/LESBIAN RELIGIOUS ORGANIZATIONS, CHURCHES, ETC.: 2

GAY/LESBIAN BOOKSTORES: 0

GAY/LESBIAN PUBLICATIONS: 2

COMPANIES THAT PROHIBIT DISCRIMINATION: N/A

INFORMATION NUMBER: 601-924-3333 COMMUNITY SERVICES

TOTAL CRIMES: 24,968

VIOLENT = (MURDER = 83, RAPE = 173, ROBBERY = 1,505, ASSAULT = 1,019)

PROPERTY = (BURGLARY = 7,071, LARCENY = 11,063, MOTOR VEHICLE THEFT = 4,054, ARSON = N/A)

Things to Do!!!

(1) State Capitol, (2) The Oaks, (3) Manship House, (4) State Historical Museum, (5) Governor's Mansion, (6) Davis Planetarium, (7) Mississippi Museum of Art, (8) Smith Robertson Museum, (9) Museum of Natural Science, (10) Municipal Art Gallery, (11) Mynelle Gardens, (12) Battlefield Park, (13) Mississippi Agricultural & Forestry Museum and National Agricultural Aviation Museum, (14) Mississippi Petrified Forest, (15) Ross R. Barnett Reservoir, (16) Jackson Zoological Park. ANNUAL EVENTS: (1) Dixie National Livestock Show, (2) Mississippi State Horse Show, (3) Mississippi State Fair.

POPULATION: 196,231 PERSONS—W = 85,675, B = 109,620, AI/E/A = 191, C = 255, F = 36, M = 283, PR = 60

POPULATION GROWTH: - 3.3%

AGE OF POPULATION: (21-24) = 6.5%, (25-34) = 17.7%, (35-44) = 14.3%, (45-54) = 8.8%, (55-64) = 7.8%, (65-74) = 6.6%, (75 AND OVER) = 5.0%

HOUSING COST: OWNING = $54,600   RENTAL = $388

COMMUNITY HOSPITALS: 7 = 2,118 BEDS

CLIMATE: JAN—AVG. (44.1 DEGREES), JULY—AVG. (81.5 DEGREES), ANNUAL PRECIPITATION (55.3 INCHES)

PER CAPITA INCOME: $12,216

UNEMPLOYMENT RATE: 6.0%

JOB GROWTH SINCE 1980: - .7%

COST OF LIVING: 95.9

EDUCATION: BETHANY COLLEGE, JACKSON STATE UNIVERSITY

MISSOURI

STATE LAWS REGARDING HOMOSEXUALITY:

Homosexual sodomy is illegal and carries a possible 15 year maximum sentence.

CITIES: (60,000 AND UP)

▼KANSAS CITY

Gay Civil Rights: Bans discrimination based on sexual orientation in public and private employment, housing and union practices.

What the Locals Say . . .

The Kansas City gay and lesbian community is certainly not closeted, although not as open as San Francisco. The largest part of the general population is very laid back. The best place for gay and lesbians to live in K.C. Missouri is Hyde Park. Hyde Park is bounded north by Armour Blvd (35th street), east by Troost, and west by Main and south by 47th Street. This area is comprised of older, larger restored homes. The Hyde Park area is safe and very enjoyable. The Midtown area (also includes Hyde Park) is bounded north by 20th Street, south by 47th Street, east by Troost, west by State Line. Midtown is the largest population area for lesbians and gays in the Kansas City area. An advantage to Midtown is the easy accessibility to both sides of the state line for shopping, sporting and cultural events, and the downtown office area. Brookside is a small community with all the amenities of a large city. Brookside is bounded north by 47th Street, south by 85th Street, east by Rockhill Road, west by State Line. The best places for gays and lesbians to live in Kansas City, Kansas is the Midtown area bounded north by Minnesota, south by I-70, east by 43rd Street, west by State Line. Midtown is made up of older, single and multiple-family, low income homes. This area provides easy access to all metropolitan areas. A growing neighborhood for women called "Womantown" covers a 10 square block area. The Plaza is the worlds oldest shopping center; it is also a place to see and be seen. The affluent and hip shop here. Housing is expensive. The "Classic Cup Cafe" and "The Metroplex" are popular restaurants for gays and lesbians. Political groups include The Human Rights Project which focuses on gay and lesbian rights throughout the state of Missouri. ACT-UP and Gay and Lesbian Alliance against defamation are also local political organizations. There is a Woman Source Sport Group, and a Women's Sport Group of Kansas City, Gay Men's Sport Group, Gay and Lesbian Couples Sport Group, and Passages- a youth sport group. There are numerous additional recreational groups including: Frontrunners/Walkers group, Kansas City Outdoor Club for camping and hiking, Kansas City Gay Rodeo, Kansas City Coed Darts, Different Spokes, Pete's Sunday Bowling League, and a volleyball group. Kansas City also has Gay and Lesbian Parents Coalition, and Gay and Married Men's Association. Musical groups include Heartland Men's Chorus, Misericord, and Pontifical Choir of Kansas City. "This Way Out," "The 10th Voice," "Willow Time," "Aware"and "Gaydar Show" are radio programs for the gay and lesbian community. There is a Men of all Colors group, an Alternative Business Alliance, and an Alternative Professional Together social networking group. "Larry's Cards and Gifts" and "Phoenix Books" are the gay and lesbian bookstores in Kansas City. Some of the most popular men's gay bars are "Cabaret" (drag shows), and "Dixie Bell" (leather and Levi bar). Some of the most popular gay and lesbian bars are "The Edge"- a dance bar which attracts the younger crowd, "The Other Side"- a neighborhood bar which has a predominately male clientele, although some women go, "Tootsies"- a lesbian bar, and "Sidekicks Saloon"- for men. "Jamie's Sports Bar" is a lesbian neighborhood dance bar, "Illusions" is a women's country and western dance bar. The Good Samaritan Organization disperses money to other organizations in the community. The Save Foundation is a home and hospice, and the Heartland AIDS Resource Center provides food and other necessities, sponsors the Condom Crusaders who distribute condoms, and also sponsors the gay Alcoholic Anonymous groups. Some publications are: *Current News* and *News Telegraph*. The following religious groups meet regularly: Presbyterians for Lesbians and Gay Concerns, Affirmations group, GLAD, Kansas City Disciples of Christ, Integrity, Interfaith Coalition, and a Jewish group. There are several Churches in Kansas City that are open and affirming to gays and lesbians including: A.G.A.P.E. of Greater Kansas City Independent Christian Church, United Methodist, Abiding Peace Lutheran Church, Grace & Holy Trinity Cathedral, Gentle Souls MCC, MCC Kansas City, MCC Johnson County.

LOCATION: KANSAS CITY IS LOCATED IN THE WESTERN REGION OF MISSOURI ALONGSIDE THE KANSAS BORDER.

GAY/LESBIAN FRIENDLY BUSINESSES: 100 +

GAY/LESBIAN BARS AND RESTAURANTS: 15

GAY/LESBIAN ORGANIZATIONS: 30

GAY/LESBIAN RELIGIOUS ORGANIZATIONS, CHURCHES, ETC.: 13

GAY/LESBIAN BOOKSTORES: 2

GAY/LESBIAN PUBLICATIONS: 1

COMPANIES THAT PROHIBIT DISCRIMINATION: SEE STATE LAW AND GAY CIVIL RIGHTS

INFORMATION NUMBER: 816-931-4470 GAY TALK

TOTAL CRIMES: 55,165

VIOLENT = (MURDER = 153, RAPE = 515 ROBBERY = 3,891, ASSAULT = 6,402)

PROPERTY = (BURGLARY = 12,106, LARCENY = 23,611, MOTOR VEHICLE THEFT = 8,487, ARSON = 527)

Things to Do!!!

(1) Kansas City Art Institute, (2) Country Club Plaza, (3) Worlds of Fun, (4) Oceans of Fun, (5) Jesse James Bank Museum, (6) Benjamin Ranch, (7) Board of Trade, (8) Westport Square, (9) Kansas City Museum, (10) Nelson-Atkins Museum of Art, (11) John Wornall House Museum, (12) Liberty Memorial Museum, (13) Government Buildings, (14) Antiques and Art Center, (15) Union Cemetery, (16) City Market, (17) Kansas City Zoo, (18) Crown Center, (19) Toy & Miniature Museum. ANNUAL EVENTS: (1) St. Patrick's Day Parade, (2) Kansas City Rodeo, (3) Kansas City Jazz Festival, (4) American Royal Livestock, Horse Show and Rodeo. SEASONAL EVENTS: (1) Missouri Repertory Theatre, (2) Lyric Opera, (3) Kansas City Symphony, (4) Coterie Children's Theater, (5) Professional Sports: Royals (baseball), Chiefs (NFL football), Comets (soccer).

POPULATION: 431,553 PERSONS—W = 290,572, B = 128,768, AI/E/A = 2,144, C = 673, F = 837, M = 13,306, PR ♣ 448

POPULATION GROWTH: - 3.7%

AGE OF POPULATION: (21-24) = 6.0%, (25-34) = 19.4%, (35-44) = 14.6%, (45-54) = 9.6%, (55-64) = 8.6%, (65-74) = 7.3%, (75 AND OVER) = 5.6%

HOUSING COST: OWNING = $56,100   RENTAL = $404

COMMUNITY HOSPITALS: 12 = 3,149 BEDS

CLIMATE: JAN—AVG. (25.7 DEGREES), JULY—AVG. (78.5 DEGREES), ANNUAL PRECIPITATION (37.62 INCHES)

PER CAPITA INCOME: $13,799

UNEMPLOYMENT RATE: 6.9%

JOB GROWTH SINCE 1980: + 1.4%

COST OF LIVING: 97.1

EDUCATION: UNIVERSITY OF MISSOURI-KANSAS CITY, ROCKHURST COLLEGE

▼ST. LOUIS

Gay Civil Rights: Bans discrimination based on sexual orientation in public and private employment, public accommodations, education, housing and credit.

What the Locals Say . . .

St. Louis is open for the Midwest. Due to crime, there seems to be a lot of people moving out of the county. St. Louis for the most part is conservative and Catholic. The Central West End is 5-10 minutes from downtown and has the greatest concentration of gays and lesbians. The historic neighborhoods of Lafayette Square and Tower Grove have a high number of gay and lesbian residents. Forest Park is very popular for rollerblading and cycling on the bike path. The Botanical Gardens are a very popular place as well. St. Louis has a men's and women's chorus, opera theatre, and symphony. There is a bowling league, dart league, softball league and a St. Louis Lesbian Gay Outdoor Club. "Our World" is a bookstore which is the core of the community. "Friends & Luvers" is gay and lesbian variety show in St. Louis. The "Blue Moon Coffee House" and "Mokabe's Coffee House" are popular with gays and lesbians. There are numerous support groups in St. Louis. The Gateway Men's Chorus, Codependents Anonymous, AA groups, Women Who Love Women, The Lesbian Avengers, FLAG, People of All Colors Group and Alive and Living Well are some of the groups. The Gateway Business and Professional Alliance is an organization of gay, lesbian and gay friendly businesses. "Meet Me in St. Louis" is an alternative introduction service. There is a Gay Lesbian & Straight Teachers Network and the Privacy Rights Education Project. St. Louis is a little bit cliquish, in that there are several small groups that frequently get together, but are slow to let anyone new into their group. The bar scene is pretty much mixed. "Magnolias'" is a two story building with a dance floor downstairs. There are drag shows and also a cabaret. "Little Bit of Everything" is a section where the leather people hang out. "The Complex" is just that - a complex with several bars and restaurants. The health care community responds very well to the gay and lesbian community. "Effort for AIDS" and "Food Outreach" are two very successful programs. "Food Outreach" prepares food on Saturdays and delivers it throughout the week. *The Lesbian & Gay Telegraph News* is published twice a month, *Les Talk* is published monthly. There are two gay and lesbian radio shows: "Coming Out of Hiding" which consists of interviews and conversations and "Out and Open," a talk show for lesbians and gays and family and friends. "Aware" is a HIV/AIDS talk show which addresses medical, legal and social issues. The religious groups: Dignity, and Unitarian Universalists for Lesbian and Gay Concerns welcomes gays and lesbians. The MCC of Living Faith Bethel, Lutheran Church, 1st Unitarian, MCC of Greater St. Louis, AGAPE Church of St. Louis, and UCC churches are very open to the gay and lesbian community. The UCC sponsors a theatre group.

LOCATION: ST. LOUIS IS LOCATED NEAR THE CONFLUENCE OF THE MISSOURI AND MISSISSIPPI RIVERS IN EASTERN MISSOURI.

GAY LESBIAN FRIENDLY BUSINESSES: 33

GAY/LESBIAN BARS AND RESTAURANTS: 16

GAY/LESBIAN ORGANIZATIONS: 25

GAY/LESBIAN RELIGIOUS ORGANIZATIONS, CHURCHES, ETC.: 8

GAY/LESBIAN BOOKSTORES: 1

GAY/LESBIAN PUBLICATIONS: 2

COMPANIES THAT PROHIBIT DISCRIMINATION: SEE STATE LAW AND GAY CIVIL RIGHTS

INFORMATION NUMBER: 314-367-0084 CHALLENGE METRO GAY AND LESBIAN HOTLINE

TOTAL CRIMES: 64,438

VIOLENT = (MURDER = 267, RAPE = 319, ROBBERY = 6,223, ASSAULT = 8,189)

PROPERTY = (BURGLARY = 12,400, LARCENY = 26,975, MOTOR VEHICLE THEFT = 10,065, ARSON = 806)

Things to Do!!!

(1) National Bowling Hall of Fame and Museum, (2) Grants Farm, (3) Missouri Botanical Garden, (4) The Magic House, (5) Jefferson Barracks Historical Park, (6) Forest Park—(St. Louis Science Center, Missouri Historical Society, St. Louis Zoological Park, The St. Louis Art Museum, Jewel Box Floral Conservatory, Steinberg Memorial Skating Rink), (7) Riverfront Area (Eads Bridge, Riverboat President, Old Courthouse, American Emporium, Eugene Field House and Toy Museum, River Excursions, Laclede's Landing, Jefferson National Expansion Memorial, Delta and Mississippi Queen, Goldenrod Showboat, Old Cathedral, St. Louis Hall of Fame), (8) Christ Church Cathedral, (9) St. Louis Cathedral, (10) Campbell House Museum, (11) Mercantile Money Museum, (12) Powell Symphony Hall, (13) Aloe Plaza, (14) National Museum of Transport, (15) The Dog Museum, (16) Craft Alliance Gallery, (17) Purina Farms, (18) Florisant, (19) Hidden Valley Ski Area, (20) Six Flags Over Mid-America, (21) County Parks (Edgar M. Queeny Park, Lone Elk Park, Laumeier Sculpture Park), (22) Mastodon State Park, (23) Dr. Edmund A. Babler Memorial State Park, (24) Anheuser-Busch, Inc. ANNUAL EVENTS: (1) National Classic Jazz and Ragtime Festival, (2) VP Fair, Strassenfest, (3) Hot Air Balloon Race. SEASONAL EVENTS: (1) Saint Louis Symphony Orchestra, (2) Repertory Theatre of St. Louis, (3) Muny Opera, (4) Theatre Project Company, (5) Professional Sports: Cardinals (baseball), Blues (hockey).

POPULATION: 383,733 PERSONS—W = 202,085, B = 188,408, AI/E/A = 950, C = 785, F = 403, M = 2,442, PR = 327

POPULATION GROWTH: -15.3%

AGE OF POPULATION: (21-24) = 6.1%, (25-34) = 18.3%, (35-44) = 12.8%, (45-54) = 8.0%, (55-64) = 8.5%, (65-74) = 8.4%, (75 AND OVER) = 8.2%

HOUSING COST: OWNING = $50,700   RENTAL = $342

COMMUNITY HOSPITALS: 21 = 7,814 BEDS

CLIMATE: JAN—AVG. (28.4 DEGREES), JULY—AVG. (78.4 DEGREES), ANNUAL PRECIPITATION (37.86 INCHES)

PER CAPITA INCOME: $10,798

UNEMPLOYMENT RATE: 9.0%

JOB GROWTH SINCE 1980: -6.9%

COST OF LIVING: 98.2

EDUCATION: ST. LOUIS UNIVERSITY, WASHINGTON UNIVERSITY, UNIVERSITY OF MISSOURI-ST. LOUIS.

MONTANA

STATE LAWS REGARDING HOMOSEXUALITY:

Homosexual sodomy is illegal and punishable by up to ten years in prison.

CITIES: (60,000 AND UP)
MISSOULA

Gay Civil Rights: None

What the Locals Say . . .

The Missoula gay community is fairly open. The city is a gay-friendly, very liberal, and very progressive. Both the mayor and the city council are supportive. The police, at the top, are also supportive; however, they may be less so out in the field. The state is experiencing a ten percent influx of people yearly, mostly from California and mostly from white flight. The second and third generation Montanans are not too happy about all these new people coming in. There are no particular neighborhoods which are better to live for gays. PRIDE!, the state's Gay and Lesbian organization meets monthly. It is working very hard for removal of the state's Deviate Sexual Conduct Statute. PRIDE! fully expects it to be removed in 1995. There is a Lambda Alliance at the University of Montana which sponsors a Gay/Lesbian Support Group and a Gay Therapy Group. "Am-Vets" serving both gays and lesbians is the one, mostly gay, bar in town. The Catalyst is a popular, gay friendly, downtown coffeehouse spot. The two bookstores having a good selection of gay/lesbian books are: "Freddy's Feed and Read" and "Fact and Fiction." *Pride Nooz,* a newspaper, published quarterly in Helena, Montana, serves the whole state and keeps abreast of Missoula happenings. The University Congregational Church is gay friendly and supportive of our community.

LOCATION: MISSOULA IS LOCATED IN WESTERN MONTANA.

GAY/LESBIAN FRIENDLY BUSINESSES: 4

GAY/LESBIAN BARS AND RESTAURANTS: 1

GAY/LESBIAN ORGANIZATIONS: 3

GAY/LESBIAN RELIGIOUS ORGANIZATIONS, CHURCHES, ETC.: 1

GAY/LESBIAN BOOKSTORES: 2

GAY/LESBIAN PUBLICATIONS: 1

COMPANIES THAT PROHIBIT DISCRIMINATION: U. F. WEST, UNIVERSITY OF MONTANA, MONTANA EDUCATION ASSOCIATION, AND THE MONTANA A.F.C.I.O.

INFORMATION NUMBER: LAMBDA, 406-243-4153 OR PRIDE NOOZ , 406-442-9322

TOTAL CRIMES: 3,135

VIOLENT = (MURDER = 1 , RAPE = 14, ROBBERY = 22 , ASSAULT = 35)

PROPERTY = (BURGLARY = 274, LARCENY = 2,645, MOTOR VEHICLE THEFT = 144, ARSON = N/A)

Things to Do!!!

Missoula is surrounded by Lolo National Forest. Other points of interest include: (1) Paxson Paintings, (2) Missoula Public Library, (3) Historical Museum at Fort Missoula, (4) Aerial Fire Depot. ANNUAL EVENTS: (1) International Wildlife Film Festival, (2) Western Montana Quarter Horse Show, (3) Western Montana Fair.

POPULATION: 44,522 - W = 40,983, B = 148, AI/E/A = 1,045, C = 137, F = 37, M = 315, PR = 25

POPULATION GROWTH: +33.5%

AGE OF POPULATION: (21-24) = 9.4%, (25-34) = 17.6%, (35-44) = 16.0%, (45-54) = 8.2%, (55-64) = 6.3%, (65-74) = 6.3%, (75 AND OVER) = 6.0%

HOUSING COST: OWNING = $64,500   RENTAL = $324

COMMUNITY HOSPITALS: 2 = 336 BEDS

CLIMATE: JAN—AVG. (22.7 DEGREES), JULY—AVG. (66.8 DEGREES), ANNUAL PRECIPITATION (13.46 INCHES)

PER CAPITA INCOME: $11,759

UNEMPLOYMENT RATE: 6.4%

JOB GROWTH SINCE 1980: +33.8%

COST OF LIVING: 103.5

EDUCATION: UNIVERSITY OF MONTANA

NEBRASKA

STATE LAWS REGARDING HOMOSEXUALITY:

In 1977, sodomy laws were repealed.

CITIES: (60,000 AND UP)

LINCOLN

Gay Civil Rights: None

What the Locals Say . . .

Lincoln's gay and lesbian community is a mixture of being out and being closeted. The University of Nebraska is pretty open. The politicians in general are pro-gay or tolerant at the least. Lincoln does not have an area where a lot of gays and lesbians live. However, close to downtown (near south) has quite a large population of yuppies and queens. Lincoln Citizens for Equal Protection is a local political group. There are informal sport groups (bowling, softball, and golf) in Omaha that family members can participate in. There is a lesbian discussion group and a gay discussion group, a FLAG group, a group for older gay people and a Gay and Lesbian Resource Center. The "Mill" in downtown, and "The Coffeehouse" are gay-friendly coffeehouses. "La Cafe Shakes" is a coffeehouse that is open later, and "Kind of Coffee" is a coffee/sandwich place that caters to the under-21 crowd. The restaurant "Crain River" is gay-friendly. "Q" is a predominately gay and lesbian bar, but sometimes there are some straight people there. "Panic" is the oldest bar in town and draws both gays and lesbians. The Nebraska AIDS Project branch out of Omaha has case workers and offers other services in Lincoln. *The New Voice* out of Omaha is the gay and lesbian publication. The MCC in Omaha and the Unitarian Church in Omaha/Lincoln welcomes gays and lesbians.

LOCATION: LINCOLN IS LOCATED IN SOUTHEASTERN NEBRASKA.

GAY/LESBIAN FRIENDLY BUSINESSES: 5

GAY/LESBIAN BARS AND RESTAURANTS: 3

GAY/LESBIAN ORGANIZATIONS: 5

GAY/LESBIAN RELIGIOUS ORGANIZATIONS, CHURCHES, ETC.: 2

GAY/LESBIAN BOOKSTORES: 1

GAY/LESBIAN PUBLICATIONS: 1

COMPANIES THAT PROHIBIT DISCRIMINATION: N/A

INFORMATION NUMBER: 402-472-5644 GAY/LESBIAN RESOURCE CENTER

TOTAL CRIMES: 13,561

VIOLENT = (MURDER = 4, RAPE = 83, ROBBERY = 127, ASSAULT = 911)

PROPERTY = (BURGLARY = 1,984, LARCENY = 10,023, MOTOR VEHICLE THEFT = 429, ARSON = 76)

Things to Do!!!

Many of the activities are centered around state government and the University of Nebraska. Specific points of interest include: (1) State Capital, (2) Museum of Nebraska, (3) National Museum of Roller Skating, (4) Numerous Parks- Pawnee Lake State Recreational Area, Conestoga Lake State Recreational Area, Branches Oak Lake State Recreational Area, Bluestem Lake State Recreation Area. Mahoney State Park.

POPULATION: 197,488 - W = 181,320, B = 4,515, AI/E/A = 1,150, C = 772, F = 114, M = 2,666, PR = 141

POPULATION GROWTH: +14.9%

AGE OF POPULATION: (21-24) = 9.0%, (25-34) = 18.8%, (35-44) = 15.0%, (45-54) = 8.4%, (55-64) = 7.0%, (65-74) = 5.9%, (75 AND OVER) = 5.1%

HOUSING COST: OWNING = $61,700   RENTAL = $379

COMMUNITY HOSPITALS: 3 = 778 BEDS

CLIMATE: JAN—AVG. (21.3 DEGREES), JULY—AVG. (78.2 DEGREES), ANNUAL PRECIPITATION (28.26 INCHES)

PER CAPITA INCOME: $13,720

UNEMPLOYMENT RATE: 2.3%

JOB GROWTH SINCE 1980: +16.4%

COST OF LIVING: 90.2

EDUCATION: UNIVERSITY OF NEBRASKA

OMAHA

Gay Civil Rights: None

What the Locals Say . . .

The gay and lesbian community in Omaha is mixed with some that are very open and some that are mostly closeted and there is everything in between. The environment over-all is "don't ask, don't tell." The politicians, for the most part, are tolerant of gays and lesbians. The Downtown/Mutual area where there are primarily apartments and businesses has a high concentration of gays and lesbians. Many gays and lesbians also live in the Cathedral area which is primarily residential. "Downtown Ground" is a popular coffeehouse. The bookstore,"New Realities," has a good section of gay and lesbian titles. Omaha has an annual Pride Celebration that includes a parade, a festival and a picnic. There are numerous groups in Omaha including, a P-FLAG group, Gay and Lesbian Parents Group, Onyx Images,

Achieving New Gay/Lesbian Endeavors (ANGLE), Prime Timers, Imperial Court of Nebraska and Women of the Plains. ANGLE has a resource guide that lists gay businesses as well as realtors, doctors, lawyers and other gay friendly professionals. Omaha also has an Alcoholics Anonymous group for gay men and lesbians, and a youth support group and a women's support group. Citizens for Equal Protection is a political action group and so is The Coalition For Gay and Lesbian Civil Rights. Frontrunners and Walkers, and River City Mixed Bowling League, River City Mixed Chorus are some of the recreational organizations in Omaha. " D.C.'s" and "Gilligan's Pub" are both mixed gay and lesbian bars. The Nebraska AIDS Project offers various services and the Omaha Meatpackers is an AIDS fund raising organization. *The New Voice* is a regional gay and lesbian publication that comes out monthly. Most organizations have their own newsletter as well. There are several churches and religious organizations that are open and affirming to gays and lesbians including the MCC of Omaha, Lutherans Concerned, Gay Lesbian & Affirming Disciples, Presbyterians for Lesbian and Gay Concerns and 7th Day Adventist Kinship Inc.

LOCATION: OMAHA IS LOCATED IN SOUTHEASTERN NEBRASKA, NORTH OF LINCOLN.

GAY/LESBIAN FRIENDLY BUSINESSES: 50 +

GAY/LESBIAN BARS AND RESTAURANTS: 6

GAY/LESBIAN ORGANIZATIONS: 8

GAY/LESBIAN RELIGIOUS ORGANIZATIONS, CHURCHES, ETC.: 9

GAY/LESBIAN BOOKSTORES: 1

GAY/LESBIAN PUBLICATIONS: 2

COMPANIES THAT PROHIBIT DISCRIMINATION: UNIVERSITY OF NEBRASKA AT OMAHA, NORTHWEST BANK (IS DEVELOPING ONE), 1ST NATIONAL BANK, AND US WEST HAS EMPLOYEE GROUP.

INFORMATION NUMBER: 402-558-5303 ANGLE

TOTAL CRIMES: N/A

VIOLENT = N/A

PROPERTY = N/A

Things to Do!!!

There are a variety of recreational areas and activities including: Fontenelle Forest Nature Center, Heartland Park, Peony Park, Louisville State Recreation Area, Two Rivers State Recreation Area, Schramm Park State Recreation Area, Platte River State Park, Henry Doorly Zoo. Other areas of interest include: (1) Boys Town, (2) Joslyn Art Museum, (3) Great Plains Black Museum, (4) Omaha Children's Museum, (5) Union Pacific Historical Museum, (6) Western Hermitage Museum, (7) Strategic Air Command Museum, (8) Gerald Ford Birth site. ANNUAL EVENTS: (1) NCAA College Baseball

World Series, (2) World Championship Rodeo, (3) River City Roundup, (4) Christmas at Union Station.

POPULATION: 339,671 PERSONS—W = 281,603, B = 43,989, AI/E/A/ = 2,274, C = 553, F = 410, M = 8,222, PR = 326

POPULATION GROWTH: +8.2%

AGE OF POPULATION: (21-24) = 6.7%, (25-34) = 18.3%, (35-44) = 14.1%, (45-54) = 9.5%, (55-64) = 8.6%, (65-74) = 7.3%, (75 AND OVER) = 5.6%

HOUSING COST: OWNING = $54,600   RENTAL = $386

COMMUNITY HOSPITALS: 9 = 2,889 BEDS

CLIMATE: JAN—AVG. (21.1 DEGREES), JULY—AVG. (76.9 DEGREES), ANNUAL PRECIPITATION (29.86 INCHES)

PER CAPITA INCOME: $13,957

UNEMPLOYMENT RATE: 3.2%

JOB GROWTH SINCE 1980: + 14.9%

COST OF LIVING: 92.2

EDUCATION: UNIVERSITY OF NEBRASKA AT OMAHA

NEVADA

STATE LAWS REGARDING HOMOSEXUALITY:

In 1993, all sodomy laws were repealed. Also the state passed a hate crimes law that includes sexual orientation.

CITIES: (60,000 AND UP)

LAS VEGAS

Gay Civil Rights: None

What the Locals Say . . .

Las Vegas has a large gay population but most gay people are still in the closet. The government tends to be homophobic which intensifies everyone's fears about coming out of the closet. The cosmopolitan attitude on the casino strip ends once you leave the strip. Interestingly, though, the sheriff is against gay discrimination and there are some openly gay police officers. There is no particular place where gays and lesbians live, although, Green Valley within the boundaries of Henderson, NV. seems to be attracting gays. The Center, the gay and lesbian community center, is funded by private funds. The Center's meetings and events include six or seven women's groups, several men's groups, and a Gay Pride Festival on Memorial Day Weekend which attracts approximately 3,000 people. "Faces" is the only lesbian bar. There are about ten or so men's bars with "Gypsy's" and "Angles" being a couple of popular ones. "Backstreet" is mixed. Health care in the area is excellent. Care is given regardless of sexual orientation. Aid for AIDS/Nevada (AFAN) provides food, housing and medical care for PWAs. The Las Vegas Bugle is published monthly. Churches and religious organizations are: MCC, Dignity Las Vegas, Episcopal Church, Unitarian Church, Gay Mormons, and Agape Love Center.

LOCATION: LAS VEGAS IS LOCATED ON A PLAIN ENCIRCLED BY DISTANT MOUNTAINS WITH THE DESERT ON THE OUTSKIRTS OF TOWN.

GAY/LESBIAN FRIENDLY BUSINESSES: 10

GAY/LESBIAN BARS AND RESTAURANTS: 12

GAY/LESBIAN ORGANIZATIONS: 18

GAY/LESBIAN RELIGIOUS ORGANIZATIONS, CHURCHES, ETC.: 6

GAY/LESBIAN BOOKSTORES: 1

GAY/LESBIAN PUBLICATIONS: 1

COMPANIES THAT PROHIBIT DISCRIMINATION: N/A

INFORMATION NUMBER: 702-733-9990 THE COMMUNITY CENTER SWITCHBOARD

TOTAL CRIMES: 48,365

VIOLENT = (MURDER = 91, RAPE = 435, ROBBERY = 3,572, ASSAULT = 3,183)

PROPERTY = (BURGLARY = 9,783, LARCENY = 23,855, MOTOR VEHICLE THEFT = 7,446, ARSON = 459)

Things to Do!!!

Las Vegas is famous for the glittering gambling casinos, nightclubs and plush hotels, although it also offers tennis, bowling, racquetball, water skiing, fishing, hunting, golf, hiking and riding trails. Specific points of interest include: (1) The Strip, (2) Convention Center, (3) Las Vegas Natural History Museum, (4) Nevada State Historical Society, (5) Guiness World of Records Museum, (6) Liberace Museum, (7) Wet 'n Wild, (8) Red Canyon National Conservation Area, (9) Mt. Charleston Area, (10) Floyd Lamb State Park, (11) Valley of Fire State Park, (12) Southern Nevada Zoological Park. (13) Las Vegas Art Museum . ANNUAL EVENTS: (1) Helldorado Festival, (2) National Finals Rodeo.

POPULATION: 295,516 PERSONS—W = 202,549, B = 29,529, AI/E/A = 2,282, C = 1,647, F = 3,247, M = 22,167, PR = 1,162

POPULATION GROWTH: + 79.5%

AGE OF POPULATION: (21-24) = 6.2%, (25-34) = 19.6%, (35-44) = 15.4%, (45-54) = 10.7%, (55-64) = 8.9%, (65-74) = 6.9%, (75 AND OVER) = 3.4%

HOUSING COST: OWNING = $89,200 RENTAL = $490

COMMUNITY HOSPITALS: 5 = 1,776 BEDS

CLIMATE: JAN—AVG. (45.5 DEGREES), JULY—AVG. (91.1 DEGREES), ANNUAL PRECIPITATION (4.13 INCHES)

PER CAPITA INCOME: $14,737

UNEMPLOYMENT RATE: 6.1%

JOB GROWTH SINCE 1980: + 61.4%

COST OF LIVING: 103.7

EDUCATION: UNIVERSITY OF NEVADA AT LAS VEGAS

NEW HAMPSHIRE

STATE LAWS REGARDING HOMOSEXUALITY:

In 1975, Governor Meldrim Thompson signed into law a bill that reformed the state's rape statute. Inadvertently, the bill also included a repeal of the sodomy law. There was an uproar, although the bill was never appealed. In 1987, Governor John Sununu signed a bill prohibiting lesbian and gay men from becoming foster or adoptive parents. New Hampshire does have a hate crimes law that includes crimes based on sexual orientation.

CITIES: (60,000 AND UP)

PORTSMOUTH

Gay Civil Rights: None

What the Locals Say . . .

Portsmouth is very liberal and gay friendly. There is also a certain amount of openness throughout the gay/lesbian community. The younger gays tend to be more "Out," and some of them would certainly feel comfortable holding hands in public. The more mature ones tend to be a little more closed. New Hampshire has a state hate crimes law which includes sexual orientation. Portsmouth is an "Artsy" community and you would feel quite safe and comfortable living in any neighborhood. Ogunquit, Maine, an "artsy" resort area with a large gay/lesbian population, is only 10 minutes from Portsmouth. Groups in the area are: Seacoast Gay Men; Out and About, a weekly social/support group for Lesbians; and AIDS Response of the Seacoast. "Members" is a mixed bar and "Desert Hearts" is for women. Health care is good. Parkland Hospital has AIDS staff. There are no local publications. Gay friendly churches are the Unitarian Universalist and the Congregational Church. The Unitarian Universalist church hosts gay events and sponsors fundraisers.

LOCATION: PORTSMOUTH IS LOCATED IN SOUTHEASTERN NEW HAMPSHIRE, ON THE ATLANTIC COAST.

GAY/LESBIAN FRIENDLY BUSINESSES: 5

GAY/LESBIAN BARS AND RESTAURANTS: 2

GAY/LESBIAN ORGANIZATIONS: 3

GAY/LESBIAN RELIGIOUS ORGANIZATIONS, CHURCHES, ETC.: 4

GAY/LESBIAN BOOKSTORES: 1

GAY/LESBIAN PUBLICATIONS: 0

COMPANIES THAT PROHIBIT DISCRIMINATION: BLUE CROSS BLUE SHIELD AND UNUM

INFORMATION NUMBER: 603-224-1686 GAY INFO LINE OF NEW HAMPSHIRE

TOTAL CRIMES: 1,021

VIOLENT = (MURDER = 0, RAPE = 31, ROBBERY = 14, ASSAULT = 34)

PROPERTY = (BURGLARY = 171, LARCENY = 701, MOTOR VEHICLE THEFT = 70, ARSON = 9)

Things to Do!!!

(1) Portsmouth Trail, (2) Fort Constitution, (3) Fort Stark State Historic Site, (4) Old Harbor Area, (5) Strawberry Bank Museum, (6) Portsmouth Harbor Cruises. ANNUAL EVENTS: Portsmouth Fair Festival.

POPULATION: 25,925—W = 24,014, B = 1,193, AI/E/A = 71, C = 71, F = 87, M = 189, PR = 151

POPULATION GROWTH: -21.1%

AGE OF POPULATION: (21-24) = 8.4%, (25-34) = 23.8%, (35-44) = 14.6%, (45-54) = 7.9%, (55-64) = 7.2%, (65-74) = 6.4%, (75 AND OVER) = 5.7%

HOUSING COST: OWNING = $137,600   RENTAL = $553

COMMUNITY HOSPITALS: 1 = 114 BEDS

CLIMATE: JAN—AVG. (22.2 DEGREES), JULY—AVG. (69.8 DEGREES), ANNUAL PRECIPITATION (42.18 INCHES)

PER CAPITA INCOME: $15,557

UNEMPLOYMENT RATE: 5.7%

JOB GROWTH SINCE 1980: + 10.0%

COST OF LIVING: N/A

EDUCATION: UNIVERSITY OF NEW HAMPSHIRE

NEW JERSEY

STATE LAWS REGARDING HOMOSEXUALITY:

In 1978, sodomy laws were repealed in New Jersey. In 1992, Governor James Florio signed a bill banning discrimination based on sexual orientation in housing, employment, public accommodations, credit, and public contracts.

TOWNS (5,000—60,000)

▼ASBURY PARK

Gay Civil Rights: Bans discrimination based on sexual orientation in housing, employment, public accommodations, credit and public contracts.

What the Locals Say . . .

Asbury Park has a very large and open gay community. Both the local police and city government are gay friendly and supportive. The City Council has three gay members and there is also a gay judge. Ocean Grove, located one half mile away, is filled with gays. Jersey Shore Gay & Lesbian Community Center and Pride Store offers a myriad of groups and activities for the gay community. It holds open Board meetings every third Monday and Social and Sober dances with a DJ every third Friday. The NEW Group, is a community oriented social group. Jersey Pride, Inc. (JPI), the independent, all volunteer, non-profit, organization produces the annual Gay Pride Celebration in Asbury Park. They also host fundraisers like tea-dances, Spring Brunches, and Casino Nights. The Center, an all volunteer AIDS service organization, sponsors the Annual AIDS Walk. Other groups in the area are: PFLAG, Jersey Shore Professional Network, and the Gay Officers League. The community is also in the process of establishing a Gay Business Guild. "Down The Street" is a men's dance bar. "M. & K," and "Bond Street Bar" are both women's bars. Health care is excellent. Jersey Shore Medical Center is very much oriented toward addressing gay needs. *Network* published in New Brunswick covers the Asbury Park area. Also, The New Group, puts out a newsletter called *G.O.A.L.S.. News Jersey*, out of New Brunswick also covers the Asbury Park area.

LOCATION: ASBURY PARK IS LOCATED ON THE SHORES OF THE ATLANTIC OCEAN.

GAY/LESBIAN FRIENDLY BUSINESSES: 5

GAY/LESBIAN BARS AND RESTAURANTS: 4

GAY/LESBIAN ORGANIZATIONS: 8

GAY/LESBIAN RELIGIOUS ORGANIZATIONS, CHURCHES, ETC.: 5

GAY/LESBIAN BOOKSTORES: 0

GAY/LESBIAN PUBLICATIONS: 3

COMPANIES THAT PROHIBIT DISCRIMINATION: A. T. & T., SEE STATE LAW AND GAY CIVIL RIGHTS

INFORMATION NUMBER: 908-774-1809, JERSEY SHORE GAY & LESBIAN COMMUNITY CENTER.

TOTAL CRIMES: 1,470

VIOLENT = (MURDER = 2, RAPE = 19, ROBBERY = 150, ASSAULT = 151)

PROPERTY = (BURGLARY = 221, LARCENY = 786, MOTOR VEHICLE THEFT = 141, ARSON = 2)

Things to Do!!!

(1) Atlantic Ocean and shoreline, (2) Long Branch Historical Museum, ANNUAL EVENTS: Jazz Fest

POPULATION: 16,799 PERSONS—W = 5,950, B = 9,977, AI/E/A = 49, A/P/I = 123, H = 1,533

POPULATION GROWTH: N/A

AGE OF POPULATION: (21-24) = 1,036, (25-34) = 5,258, (35-44) = 1,430, (45-54) = 638, (55-64) = 669, (65-74) = 2,701, (75 AND OVER) = 1,723

HOUSING COST: OWNING = $102,900   RENTAL = $502

COMMUNITY HOSPITALS: N/A

CLIMATE: N/A

PER CAPITA INCOME: N/A

UNEMPLOYMENT RATE: N/A

JOB GROWTH SINCE 1980: N/A

COST OF LIVING: N/A

EDUCATION: NONE

▼NEW BRUNSWICK

Gay Civil Rights: Bans discrimination based on sexual orientation in housing, employment, public accommodations, credit and public contracts.

What the Locals Say . . .

New Brunswick has a large younger population. The city government and police seem to have no adverse reaction to gays; and, the police, during their training, take a course which includes sensitivity training for gay/lesbian issues. Some of the younger gays do feel perfectly comfortable walking down the street holding hands. Since Rutgers University is located in New Brunswick, it is estimated that probably one third of the population is students. The population is very heterogeneous with many students being Hispanic and Black.

The Highland Park area is a good area for gays and lesbians; although, you could be very comfortable and safe living almost anywhere in New Brunswick. The New Brunswick Gay/Lesbian community is progressive and active. The Pride Center, the local gay/lesbian community center, is home to many diverse groups and activities all established to enrich the lives of the gay/lesbian community. Groups include: the Lesbian Avengers, Overeaters Anonymous, Bisexual Network of New Jersey, Men's Support Group, Womyn's Support Group, Mixed Support Group, Men's Coming out Group, Women's Movie Night, Log Cabin Club of Central New Jersey, Gay Roller Skating, Lesbian, Gay, and Bisexual Caucus, Lesbian Mother's Support Group, S.A.G.E. Group, P-FLAG Groups, AIDS Walk, Brunches, Casino Nights, G/L/B Writers Group, New Jersey Education Association Gay and Lesbian Caucus, Lesbians Considering Motherhood Group, Non-Monogamy Discussion Group, and Gay Square Dancing. Other area groups are: Gallivanting, a social group; Rainbow Place, also a social group with coffee hours, hiking trips etc.; a Lambda organization; and Lesbians and Gay Men of New Brunswick. There is an annual Pride Parade, Rally and Festival. Rutgers has a GALA (alums), Rutgers BiGLARU, and Rutgers G/L/B Hotline. "The Den" is a mixed night club/bar meeting place. It has four bars, huge dance floor, and intimate clean space. "The Coliseum" and the "Cactus Club" are also in the area. "The Coliseum" sometimes holds T-Dances benefiting The Pride Center. Health Care is good. The AIDS Network provides support and practical assistance to persons affected with HIV. The Hyacinth Foundation is a statewide AIDS referral service with an office in New Brunswick. They provide a Hotline, Support Group, Counseling Buddies, Testing Sites, Meals Program, and Direct Emergency Service providing emergency rent for those in need They also have a recreational program which provides free tickets to area events. Chapter One Books is a great gay/lesbian bookstore. Publications include the *News Jersey*, put out monthly by the NJLGC/PLF. The Lesbians and Gay Men of New Brunswick also send out a newsletter and there's also the monthly, *Lavender Express*. Churches and religious groups in the area include a MCC, Dignity of New Brunswick, and a gay Jewish group.

LOCATION: NEW BRUNSWICK IS LOCATED ON THE SOUTH BANK OF THE RARITAN RIVER IN EASTERN NEW HAMPSHIRE.

GAY/LESBIAN FRIENDLY BUSINESSES: 10+

GAY/LESBIAN BARS AND RESTAURANTS: 4

GAY/LESBIAN ORGANIZATIONS: 30+

GAY/LESBIAN RELIGIOUS ORGANIZATIONS, CHURCHES, ETC.: 6

GAY/LESBIAN BOOKSTORES: 1

GAY/LESBIAN PUBLICATIONS: 3

COMPANIES THAT PROHIBIT DISCRIMINATION: SEE STATE LAW AND GAY CIVIL RIGHTS

INFORMATION NUMBER: 908-846-2232, THE PRIDE CENTER

TOTAL CRIMES: 3,712

VIOLENT = (MURDER = 5, RAPE = 18, ROBBERY = 311, ASSAULT = 289)

PROPERTY = (BURGLARY = 797, LARCENY = 1,955, MOTOR VEHICLE THEFT = 337, ARSON = 19)

Things to Do!!!

(1) George Street Playhouse, (2) Crossroad Theatre, (3) Rutgers University—Display Gardens, Geology Museum, Jane Voorhees Zimmerli Art Museum. ANNUAL EVENTS: Middlesex County Fair. SEASONAL EVENTS: Rutgers SummerFest.

POPULATION: 42,387 PERSONS—W = 23,929, B = 12,337, AI/E/A = 130, C = 445, F = 225, M = 914, PR = 3,715

POPULATION GROWTH: + 2.3%

AGE OF POPULATION: (21-24) = 17.2%, (25-34) = 18.6%, (35-44) = 10.1%, (45-54) = 5.8%, (55-64) = 5.2%, (65-74) = 5.4%, (75 AND OVER) = 4.0%

HOUSING COST: OWNING = $126,000   RENTAL = $640

COMMUNITY HOSPITALS: 3 = 822 BEDS

CLIMATE: JAN—AVG. (29.0 DEGREES), JULY—AVG. (74.6 DEGREES), ANNUAL PRECIPITATION (47.02 INCHES)

PER CAPITA INCOME: $11,252

UNEMPLOYMENT RATE: 8.3%

JOB GROWTH SINCE 1980: + 15.9%

COST OF LIVING: N/A

EDUCATION: RUTGERS

▼PLAINFIELD

Gay Civil Rights: Bans discrimination based on sexual orientation in housing, employment, public accommodations, credit and public contracts.

What the Locals Say . . .

Plainfield is located between New York and Philadelphia. It's a unique community which is really a series of seven neighborhoods. Probably more than 20% of the population in the East End is gay/lesbian. Although there is a statewide anti-discrimination law which includes discrimination based on sexual orientation, you won't see many people walking down the street holding hands. It just doesn't "fit" in Plainfield. There are some neighborhoods, though, where you would feel very comfortable being "Out" to your neighbors; it's just that in this area of the country public displays of affection by anyone are not common. The East End with its old Victorian homes and Highland Park both have a lot of gays. An interesting and humorous aside is that Plainfield was known as the "Queen City" a long time before the word "Queen" was used in the gay community. Groups and organizations in the area include: Central Jersey Alliance of Gay, Lesbian and Bisexual People; a bowling group called Pride of the Lanes; a N.J. Lesbian/Gay Havurah Group; a cartoonist network group; a Roller Skating Evening Group; PFLAG Groups; and a lesbian group called, More Than You Can Count. Since Plainfield is so close to New Brunswick, N. J., Asbury Park, N. J., and New Hope, Penn., most people go to these cities for the bar scene. New Brunswick, only fifteen minutes away, has The Pride Center which is a wonderful community center for gays and lesbians. The Pride Center offers all kinds of activities and groups for gays in the area. J. F. K. Medical Center, Robert Woods Johnson, and St Peter's Hospital all provide excellent medical care. Finding a good gay friendly doctor is mainly a word of mouth process. There are several different religious denominations in the area which are gay-friendly and gay-supportive including: three Dignity Groups, a First Unitarian Church which has an outreach program for gays, and the MCC. *The Network*, published monthly out of New Brunswick covers Plainfield. The Pride Center in New Brunswick also puts out a newsletter called, *The Pride Center News.*

LOCATION: PLAINFIELD IS LOCATED SOUTH OF THE WATCHUNG MOUNTAINS.

GAY/LESBIAN FRIENDLY BUSINESSES: 8

GAY/LESBIAN BARS AND RESTAURANTS: 1

GAY/LESBIAN ORGANIZATIONS: 7

GAY/LESBIAN RELIGIOUS ORGANIZATIONS, CHURCHES, ETC.: 3

GAY/LESBIAN BOOKSTORES: 0

GAY/LESBIAN PUBLICATIONS: 2

COMPANIES THAT PROHIBIT DISCRIMINATION: A. T. & T., SEE STATE LAW AND GAY CIVIL RIGHTS

INFORMATION NUMBER: 908-846-2232, THE PRIDE CENTER IN NEW BRUNSWICK

TOTAL CRIMES: 3,683

VIOLENT = (MURDER = 9, RAPE = 28, ROBBERY = 377, ASSAULT = 286)

PROPERTY = (BURGLARY = 924, LARCENY = 1,609, MOTOR VEHICLE THEFT = 424, ARSON = 16)

Things to Do!!!

(1) Drake House Museum

POPULATION: 45,356 PERSONS—W = 12,338, B = 39,573,AI/E/A = 252, C = 46, F = 86, M = 253, PR = 1,897

POPULATION GROWTH: - 4.0%

AGE OF POPULATION: (21-24) = 6.9%, (25-34) = 19.3%, (35-44) = 15.3%, (45-54) = 10.4%, (55-64) = 7.4%, (65-74) = 5.6%, (75 AND OVER) = 4.3%

HOUSING COST: OWNING = $141,400   RENTAL = $627

COMMUNITY HOSPITALS: 1 = 385 BEDS

CLIMATE: JAN-AVG. (29.4 DEGREES), JULY- AVG. (75.0 DEGREES), ANNUAL PRECIPITATION (49.0 INCHES)

PER CAPITA INCOME: $14,742

UNEMPLOYMENT RATE: 9.3%

JOB GROWTH SINCE 1980: + 15.5%

COST OF LIVING: N/A

EDUCATION: NONE

COUNTIES:

ESSEX COUNTY

Gay Civil Rights: Bans discrimination based on sexual orientation in public employment.

Towns and Cities Included in Essex County:

Belleville Town
Bloomfield Town
Caldwell Borough Fairfield Township
Cedar Grove Township
East Orange City
Essex Fells Borrough
Glen Ridge Borrough
Irvington Township
Livingston Township
Maplewood Township
Milburn Township
Montclair Township
Newark City
North Caldwell Borrough
Nutley Township
Orange City
Roseland Borrough
South Orange Village
Verona Borrough

West Caldwell Borrough
West Orange Town

NEW MEXICO

STATE LAWS REGARDING HOMOSEXUALITY:

In 1975 sodomy laws were repealed. The state of New Mexico bans anti-gay discrimination in public employment.

CITIES: (60,000 AND UP)

▼ALBUQUERQUE

Gay Civil Rights: The state of New Mexico bans anti-gay discrimination in public employment.

What the Locals Say . . .

What a wonderful and beautiful state, where the sun shines 365 days every year. Albuquerque has a large diverse community with a "live and let live" attitude. The present mayor is openly gay supportive. If you are tired of the rush, rush, rush life in the big cities, this is the place to be. You can, most certainly, live a laid-back kind of life in Albuquerque, New Mexico, the land of Montezuma. Being gay in this city is mostly a non-issue as it is a very liberal city. Albuquerque is a large city with a small city feel. Some gays and lesbians hold hands in public but most are not inclined to do so. Good areas to live are: South Valley, Downtown, University, and Knob Hill. Lesbian Avengers Group, Gay and Lesbian Political Alliance, University of New Mexico Support Groups, New Mexico AIDS Services, New Mexico Association of People Living with AIDS, New Mexico Gay Men's Health Project, Duke City Professional Association, and New Mexico Outdoors are all area groups. Common Bond Inc. Community Center is the gay/lesbian community center in Albuquerque hosting such activities as a Women's Over Thirty Coffeehouse Night, and a Board Game Night for Women. Most of the bars are mixed. "Albuquerque Mining Co.," "Albuquerque Social Club,""Club on Center," and "Foxes Lounge" are all mixed. "The Ranch" is more for men and "Corky's" is for the women. Sisters and Brothers is a nationally known gay/lesbian bookstore. University Hospital is excellent for treating people living with AIDS. There is a need for more openly gay doctors. *Out Magazine* is published in Albuquerque. *Hembre* is a biweekly women's magazine with lesbian issues. *Rainbow* is another biweekly. There are a couple of gay BBS's in Albuquerque. There are several gay friendly and gay supportive churches and religious organizations in the area including: the MCC, the First Unitarian Church, Gay Men's Spirituality Group, Holy Resurrection Eastern Orthodox, Kinship, and Jewish Gay and Lesbian Group.

LOCATION: SURROUNDED BY MOUNTAINS ALBUQUERQUE IS LOCATED IN THE CENTRAL REGION OF NEW MEXICO.

GAY/LESBIAN FRIENDLY BUSINESSES: 13

GAY/LESBIAN BARS AND RESTAURANTS: 5

GAY/LESBIAN ORGANIZATIONS: 11

GAY/LESBIAN RELIGIOUS ORGANIZATIONS, CHURCHES, ETC.: 6

GAY/LESBIAN BOOKSTORES: 2

GAY/LESBIAN PUBLICATIONS: 4

COMPANIES THAT PROHIBIT DISCRIMINATION: UNIVERSITY OF NEW MEXICO, INTELL, SEE STATE LAW

INFORMATION NUMBER: 505-266-8041 COMMON BOND INFORMATION LINE

TOTAL CRIMES: 39,025

VIOLENT = (MURDER = 50, RAPE = 259, ROBBERY = 1,522, ASSAULT = 4,835)

PROPERTY = (BURGLARY = 294, LARCENY = 968, MOTOR VEHICLE THEFT = 43, ARSON = 7)

Things to Do!!!

The air is dry and the sunshine plentiful which provides an excellent environment for a variety of outdoor activities. Points of interest include: (1) Albuquerque Museum, (2) Telephone Pioneer Museum, (3) Indian Pueblo Cultural Center, (4) New Mexico Museum of Natural History, (5) National Atomic Museum, (6) Rio Grande Nature Center, (7) Old Town, (8) Isleta Pueblo, (9) Indian Petroglyph State Park, (10) Coronado State Monument, (11) Cibola National Forest, (12) Sandia Peak Ski Area. ANNUAL EVENTS: (1) New Year's Celebration, (2) Kings' Day, (3) Corn and Turtle Dances, (4) Spring Corn Dances, (5) Old Town Fiesta, (6) San Pedro Day, (7) New Mexico Arts and Crafts Fair, (8) St. Ann's Day, (9) Pecos Feast, (10) Our Lady of Assumption Feast, (10) Fiesta Artistica, (11) Spanish Fiesta and St. Augustine's Day, (12) New Mexico State Fair, (13) International Balloon Festival, (14) Indian National Finals Rodeo, (15) San Diego Feast Day, (16) Luminaria Tour, (17) Dances. SEASONAL EVENTS: (1) New Mexico Symphony Orchestra, (2) Albuquerque Little Theatre, (3) Albuquerque Civic Light Opera, (4) New Mexico Repertory Theatre, (5) Southwest Ballet Company.

POPULATION: 398,492 - W = 301,010, B = 11,484, AI/E/A = 11,708, C = 1,401, F = 720, M = 70,380, PR = 944

POPULATION GROWTH: + 19.7%

AGE OF POPULATION: (21-24) = 6.3%, (25-34) = 18.9%, (35-44) = 16.2%, (45-54) = 9.9%, (55-64) = 7.9%, (65-74) = 6.7%, (75 AND OVER) = 4.4%

HOUSING COST: OWNING = $85,900   RENTAL = $402

COMMUNITY HOSPITALS: 10 = 1,726 BEDS
CLIMATE: JAN—AVG. (34.2 DEGREES), JULY—AVG. (78.5 DEGREES)
ANNUAL PRESCIPITATION: (8.8 INCHES)
PER CAPITA INCOME: $14,013
UNEMPLOYMENT RATE: 5.0%
JOB GROWTH SINCE 1980: +23.9%
COST OF LIVING: 104.0
EDUCATION: UNIVERSITY OF NEW MEXICO

▼SANTA FE

Gay Civil Rights: The state of New Mexico bans anti-gay discrimination in public employment.

What the Locals Say . . .

The Santa Fe gay and lesbian community is an established community that is fairly open. The State Capital is located in Santa Fe. Many artists live in Santa Fe and there is a constant stream of tourists, which might be the reason the city seems to be more accepting of lesbians and gays. The downtown area is open enough for it not to be unusual to see two lesbians holding hands. There isn't a specific area where gays and lesbians live, although there are many gays and lesbians living throughout town. Housing tends to be expensive in town. If you go just a little way out of town, prices tend to be lower. The Santa Fe Lesbian and Gay Pride Committee organizes the Pride Festival and the Lesbian and Gay Film Festival. Gay Pride is always the Sunday after July 4th. There are a number of events prior to Gay Pride Day, including: speakers, dances, media training, gay town hall meeting, performances by The Gay Men's Chorus and Gay Square Dancing Group and various other activities. The Human Rights Alliance is an educational organization that lends a hand when needed. When the legislature or some other group takes a position against the gay and lesbian community, The Human Rights Alliance is there to run ads in the paper and speak out against the oppression. The Alliance has a couple of dances during the year to raise money for the financial needs of the group. The Human Rights Election Fund is a political action group which raises approximately $20,000 a year to disseminate pertinent election information. There are many national political gays and lesbians who visit Santa Fe. Gays Lesbians Straight Teachers Education Network (GLISTEN) is another politically active group. PFLAG has a chapter here too. The Gay Men's Health Project has a number of support groups including men's support groups and safer sex groups as well as many others. Santa Fe is also home to the Lambda Eldorado Group which is a social/potluck group. One of the leaders of the community puts an annual Easter surprise together each year where approximately 50 Easter baskets are made and delivered to battered and homeless kids on Easter morning in Santa Fe. There is a gay radio talk show called, "Out Loud and Proud," which showcases the gay and lesbian community. The bar in town is called "Bad Lands" and is mixed with gays and straights, although it is predominately men. Santa Fe Cares is an umbrella AIDS Agency that raises $250,000 a year of private money to fund a spectrum of AIDS services throughout Santa Fe. Santa Fe Cares gives quarterly allotments to the different agencies serving AIDS patients which prevents duplication of services, and it also fills in the gaps of where needed. St. Bede's Episcopal Church and the Unitarian Church are gay friendly, the 1st Presbyterian Church has a pro-gay minister.

LOCATION: SANTA FE IS LOCATED AT THE BASE OF THE SANGRE DE CRISTO MOUNTAINS IN NORTH CENTRAL NEW MEXICO.

GAY/LESBIAN FRIENDLY BUSINESSES: 8

GAY/LESBIAN BARS AND RESTAURANTS: 1

GAY/LESBIAN ORGANIZATIONS: 4

GAY/LESBIAN RELIGIOUS ORGANIZATIONS, CHURCHES, ETC.: 3

GAY/LESBIAN BOOKSTORES: 0

GAY/LESBIAN PUBLICATIONS: 2

COMPANIES THAT PROHIBIT DISCRIMINATION: SEE STATE LAW

INFORMATION NUMBER: BADLANDS 505—986-1700

TOTAL CRIMES: N/A

VIOLENT = N/A

PROPERTY = N/A

Things to Do!!!

There are numerous and varied activities in Santa Fe. Points of interest include: (1) Old Cienega Village Museum, (2) Institute of American Indian Arts Museum, (3) Santuario de Guadalupe, (4) Canyon Road Tour-Canyon Road, Camino del Monte Sol, St. Francis School, National Park Service, Southwest Regional Office, Museum of Indian Arts and Culture, Museum of International Folk Art, Wheelwright Museum, (5) Walking Tour-State Capital, Oldest House, The Famous Staircase, Footsteps Across New Mexico, Loretto Chapel, La Fonda Hotel, Cathedral of St. Francis, San Miguel Mission, Palace of the Governors, Museum of Fine Arts, The Plaza, Sena Plaza and Prince Plaza, Scottish Rite Temple, Federal Court House, (6) San Ildefonso Pueblo, (7) Hyde Memorial State Park, (8) Santa Fe Ski Area, (9) Santa Fe National Forest, (10) Pecos National Monument. ANNUAL EVENTS: (1) Buffalo and Comanche Dances, (2) Candelaria Day Celebration, (3) Spring Corn Dances, (4) Fiesta and Green Corn Dances, (5) Riverman Day, (6) War Dances and Footraces, (7) Santa Fe Rodeo, (8) Fiesta at Cochiti Pueblo, (9) Spanish Market, (10) Fiesta at Santa Domingo, (11) St. Lawrence

Feast, (12) Indian Market, (13) Invitational Antique Indian Art Show, (14) Santa Fe Fiesta, (15) Christmas Eve Celebration. SEASONAL EVENTS: (1) Horse Racing, (2) Folk Art Festival, (3) Sante Fe Opera, (4) Orchestra of Santa Fe, (5) Chamber Music Festival.

POPULATION: 59,004 PERSONS—W = 45,359, B = 332, AI/E/A = 1,249, C = 109, F = 34, M = 8,918, PR = 87

POPULATION GROWTH: + 20.0%

AGE OF POPULATION: (21-24) = 5.1%, (25-34) = 15.6%, (35-44) = 18.5%, (45-54) = 12.0%, (55-64) = 8.7%, (65-74) = 7.4%, (75 AND OVER) = 5.3%

HOUSING COST: OWNING = $99,000   RENTAL = $496

COMMUNITY HOSPITALS: 1 = 226 BEDS

CLIMATE: JAN—AVG. (30.4 DEGREES), JULY—AVG. (69.0 DEGREES), ANNUAL PRECIPITATION (16.37 INCHES)

PER CAPITA INCOME: $16,554

UNEMPLOYMENT RATE: 4.2%

JOB GROWTH SINCE 1980: + 28.3%

COST OF LIVING: N/A

EDUCATION: COLLEGE OF SANTA FE, ST. JOHN'S COLLEGE IN SANTA FE

NEW YORK

STATE LAWS REGARDING HOMOSEXUALITY:

In 1980, the State Supreme Court struck down the sodomy ruling. New York also has a law that doesn't allow discrimination in public employment. Governor Cuomo signed an executive order that allows for domestic partnerships.

CITIES: (60,000 and Up)

▼ALBANY

Gay Civil Rights: **Bans discrimination based on sexual orientation in public and private employment, public accommodations, education and housing.**

What the Locals Say . . .

The gays and lesbians in Albany are out and open in some areas and not in others. The political climate was very good until the 1994 Republican Sweep. The first black, openly gay alderman is no longer on the city council. The Center Square area is a highly concentrated area for gays and lesbians. This area (Madison-Lancaster-Swan-Lark Street) is five blocks by 3 blocks and consists of a residential area as well as gay bars. The Capitol District Gay and Lesbian Community Center (CDGLCC)has several groups that either meet in the facility or are sponsored by the CDGLCC. There is a leather group, a transgender group, men's AA, women's AA, AIDS support group, youth support group as well as a cruise on the Hudson River at Midnight. There is a Two Rivers Outdoor Club, Bi-sexual Support group, and a Stonewall group in Albany. Lesbian/Gay/Bisexual Caucus and the Lesbian/Gay/Bisexual Alliance SUNY Albany are other organizations in Albany. Gay and Lesbian Club Nite at "Mother Earth Cafe" is a popular activity. "Companions" is a dating service and social network for lesbians and gays. "Lifestyle Books" is a lesbigay bookstore. "Cafe LuLu" is gay-friendly. "Stone Ends," an elegant restaurant, and "Cafe Hollywood" are both gay-friendly. "Waterworks" is predominately a gay male crowd, "OH Bar" is a neighborhood bar that draws a mixed crowd, "Power Company" is a mixed bar and the "Longhorn" is a country/western bar that attracts mostly men. The AIDS Council provides many services including a service for homebound HIV/AIDS individuals. Albany Medical Center is a large hospital that has an AIDS unit. *Community* is a monthly gay and lesbian publication. "Face The Music" is a feminist radio program and Homo Radio is a lesbian gay radio program. The MCC, Unitarian Congregation, Lighthouse Apostolic Church, Dignity and Integrity are churches and religious groups that welcomes gays and lesbians.

LOCATION: ALBANY IS LOCATED ON THE HUDSON RIVER IN EASTERN NEW YORK.

GAY/LESBIAN FRIENDLY BUSINESSES: 21

GAY/LESBIAN BARS AND RESTAURANTS: 6

GAY/LESBIAN ORGANIZATIONS: 12

GAY/LESBIAN RELIGIOUS ORGANIZATIONS, CHURCHES, ETC.: 5

GAY/LESBIAN BOOKSTORES: 1

GAY/LESBIAN PUBLICATIONS: 1

COMPANIES THAT PROHIBIT DISCRIMINATION: SEE STATE LAW AND GAY CIVIL RIGHTS

INFORMATION NUMBER: 518-462-6138 THE CAPITOL DISTRICT GAY AND LESBIAN COMMUNITY CENTER

TOTAL CRIMES: 7,802

VIOLENT = (MURDER = 6, RAPE = 59, ROBBERY = 481, ASSAULT = 692)

PROPERTY = (BURGLARY = 2,063, LARCENY = 4,030, MOTOR VEHICLE THEFT = 471, ARSON = 45)

Things to Do!!!

(1) State Capitol, (2) New York State Museum, (3) Albany Institute of History and Art, (4) Historic Cherry Hill, (5) Rensselaerville, (6) Empire State Plaza.

POPULATION : 99,708 PERSONS—W = 76,323, B= 20,869, AI/E/A = 277, C = 801, F = 137, M = 207, PR = 1,704

POPULATION GROWTH: -2.0%

HOUSING COST: OWNING = $101,800   RENTAL = $ 456

COMMUNITY HOSPITALS: 4 = 1,246 BEDS

CLIMATE: JAN—AVG. (20.6 DEGREES), JULY—AVG. (71.8 DEGREES), ANNUAL PRECIPITATION (36.17 INCHES)

PER CAPITA INCOME: $13,742

AGE OF POPULATION: (21-24) = 11.2%, (25-34) = 18.7%, (35-44) = 12.9%, (45-54) = 7.6%, (55-64) = 7.3%, (65-74) = 7.5%, (75 AND OVER) = 7.8%

UNEMPLOYMENT RATE: 5.5%

JOB GROWTH SINCE 1980: + 9.3%

COST OF LIVING: 106

EDUCATION: UNIVERSITY AT ALBANY, STATE UNIVERSITY OF NEW YORK

▼BUFFALO

Gay Civil Rights: Bans discrimination based on sexual orientation in public employment and businesses who do business with city.

What the Locals Say . . .

The gay and lesbian community in Buffalo is undergoing an evolution. There was a period of time when Buffalo had a conservative mayor who was anti-gay. The mayor closed gay bars. The gay and lesbian community center was flooded with people at that time; but when the bars reopened, many went back and the community center suffered financially. Periodically, the community center opens and closes. Currently the Community Center has a mailing list of 1,500 and is sharing space with an AIDS organization. The highest concentration of gays and lesbians is in the Allentown area. Allentown is kind of an artsy area with nice old mansions. The lower westside area has lower housing rates. Couples tend to live more north in Richmond or Elmwood Village. Buffalo has a PFLAG group, Gay Positive of Buffalo, Gay and Lesbian Youth Service, City of Good Neighbors Chorale, and Queer Nation of Buffalo. *Outworks, Western New York Sentinel,* and *Pride Path* are gay and lesbian publications out of Buffalo. "Cathode Ray" is a video bar that attracts gays and lesbians, "Stage Door" is predominately men, and "Zippers/Backpocket" has a women's bar on the first floor and the men's bar on the 2nd floor. Dignity, Integrity and the Pink Triangle Christian Fellowships are gay and lesbian religious groups in Buffalo.

LOCATION: BUFFALO IS AT THE EASTERN END OF LAKE ERIE IN WESTERN NEW YORK.

GAY/LESBIAN FRIENDLY BUSINESSES:13

GAY/LESBIAN BARS AND RESTAURANTS: 9

GAY/LESBIAN ORGANIZATIONS: 11

GAY/LESBIAN RELIGIOUS ORGANIZATIONS, CHURCHES, ETC.: 3

GAY/LESBIAN BOOKSTORES: 4

GAY/LESBIAN PUBLICATIONS: 3

COMPANIES THAT PROHIBIT DISCRIMINATION:: UNIVERSITY OF BUFFALO, COMMUNITY COLLEGES, STATE, CITY AND COUNTY

INFORMATION NUMBER: 716-883-4750 INFORMATION LINE

TOTAL CRIMES: 31,871

VIOLENT = (MURDER = 76, RAPE = 295, ROBBERY = 2,898, ASSAULT = 2,772)

PROPERTY = (BURGLARY = 7,597, LARCENY = 12,714, MOTOR VEHICLE THEFT = 5,519, ARSON = 434)

Things to Do!!!

(1) Theodore Roosevelt Inaugural National Historic Site, (2) Albright-Knox Art Gallery, (3) Studio Arena Theatre, (4) Shea's Buffalo Theatre, (5) City Hall/Observation Tower, (6) Buffalo Museum of Science, (7) Buffalo Zoological Gardens, (8) Buffalo

Raceway, (9) Boat Trips, (10) Buffalo Philharmonic Orchestra, (11) Professional Sports: Football - Bills, Hockey - Sabres. ANNUAL EVENTS: Erie County Fair

POPULATION: 323,284 PERSONS—W = 212,449, B = 100,579, AI/E/A =2,547, C = 963, F = 162, M = 907, PR = 12,978

POPULATION GROWTH: 9.7%

AGE OF POPULATION: (21-24) = 7.5%, (25-34) = 18.4%, (35-44) = 13.0%, (45-54) = 8.2%, (55-64) = 8.6%, (65-74) = 8.4%, (75 AND OVER) = 6.5%

HOUSING COST: OWNING = $46,700   RENTAL = $352

COMMUNITY HOSPITALS: 9 = 3,838 BEDS

CLIMATE: JAN—AVG. (23.6 DEGREES), JULY—AVG. (71.1 DEGREES), ANNUAL PRECIPITATION (38.58 INCHES)

PER CAPITA INCOME: $10,445

JOB GROWTH SINCE 1980: .2%

COST OF LIVING: N/A

EDUCATION: STATE UNIVERSITY COLLEGE AT BUFFALO, CANIAIUS COLLEGE

▼NEW YORK

Gay Civil Rights: Bans discrimination based on sexual orientation in public and private employment, public accommodations, education, housing and union practices.

What the Locals Say . . .

New York City is considered by many to be the gay mecca of the world. In fact, New York City attracts many gays and lesbians who have hopes of finding acceptance through being surrounded by other lesbians and gays with the same needs and desires. New York City has something to offer everyone. It is composed of five boroughs (Bronx, Brooklyn, Manhattan, Queens and Staten Island). The population of these five boroughs is over 7 million people. There are literally thousands of gay/lesbian/bisexual activities, organizations, groups, events, and businesses that overlap among the boroughs. Although there are many advantages to living in New York City, there are also some disadvantages. A major one being that there is a lot of violence against gays, and another one being that New York City is so large and diverse that it is easy to become overwhelmed and to feel isolated and confused. Not to worry though, since there is every type of resource imaginable in New York City for gays and lesbians. An excellent starting point for the newly out or newly relocated gay or lesbian in New York City would be The Lesbian and Gay Community Center (TLGCC). The TLGCC is located in Greenwich Village and has over 300 gay and lesbian community groups which meet at that facility regularly, including: ethnic groups, AIDS groups, gay family groups, political groups, professional groups, religious groups, sport groups, sexuality groups and women's groups The Center itself offers numerous programs including social service, outreach and education, public policy, recreation, quality of life and cultural organizations. But perhaps, to a newcomer, the most helpful program is called "Center Orientation." Orientation offers those newly out a broad introduction to the New York lesbian and gay community. The Center also offers an "Orientation on the Road" program which functions as a welcome wagon for gays and lesbians. The Gay Pride Event in New York is attended by many thousands. There is an Annual Center Garden Party, rally, march, Pride Fest, and Dance as well as many other activities. The AIDS projects in New York are among the world's finest. Some of them include The Men's Health Crisis, The National AIDS Hotline, The New York State AIDS Project, and the PWA Coalition of New York.

LOCATION: NEW YORK CITY IS COMPRISED OF FIVE BOROUGHS WHICH ARE ALL LOCATED IN THE SOUTHEASTERN PENINSULA OF THE STATE OF NEW YORK.

GAY/LESBIAN FRIENDLY BUSINESSES: 1,000 +

GAY/LESBIAN BARS AND RESTAURANTS: 225+

GAY/LESBIAN ORGANIZATIONS: 400 +

GAY/LESBIAN RELIGIOUS ORGANIZATIONS, CHURCHES, ETC.: 50+

GAY/LESBIAN BOOKSTORES: 15

GAY/LESBIAN PUBLICATIONS: 20+

COMPANIES THAT PROHIBIT DISCRIMINATION: STATE, CITY AND COUNTY

INFORMATION NUMBER: 212-620-7310 LESBIAN & GAY COMMUNITY CENTER

TOTAL CRIMES: N/A

VIOLENT = N/A

PROPERTY = N/A

▼BRONX

Gay Civil Rights: See New York City

What the Locals Say . . .

The Bronx is heavily Hispanic. The largest women's organization is Bronx Lesbians United in Sisterhood and the largest men's organization is Gay Men of the Bronx (GMOB). There aren't very many bars in the Bronx so most everyone either goes to Manhattan or Westchester. The neighborhoods farthest away from Manhattan are the nicest areas to live. St. Ann's Church of Morrisania is a gay and lesbian Ministry.

LOCATION: THE BRONX IS ONE OF FIVE BOROUGHS IN NEW YORK CITY AND IS LOCATED NORTH OF MANHATTAN.

Things to Do!!!

(1) Museum of Bronx History, (2) Bronx Museum of the Arts, (3) Edgar Allen Poe Cottage, (4) Yankee Stadium, (5) Bronx Zoo/International Wildlife Conservation Park, (6) The New York Botanical Garden, (7) City Island, (8) Pelham Bay Park, (9) Wave Hill, (10) Professional Sports: Baseball- New York Yankees.

POPULATION: 1,194,614 PERSONS—W = 430,077, B = 449,399, AI/E/A = 6,069, C = 7,015, F = 3,497, M = 12,481 , PR = 34,115

POPULATION GROWTH: + 2.2%

AGE OF POPULATION: (21-24) = 6.3%, (25-34) = 18.7%, (35-44) = 15.2 %, (45-54) = 10.6%, (55-64) = 8.8%, (65-74) = 7.3%, (75 AND OVER) = 5.8%

HOUSING COST: OWNING = $173,900   RENTAL = $443

COMMUNITY HOSPITALS: 9 = 4,871 BEDS

CLIMATE: JAN—AVG. (31.5 DEGREES), JULY—AVG. (76.8 DEGREES), ANNUAL PRECIPITATION (47.25 INCHES)

PER CAPITA INCOME: $10,535

UNEMPLOYMENT RATE: 10.1%

JOB GROWTH SINCE 1980: +13.0%

COST OF LIVING: N/A

EDUCATION: FORDHAM UNIVERSITY, CITY UNIVERSITY OF NEW YORK-HERBERT H. LEHMAN COLLEGE

▼BROOKLYN

Gay Civil Rights: See New York City

What the Locals Say . . .

Brooklyn is the most populated of the five boroughs and is vastly different from the sophistication and glamour of Manhattan. A lot of individuals new to the area move to Brooklyn Heights or Park Slope. Brooklyn Heights is a historic neighborhood composed of Victorian architecture and beautiful landscaping. Park Slope is more of a lesbian neighborhood, although many gay men are moving in. The Park Slope population is considered 40% lesbian and gay. There are numerous restored brownstones and beautiful trees throughout the neighborhood. Park Slope touts that it offers all the basic needs a person could need and at a lower cost than Manhattan. There are gay and lesbian cafes, restaurants, a bookstore, and a variety of shops, as well as a couple of gay and lesbian bars. "Roost" is a popular gay bar; and "La Papaya," "Aunt Sonia" and "New Prospect Cafe" are popular restaurants. "A Room of Our Own Bookstore" is the unofficial gay community center of Park Slope. The Lesbian Herstory Archives is a focal point of the community and is located in Park Slope. There are numerous organizations in Brooklyn including: Brooklyn Women's Martial Arts Group, Gay and Lesbian Ballroom Dance Metro, Women's Golf Club, Slope Activities for Women, and Brooklyn Men's Support Group to name just a few. The Metropolitan Community Church of Brooklyn, The First Unitarian Church of Brooklyn, Lesbian, Gay, Bisexual Concerns Committee and the group Dignity meet regularly.

LOCATION: BROOKLYN IS ONE OF THE FIVE BOROUGHS OF NEW YORK CITY AND IS SITUATED SOUTH OF MANHATTAN.

Things to Do!!!

(1) Brooklyn Academy of Music, (2) Brooklyn Museum, (3) Coney Island, (4) Brooklyn's History Museum (5) Prospect Park, (6) Gateway National Recreation Area.

POPULATION: 2,286,167 PERSONS—W = 1,078,549, B = 872,305, AI/E/A = 7,969, C = 68,191, F = 5,776, M = 21,623, PR = 274,530

POPULATION GROWTH: + 2.5%

AGE OF POPULATION: (21-24) = 6.8%, (25-34) = 17.7%, (35-44) = 13.7%, (45-54) = 9.8%, (55-64) =7.9 %, (65-74) = 6.2%, (75 AND OVER) = 5.4

HOUSING COST: OWNING = $196,100   RENTAL = $ 477

COMMUNITY HOSPITALS: 9 = 4,871 BEDS

CLIMATE: JAN—AVG. (31.5 DEGREES), JULY—AVG. (76.8 DEGREES), ANNUAL PRECIPITATION (47.25 INCHES)

PER CAPITA INCOME: $12,388

UNEMPLOYMENT RATE: 9.5%

JOB GROWTH SINCE 1980: + 14.8%

COST OF LIVING: N/A

EDUCATION: BROOKLYN CAMPUS OF LONG ISLAND, CITY UNIVERSITY OF NEW YORK BROOKLYN COLLEGE

MANHATTAN
Gay Civil Rights: See New York City

What the Locals Say . . .

Many people feel that Manhattan is the center of the gay mecca of the world. Manhattan is a very open society. There are tons of resources for lesbians and gays in Manhattan. The Lesbian and Gay Community Center is located in Manhattan's renowned Greenwich Village. There are several neighborhoods that have a large gay and lesbian presence in Manhattan including Greenwich Village, Chelsea, Midtown, Inwood and Washington Heights. Greenwich Village is composed of the West Village and the East Village. The boundaries of the West Village is the area of downtown south of 14th Street, west of Broadway. The West Village is very pricey and is still considered by many "the place to live" if you are gay or lesbian. "Christopher Street" is a street that has numerous piano bars and shops catering to the gay and lesbian community. "Grove Street" is livelier and contains several new bars, restaurants, and shops. "The Monster" is a popular gay bar, and "Henrietta Hudson" is a popular lesbian bar in the West Village. There are several wonderful restaurants in the West Village, including "Orbit," Rubyfruit Bar & Grill," "Blacksheep" and "Mary's." The geographical definition of the East Village is: it is east of Broadway, north of east Houston, and south of 14th Street. East Village residents are perhaps more diverse and tend to draw more of an alternative/trendy crowd than their neighbors to the west. The East Village is also known for having straights mixed in with gays and lesbians. "Wig Stock" is a annual drag celebration in the East Village. Chelsea is considered by many to be the most gay friendly neighborhood to live in. The geographical boundaries of Chelsea is the area of West Side south of 31st Street, west of Sixth Avenue, north of 14th Street and east of the Hudson River. Chelsea is very yuppie, very gay, and very nice. "The Food Bar" and "Viceroy" are popular restaurants. "Rawhide" and "The Break" are popular gay bars, and "Verso Books" and"A Different Light" are gay and lesbian bookstores. A $100 million sports center project currently under construction in Chelsea will give residents access to a nearby running track, pool, ice skating rink, and a golf driving range. The Midtown area is located between 59th Street and 34th Street and the East and Hudson rivers; south of 59th Street, west of Eighth Avenue, north of 34th Street, and east of Lexington Avenue. There are several new bars and restaurants opening up in the Midtown area. "Nocturnal" is a popular gay bar and "Julie's" is a popular lesbian bar in Midtown. "Cafe' Un Deux Trois," "Chez Josephine," and "Uncle Nicks" are popular restaurants in Midtown. New arrivals to Manhattan are moving in and fixing up run-down homes in the Washington Heights area. There is also a good selection of large apartments that are inexpensive compared to other neighborhoods. The Inwood neighborhood is nicer than Washington Heights and offers huge apartments that are inexpensive. The Upper East and the Upper West Sides of Manhattan are not primarily gay neighborhoods, but they are very wealthy, nice neighborhoods that have some gay and lesbian residents. *The New York Native* and *Stonewall News* are publications out of Manhattan. *The Metro Source* is an excellent source book for gays and lesbians in New York.

LOCATION: MANHATTAN IS LOCATED IN THE NORTHWESTERN SECTION OF NEW YORK CITY. MANHATTAN IS 12 1/2 MILES LONG AND 2 1/2 MILES WIDE AT ITS WIDEST POINT.

Things to Do!!!

Manhattan has arguably the best city parks (Central Park), best theater district, and in general the most sophisticated of almost everything. Specific points of interest include: (1) Downtown Manhattan - New York Stock Exchange, Federal Reserve Bank of New York, Brooklyn Bridge, Woolworth Building, World Trade Center, (2) Statue of Liberty National Monument, (3) The Garment District, (4) Greenwich Village, (5) Madison Square Garden, (6) Empire State Building, (7) Rockefeller Center, (8) Lincoln Center for the Performing Arts, (9) Times Square and the Theater District, (10) Carnegie Hall, (11) Metropolitan Museum of Art, (12) Cooper-Hewitt, National Museum of Design, Smithsonian Institution, (13) The Museum of Modern Art, (14) Museum of the City of New York, (15) Jewish Museum, (16) Intrepid Sea-Air Space Museum, (17) The Museum of Television and Radio, (18) Police Museum, (19) Macy's Herald Square, (20) World Financial Center, (21) Bloomingdale's, (22) Professional Sports: Basketball - Knickerbockers, Hockey - Rangers. ANNUAL EVENTS: (1) Chinese New Year, (2) St. Patrick's Day Parade, (3) Ninth Avenue International Food Festival, (4) JVC Jazz Festival-New York, (5) New York City Marathon, (6) Thanksgiving Parade.

POPULATION: 1,489,066 PERSONS—W = 867,227 , B = 326,967, AI/E/A = 5,728, C = 71,723, F = 8,116, M = 12,800 , PR = 154,978

POPULATION GROWTH: + 4.3%

AGE OF POPULATION: (21-24) = 6.5%, (25-34) = 21.6 %, (35-44) = 17.6 %, (45-54) = 11.7%, (55-64) = 9.1%, (65-74) = 7.2%, (75 AND OVER) = 6.1

HOUSING COST: OWNING = $800,000   RENTAL = $850

COMMUNITY HOSPITALS: 23 = 13,746 BEDS

CLIMATE: JAN—AVG. (31.5 DEGREES), JULY—AVG. (76.8 DEGREES), ANNUAL PRECIPITATION (47.25 INCHES)

PER CAPITA INCOME: $27,862

UNEMPLOYMENT RATE: 7.3%

JOB GROWTH SINCE 1980: + 10.9%

COST OF LIVING: N/A

EDUCATION: MANHATTAN COLLEGE

▼STATEN ISLAND

Gay Civil Rights: See New York City

What the Locals Say . . .

Staten Island is more of a bedroom community and the gay and lesbian community is less visible than in Manhattan. Staten Island is the farthest removed from Manhattan and the least gay friendly of the five boroughs. There aren't really that many clubs or social activities, so many go to Manhattan for that.

LOCATION: STATEN ISLAND IS ONE OF THE FIVE BOROUGHS AND IS LOCATED SOUTHWEST OF MANHATTAN.

Things to Do!!!

(1) Jacques Marchais Museum of Tibetan Art, (2) Historic Richmond Town, (3) The Greenbelt/High Rock, (4) Snug Harbor Cultural Center, (5) Staten Island Zoo.

POPULATION: 391,085 PERSONS—W = 322,043 , B = 30,630, AI/E/A = 715, C = 5,105, F = 3,516 , M = 1,476 , PR = 17,730

POPULATION GROWTH: +11.1%

AGE OF POPULATION: (21-24) = 6.2%, (25-34) = 17.5%, (35-44) = 16.1%, (45-54) = 11.3%, (55-64) = 8.5%, (65-74) = 6.6%, (75 AND OVER) = 4.6

HOUSING COST: OWNING = $ 186,300   RENTAL = $578

COMMUNITY HOSPITALS: 4 = 1,374 BEDS

CLIMATE: JAN—AVG. (30.7 DEGREES), JULY—AVG. (75.5 DEGREES), ANNUAL PRECIPITATION (47.24 INCHES)

PER CAPITA INCOME: $17,507

UNEMPLOYMENT RATE: 8.3%

JOB GROWTH SINCE 1980: + 23.1%

COST OF LIVING: N/A

EDUCATION: CITY UNIVERSITY OF NEW YORK, COLLEGE OF STATEN ISLAND

▼QUEENS

Gay Civil Rights: See New York City

What the Locals Say . . .

Queens has a very large gay and lesbian Hispanic and African

American population. Queens is gay friendly but not quite as open as Brooklyn. There is a large gay and lesbian community in Queens, although the majority of residents are heterosexual. The Jackson Heights/Kew Gardens neighborhood is home to many lesbians and gays in the airline industry since La Guardia Airport is nearby. Queens tends to be less expensive than the other boroughs. The religious group, Queens Lesbian and Gay Christians, meets on a regular basis. Unitarian Universalist Church of Flushing is open and affirmative to gays and lesbians.

LOCATION: QUEENS IS THE LARGEST GEOGRAPHICALLY OF THE FIVE BOROUGHS AND IS LOCATED EAST OF MANHATTAN ON LONG ISLAND.

Things to Do!!!

(1) La Guardia Airport, (2) John F. Kennedy Airport, (3) Flushing Meadow Corona Park, (4) Queens Botanical Garden, (5) Shea Stadium, (6) Forest Hills, (7) Professional Sports: Baseball- Mets, Football-Jets. ANNUAL EVENTS: (1) US Open Tennis

POPULATION: 1,951,034 PERSONS—W = 1,129,192, B = 423,211, AI/E/A = 7,050, C = 86,885, F = 22,324 , M = 13,342, PR = 100,410

POPULATION GROWTH: + 3.2%

AGE OF POPULATION: (21-24) = 6.2%, (25-34) = 18.6%, (35-44) =14.9 %, (45-54) = 10.9%, (55-64) = 9.7%, (65-74) = 8.3%, (75 AND OVER) = 6.4

HOUSING COST: OWNING = $191,000   RENTAL = $560

COMMUNITY HOSPITALS: 13 = 5,880 BEDS

CLIMATE: JAN—AVG. (31.3 DEGREES), JULY—AVG. (76.4 DEGREES), ANNUAL PRECIPITATION (42.12 INCHES)

PER CAPITA INCOME: $15,348

UNEMPLOYMENT RATE: 8.0%

JOB GROWTH SINCE 1980: + 12.0%

COST OF LIVING: N/A

EDUCATION: CITY UNIVERSITY OF NEW YORK, QUEENS COLLEGE

▼SYRACUSE

Gay Civil Rights: Bans discrimination based on sexual orientation in public and private employment, public accommodations, education and housing.

What the Locals Say . . .

The gay and lesbian community in Syracuse is fairly closeted. While there are laws that protect gay rights, many feel the politicians are for the most part just tolerant. There doesn't seem to be a specific area where gays and lesbians live. "My Sisters' Words" is a feminist bookstore which has a good selection of lesbian and feminist publications. The Gay and Lesbian Alliance of Syracuse sponsors a help line. There are a couple of organizations on the Syracuse Campus; the Syracuse University Gay, Lesbian and Bisexual Student Association and the Gay and Lesbian University Employees group. There are gay and lesbian volleyball and softball teams and the Syracuse Gay and Lesbian Chorus. Lambda Youth Services is an organization for gay and lesbian youth. "Ryan's Someplace Else," "My Bar," "Sassy's," and "Screamers" are gay and lesbian bars in Syracuse. The Central AIDS Office offers information and some counseling. *The Pink Paper* is a gay and lesbian publication in Syracuse and comes out every other month. The Ray of Hope Metropolitan Community Church and the May Memorial Unitarian Universalists for Lesbian and Gay concerns is open and affirming to gays and lesbians.

LOCATION: SYRACUSE IS LOCATED IN NORTH CENTRAL NEW YORK.

GAY/LESBIAN FRIENDLY BUSINESSES: 6

GAY/LESBIAN BARS AND RESTAURANTS: 7

GAY/LESBIAN ORGANIZATIONS: 23

GAY/LESBIAN RELIGIOUS ORGANIZATIONS, CHURCHES, ETC.: 2

GAY/LESBIAN BOOKSTORES: 1

GAY/LESBIAN PUBLICATIONS: 2

COMPANIES THAT PROHIBIT DISCRIMINATION: STATE, CITY AND COUNTY

INFORMATION NUMBER: 315-422-5732 GAY AND LESBIAN ALLIANCE OF SYRACUSE

TOTAL CRIMES: 11,115

VIOLENT = (MURDER = 18, RAPE = 79, ROBBERY = 561, ASSAULT = 703)

PROPERTY = (BURGLARY = 2,824, LARCENY = 6,358, MOTOR VEHICLE THEFT = 572, ARSON = 116)

Things to Do!!!

(1) Everson Museum of Art, (2) Erie Canal Museum, (3) Landmark Theatre, (4) Onondaga Lake Park, (5) Beaver Lake Nature Center, (6) Green Lakes State Park, (7) Burnet Park Zoo, (8) New York State Canal Cruises.

POPULATION: 162,835 PERSONS—W = 122,867, B = 33,320, AI/E/A = 2,062, C = 933, F = 221, M = 426, PR = 3,925

POPULATION GROWTH: - 4.3%

AGE OF POPULATION: (21-24) = 9.2%, (25-34) = 18.3%, (35-44) = 12.2%, (45-54) = 7.3%, (55-64) = 7.1%, (65-74) = 7.6%, (75 AND OVER) = 7.3%

PER CAPITA INCOME: $11,351

HOUSING COST: OWNING = $67,600   RENTAL = $409

COMMUNITY HOSPITALS: 4 = 1,668 BEDS

CLIMATE: JAN—AVG. (22.4 DEGREES), JULY—AVG. (70.4 DEGREES), ANNUAL PRECIPITATION (38.93 INCHES)

UNEMPLOYMENT RATE: 6.9%

JOB GROWTH SINCE 1980: - .6%

COST OF LIVING: 104.7

EDUCATION: SYRACUSE UNIVERSITY, LE MOYNE COLLEGE

TOWNS: (5,000—60,000)

▼ITHACA

Gay Civil Rights: Bans discrimination based on sexual orientation in public and private employment, public accommodations, education, housing, credit, and union practices.

What the Locals Say . . .

Ithaca is a pretty open community. It is a strong lesbian and women's community. They held a women's town meeting sponsored by thirty-two organizations where over 200 women attended. Ithaca also has a great city bus system. The political climate in Ithaca is liberal. The outlying towns are very conservative. The downtown area of Ithaca is safe, or rather, as safe as it can be anywhere. In fact you sometimes get a false sense of security. Cornell University has a pro-gay campus and is located in Ithaca. Cornell provides same sex partner health care benefits. The downtown area is a great place for lesbians and gays to live. In particular, Falls Creek a small neighborhood is very gay-friendly. "Common Ground" is the only gay/lesbian bar in town. Tuesdays, it is a singing bar, Wednesday, a country western bar, Thursday, a disco. "Common Ground" also serves as the focal point of the community since many events and meetings are held there. The Ithaca Gay and Lesbian Task Force runs the switchboard, has a monthly coffeehouse, publishes a quarterly newsletter, and maintains a mailing list of over 600. The Ithaca Gay and Lesbian Activities Board meets at the bar and has an adopt a highway program and sometimes has progressive dinners. "Borealis" is a bookstore that has a huge lesbian and gay section. There is a women's softball league which has a large number of lesbians participating, and there's also a bowling league in Ithaca. The social atmosphere in Ithaca is a little cliquish. The older gays and lesbians tend to be self-organized and frequently have potlucks, etc. The Society of Honorary Lesbians organizes a big New Year's Eve Party by arranging for two restaurants to allow the group use of the bar after the dinner hour. The Anti-Homophobia and Racism Commission is a non-profit organization. Endorsing candidates is not allowed, but the Commission does work on reducing homophobia and racism. The Empire State Pride Agenda is a group that lobbies for gay and lesbian bills and fights anti-gay bills. The Cornell Gay and Lesbian Alliance is a very active campus organization. The Alliance sponsors a Men Supporting Men Group, Women Supporting Women Group, and Bridge, (a group of bisexual people). Match 101 Program is sponsored by the research office. It matches someone gay or lesbian with someone who has questions or is unsure if they are gay or lesbian. Instead of celebrating Gay History Month in June, Ithaca celebrates it in April when the students are on campus and it is called Gaypril. The Gay and Lesbian Coalition is a political group and it sponsors LBQ and DASH-Direct Action to Stop Homophobia. Out-N-The Wild is a social group that has picnics, barbecues, dances, hiking trips, etc. AIDS Work is a non-profit organization that assists those with AIDS. *Outlines* is a gay and lesbian quarterly publication. The Unitarian Church is open to gay and lesbians and The Alternate Spiritual Community is a non-denominational group of 10-20 people that get together regularly.

LOCATION: ITHACA IS BUILT ON THE HILLS AT THE HEAD OF CAYUGA LAKE, THE CITY HAS SEVERAL CREEKS, GORGES, AND WATERFALLS THAT CASCADE THROUGH THE TOWN.

GAY/LESBIAN FRIENDLY BUSINESSES: 10 +

GAY/LESBIAN BARS AND RESTAURANTS: 2

GAY/LESBIAN ORGANIZATIONS: 4

GAY/LESBIAN RELIGIOUS ORGANIZATIONS, CHURCHES, ETC.: 2

GAY/LESBIAN BOOKSTORES: 1

GAY/LESBIAN PUBLICATIONS: 1

COMPANIES THAT PROHIBIT DISCRIMINATION: CORNELL UNIVERSITY, SEE STATE LAW, COUNTY LAW AND GAY CIVIL RIGHTS

INFORMATION NUMBER: 607-277-4614 ITHACA GAY AND LESBIAN TASK FORCE AND 607-255-6482 CORNELL LESBIAN GAY BISEXUAL ALLIANCE

TOTAL CRIMES: 2,224

VIOLENT = (MURDER = 0, RAPE = 12, ROBBERY = 58, ASSAULT = 33)

PROPERTY = (BURGLARY = 434, LARCENY = 1,654, MOTOR VEHICLE THEFT = 33, ARSON = 3)

Things to Do!!!

(1) Dewitt Historical Society and Museum, (2) Buttermilk Falls, (3) Allan H. Treman State Marine park, (4) Taughannock Falls, (5) Stewart Park, (6) Six Mile Creek Vineyard. ANNUAL EVENTS: Groton Festival.

POPULATION: 29,389 PERSONS—W = 24,166, B = 1,916, AI/E/A = 102, C = 1,241, F = 114, M = 165, PR = 299

POPULATION GROWTH: + 2.3%

AGE OF POPULATION: (21-24) = 23.7%, (25-34) = 14.8%, (35-44) = 8.6%, (45-54) = 4.1%, (55-64) = 3.7%, (65-74) = 3.7%, (75 AND OVER) = 4.0%

HOUSING COST: OWNING = $95,600   RENTAL = $493

COMMUNITY HOSPITALS: 1 = 191 BEDS

CLIMATE: JAN—AVG. (21.5 DEGREES), JULY—AVG. (68.6 DEGREES), ANNUAL PRECIPITATION (35.40 INCHES)

PER CAPITA INCOME: $9,213

UNEMPLOYMENT RATE: 3.8%

JOB GROWTH SINCE 1980: + 3.9%

COST OF LIVING: N/A

EDUCATION: CORNELL UNIVERSITY, ITHACA COLLEGE

▼TROY

Gay Civil Rights: Bans discrimination based on sexual orientation in public employment.

What the Locals Say . . .

Troy is a rural area across the river from Albany. A lot of gay and lesbians want to go out, so they have been flocking to Albany. However, the gay and lesbian community in Troy is growing and there are more societal events, meetings, etc. getting started. The City of Troy is currently not economically stable. There are several businesses that are gay supportive. There is a large concentration of gays and lesbians that live in downtown Troy. The downtown is very commercial and runs alongside the Hudson River. Lansingburg residential area is filled with old Colonial homes. Watervliet has a lot of apartments where gays and lesbians live. There aren't any gay bars in Troy. The Troy Chapter of the Capitol District Lesbian and Gay Community Center holds meetings, and sponsors social events every other month. There is a Valentine's Day and St. Patrick's Day Dance, and rafting down the river. A Theatre production is currently in the works for 1996. Everyone goes to Albany approximately 15 minutes away if they want to go to a gay bar. The Samaritan Hospital has an HIV/AIDS Unit. The 1st United Presbyterian is open to gays and lesbians.and the pastor is very welcoming.

LOCATION: TROY IS LOCATED APPROXIMATELY 15 MILES NORTH OF ALBANY, NEW YORK.

GAY/LESBIAN FRIENDLY BUSINESSES: 12

GAY/LESBIAN BARS AND RESTAURANTS: 0

GAY/LESBIAN ORGANIZATIONS: 2

GAY/LESBIAN RELIGIOUS ORGANIZATIONS, CHURCHES, ETC.: 1

GAY/LESBIAN BOOKSTORES: 0

GAY/LESBIAN PUBLICATIONS: 0

COMPANIES THAT PROHIBIT DISCRIMINATION: SEE STATE LAW AND GAY CIVIL RIGHTS

INFORMATION NUMBER: 518-462-6138 #46 CAPITAL DISTRICT LESBIAN & GAY COMMUNITY CENTER

TOTAL CRIMES: N/A

VIOLENT = N/A

PROPERTY = N/A

Things to Do!!!

(1) RiverSpark Visitor Center, (2) Rensselaer County Historical Society, (3) Troy Savings Bank Music Hall.

POPULATION:54,153 PERSONS—W = 47,944, B = 4,132, AI/E/A = 123, C = 558, F = 85

POPULATION GROWTH: - 4.4%

AGE OF POPULATION: (21-24) = 10.1%, (25-34) = 18.0%, (35-44) = 11.3%, (45-54) = 7.5%, (55-64) = 7.7%, (65-74) = 7.3%, (75 AND OVER) = 6.7%

HOUSING COST: OWNING = $84,400   RENTAL = $396

COMMUNITY HOSPITALS: 3 = 616

CLIMATE: JAN—AVG. (21.3 DEGREES), JULY—AVG. (73.0 DEGREES), ANNUAL PRECIPITATION (36.18 INCHES)

PER CAPITA INCOME: $11,704

UNEMPLOYMENT RATE: 8.1%

JOB GROWTH SINCE 1980: + 10.2%

COST OF LIVING: N/A

EDUCATION: RENSSELAER POLYTECHNIC INSTITUTE, RUSSELL SAGE COLLEGE

COUNTIES:

SUFFOLK COUNTY

Gay Civil Rights: Bans discrimination based on sexual orientation in public employment.

Towns and Cities Included in Suffolk County:

Amangansett
Amityville Village
Asharoken Village
Bay Shore
Commack

East Hampton Town
East Hampton Village
Greenport Village
Hauppauge
Head of Harbor Village
Huntington
Lloyd Harborville
Matic Beach
Medford
Nisequogue Village
Northport Village
Ocean Beach Village
Quogue Village
Port Jefferson
Riverhead Town
Ronkonkoma
Sag Harbor Village
Saltaire Village
Shelter Island Town
Shirley
Smithtown
Stoney Brook
Sound Beach
Southampton Town
Southampton Village
South Old Town
West Hampton Beach Village
Wyandanch

TOMPKINS COUNTY

Gay Civil Rights: Bans discrimination based on sexual orientation in public and private employment, public accommodations, education, housing, credit, and union practices.

Cities and Towns Included in Tompkins County:

Cayuga Heights Village
Dryden Village
Freeville Village
Groton Village

Ithaca
Trumansburg Village
West Danby

NORTH CAROLINA

STATE LAWS REGARDING HOMOSEXUALITY:

Heterosexual and homosexual sodomy is illegal and carries a maximum sentence of up to ten years.

CITIES: (60,000 AND UP)

▼ASHEVILLE
Gay Civil Rights: Bans discrimination based on sexual orientation in public employment.
What the Locals Say . . .

Asheville's gay and lesbian community is not closeted, but it isn't in your face all the time either. Four out of seven members on the city council are very gay-friendly. The towns surrounding Asheville are rural and very conservative. The areas of Asheville that have the highest concentration of gays and lesbians are the downtown and the Montford area. Downtown has a lot of businesses that are gay-friendly, but the residential area here is not very large. Some gays and lesbians feel comfortable enough in downtown to hold hands with their partner. Montford is a mixed area going through a transition period. It is a historical district where homes are being refurbished. Perhaps one of the strongest groups in the gay and lesbian community is the group, Affirmations. They sponsor CLOSER and OUTFIT. CLOSER is a support group for gays and lesbians. Anything that deals with gay and lesbian issues, CLOSER gets together and discusses them in a social atmosphere. CLOSER is careful to maintain confidentiality for those who cannot afford to be out. OUTFIT is a youth group that basically does the same thing, just with youth. Affirmations also offers ministry to those with HIV/AIDS. Asheville is a very artsy city. There are hundreds of artists and numerous galleries throughout the area. The largest gay-owned ones are: Blue Spiral I, New Morning Gallery and Bellagio. "Malaprops Books and Cafe" has gay and lesbian books, literature and a light food menu. "Cahootz" and "Bean Streets" are gay-friendly restaurants. Asheville has a Lesbian AA group, a Gay Fathers Group, Men's Spirituality Support Group, Alternative Lifestyles Families United Network (ALFUN), a group for partners/spouses who are homosexual, GLAD—a youth group, Gay Men's Chorus, Women's Outdoor Group, Women's Softball Team and GLAPAC—Gay Lesbian Parents & Their Kids. Asheville also has a relationship support group of lesbian and bisexual women, and a Phoenix Transgender group. Southern Appalachian Lesbian & Gay Association (SALGA) is a political action organization working to achieve full human rights for lesbians and gay men. Pride Day activities include a picnic, rafting, numerous booths and a variety of other activities. The

"Hairspray Cafe Bar," "O'Henry's," "Metropolis" and "Scandals" are mixed bars that draw gays and lesbians. Western North Carolina AIDS Project provides many services for those individuals with HIV/AIDS. Kennelworth Wellness Center is a free clinic. *Community Connections* is a monthly publication. All Souls Cathedral and Gay and Lesbian Affirming Ministries are religious organizations in Asheville. MCC/Asheville, Unitarian Church, Unity Center, Jubilee Community Church, St. Serephin Orthodox Church and St. Joan of Arc Catholic Church are open and affirming to gays and lesbians. There is also the Asheville Religious Network For Gay and Lesbian Equality.

LOCATION: ASHEVILLE IS LOCATED IN THE BLUE RIDGE MOUNTAINS IN WESTERN NORTH CAROLINA.

GAY/LESBIAN FRIENDLY BUSINESSES: 20

GAY/LESBIAN BARS AND RESTAURANTS: 4

GAY/LESBIAN ORGANIZATIONS: 12

GAY/LESBIAN RELIGIOUS ORGANIZATIONS, CHURCHES, ETC.: 8

GAY/LESBIAN BOOKSTORES: 1

GAY/LESBIAN PUBLICATIONS: 1

COMPANIES THAT PROHIBIT DISCRIMINATION: CITY EMPLOYMENT

INFORMATION NUMBER: 704-645-5908 SALGA

TOTAL CRIMES: 5,268

VIOLENT = (MURDER = 9, RAPE = 44, ROBBERY = 142, ASSAULT = 261)

PROPERTY = (BURGLARY = 1,148, LARCENY = 3,311, MOTOR VEHICLE THEFT = 353, ARSON = 8)

Things to Do!!!

There are many cultural and recreational opportunities in this picturesque mountain city. Specific points of interest include: (1) Biltmore Estates, (2) Biltmore Homespun Shops, (3) Thomas Wolfe Memorial, (4) Asheville Community Theatre, (5) Pack Place Education, Art and Science Center, (6) Botanical Gardens of Asheville, (7) Folk Art Center, (8) Wolf Laurel Ski Resort, (9) River Rafting, (10) Western North Carolina Nature Center, (11) Chimney Rock Park. ANNUAL EVENTS: (1) Shindig-on-the-Green, (2) Southern Highland Handicraft Guild Fair, (3) Mountain Dance and Folk Festival. SEASONAL EVENTS: SHAKESPEARE In The Park.

POPULATION: 61,607 PERSONS—W = 48,726, B = 12,207, AI/E/A = 165, C = 81, F = 51, M = 215, PR = 83

POPULATION GROWTH: + 16.3%

AGE OF POPULATION: (21-24) = 5.4%, (25-34) = 15.2 %, (35-44) = 14.6%, (45-54) = 9.8%, (55-64) = 10.1%, (65-74) = 10.8%, (75 AND OVER) = 9.2%

HOUSING COST: OWNING = $57,000   RENTAL = $365
COMMUNITY HOSPITALS: 2 = 725 BEDS
CLIMATE: JAN—AVG. (35.7 DEGREES), JULY—AVG. (72.8 DEGREES),
ANNUAL PRECIPITATION (47.59 INCHES)
PER CAPITA INCOME: $13,079
UNEMPLOYMENT RATE: 5.8%
JOB GROWTH SINCE 1980: + 21.5%
COST OF LIVING: 104.6
EDUCATION: UNIVERSITY OF NORTH CAROLINA AT ASHEVILLE

▼DURHAM

Gay Civil Rights: Bans discrimination based on sexual orientation in public employment.

What the Locals Say . . .

The Durham gay and lesbian community considers itself the most active and organized of the Triangle Cities (Durham, Raleigh, Chapel Hill). Lavender Hill is an upscale neighborhood for gays and lesbians to live. Watts is an area where gay and lesbian professionals live. Trendy Parks has older homes where gays and lesbians tend to congregate. "Southern Sisters" is a feminist bookstore. Durham has a Women Over 40 Group, Women Over 35 Potluck Group, Old Lesbians Organizing For Change, Lesbian Avengers, the Mentor Program for men that came out at an older age, the Mary Renault Society—a wealthy white professional male group, Men Of Colors Together, and Cedar Chest—a group for black lesbians. The Menshi Project is an advocacy group for gay men's issues. The North Carolina Veterans Coalition and the North Carolina Center for Lesbian and Gay Equality (Nickel Giggle) is a statewide advocacy group. Durham also has a Gay Men's Support Group, Lesbian Support Group, Bisexual Women's Support Group, Gay and Lesbian AA Group, and a Gay Married Men Group. Southern Exposure is a women's professional business network. "Boxers" is a predominately men's professional money crowd bar, "Power Company" is a men's and women's complex with three bars. "Competition" is a lesbian bar. The Lesbian Health Center offers medical treatment and referrals. The Lesbian and Gay Health Project, AIDS Community Residence Association, and Early HIV Intervention Clinic all provide services for persons with HIV/AIDS. Durham has several HIV and AIDS support groups. "An Evening With Friends" is an annual HIV/AIDS fundraiser that raised $200,000 in 1995. *The Front Page* and *"Q" Notes* are lesbian and gay publications that come out twice a month. The Eno River Unitarian Church welcomes gays and lesbians into their congregation. The religious groups Lesbians and Gay Shabaat and a chapter of Dignity meet regularly.

LOCATION: DURHAM IS LOCATED IN EASTERN NORTH CAROLINA, NORTH OF RALEIGH AND EAST OF CHAPEL HILL.

GAY/LESBIAN FRIENDLY BUSINESSES: 70

GAY/LESBIAN BARS AND RESTAURANTS: 5

GAY/LESBIAN ORGANIZATIONS: 11

GAY/LESBIAN RELIGIOUS ORGANIZATIONS, CHURCHES, ETC.: 3

GAY/LESBIAN BOOKSTORES: 1

GAY/LESBIAN PUBLICATIONS: 2

COMPANIES THAT PROHIBIT DISCRIMINATION: SEE GAY CIVIL RIGHTS

INFORMATION NUMBER: 919-821-0055 GAY & LESBIAN HELPLINE OF WAKE COUNTY

TOTAL CRIMES: 14,980

VIOLENT = (MURDER = 4,851, RAPE = 109, ROBBERY = 848, ASSAULT = 724)

PROPERTY = (BURGLARY = 4,851, LARCENY = 7,471, MOTOR VEHICLE THEFT = 951, ARSON = 90)

Things to Do!!!

(1) North Carolina Museum of Life and Science, (2) Duke University- Duke Chapel, Duke Medical Center, Duke Libraries, Art Museum, Duke's Wallace Wade Stadium, Sarah P. Duke Gardens, (3) West Point On The Eno. ANNUAL EVENTS: Center Fest.

POPULATION: 140,926 PERSONS—W = 70,640, B = 62,449, AI/E/A = 334, C = 841, F = 173, M = 579, PR = 238

POPULATION GROWTH: + 39.3%

AGE OF POPULATION: (21-24) = 8.4%, (25-34) = 21.5%, (35-44) = 15.4%, (45-54) = 7.8%, (55-64) = 6.6%, (65-74) = 6.2%, (75 AND OVER) = 5.1%

HOUSING COST: OWNING = $80,600   RENTAL = $440

COMMUNITY HOSPITALS: 3 = 1,496 BEDS

CLIMATE: JAN—AVG. (37.1 DEGREES), JULY—AVG. (77.1 DEGREES), ANNUAL PRECIPITATION (48.10 INCHES)

PER CAPITA INCOME: $14,498

UNEMPLOYMENT RATE: 4.3%

JOB GROWTH SINCE 1980: + 51.8%

COST OF LIVING: 98.6

EDUCATION: DUKE UNIVERSITY

▼RALEIGH

Gay Civil Rights: Bans discrimination based on sexual orientation in public employment.

What the Locals Say . . .

The gay and lesbian community is not that visible. The local politicians are rather split; some being pro-gay and some being anti-gay. The political atmosphere was more pro-gay before the 1994 elections. This is also the hometown of anti-gay Senator, Jesse Helms. The Five Points area is a neighborhood that has a high concentration of gays and lesbians. The homes are older and there are also some gay businesses in the area. Carom Court is an apartment complex near North Carolina State University on Hillsborough. Mordecia, which tends to be more expensive, is another gay and lesbian neighborhood; it has older homes and parks throughout. Historic Oakwood area is in the outskirts of downtown Raleigh and is also a rather expensive neighborhood. Raleigh has a Kings and Queens Gay bowling League, Tennis and Racquetball Society, Literary Social Group, Lesbian and Thespians, a women's potluck group, and ASPYN and OUTRIGHT youth groups. Some of the most popular support groups are Gay/Bisexual Married Men, Gay Men With HIV/AIDS, Couples Affected by HIV, Triangle Bisexual Network, Gay Fathers and Partners of Bisexuals. The Realto Theatre shows gay and lesbian films. There is the Triangle Business and Professional Guild for Raleigh, Durham and Chapel Hill. The North Carolina Pride Pac For Gay and Lesbian Equality and the Human Rights Campaign Fund are strong political groups in Raleigh. The "White Rabbit Bookstore" sells gay and lesbian literature. "Lilly's Pizza" and "Third Place" are gay friendly restaurants. "Cup of Jo" is a gay-friendly coffeehouse. "Man Bites Dog" is a theatre group that does gay and lesbian themes. "Legend's" is a men and women's bar, "CC's" is predominately a leather bar, "1622" is a predominately men's bar except for Thursdays. The Wake County Department of Health provides HIV counseling and testing and HIV early intervention case management. *The Front Page* is a gay and lesbian publication, *Independent Weekly* is a left slanted newspaper that lists upcoming events, and *The Newsletter* is a women only publication. The MCC, St. Johns Community Church and the Unitarian Church are open to gays and lesbians. The Raleigh Religious Network for gay and lesbian equality, Integrity, Lutherans Concerned and the group Affirmations have chapters in Raleigh.

LOCATION: RALEIGH IS LOCATED IN EASTERN NORTH CAROLINA, SOUTH OF DURHAM.

GAY/LESBIAN FRIENDLY BUSINESSES: 40

GAY/LESBIAN BARS AND RESTAURANTS: 4

GAY/LESBIAN ORGANIZATIONS: 11

GAY/LESBIAN RELIGIOUS ORGANIZATIONS, CHURCHES, ETC.: 7

GAY/LESBIAN BOOKSTORES: 1

GAY/LESBIAN PUBLICATIONS: 3

COMPANIES THAT PROHIBIT DISCRIMINATION: SEE GAY CIVIL RIGHTS

INFORMATION NUMBER: 919-821-0055 GAY& LESBIAN HELPLINE OF WAKE COUNTY

TOTAL CRIMES: 15,255

VIOLENT = (MURDER = 27, RAPE = 94, ROBBERY = 795, ASSAULT = 1,114)

PROPERTY = (BURGLARY = 2,947, LARCENY = 9,395, MOTOR VEHICLE THEFT = 883, ARSON = 23)

Things to Do!!!

(1) State Capital, (2) Capitol Area Visitors Center, (3) North Carolina Museum of Art, (4) State Museum of Natural Science, (5) William B. Umstead State Park, (6) Falls Lake, (7) Research Triangle Park. ANNUAL EVENTS: (1) Great Raleigh festival, (2) Artsplosure, (3) State Fair.

POPULATION: 220,524 PERSONS—W = 143,862, B = 57,354, AI/E/A = 584, C = 1,440, F = 225, M = 897, PR = 474

POPULATION GROWTH: +46.8%

AGE OF POPULATION: (21-24) = 10.3%, (25-34) = 22.5%, (35-44) = 15.8%, (45-54) = 9.0%, (55-64) = 6.6%, (65-74) = 5.2%, (75 AND OVER) = 3.6%

HOUSING COST: OWNING = $96,600   RENTAL = $479

COMMUNITY HOSPITALS: 3 = 1,199 BEDS

CLIMATE: JAN—AVG. (38.8 DEGREES), JULY—AVG. (78.6 DEGREES), ANNUAL PRECIPITATION (44.97 INCHES)

PER CAPITA INCOME: $16,896

UNEMPLOYMENT RATE: 4.1%

JOB GROWTH SINCE 1980: + 54.7%

COST OF LIVING: 98.6

EDUCATION: NORTH CAROLINA STATE UNIVERSITY, MEREDITH COLLEGE

TOWNS: (5,000—60,000)

▼CHAPEL HILL

Gay Civil Rights: Bans discrimination based on sexual orientation in public employment. There is a domestic partnership ordinance on the books.

What the Locals Say . . .

Chapel Hill is a very collegiate town; home of University of North Carolina at Chapel Hill. There is a very open gay and lesbian college community, although the post college gay and lesbian community is quite closeted. "Cafe Trio" is gay-friendly and attracts more gays and lesbians on the weekends. The Orange County Women's Center has support groups and peer counseling. There is a Sappho group that has lunches on Friday at UNC Chapel Hill. BGLAD (Bisexuals, Gay Men, Lesbians and Allies for Diversity) is located at UNC Chapel Hill, although they welcome people outside of the University as well. Chapel Hill has a PFLAG group, Crepe Myrtle Festival Group, Gay/Lesbian/Bisexual Over 35 group, Men Of All Colors Together The Quest Discussion Group, and a Pink Triangle Al-Anon group. "International Books" has a good selection of gay and lesbian books. There are some gay-friendly bars, although most gays and lesbians go to Durham if they want to go to a gay bar. The AIDS Service Center is located in Chapel Hill. The Orange County Health Department has significant HIV/AIDS services as well as free and anonymous testing. There is a Lesbian and Gay Democrat Club of Chapel Hill. *The Independent Weekly* is primarily an arts and entertainment publication, but it does have same sex personal ads. The Unitarian Community Church, Church of Reconciliations and Unity Center of Peace, Brinkley Baptist Church are open to gays and lesbians. American Baptists Concerned and Jewish Gay Lesbian/Bisexuals are religious gay and lesbian groups in Chapel Hill.

LOCATION: CHAPEL HILL IS LOCATED IN EASTERN NORTH CAROLINA, SOUTH OF DURHAM.

GAY/LESBIAN FRIENDLY BUSINESSES: 4

GAY/LESBIAN BARS AND RESTAURANTS: 2

GAY/LESBIAN ORGANIZATIONS: 5

GAY/LESBIAN RELIGIOUS ORGANIZATIONS, CHURCHES, ETC.: 6

GAY/LESBIAN BOOKSTORES: 1

GAY/LESBIAN PUBLICATIONS: 0

COMPANIES THAT PROHIBIT DISCRIMINATION: UNIVERSITY OF NORTH CAROLINA CHAPEL HILL, SEE GAY CIVIL RIGHTS

INFORMATION NUMBER: 919-942-1740 INTERNATIONAL BOOKS

TOTAL CRIMES: 2,699

VIOLENT = (MURDER = 1, RAPE = 15, ROBBERY = 100, ASSAULT = 203)

PROPERTY = (BURGLARY = 516, LARCENY = 1,766, MOTOR VEHICLE THEFT = 98, ARSON = 14)

Things to Do!!!

(1) University of North Carolina at Chapel Hill, (2) Coker Arboretum, (3) Kenan Stadium, (4) Louis Round Wilson Library, (5) Morehead Planetarium, (6) Playmaker Theatre, (7) Paul Green Theatre, (8) North Carolina Botanical Garden, (9) Chapel of The Cross.

POPULATION: 43,215 PERSONS—W = 31,875, B = 4,853, AI/E/A = 123, C = 659, F = 48, M = 163, PR = 59

POPULATION GROWTH: + 33.3%

AGE OF POPULATION: (21-24) = 16.6%, (25-34) = 17.4%, (35-44) = 11.6%, (45-54) = 7.1%, (55-64) = 5.0%, (65-74) = 4.7%, (75 AND OVER) = 3.9%

HOUSING COST: OWNING = $141,100   RENTAL = $489

COMMUNITY HOSPITALS: 1 = 592 BEDS

CLIMATE: JAN—AVG. (37.2 DEGREES), JULY—AVG. (76.8 DEGREES), ANNUAL PRECIPITATION (46.02 INCHES)

PER CAPITA INCOME: $16,288

UNEMPLOYMENT RATE: 2.7%

JOB GROWTH SINCE 1980: + 36.2%

COST OF LIVING: 107.3

EDUCATION: UNIVERSITY OF NORTH CAROLINA AT CHAPEL HILL

NORTH DAKOTA

STATE LAWS REGARDING HOMOSEXUALITY:

The sodomy law in North Dakota was repealed in 1975.

CITIES: (60,000 AND UP)

FARGO

Gay Civil Rights: None

What the Locals Say . . .

The community as a whole in Fargo, North Dakota, and in Moorhead, Minnesota (a sister city just across the state line), is still quite closed. The gay/lesbian community ranges from middle-of-the-road to closeted. The new mayor of Fargo was voted in on a, "we need to get back to traditional values" platform; however, the former mayor was open to gay issues. People who are really open probably would not move to this part of the country to live an "Out" lifestyle. Anywhere is all right to live as there are no particular neighborhoods which would be better for gays than others. Gays do frequent "Ralph's Corner Bar," but it is not exclusively gay. In Moorhead, there's a place called, "The Frying Pan," which is gay-friendly. Dances sponsored by individuals are sometimes held at the "Bowler," a restaurant. There is a gay group in the area called The Round Table; they are a support/social group. They have meetings on Sunday nights and activities on Thursday nights. Moorhead State University has a 10% Society. There is also the West Central AIDS Project operated out of the Clay County Health Department located in Moorhead. Health care in the area is good; however, the medical community in general is ignorant of gay issues. The Community Health Center in Fargo does AIDS testing.

LOCATION: FARGO IS LOCATED IN THE RED RIVER VALLEY IN EASTERN NORTH DAKOTA.

GAY/LESBIAN FRIENDLY BUSINESSES: 2

GAY/LESBIAN BARS AND RESTAURANTS: NONE SPECIFICALLY

GAY/LESBIAN ORGANIZATIONS: 3

GAY/LESBIAN RELIGIOUS ORGANIZATIONS, CHURCHES, ETC.: 0

GAY/LESBIAN BOOKSTORES: 0

GAY/LESBIAN PUBLICATIONS: 0

COMPANIES THAT PROHIBIT DISCRIMINATION: A.T.&T.

INFORMATION NUMBER: 701-235-7335 THIS IS A GENERAL HOT LINE NUMBER, THEY WILL GIVE YOU A NUMBER FOR THE ROUND TABLE.

TOTAL CRIMES: 3,919

VIOLENT = (MURDER = 0, RAPE = 37, ROBBERY = 17, ASSAULT = 44)

PROPERTY = (BURGLARY = 428, LARCENY = 3,176, MOTOR VEHICLE THEFT = 217, ARSON = N/A)

Things to Do!!!

There are approximately 30 casinos in Fargo. Other things to see and do include: (1) Bonanzaville, USA, (2) Fargo-Moorhead Community Theatre, (3) Fargo Theatre, (4) Roger Maris Museum. ANNUAL EVENTS: (1) Red River Valley Fair, (2) Pioneer Days.

POPULATION: 77,052 PERSONS—W = 71,968, B = 260, AI/E/A = 796, C = 188, F = 63, M = 331, PR = 20

POPULATION GROWTH: + 25.5%

AGE OF POPULATION: (21-24) = 10.9%, (25-34) = 20.1%, (35-44) = 14.6%, (45-54) = 7.9%, (55-64) = 6.7%, (65-74) = 5.2%, (75 AND OVER) = 4.8%

HOUSING COST: OWNING = $70,300   RENTAL = $355

COMMUNITY HOSPITALS: 3 = 643 BEDS

CLIMATE: JAN—AVG. (5.9 DEGREES), JULY—AVG. (71.1 DEGREES), ANNUAL PRECIPITATION (19.45 INCHES)

PER CAPITA INCOME: $13,554

UNEMPLOYMENT RATE: 2.6%

JOB GROWTH SINCE 1980: + 26.6%

COST OF LIVING: 102.7

EDUCATION: NORTH DAKOTA STATE

OHIO

STATE LAWS REGARDING HOMOSEXUALITY:

In 1974, Governor John Gilligan signed an extension of the criminal code which repealed the sodomy law. Legislation was also passed which bans anti-gay discrimination in public employment.

CITIES: (60,000 AND UP)

CINCINNATI

Gay Civil Rights: None

What the Locals Say . . .

Cincinnati is a fairly modern city; but politically, it is mostly conservative. The gay and lesbian community is very open, although the current sheriff is said to be homophobic. The main newspaper gave whole page coverage to a male union which did cause some controversy. The Northside neighborhood has a high concentration of gays and lesbians and is becoming increasingly popular. The "Crazy Ladies" is a gay and lesbian bookstore located upstairs in the Cincinnati Women's Center. The "Pink Pyramid" is a gay/lesbian bookstore that sells books, magazines and cards. Cincinnati has the organizations: Gays and Lesbians United for Educations (GLUE), and the "Suns"(a nudist group). River City Sports is a large organization that consists of a bowling league, 10-12 baseball teams, a soccer league, tennis league, volleyball league, camping and hiking group, and aerobics. Cincinnati has Frontrunners, a group for runners, although walkers are welcome. The Gays Men's Chorus is popular and funded by the City of Cincinnati. Brother II Brother is an Afro-American organization, and there is a group for lesbians called, "Slightly Older Lesbians." The Log Cabin Republican Club and the Stonewall Democratic Club are two of the political organizations in Cincinnati. The Pride Committee organizes the Pride Celebration, which includes a boat ride, gay day at Kings Island, a parade in downtown, a festival and a gay only picnic. "Gay Day" at Kings Island, a theme park, is a yearly event that draws thousands of gays and lesbians. Queer City Association is a group of several hundred professionals who band together and publish a resource book which offers services and discounts to the gay and lesbian community. Some of the most popular cafes are: "Carols Corner Cafe" which is very popular and serves excellent food and attracts a mixed crowd; "Peterson's Restaurants" with three locations are all good choices; a newly opened "Jimmy's" in the downtown area and "G.J. Gaslight." "Highland" and "Grazi" are coffeehouses that draw a mixed crowd. Kalde's is a coffeehouse and a bookstore as well. Predominantly gay men's bars include: the "Subway"—a drag bar, "Spurs"—a soft leather bar, "Shooters"—a country bar, and the

"Dock"—a disco bar where something different is happening every night. "Bull Fishes Tavern" and "Chasers" are lesbian bars, "Shirley's Tight End" is a neighborhood dance bar, and "Companions" is a gay dating/introduction service. The AIDS care in Cincinnati is very good; and, in fact, there is a whole wing of a hospital dedicated to AIDS patients. The Caracole is an AIDS hospice house that is staffed 24 hours a day. AIDS Volunteers of Cincinnati (AVOC) is a very powerful organization with excellent outreach. Their services include education, meals on wheels, and a network of nurses. *Gay Beat* is the Cincinnati gay and lesbian newspaper published twice a month. The New Spirit MCC, Mt. Auburn Presbyterian Church, Church of our Savior and two or three St. John Unitarians Churches are open to gays and lesbians. The groups Integrity and Dignity welcome gays and lesbians as well.

LOCATION: CINCINNATI IS LOCATED IN SOUTHWESTERN OHIO WITH THE OHIO RIVER FLOWING THROUGH THE CITY.

GAY/LESBIAN FRIENDLY BUSINESSES: 10

GAY/LESBIAN BARS AND RESTAURANTS:10

GAY/LESBIAN ORGANIZATIONS: 18

GAY/LESBIAN RELIGIOUS ORGANIZATIONS, CHURCHES, ETC.: 7

GAY/LESBIAN BOOKSTORES: 2

GAY/LESBIAN PUBLICATIONS: 1

COMPANIES THAT PROHIBIT DISCRIMINATION: SEE STATE LAW

INFORMATION NUMBER: 513-651-0070 SWITCHBOARD

TOTAL CRIMES: 30,923

VIOLENT = (MURDER = 39, RAPE = 449, ROBBERY = 2,327, ASSAULT = 2,806)

PROPERTY = (BURGLARY = 6,154, LARCENY = 17,085, MOTOR VEHICLE THEFT = 2,063, ARSON = 581)

Things to Do!!!

Cincinnati is filled with cultural and recreational opportunities. The downtown has been refurbished and offers many activities. Specific sites to see and things to do include: (1) Cincinnati Art Museum, (2) Museum of Natural History, (3) Cincinnati Convention Center and Skywalk, (4) Cincinnati Fire Museum, (5) Contemporary Arts Center, (6) Cincinnati Historical Society, (7) John Hauck House Museum, (8) Fountain Square Plaza, (9) Union Terminal, (10) Hamilton House Courthouse, (11) Mt. Adams, (12) Cincinnati Opera, (13) Cincinnati Ballet, (14) Cincinnati Symphony Orchestra, (15) Cincinnati Zoo and Botanical Garden, (16) Airport Playfield, (17) Paramount's Kings Island, (18) River Cruises, (19) Bicentennial Commons at Sawyer Point, (20) Eden Park, (21) Mount Airy Forest & Arboretum, (22) Civic Garden Center of Greater Cincinnati, (23) East Fork State Park, (24) Professional Sports: Baseball - Reds, Football - Bengals. ANNU-

AL EVENTS: (1) May Festival, (2) Riverfront Stadium Festival, (3) Riverfest, (4) International Folk Festival, SEASONAL EVENTS: (1) River Downs Race Track, (2) Turfway Park Race Course.

POPULATION: 364,278 PERSONS—W = 220,285, B = 138,132, AI/E/A = 660, C = 1,086, F = 424, M = 704, PR = 376

POPULATION GROWTH: - 5.5%

AGE OF POPULATION: (21-24) = 7.6%, (25-34) = 19.4%, (35-44) = 13.0%, (45-54) = 7.8%, (55-64) = 7.8%, (65-74) = 7.2%, (75 AND OVER) = 6.7%

HOUSING COST: OWNING = $61,900   RENTAL = $329

COMMUNITY HOSPITALS:13 = 4,683 BEDS

CLIMATE: JAN—AVG. (29.8 DEGREES), JULY—AVG. (76.4 DEGREES), ANNUAL PRECIPITATION (40.70 INCHES)

PER CAPITA INCOME: $12,547

UNEMPLOYMENT RATE: 5.9%

JOB GROWTH SINCE 1980: - 1.2%

COST OF LIVING: 100.8

EDUCATION: UNIVERSITY OF CINCINNATI, XAVIER UNIVERSITY, HEBREW UNION COLLEGE-JEWISH INSTITUTE OF RELIGION

CLEVELAND

Gay Civil Rights: None

What the Locals Say . . .

For the most part, Cleveland is closeted, although the gay and lesbian community seems to be coming out of the closet somewhat. The Lakewood area has the largest concentration of gays and lesbians. There are coffeeshops, cafes, restaurants, card shops, bookstores and other gay and lesbian owned businesses in Lakewood. The Community Center offers support groups for gay and lesbian youths; a homes group, which is a coming out group; and a 20-something group. Next door to the community center is a place for HIV patients to come to get a haircut, sleep, TLC, or have various other needs met. Cleveland has several gay and lesbian politicians. Volunteering at various organizations is very popular with gays and lesbians in Cleveland. Cleveland has a gay and lesbian veterans group, gay and lesbian bowling league, Lesbian Business Association, Speak Out, ACT UP, Stonewall Union Lesbian and Gay Reports (a Television Show), and a Catholic Lesbian Support Group. The Gay Pride Festival and Dancing in the Streets are two of the year's biggest events. Edgewater Park (though not officially) is predominately gay, especially near the beach and water. The bar scene offers something for everyone. "U 4 IA" is a mixed dance bar, and "Ohio City Oasis" is a mixed bar as well. "Numbers" and "Rockies" are predominately gay dance bars. "5 cent

Decision" is a lesbian bar, while "Paradise Inn" is a lesbian dance bar. Health care for the gay and lesbian community is about average compared to the rest of the United States. *The Gay Peoples Chronicles* is a twice a month publication. *The Gay Peoples Chronicles* also offers a resource directory of various gay friendly and gay and lesbian owned businesses and services. The only church that is specifically gay is the MCC.

LOCATION: CLEVELAND IS LOCATED ON LAKE ERIE IN NORTHERN OHIO.

GAY/LESBIAN FRIENDLY BUSINESSES: 13

GAY/LESBIAN BARS AND RESTAURANTS: 19

GAY/LESBIAN ORGANIZATIONS: 15

GAY/LESBIAN RELIGIOUS ORGANIZATIONS, CHURCHES, ETC.: 4

GAY/LESBIAN BOOKSTORES: 5

GAY/LESBIAN PUBLICATIONS: 3

COMPANIES THAT PROHIBIT DISCRIMINATION: SEE STATE LAW

INFORMATION NUMBER: 216-522-1999 LESBIAN GAY COMMUNITY SERVICES CENTER

TOTAL CRIMES: 40,005

VIOLENT = (MURDER = 167, RAPE = 834, ROBBERY = 4,297, ASSAULT = 3,012)

PROPERTY = (BURGLARY = 8,031, LARCENY = 13,494, MOTOR VEHICLE THEFT = 10,170, ARSON = 656)

Things to Do!!!

The Cuyahoga River Flats area is the dining and entertainment center of the city. There are 39 city parks with over 17,500 acres set aside for recreation. Other sites to see and things to do include: (1) Downtown Area -The Cleveland Arcade, USS COD, Steamship William G. Mather Museum, Tower City Center, Playhouse Square Center, Hanna Fountain Mall, (2) Western Reserve Museum, (3) The Cleveland Museum of Art, (4) Cleveland Health Education Museum, (5) Dunham Tavern Museum, (6) Temple Museum of Religious Art, (7) Dittrick Museum of Medical History, (8) Cleveland Orchestra, (9) Karamu House and Theatre, (10) Cleveland Play House, (11) Parks-Wildwood Park, Rockefeller Park, Wade Park, Brookside Park, Edgewater Park, (12) Professional Sports: Football - Browns, Baseball - Indians, Basketball - Cavaliers, Soccer - Crunch. ANNUAL EVENTS: (1) Tri-City JazzFest, (2) Slavic Village Harvest Festival, (3) Cuyahoga County Fair, (4) Cleveland National Air Show.

POPULATION: 502,539, PERSONS—W = 250,234, B = 235,405, AI/E/A = 1,562, C = 1,645, F = 650, M = 1,991, PR = 17,829

POPULATION GROWTH: -12.4%

AGE OF POPULATION: (21-24) = 6.1%, (25-34) = 18.0%, (35-44) = 12.7%, (45-54) = 8.7%, (55-64) = 9.0%, (65-74) = 8.2%, (75 AND OVER) = 5.8%

HOUSING COST: OWNING = $40,900   RENTAL = $322

COMMUNITY HOSPITALS: 15 = 5,586 BEDS

CLIMATE: JAN—AVG. (24.8 DEGREES), JULY—AVG. (71.9 DEGREES), ANNUAL PRECIPITATION (36.63 INCHES)

PER CAPITA INCOME: $9,258

UNEMPLOYMENT RATE: 8.5%

JOB GROWTH SINCE 1980: -11.7%

COST OF LIVING: 105.7

EDUCATION: CLEVELAND STATE UNIVERSITY, JOHN CARROLL UNIVERSITY

▼COLUMBUS

Gay Civil Rights: Bans discrimination based on sexual orientation in public and private employment, public accommodations, education, housing and credit.

What the Locals Say . . .

Columbus boasts it has the largest gay and lesbian population in Ohio. Like many cities, part of the city is openly gay-friendly while other areas are not. The best areas to live in if you are a gay man are German Village, Victorian Village, and Italian Village. The best area to live in if you are a lesbian is Clintonville. Pride Flags and other signs of gays and lesbians are prevalent throughout those areas. Columbus is touted as having the largest gay and lesbian bowling league contingency in the United States. There are four winter leagues and one summer league. Softball is also very popular in Columbus. The Pride March and Gay Fest was attended by approximately 11,000 individuals in 1994. Other activities in the Columbus area include: Gay Men's Chorus, Women's Chorus, Columbus Stompers, Capital City Cycling Club, Columbus Owls, Volleyball Leagues- (recreation, amateur, competitive), Lambda Car Club, Lambda Sci Fi Club, Women's Rugby, Women's Martial Arts, and a newly forming Tennis Organization. The bars are mainly mixed. Some of the most popular gay bars for men are: the "Columbus Eagle," "Eagle in Exile," and "Tradewinds II." The most popular lesbian bars are: "Summit Station" and "Wallstreet." Columbus has three gay and lesbian newspapers. *The Stonewall Union Journal* is published monthly, while the *Gay Beat* and the *Gay Peoples Chronicle* are published twice monthly. There are at least 23 different churches who welcome gays and lesbians into their congregations. Some congregations consist of only gays and lesbians.

LOCATION: COLUMBUS IS LOCATED IN CENTRAL OHIO.

GAY/LESBIAN FRIENDLY BUSINESSES: 234

GAY/LESBIAN BARS AND RESTAURANTS: 14

GAY/LESBIAN ORGANIZATIONS: 31

GAY/LESBIAN RELIGIOUS ORGANIZATIONS, CHURCHES, ETC.: 9

GAY/LESBIAN BOOKSTORES: 2

GAY/LESBIAN PUBLICATIONS: 7

COMPANIES THAT PROHIBIT DISCRIMINATION: SEE STATE LAW AND GAY CIVIL RIGHTS

INFORMATION NUMBER: 614-299-7764 STONEWALL UNION HOTLINE

TOTAL CRIMES: 56,322

VIOLENT = (MURDER = 105, RAPE = 658, ROBBERY = 3,887, ASSAULT = 2,496)

PROPERTY = (BURGLARY = 13,055, LARCENY = 29,051, MOTOR VEHICLE THEFT = 2,070, ARSON = 1,029)

Things to Do!!!

Columbus residents tend to focus on government and education, although sports and culture are still a very big part of the community. (1) Columbus Museum of Art, (2) Ohio Historical Center, (3) Santa Maria Replica, (4) Ohio State Capital, (5) The Columbus Symphony Orchestra, (6) Ballet Met, (7) Ohio Prehistoric Indian Mounds. (8) Park of Roses, (9) Columbus Zoological Gardens. ANNUAL EVENTS: (1) Greater Columbus Arts Festival, (2) Ohio State Fair, (3) Columbus Day Celebration.

POPULATION: 642,987 PERSONS—W = 471,025, B = 142,748, AI/E/A = 1,469, C = 3,412, F = 943, M = 2,090, PR = 1,406

AGE OF POPULATION: (21-24) = 9.5%, (25-34) = 22.2%, (35-44) = 14.3%, (45-54) = 8.1%, (55-64) = 6.9%, (65-74) = 5.4%, (75 AND OVER) = 3.8%

POPULATION GROWTH: + 13.8%

HOUSING COST: OWNING = $66,000   RENTAL = $422

COMMUNITY HOSPITALS: 8 = 3,857 BEDS

CLIMATE: JAN—AVG. (26.4 DEGREES), JULY—AVG. (73.2 DEGREES), ANNUAL PRECIPITATION (38.09 INCHES)

PER CAPITA INCOME: $13,151

UNEMPLOYMENT RATE: 4.8%

JOB GROWTH SINCE 1980: + 23.7%

COST OF LIVING: 102.7

EDUCATION: OHIO STATE UNIVERSITY

▼DAYTON

Gay Civil Rights: Bans discrimination based on sexual orientation in public employment.

What the Locals Say . . .

Being gay in Dayton is not really a hot issue. There is a large and pretty open community of gays/lesbians. Police respond well to the gay community. St. Ann's Hill District, a historical district, is a popular area for family. Dayton enjoys a world of religious, political, recreational, and support groups, with many of them meeting in the Dayton Lesbian and Gay Center located at 1424 W. Dorothy Lane. Groups meeting at the center include the Miami Men's Chorus, Parents with Pride, the Natalie Barney Literary Salon, The Women's Hour, etc. Outside the community center, there are a multitude of organizations and activities to choose from. There is Team Dayton, the umbrella organization for most athletic activities in the area. Dayton has gay bowling, volleyball, softball, and tennis. Some of the religious and church groups are, BGLAD, MCC, Community Gospel Church, Community Unity and Wholeness Project, Dignity Dayton, and the First United Methodist Church Outreach. Dayton has a Parents with Pride group, the AIDS Foundation of Miami Valley, a group called the Couples of the Miami Valley, a Youth Quest group, and a group named URSUS which is a group of leather men who raise funds for other gay groups. The organizations and groups mentioned are only a sampling of what's available in Dayton. Pick up a copy of *The Dayton SPECTRUM* at any bar or the community center for a listing of what's going on in Dayton. "Jessies" is primarily a men's dance bar, "The Edge, Inc." is a men's bar and has a leather shop, the "Detour" is a mixed and sometimes alternative bar, and the "Dugout" is mostly women. In all, there are thirteen bars in the Dayton area. There are at least three "out" doctors in Dayton and one is primarily treating HIV patients. If you are just moving to the area, a great place to get started would be to check out the Dayton Lesbian and Gay Center. All in all, the gay community in Dayton seems to be very well rounded, and progressive.

LOCATION: DAYTON IS LOCATED AT THE FORK OF THE GREAT MIAMI RIVER IN SOUTHWESTERN OHIO.

GAY/LESBIAN FRIENDLY BUSINESSES: 25+

GAY/LESBIAN BARS AND RESTAURANTS: 13

GAY/LESBIAN ORGANIZATIONS: 50+

GAY/LESBIAN RELIGIOUS ORGANIZATIONS, CHURCHES, ETC.: 3

GAY/LESBIAN BOOKSTORES: 0

GAY/LESBIAN PUBLICATIONS: 2

COMPANIES THAT PROHIBIT DISCRIMINATION: KINKOS, MEAD DATA CENTRAL, AT&T

INFORMATION NUMBER: HOTLINE (DLGC) 513-274-1776

VIOLENT = (MURDER = 49, RAPE = 269, ROBBERY = 1,475, ASSAULT = 1,129)

PROPERTY = (BURGLARY = 4,303, LARCENY = 9,473, MOTOR VEHICLE THEFT = 2,929, ARSON = 260)

Things to Do!!!

(1) United States Air Force Museum, (2) The Dayton Art Institute, (3) Dayton Museum of Natural History, (4) Sun Watch Archaeological Park, (5) Eastwood Lake. ANNUAL EVENTS: (1) US Air & Trade Show, (2) Dayton Horse Show, (3) Montgomery County Fair.

POPULATION: 183,189 PERSONS—W = 106,258, B = 73,595, AI/E/A = 410, C = 162, F = 113, M = 528, PR = 270

POPULATION GROWTH: - 5.3%

AGE OF POPULATION: (21-24) = 7.3%, (25-34) = 18.0%, (35-44) = 13.0%, (45-54) = 8.3%, (55-64) = 8.5%, (65-74) = 7.8%, (75 AND OVER) = 5.3%

HOUSING COST: OWNING = $43,200   RENTAL = $329

COMMUNITY HOSPITALS: 5 = 2,428 BEDS

CLIMATE: JAN—AVG. (26.0 DEGREES), JULY—AVG. (74.2 DEGREES), ANNUAL PRECIPITATION (36.64 INCHES)

PER CAPITA INCOME: $9,946

UNEMPLOYMENT RATE: 8.7%

JOB GROWTH SINCE 1980: - 9.0%

COST OF LIVING: 99.1

EDUCATION: UNIVERSITY OF DAYTON

COUNTIES:

CAYAHOGA COUNTY

Gay Civil Rights: Bans discrimination based on sexual orientation in public employment.

Towns and Cities Included Within Cayahoga County:

Bay Village
Beachwood
Bedford
Bedford Heights
Berea

Brecksville
Broadview Hieghts
Brooklyn
Brook Park
Cleveland
Cleveland Hieghts
East Cleveland
Euclid
Fairview Park
Garfield Heights
Highland Heights
Independence
Lakewood
Lyndhurst
Maple Heights
Mayfield Heights
Middleburg Heights
North Olmstead
North Royalton
Olmsted Falls
Parma
Parma Heights
Pepper Pike
Richmond Heights
Rocky River
Seven Hills
Shaker Heights
Solon
South Euclid
Strongsville
Universal Heights
Warrensville Heights
Westlake
West Lake

OKLAHOMA

STATE LAWS REGARDING HOMOSEXUALITY:

Heterosexual and homosexual sodomy is illegal and carries a maximum ten year sentence.

❧

CITIES: (60,000 AND UP)

OKLAHOMA CITY

Gay Civil Rights: None

What the Locals Say . . .

The gay and lesbian community within itself is very open, although to the outside community it isn't very visible. There is a gay and lesbian district between 39th and 36th Streets, and Pennsylvania and May Streets. This area has several bars nearby, the Oasis Resource Center for gays and lesbians, various restaurants, and a residential neighborhood. 39th Street is the strip that has eight bars. "Gushers Bar," The "Wreck Room," and "Angles," all have a mixed crowd of gays and lesbians, "Tramps," "The Park" and "Bunk House" draw predominately men, "Porthole" and "The Coyote Club" are predominately lesbian bars. "The Habana Inn" is a gay hotel that has a two mixed bars; "The Finish Line" and "Gushers." "Gushers" also has a restaurant. There are several gay/lesbian restaurants in Oklahoma City: "The Kitchen" (often referred to as The Diner), "The Bunkhouse," "La Roca" (a Mexican restaurant), "The Buckboard Restaurant," "The Patio Cafe," and "The Greatful Bean." "Dreamland," "Elite Bookstore," and "Whittier Bookstore" carry gay and lesbian literature. Gay May Day, sponsored by Pride Network, is a community festival event featuring crafts, merchandise, gifts, information booths and a ongoing variety of entertainment. There are several gay and lesbian organizations in Oklahoma City such as the Lambda Bowling League, Primetimers group, The Oklahoma Gay Rodeo Association, The Gay Trail Ride Group, Finishline Dancers, and the Finishline Cloggers. The Oasis Resource Center offers several support groups including: AA, NA, and Overeaters Anonymous. There is also a Young Gay and Lesbian Alliance out of the Oasis Center. The political group, Oklahoma Gay and Lesbian Political Caucus, helps the gay and lesbian community stay abreast of current gay and lesbian issues in the state. The Pride Network organizes the week long Gay Pride Festival. The Pride Festival consists of a block party, a picnic in Memorial Park, a drag show in the amphitheater, a parade, and a pool party at the Habana Inn. The Carpenter Square Theatre is a gay-friendly dramatic theatre. "Gene Barons Gifts and Books" offers self help books as well as gay and lesbian titles. Oklahoma City also has a gay television program called, "Gay News Break." Testing the Limits is a free anonymous testing site for HIV. Red Rock Mental Health Clinic offers HIV/AIDS Gay & Lesbian Outreach, adult gay and lesbian support groups, and Young Gay and Lesbian Alliance. The AIDS Coalition of Central Oklahoma AIDS Task Force, Triangle Association, Open Your Heart Foundation, and Hospice Care of Oklahoma all offer AIDS related services. *The Gayly Oklahoman* is published twice a month. There are many churches that are open and affirming to gays and lesbians. The Holy Union Specialists do just that, perform holy unions for gays and lesbians. The Holy Trinity Church, Lambda Church of Christ for Gays, The Lighthouse MCC and the Unitarian Church, and The Jewish Synagogue Reformed Temple Bnai are open to gays and lesbians. The groups Gay Christian Ecumenical Council, Affirmation, Dignity/Integrity, The Religious Society of Friends (Quaker) are open and affirming to gays and lesbians.

LOCATION: OKLAHOMA CITY LOCATED ATOP ONE OF THE NATION'S LARGEST OIL FIELDS IN CENTRAL OKLAHOMA.

GAY/LESBIAN FRIENDLY BUSINESSES: 9

GAY/LESBIAN BARS AND RESTAURANTS: 16

GAY/LESBIAN ORGANIZATIONS: 13

GAY/LESBIAN RELIGIOUS ORGANIZATIONS, CHURCHES, ETC.: 10

GAY/LESBIAN BOOKSTORES: 1

GAY/LESBIAN PUBLICATIONS: 1

COMPANIES THAT PROHIBIT DISCRIMINATION: N/A

INFORMATION NUMBER: 405-525-2437 OASIS RESOURCE CENTER

TOTAL CRIMES: 51,335

VIOLENT = (MURDER = 80, RAPE = 515, ROBBERY = 1,724, ASSAULT = 4,161)

PROPERTY = (BURGLARY = 10,000, LARCENY = 29,316, MOTOR VEHICLE THEFT = 5,539, ARSON = 420)

Things to Do!!!

(1) Civic Center Music Hall, (2) Oklahoma Art Center, (3) Artsplace, (4) Kirkpatrick Center, (5) Harn Homestead and 1889er Museum, (6) 45th Infantry Division Museum, (7) Enterprise Square, USA, (8) Metro Concourse, (9) State Capital, (10) National Softball Hall of Fame and Museum and Stadium Complex, (11) National Cowboy Hall of Fame and Western Heritage Center, (12) Oklahoma Firefighters Museum, (13) Oklahoma Museum of Art, (14) Oklahoma City Zoo, (15) Garden Exhibition Building and Horticulture Gardens, (16) Frontier City, (17) Oklahoma National Stock Yards, (18) White Water. ANNUAL EVENTS: (1) Festival of the Arts, (2) Red Earth Days, (3) Festfall, (4) State Fair of Oklahoma, (5) World Championship Quarter Horse Show. SEASONAL EVENTS: (1) Oklahoma Philharmonic Orchestra, (2) Ballet Oklahoma, (3) Lyric

Theatre.

POPULATION: 453,995 PERSONS—W = 332,539, B = 71,064, AI/E/A = 18,794, C = 1,376, F = 608, M = 17,626, PR = 656

POPULATION GROWTH: + 12.4%

AGE OF POPULATION: (21-24) = 6.0%, (25-34) = 18.7%, (35-44) = 15.0%, (45-54) = 10.0%, (55-64) = 8.4%, (65-74) = 6.8%, (75 AND OVER) = 5.1%

HOUSING COST: OWNING = $54,900   RENTAL = $364

COMMUNITY HOSPITALS: 10 = 3,087 BEDS

CLIMATE: JAN—AVG. (35.9 DEGREES), JULY—AVG. (82.0 DEGREES), ANNUAL PRECIPITATION (33.36 INCHES)

PER CAPITA INCOME: $13,528

UNEMPLOYMENT RATE: 6.1%

JOB GROWTH SINCE 1980: + 14.1%

COST OF LIVING: 92.5

EDUCATION: OKLAHOMA CITY UNIVERSITY

OREGON

STATE LAWS REGARDING HOMOSEXUALITY:

In 1972, homosexual acts between consenting adults became legal. Oregon considers crimes based on sexual orientation to be hate crimes.

CITIES: (60,000 AND UP)

▼PORTLAND

Gay Civil Rights: **Bans discrimination based on sexual orientation in public and private employment, public accommodations and housing.**

What the Locals Say . . .

Portland is a fairly open city, although there is some animosity from the heterosexual community. The best part of town for gay men to live in is the northwest quadrant. The best area for lesbians is the southeast quadrant. Hawthorne Boulevard is an area that is filled with coffeehouses and gay-owned and gay-friendly shops. Waterfront Park is not specifically gay, although it is very open. There are numerous activities available in Portland including: dances, pool tournaments, softball leagues, bowling leagues, youth groups, couple and individual support groups, and a Pride Celebration. Some of the bars are mixed with heterosexual and homosexual clientele. Among some of the most popular are: "Panorama" a dance club, and "Embers"—a dance club and drag show. Some of the best exclusively gay bars are: "Starkey's" bar and restaurant; and the lesbian dance club, "Choices." The Cascade AIDS Project is a very large and very well respected organization. It offers many outreach and educational services throughout the state. Individuals can contact Phoenix Rising to find a resource list of individuals for practically any service needed. *Just Out* is the major gay and lesbian newspaper and is distributed as far north as Vancouver and as far south as Eugene. *Just Out* is published every two weeks. Several churches are very accepting and open to gay and lesbians including: Unitarian, MCC, Methodist and a whole range of other denominations.

LOCATION: PORTLAND IS LOCATED ACROSS BOTH BANKS OF THE WILLAMETTE RIVER, JUST SOUTH OF WHERE IT MEETS THE COLUMBIA RIVER.

GAY/LESBIAN FRIENDLY BUSINESSES: 33

GAY/LESBIAN BARS AND RESTAURANTS: 18

GAY/LESBIAN ORGANIZATIONS: 28

GAY/LESBIAN RELIGIOUS ORGANIZATIONS, CHURCHES, ETC.: 9

GAY/LESBIAN BOOKSTORES: 1

GAY/LESBIAN PUBLICATIONS: 2

COMPANIES THAT PROHIBIT DISCRIMINATION: SEE GAY CIVIL RIGHTS

INFORMATION NUMBER: 503-223-8299 PHOENIX RISING

TOTAL CRIMES: 51,765

VIOLENT = (MURDER = 58, RAPE = 479, ROBBERY = 2,305, ASSAULT = 5,603)

PROPERTY = (BURGLARY = 7,845, LARCENY = 27,016, MOTOR VEHICLE THEFT = 8,459, ARSON = 604)

Things to Do!!!

Waterfalls, forests, ski slopes, fishing streams, hunting and camping areas are within easy access. Specific points of interest include: (1) Washington Park, (2) Mt. Hood, (3) Columbia River Gorge, (4) World Forestry Center, (5) Council Crest Park, (6) Peninsula Park and Community Center, (7) Oregon Museum of Science & Industry, (8) American Advertising Museum, (9) Portland Art Museum, (10) Professional Sports: Basketball- Trail Blazers, Hockey - Winter Hawks. ANNUAL EVENTS: (1) Portland Rose Festival, (2) Multnomah County Fair, (3) Mt. Hood Festival of Jazz, (4) Portland Marathon, (5) Christmas Boat Parade. SEASONAL EVENTS: (1) Horse racing, (2) Oregon Shakespeare Festival.

POPULATION: 445,458 PERSONS—W = 370,135, B = 33,530, AI/E/A = 5,399, C = 5,524, F = 1,973, M = 8,631, PR = 591

POPULATION GROWTH: + 21%

AGE OF POPULATION:(21-24) = 6.1%, (25-34) = 18.8%, (35-44) = 17.7%, (45-54) = 9.3%, (55-64) = 7.5%, (65-74) = 7.8%, (75 AND OVER) = 6.8%

HOUSING COST: OWNING = $59,200   RENTAL = $397

COMMUNITY HOSPITALS: 11 = 2,901 BEDS

CLIMATE: JAN—AVG. (39.6 DEGREES), JULY—AVG. (68.2 DEGREES), ANNUAL PRECIPITATION (36.30 INCHES)

PER CAPITA INCOME: $14,478

UNEMPLOYMENT RATE: 5.3%

JOB GROWTH SINCE 1980: + 24.7%

COST OF LIVING: N/A

EDUCATION: PORTLAND STATE UNIVERSITY, UNIVERSITY OF PORTLAND

PENNSYLVANIA

STATE LAWS REGARDING HOMOSEXUALITY:

In 1982, the state sodomy laws were repealed. The state bans anti-gay discrimination in public employment.

CITIES: (60,000 AND UP)

▼PHILADELPHIA

Gay Civil Rights: Bans discrimination based on sexual orientation in public and private employment, public accommodations, housing, credit and union practices.

What the Locals Say . . .

The gay and lesbian community in Philadelphia is very big and fairly open. Philadelphia is unique in that among major cities, it has a large center city population that happens to be heavily gay. The politicians, for the most part, are pro-gay. The neighborhood that has the largest gay and lesbian concentration is, of course, Center City. Center City has bars, businesses and older three story homes. Fairmount is near the Parkway and is another area that has a lot of gay and lesbian residents. Pride Fest is a huge gay pride celebration. In 1995, there were over 40 informational programs and over 11 social events. Some of the activities included several dances (CelebrASIAN, Cinco de Mayo, Tea Dance, Teen Dance, etc.), a barbecue, and an Over 40 and Fabulous Cocktail Party and Dinner Show, a brunch and, of course, a Pride Parade. The Philadelphia Gay and Lesbian Film Festival is a 10 day event that in 1995 had over 40 feature films and over 30 short films. Penguin Place, The Gay and Lesbian Community Center of Philadelphia, offers youth services including discussion groups and social outings and a library for lesbigay youth 21 years old and under. Voyage House, Inc. is a Community Center that provides individual youth counseling and youth crisis counseling for lesbigay youth 21 and under and a buddy program. There are hundreds of gay-friendly organizations, groups, restaurants, and business in Philadelphia, the following are only a sample: "Giovania" is a huge gay and lesbian bookstore. "The Cafe," "The Venture Inn," "The Philadelphian," "Ristoranti San Carol," "Rembrandt's," and "Rodz Restaurant and Cabaret" are popular lesbigay restaurants. "The Millennium" and "Balcony Cafe" are popular coffeehouses. There are several political groups in Philadelphia including the The Philadelphia Gay and Lesbian Task Force, The Philadelphia Foundation, Gay & Lesbian Democrats, Liberty Democratic Club, and the Log Cabin Republican Group. "Gay Dreams" is a gay radio program out of the University of Pennsylvania. "Fabulous" is a gay theatre company. Sport groups in

Philadelphia include a large men's and women's softball league, running group, bowling group, outdoors club, women's rugby, swim club and a wrestling club. Wilderness Women, Delaware Valley Couples Group, French Language and Italian Language group, and Unity, a gay white group, are some of the social groups in Philadelphia. Typically the bars outside of Philadelphia are mixed, while the bars within the city are separated into gay or lesbian bars. "The Lark" is a popular mixed bar, "Hepburn" is a popular lesbian bar, and "Woody's is a popular men's bar. Action AIDS provides educational outreach to people with AIDS. *The Philadelphia Gay News* and *AU Courant* are weekly gay and lesbian publications. St. Paul's Lutheran Settlement House and Bethany are safe places for gay youth. Dignity and Integrity have chapters in Philadelphia. The MCC is open and affirming to gays and lesbians.

LOCATION: PHILADELPHIA IS LOCATED IN SOUTHEASTERN PENNSYLVANIA ON THE DELAWARE RIVER.

GAY/LESBIAN FRIENDLY BUSINESSES: 500 +

GAY/LESBIAN BARS AND RESTAURANTS: 20

GAY/LESBIAN ORGANIZATIONS: 58

GAY/LESBIAN RELIGIOUS ORGANIZATIONS, CHURCHES, ETC.: 5

GAY/LESBIAN BOOKSTORES: 2

GAY/LESBIAN PUBLICATIONS: 5

COMPANIES THAT PROHIBIT DISCRIMINATION: AMERICAN FRIENDS SERVICE COMMITTEE, CORE STATES BANK, N.A., SEE STATE LAW AND GAY CIVIL RIGHTS

INFORMATION NUMBER: 215-546-7100 GAY & LESBIAN SWITCHBOARD

TOTAL CRIMES: 97,659

VIOLENT = (MURDER = 439, RAPE = 785, ROBBERY = 11,531, ASSAULT = 6,821)

PROPERTY = (BURGLARY = 15,117, LARCENY = 39,181, MOTOR VEHICLE THEFT = 23,785, ARSON = 2,282)

Things to Do!!!

(1) Independence National Historical Park - (Independence Hall, Independence Mall, Declaration House, Liberty Bell Pavilion, Independence Square, Pemberton House, The Merchant's Exchange, (2) Edgar Allen Poe National Historic Site, (3) Society Hill Area, (4) US Mint, (5) Germantown, (6) Washington Square, (7) Penn's Landing, (8) Academy of Music, (9) Philadelphia Museum of Art, (10) Please Touch Museum for Children, (11) Civil War Library and Museum, (12) Norman Rockwell Museum, (13) Fairmount Park, (14) Historic Bartram's Garden, (15) Professional Sports: Football- Eagles, Basketball - '76ers, Baseball - Phillies. ANNUAL EVENTS: (1) Mummers Parade, (2) Freedom Festival, (3) Thanksgiving Day Parade, (4) Army-Navy Football Game. SEASONAL EVENTS: (1)

American Music Theater, (2) Philadelphia Drama Guild, (3) Pennsylvania Ballet, (4) Philadelphia Orchestra, (5) Philadelphia Company, (6) The Opera Company of Philadelphia

POPULATION: 1,552,572 PERSONS—W = 848,586, B = 631,936, AI/E/A = 3,454, C = 11,691, F = 3,993, M = 3,276, PR = 67,857

POPULATION GROWTH: - 8.0%

AGE OF POPULATION: (21-24) = 6.8%, (25-34) = 17.5%, (35-44) = 13.5%, (45-54) = 9.3%, (55-64) = 9.0%, (65-74) = 8.7%, (75 AND OVER) = 6.5%

HOUSING COST: OWNING = $49,400   RENTAL = $452

COMMUNITY HOSPITALS: 36 = 9,503 BEDS

CLIMATE: JAN—AVG. (30.4 DEGREES), JULY—AVG. (76.7 DEGREES), ANNUAL PRECIPITATION (41.41 INCHES)

PER CAPITA INCOME: $12,091

UNEMPLOYMENT RATE: 8.0%

JOB GROWTH SINCE 1980: + 2.5%

COST OF LIVING: 129.6

EDUCATION: UNIVERSITY OF PENNSYLVANIA, TEMPLE UNIVERSITY, DREXEL UNIVERSITY

▼PITTSBURGH

Gay Civil Rights: Bans discrimination based on sexual orientation in public and private employment, public accommodations, housing, credit and union practices.

What the Locals Say . . .

The Pittsburgh gay and lesbian community seems to consist of two extremes, very open or very closeted. Most people are afraid to be openly affectionate with their partner. The Shady Side is a good place to live for gays and lesbians. Squirrel Hill has a lot of straight families, although there are many gays and lesbians in that area as well. There are Victorian mansions in Squirrel Hill, and it is a very nice neighborhood. The Northside, around the Mexican War Streets, is very popular. There are 100-110 community type organizations including: leather clubs, outdoor clubs, and professional clubs. There is a specific women's outdoor group, a gay and lesbian library, and a lambda Foundation. There are also many sport groups including: volleyball, tennis, softball and 5 bowling leagues. The" Sunset Strip Cafe" is on the strip in the downtown area. The Gay Pride Celebration is attended by 500-2,000. The parade was moved from downtown to Shady Side (the largest population of gays and lesbians), where there is a real park (Mellon Park) and real grass, as opposed to the concrete downtown area. Schenley Park is a huge park in Pittsburgh. Prospect Drive or what some call the Loop is an area filled with gay men in the summer.

The bar scene is mostly mixed. Most of the mixed bars are neighborhood bars and include: "Real Luck Cafe," and "Images." Some of the predominately men's bars are: "The Eagle" (a leather levi bar), "Jaze," "Pegasus" (a dance bar and the largest). Some of the most popular lesbian bars are "Bubbas" (located in a working class neighborhood), "C J Digghans" (the most popular), "Bloomers" (a non-profit bar that lost its lease and is currently trying to find a new location). The health care in Pittsburgh is very good, and in general people get whatever they need. Being gay and having AIDS is not an issue. In the early 1980's ,the University of Pittsburgh started monitoring gay men and publishing resultant statistics. Currently the Pittsburgh area is seeing a rise in infected gay males, so there is a new commission called, "Commission on AIDS Reduction Project," which pays people $50.00 to participate in educational seminars to see if that education reduces the number of newly infected individuals. Lesbian Hope is a special project that provides information for women on mammograms and other needs specifically for women. There are two local newspapers in Pittsburgh for gays and lesbians. *Out* is a monthly tabloid bar newspaper, while *Planet Queer* is a politically active newspaper that is published monthly. The religious community in the city is generally very conservative. Although, there is at least one representative group from every denomination that is open to gays and lesbians. The churches that are open to gays and lesbians are MCC, two Dignity groups, three Integrity groups, one Lutheran, and one Methodist Church that has numerous gay and lesbian events.

LOCATION: PITTSBURGH IS LOCATED IN SOUTHWESTERN PENNSYLVANIA.

GAY/LESBIAN FRIENDLY BUSINESSES: 14

GAY/LESBIAN BARS AND RESTAURANTS: 13

GAY/LESBIAN ORGANIZATIONS: 23

GAY/LESBIAN RELIGIOUS ORGANIZATIONS, CHURCHES, ETC.: 7

GAY/LESBIAN BOOKSTORES: 1

GAY/LESBIAN PUBLICATIONS: 1

COMPANIES THAT PROHIBIT DISCRIMINATION: WQED, SEE STATE LAW AND GAY CIVIL RIGHTS

INFORMATION NUMBER: 412-422-0114 GAY AND LESBIAN COMMUNITY CENTER

TOTAL CRIMES: 28,613

VIOLENT = (MURDER = 80, RAPE = 226, ROBBERY = 2,784, ASSAULT = 1,389)

PROPERTY = (BURGLARY = 4,611, LARCENY = 13,017, MOTOR VEHICLE THEFT = 6,505)

Things to Do!!!

(1) Carnegie Hall, (2) The Pittsburgh Zoo, (3) Rodef Shalom Biblical Botanical Garden, (4) The Frick Art and Historical Center,

(5) The Aviary, (6) Schenley Park, (7) Station Square, (8) Civic Arena, (9) Monongahela Incline, (10) Duquesne Incline. (11) Pittsburgh Orchestra, (12) Pittsburgh Opera, (13) Pittsburgh Ballet, (14) Phipps Conservatory, (15) Professional Sports: Football - Steelers, Baseball - Pirates, Hockey - Penguins. ANNUAL EVENTS: (1) Three Rivers Arts Festival, (2) Regatta.

POPULATION: 366,852 PERSONS—W = 266,791, B = 95,362, AI/E/A = 671, C = 1,834, F = 251, M = 926, PR = 711

POPULATION GROWTH: -13.5%

AGE OF POPULATION: (21-24) = 7.5%, (25-34) = 16.9%, (35-44) = 13.2%, (45-54) = 8.5%, (55-64) = 9.6%, (65-74) = 10.1%, (75 AND OVER) = 7.8%

HOUSING COST: OWNING = $41,200   RENTAL = $368

COMMUNITY HOSPITALS: 20 = 6,772 BEDS

CLIMATE: JAN—AVG. (26.1 DEGREES), JULY—AVG. (72.1 DEGREES), ANNUAL PRECIPITATION (36.85 INCHES)

PER CAPITA INCOME: $12,580

UNEMPLOYMENT RATE: 5.4%

JOB GROWTH SINCE 1980: 9.7%

COST OF LIVING: N/A

EDUCATION: UNIVERSITY OF PITTSBURGH

TOWNS: (5,000—60,000)

▼HARRISBURG

Gay Civil Rights: Bans discrimination based on sexual orientation in public and private employment, public accommodations, education, housing, credit, and union practices.

What the Locals Say . . .

About 50% of the gays and lesbians in Harrisburg are out, and the other half are closeted. The political climate is conservative. Harrisburg is very quiet compared to nearby Philadelphia, New York and Boston. Midtown seems to have the biggest concentration of gays and lesbians. This residential area has a lot of older townhomes. There are some gay bars on North Street. The rest of the gay community is spread throughout town. The Bisexual Gay Lesbian Youth Association of Harrisburg (BiGLYAH) is a safe environment where young adults can ask questions, get information, and simply be themselves. Harrisburg has a PFLAG group, Pennsmen group, a volleyball group and the Harrisburg Men's Chorus. The Pennsylvania Association for

Justice Campaign is a group for lesbian and gay rights. Lilly White & Company is a Drag/Theatre. Harrisburg also has a Pride Coalition, Renaissance Education Association/LSV (transgenderists and cross-dressers), Harrisburg Area Professional and Business Women, and Dialog—a gay/lesbian discussion group. The Gay and Lesbian Community Awareness Council of Central Pennsylvania is located in Harrisburg. "Court Yard" and "Beatles" are women's bars in Harrisburg. "Strawberry" is a mixed video bar and "Neptune" is a neighborhood bar. The "Paper Moon" and "Issac's" are gay-friendly restaurants. SCAAN is an AIDS organization that provides education, advocacy, support to people with HIV/AIDS and their families, buddy training and match-up, emergency financial assistance, support groups, short term counseling, case management and referrals. *The Gay & Lesbian Guide to Central Pennsylvania* and the *Lavender Letter* are both published in Harrisburg. MCC of The Spirit, MCC Vision of Hope, Unitarian Church of Harrisburg, Unity Church of Harrisburg are open and affirming to gays and lesbians.

LOCATION: HARRISBURG IS LOCATED IN THE SOUTHERN REGION OF PENNSYLVANIA.

GAY/LESBIAN FRIENDLY BUSINESSES: 10

GAY/LESBIAN BARS AND RESTAURANTS: 6

GAY/LESBIAN ORGANIZATIONS: 11

GAY/LESBIAN RELIGIOUS ORGANIZATIONS, CHURCHES, ETC.: 4

GAY/LESBIAN BOOKSTORES: 0

GAY/LESBIAN PUBLICATIONS: 1

COMPANIES THAT PROHIBIT DISCRIMINATION: SEE STATE LAW AND GAY CIVIL RIGHTS

INFORMATION NUMBER: 717-234-0328 GAY & LESBIAN SWITCHBOARD OF HARRISBURG

TOTAL CRIMES: 4,976

VIOLENT = (MURDER = 13, RAPE = 67, ROBBERY = 539, ASSAULT = 525)

PROPERTY = (BURGLARY = 1,043, LARCENY = 2,382, MOTOR VEHICLE THEFT = 407, ARSON = N/A)

Things to Do!!!

(1) State Capitol, (2) The State Museum of Pennsylvania, (3) Italian Lake, (4) Fort Hunter Park, (5) Riverfront Park. ANNUAL EVENTS: (1) Kipona, (2) Pennsylvania National Horse Show.

POPULATION: 53,430 PERSONS—W = 22,306, B = 26,502, AI/E/A = 147, C = 68, F = 27, M = 268, PR = 3,051

POPULATION GROWTH: + . 3%

HOUSING COST: OWNING = $38,400   RENTAL = $363

COMMUNITY HOSPITALS: 3 = 1,026 BEDS

CLIMATE: JAN—AVG. (28.6 DEGREES), JULY—AVG. (75.7 DEGREES), ANNUAL PRECIPITATION (40.50 INCHES)

AGE OF POPULATION: (21-24) = 6.1%, (25-34) = 18.5%, (35-44) = 14.9%, (45-54) = 8.7%, (55-64) = 7.5%, (65-74) = 6.9%, (75 AND OVER) = 6.0%

PER CAPITA INCOME: $11,037

UNEMPLOYMENT RATE: 7.2%

JOB GROWTH SINCE 1980: + 9.7%

COST OF LIVING: 105

EDUCATION: HARRISBURG COMMUNITY COLLEGE

▼LANCASTER

Gay Civil Rights: Bans discrimination based on sexual orientation in public and private employment, public accommodations, education, housing, credit, and union practices.

What the Locals Say . . .

Lancaster is relatively open, with the political climate being half pro-gay and lesbian and half anti-gay and lesbian. There is a large Amish and Mennonite community in Lancaster that doesn't tolerate homosexuality from a religious standpoint, although they do tend to support the projects of the homosexual community. There is not one area that the gays and lesbians congregate to. Everything is pretty spread out. The "Loft" is a coffeehouse that serves food and cappuccino. "Issac's Restaurant & Deli" is a popular gay-friendly restaurant. *The Lancaster County Gay Guide* is a resource book of all gay-friendly or gay and lesbian owned businesses in Lancaster County. Lancaster has a gay travel agency, and a gay dentist who gives family members a discount. There is a group of men who have a potluck dinner once a month and take-up contributions to fund the gay and lesbian information line. Lancaster Lambda and Lancaster Men's Covered Dish are two men's social groups. *The Lavender Letter* is a lesbian publication that lists 20-25 activities for lesbians to participate in each month. Susquehanna Club is a hiking, camping and outdoor activities group. The Pink Triangle Coalition is located in Lancaster. There is a PFLAG group that is active in Lancaster. There seems to be a large number of gay and lesbian teenagers in Lancaster. A city councilman has been instrumental in getting counseling into the schools for these gay and lesbian youth. There is also a 16—24 years old youth group. Lancaster County Park and Long Park are places for gays and lesbians to go. "Tallyho" is a mixed dance bar, the "Sundown" is a lesbian bar. There are several gay-friendly physicians in and around Lancaster. The Unitarian, Presbyterian, and Methodist Church are very open to gays and lesbians. The MCC has 150 members.

LOCATION: LANCASTER IS LOCATED IN SOUTHERN PENNSYLVANIA, APPROXIMATELY 50 MILES FROM HARRISBURG.

GAY/LESBIAN FRIENDLY BUSINESSES: 10 +

GAY/LESBIAN BARS AND RESTAURANTS: 4

GAY/LESBIAN ORGANIZATIONS: 8

GAY/LESBIAN RELIGIOUS ORGANIZATIONS, CHURCHES, ETC.: 4

GAY/LESBIAN BOOKSTORES: 0

GAY/LESBIAN PUBLICATIONS: 1

COMPANIES THAT PROHIBIT DISCRIMINATION: SEE STATE LAW AND GAY CIVIL RIGHTS

INFORMATION NUMBER: 717-397-0691 GAY & LESBIAN INFORMATION LINE

TOTAL CRIMES: 4,485

VIOLENT = (MURDER = 11, RAPE = 45, ROBBERY = 273, ASSAULT = 177)

PROPERTY = (BURGLARY = 882, LARCENY = 2,784, MOTOR VEHICLE THEFT = 313, ARSON = 30)

Things to Do!!!

(1) Amish & Mennonite sites, (2) Heritage Center of Lancaster County, (3) Candy Americana Museum, (4) The Watch & Clock Museum, (5) Twin Brook Winery, (6) Dutch Wonderland, (7) Fulton Opera House. ANNUAL EVENTS: (1) Sheep Shearing, (2) Victorian Circus and Fair, (3) Harvest Days, (4) Victorian Christmas Week.

POPULATION: 57,171 PERSONS—W = 39368, B = 6,802, AI/E/A = 137, C = 177, F = 25, M = 187, PR = 10,305

POPULATION GROWTH: + 4.5%

AGE OF POPULATION: (21-24) = 8.0%, (25-34) = 18.8%, (35-44) = 13.2%, (45-54) = 8.0%, (55-64) = 7.3%, (65-74) = 7.1%, (75 AND OVER) = 5.1%

HOUSING COST: OWNING = $59,200   RENTAL = $390

COMMUNITY HOSPITALS: 3 = 1,031 BEDS

CLIMATE: JAN—AVG. (27.9 DEGREES), JULY—AVG. (74.1 DEGREES), ANNUAL PRECIPITATION (41.22 INCHES)

PER CAPITA INCOME: $10,693

UNEMPLOYMENT RATE: 8.1%

JOB GROWTH SINCE 1980: + 6.7%

COST OF LIVING: 104.6

EDUCATION: FRANKLIN AND MARSHALL COLLEGE

▼YORK

Gay Civil Rights: Bans discrimination based on sexual orientation in public and private employment, public accommodations and housing.

What the Locals Say . . .

On a scale of 1-10, York rates as a 5 on being open as a gay and lesbian community. Gays and lesbians are scattered throughout the city of York. The York area Lambda has one social activity per month. Small groups throughout town have social activities frequently. Individuals who are more open go to Harrisburg or Lancaster. "Mackley's Mill" and "Issac's Restaurant & Deli" are popular gay and lesbian restaurants. York has a York Area Single Women's Potluck and a York Area Women's Potluck. York also has a gay youth group and a gay AA group. "Atland's Ranch" is the largest bar and caters to a mixed crowd of gays and lesbians and is only open Friday and Saturday nights. "14 Karat" is a mixed bar. It is not difficult to get medical treatment, although being HIV positive would not be something to discuss with your friends. *The York Area Lambda Newsletter* comes out once every two months. The United Methodist and the Unitarian churches are generally welcoming to gays and lesbians.

LOCATION: YORK IS LOCATED IN SOUTHERN PENNSYLVANIA.

GAY/LESBIAN FRIENDLY BUSINESSES: 5

GAY/LESBIAN BARS AND RESTAURANTS: 4

GAY/LESBIAN ORGANIZATIONS: 5

GAY/LESBIAN RELIGIOUS ORGANIZATIONS, CHURCHES, ETC.: 2

GAY/LESBIAN BOOKSTORES: 0

GAY/LESBIAN PUBLICATIONS: 1

COMPANIES THAT PROHIBIT DISCRIMINATION: SEE STATE LAW AND GAY CIVIL RIGHTS

INFORMATION NUMBER: 717-846-9636 YORK AREA LAMBDA

TOTAL CRIMES: 602

VIOLENT = (MURDER = 1, RAPE = 5, ROBBERY = 1, ASSAULT = 11)

PROPERTY = (BURGLARY = 105, LARCENY = 455, MOTOR VEHICLE THEFT = 20, ARSON = 4)

Things to Do!!!

History and recreation are intertwined throughout this great historical city. There are approximately 50 historic sites throughout the city of York. There are several recreational areas including: (1) Gifford Pinchot State Park, (2) Ski Roundtop. ANNUAL EVENTS: (1) The River Walk Art Festival

POPULATION: 43,301 PERSONS—W = 30,583, B = 8,968, AI/E/A = 98, C = 73, F = 20, M = 145, PR = 2,718

POPULATION GROWTH: 3.0%

AGE OF POPULATION: (21-24) = 7.5%, (25-34) = 18.7%, (35-44) = 13.1%, (45-54) = 8.5%, (55-64) = 7.7%, (65-74) = 7.4%, (75 AND OVER) = 6.1%

HOUSING COST: OWNING = $41,600   RENTAL = $357

COMMUNITY HOSPITALS: 3 = 750 BEDS

CLIMATE: JAN—AVG. (29.0 DEGREES), JULY—AVG. (74.5 DEGREES), ANNUAL PRECIPITATION (40.40 INCHES)

PER CAPITA INCOME: $10,485

UNEMPLOYMENT RATE: 7.1%

JOB GROWTH SINCE 1980: + 2.6%

COST OF LIVING: 97.8

EDUCATION: YORK COLLEGE OF PENNSYLVANIA

RHODE ISLAND

STATE LAWS REGARDING HOMOSEXUALITY:

Heterosexual and homosexual sodomy is illegal and carries a maximum twenty year sentence. In 1985, Governor DiPrete signed an executive order barring discrimination on the basis of sexual orientation in state employment. To avoid criticism, there was no public announcement. In May, 1995, Governor Almond signed into law a statewide gay civil rights law which prohibits discrimination based on sexual orientation in employment, housing, credit and public accommodations.

CITIES: (60,000 AND UP)

PROVIDENCE

Gay Civil Rights | Bans discrimination based on sexual orientation in public and private employment, public accommodations, credit and housing. (State Law)

What the Locals Say . . .

The gay and lesbian community of Providence is somewhat open and politically active. Most couples would not feel comfortable holding hands in public. The Eastside is the most gay-friendly area of town. Brown University and Rhode Island School of Design are located there. This area also has beautiful historical homes that date back to the 1600's. The Pride Week is a week long event. The Pride March attracts 5-6,000 people and includes art, comedy, performances of all kinds, and a picnic. There's a different event every night. The Gay and Lesbian Film Festival for Rhode Island is held in Providence. Social groups in Providence include Network, a little older men's group; Rhode Island Women's Group which has dances, dinners, and other activities; Enforcers, men and women into leather; cycling organization; computer group; card group; and a bowling league. "Al Forno" and "Rue de L'e Spoir" are very good gay-friendly restaurants. The "Coffee Exchange" is a coffeehouse to hang out and to see and be seen. "Adams and Steve's Garden of Eden" is a new coffeehouse gaining in popularity. Support groups include a youth group and a PFLAG group. Visions & Voices is a gay and lesbian bookstore. The Rhode Island Alliance for Lesbian/Gay Civil Rights is the largest political group in Providence. The Log Cabin, a gay Republican group; ACT-UP; and the Straight But Not Narrow Coalition, who push for gay and lesbian rights are additional political groups in Providence. The Rainbow Business Coalition advocates keeping gay and lesbian money in the family. Brown University has the Lesbian Bisexual Collective and the Lesbian Gay/Bisexual Alliance that publishes *Not Guilty*. Rhode Island College has the Gay Lesbian or Bisexual Equity Alliance. "Generation X" is the largest bar and draws a mixed crowd.

"Devilles" is a women's neighborhood dance bar. Rhode Island AIDS provides education, basic support, and assistance with food and health. *Options* is a monthly gay and lesbian publication that lists all social and political organizations. The Rhode Island Helpline provides a resource book which has a listing of gay friendly doctors, therapists, etc.. The Unitarian Church has an active gay group and is very popular. The Episcopal Church in Pawtucket is a very large and accepting church. There is also a chapter of Dignity in Providence.

LOCATION: PROVIDENCE IS LOCATED ALONG THE UPPER NARRAGANSETT BAY IN EASTERN RHODE ISLAND.

GAY/LESBIAN FRIENDLY BUSINESSES: 10 +

GAY/LESBIAN BARS AND RESTAURANTS: 6

GAY/LESBIAN ORGANIZATIONS: 18

GAY/LESBIAN RELIGIOUS ORGANIZATIONS, CHURCHES, ETC.: 3

GAY/LESBIAN BOOKSTORES: 1

GAY/LESBIAN PUBLICATIONS: 2

COMPANIES THAT PROHIBIT DISCRIMINATION: SEE STATE LAW

INFORMATION NUMBER: 401-751-3322 GAY/LESBIAN HELPLINE OF RHODE ISLAND

TOTAL CRIMES: 15,162

VIOLENT = (MURDER = 22, RAPE = 114, ROBBERY = 636, ASSAULT = 601)

PROPERTY = (BURGLARY = 4,240, LARCENY = 6,433, MOTOR VEHICLE THEFT = 3,116, ARSON = 384)

Things to Do!!!

(1) Museum of Rhode Island History at Aldrich House, (2) Roger Williams National Memorial, (3) Providence Athenaeum Library, (4) Rhode Island State House, (5) The Arcade, (6) Lincoln Woods State Park. ANNUAL EVENTS: Spring Festival of Historic Houses.

POPULATION: 155,418 PERSONS—W = 112,404, B = 23,828, AI/E/A = 1,495, C = 1,160, F = 407, M = 801, PR = 7,157

POPULATION GROWTH: -.9%

AGE OF POPULATION: (21-24) = 9.1%, (25-34) = 17.9%, (35-44) = 12.2%, (45-54) = 7.5%, (55-64) = 7.0%, (65-74) = 7.2%, (75 AND OVER) = 6.4%

HOUSING COST: OWNING = $113,000   RENTAL = $469

COMMUNITY HOSPITALS: 4 = 1,295 BEDS

CLIMATE: JAN—AVG. (27.9 DEGREES), JULY—AVG. (72.7 DEGREES), ANNUAL PRECIPITATION (45.53 INCHES)

PER CAPITA INCOME: $11,838

UNEMPLOYMENT RATE: 9.0%

JOB GROWTH SINCE 1980: +5.3%
COST OF LIVING: N/A
EDUCATION: BROWN UNIVERSITY, RHODE ISLAND SCHOOL OF DESIGN

SOUTH CAROLINA

STATE LAWS REGARDING HOMOSEXUALITY:

Heterosexual and homosexual sodomy is illegal and carries a maximum five year sentence.

CITIES: (60,000 AND UP)

▼COLUMBIA

Gay Civil Rights: Bans discrimination based on sexual orientation in public employment.

What the Locals Say . . .

Columbia has the most "out" lesbian/gay community in South Carolina. This does not mean people are "OUT" as in San Francisco, but they are "out" compared to other areas of South Carolina. The Mayor of Columbia is open minded about gay issues; but state-wide, the politics are very conservative. Most people would not be "out" at work, but would feel comfortable going to gay clubs and the gay community center. Good areas for gays to live are Murray Hill, Shandon, and Downtown. The South Carolina Gay/Lesbian Community Center has a huge volunteer base of some 200 to 250 people. It has recently received a federal grant to fund a youth group for youths under twenty one. It has all kinds of activities, puts out a newsletter, and has a Pride Shop and a library. Some groups and organizations in the area are: The South Carolina Gay and Lesbian Pride Movement, South Carolina Gay/Lesbian Business Guild, Bowling League (8 to 10 teams), Levi Leather Club (The Brigade), volleyball, softball, Les Ms (a facilitator lead education and support group), First Saturday Out, and M+B+ support group. The South Carolina Gay/Lesbian Guild is far more than a business directory; it is their "Business" to advance the various gay/lesbian causes in the area. It is an outreach organization as well as a social/business organization. The University of South Carolina has a large Gay, Lesbian, Bisexual Association. Members include both students and faculty. Health care is good generally, and there are several organizations benefiting AIDS located in the area. Some of them are Palmetto AIDS Life Support Services of South Carolina (PALSS), South Carolina AIDS Hotline, John Windum Patient Assistance Fund, and Dr. Alfred Burnside's Clinic which has HIV specialists on staff. Both Baptist and Richland Hospitals maintain AIDS hospices. There's a PFLAG Columbia. A good bookstore in Columbia is "Bluestocking Books." Some Bars are: "Affairs" (mixed) and the oldest in the area, "Metropolis" (mixed) dance and drag bar with a back bar called "DVA,"" The Candy Shop" (a primarily black drag bar), "Traxx" (women), "The Edge" (mixed), "The Arcade" (mixed), "Capitol Club" (mixed), "Shandon" (mixed), and "Lil

Rascals" (private). The South Carolina Gay/Lesbian Business Guild publishes the *Palmetto State Business,* a bimonthly newsletter with an estimated readership of over 1600. *In Unison Magazine* is a gay rag published monthly. *Virago* is the Lesbian Newsletter. There's a *Women's Yellow Pages* in the area. Columbia has a MCC, a Lutherans Concerned South Carolina, a New Hope Christian Church, and a Unitarian Universalist.

LOCATION: COLUMBIA IS LOCATED AT THE GEOGRAPHIC CENTER OF SOUTH CAROLINA. IT IS MIDWAY BETWEEN THE ATLANTIC SEASHORE AND THE APPALACHIAN MOUNTAINS.

GAY/LESBIAN FRIENDLY BUSINESSES: 50+

GAY/LESBIAN BARS, RESTAURANTS: 10

GAY/LESBIAN ORGANIZATIONS: 20

GAY/LESBIAN RELIGIOUS ORGANIZATIONS, CHURCHES, ETC.: 5

GAY/LESBIAN BOOKSTORES: 2

GAY/LESBIAN PUBLICATIONS: 4

COMPANIES THAT PROHIBIT DISCRIMINATION: A.T.&T., I.B.M., FANTAZIA, BLUE STOCKING, SEE GAY CIVIL RIGHTS

INFORMATION NUMBER: 803-771-7713 THE CENTER

TOTAL CRIMES: 12,363

VIOLENT = (MURDER = 22, RAPE = 94, ROBBERY = 666, ASSAULT = 1,422)

PROPERTY = (BURGLARY = 2,090, LARCENY = 7,316, MOTOR VEHICLE THEFT = 753, ARSON = 13)

Things to Do!!!

There are approximately 130 parks in the region. Rafting, boating, fishing and camping are available at many of the sites. Specific points of interest include: (1) Governors Mansion, (2) State House, (3) South Carolina Archives Building, (4) Towns Theatre, (5) South Carolina State Museum, (6) Columbia Museum of Art, (7) Lexington County Museum Complex, (8) Sesquicentennial Park, (9) Riverbanks Zoological Park and botanical Garden. ANNUAL EVENTS: South Carolina State Fair

POPULATION: 98,832 PERSONS—W = 52,625, B = 42,837, AI/E/A = 341, C = 404, F = 143, M = 598, PR = 565

POPULATION GROWTH: - 2.4%

AGE OF POPULATION: (21-24) = 10.8%, (25-34) = 19.9%, (35-44) = 13.0%, (45-54) = 6.7%, (55-64) = 6.0%, (65-74) = 6.6%, (75 AND OVER) = 5.3%

HOUSING COST: OWNING = $72,600   RENTAL = $392

COMMUNITY HOSPITALS: 3 = 1,207 BEDS

CLIMATE: JAN—AVG. (43.8 DEGREES), JULY—AVG. (80.8 DEGREES), ANNUAL PRECIPITATION (49.91 INCHES)

PER CAPITA INCOME: $12,210

UNEMPLOYMENT RATE: 5.5%

JOB GROWTH SINCE 1980: + 1.4%

COST OF LIVING: 95.0

EDUCATION: UNIVERSITY OF SOUTH CAROLINA

SOUTH DAKOTA

STATE LAWS REGARDING HOMOSEXUALITY:

In 1977, the sodomy law was abolished.

CITIES: (60,000 AND UP)

SIOUX FALLS

Gay Civil Rights: None

What the Locals Say . . .

The gay and lesbian community of Sioux Falls is not really open and not really closeted. Sioux Falls does seem to be very cliquish. The political atmosphere is the ,"Don't Ask, Don't Tell Policy." Sioux Falls is growing and some polls indicated in 1992 that it was the #1 best city in the country. The downtown area is coming back to life for the most part. The gay and lesbian community is spread throughout town. However, the McKinnon Park area has some gays; and the Cathedral Area, an older part of town also has some family members living there. The Sioux Falls Barnes and Noble Bookstore has a large gay and lesbian section. In fact, the gay-friendly manager had a display for Pride week. The Pride Celebration consists of the bar hosting a drag show, speakers, volleyball, picnic at the park, and short seminars. Sioux Empire Coalition is a political group that is becoming more active. They currently have a speakers group and an adopt a highway program. Queer Nation and Act-Up are other political groups in Sioux Falls. "Ciaos" is an excellent Italian restaurant that is gay friendly, and "Our House For Coffee" is also gay-friendly. There are potlucks and private dinner parties throughout town. "To Shay's" is a mixed bar for men and women. McKinnon Hospital has a good rapport with the gay and lesbian community. Beraka House is for people with AIDS. St. Francis & St. Clare MCC is a growing church and it sponsors a St Patrick's Day Parade Float.

LOCATION: SIOUX FALLS IS LOCATED AT THE FALLS OF THE SIOUX RIVER.

GAY/LESBIAN FRIENDLY BUSINESSES: 2

GAY/LESBIAN BARS AND RESTAURANTS: 2

GAY/LESBIAN ORGANIZATIONS: 2

GAY/LESBIAN RELIGIOUS ORGANIZATIONS, CHURCHES, ETC.: 1

GAY/LESBIAN BOOKSTORES: 0

GAY/LESBIAN PUBLICATIONS: 0

COMPANIES THAT PROHIBIT DISCRIMINATION: N/A

INFORMATION NUMBER: 605-332-3966 MCC

TOTAL CRIMES: 4,875

VIOLENT = (MURDER = 2, RAPE = 103, ROBBERY = 44, ASSAULT = 326)

PROPERTY = (BURGLARY = 735, LARCENY THEFT = 3,470, MOTOR VEHICLE THEFT = 195, ARSON = 29)

Things to Do!!!

(1) Earth Resource Center, (2) Sioux land Heritage Museum, (3) Sherman Park, (4) Great Plains Zoo, (5) U.S.S. South Dakota Battleship Memorial. There is also an abundant source of recreational activities such as several golf courses, an aquarium and zoo, and state parks.

POPULATION: 105,634 PERSONS—W = 97,627, B = 733, AI/E/A = 1,574, C = 98, F = 52, M = 295, PR = 32

POPULATION GROWTH: + 29.9%

AGE OF POPULATION: (21-24) = 6.8%, (25-34) = 19.8%, (35-44) = 14.8%, (45-54) = 8.7%, (55-64) = 7.7%, (65-74) = 6.5%, (75 AND OVER) = 5.2%

HOUSING COST: OWNING = $59,100   RENTAL = $380

COMMUNITY HOSPITALS: 2 = 883 BEDS

CLIMATE: JAN—AVG. (13.8 DEGREES), JULY—AVG. (74.3 DEGREES), ANNUAL PRECIPITATION (23.86 INCHES)

PER CAPITA INCOME: $13,677

UNEMPLOYMENT RATE: 2.5%

COST OF LIVING: 96.3

EDUCATION: AUGUSTA COLLEGE, SIOUX FALLS COLLEGE

COUNTIES:

MINNEHAHA COUNTY

Gay Civil Rights: Bans discrimination based on sexual orientation in public employment.

Towns and Cities included in Minnehaha County:

Baltic
Brandon
Colton
Corson
Crooks
Dell Rapids
Ellis

Hartford
Humboldt
Renner
Sioux Falls
Sherman
Valley Springs

TENNESSEE

STATE LAWS REGARDING HOMOSEXUALITY:

The homosexual sodomy law was repealed in early 1995, although it is currently under appeal.

CITIES: (60,000 AND UP)

MEMPHIS

Gay Civil Rights: None

What the Locals Say . . .

Memphis is described as being pretty closeted in some aspects, yet open in others. The area with the largest concentration of gays and lesbians is the Mid-Town area. Madison Avenue and Cooper-Young have the majority of bars and gay and lesbian owned businesses. The Gay and Lesbian Community Center is trying to get more volunteers and services for members of the community. The 3rd Saturday of each month, the Community Center hosts a potluck dinner for different organizations. Memphis also has a Lambda Center which is a 12 step recovery program. There are numerous support groups, a bowling league, a softball league, ACT UP, two square dance groups, PFLAG, and a gay teen group. Overton Park is gay dominated, but not considered a gay only park. Overton Park includes a golf course, the Memphis Zoo, and a regular park area. Coffeeshops that are frequented by gays and lesbians include the "Coffee Cellar" and "The Edge." Memphis has a Brothers and Sisters Bowling League, Memphis Gay/Lesbian Sports Association, Memphis Lambda Center, Girth & Mirth of Tennessee, Prime Timers Group of Memphis, and a Gay and Lesbian American Indian Group. There is a radio program called the "Gay Alternative." The Pride Festival consists of a boat ride on the Delta River Queen and a parade. Cafe Society and Anderton's are gay-friendly restaurants. "Lavender Earth" is a lesbian-owned business with an assortment of plants and herbs, "Botanica" is a family florist. The bar scene is somewhat mixed. "Amnesia" is a mixed dance bar, "Club 501" is predominately men, and on the other side "Club 505" is predominately women. The "Apartment Club" is a black male club, though others are welcome, "Construction Site" and "David's" are predominately men, "J Wags" is a 24 hour bar for men, "Pipeline" is a leather and Levi bar. Predominately lesbian bars are "WKRB," and "Nikita's Bar and Grill." "Crossroads" is frequented by both men and women. The Coffee Cellar is gay oriented. Friends For Life is the AIDS organization for Memphis. Recent downsizing at the "MED," the state supported hospital, has cut programs for AIDS patients. The Friends for Life Food Pantry is an additional service for AIDS patients. Meristem bookstore plays many roles in the community. It sponsors poetry and book readings, acts as a clearinghouse for information, gives discounts to AIDS patients and people with breast cancer, and stocks a wealth of books addressing the issues of homosexuality. *The Triangle News Journal* is a monthly gay and lesbian publication. The MCC meets at the Community Center. Churches that are very open include: Holy Trinity, Safe Harbor Community Church, Integrity - Calvary Trinity Church and Neshoba Unitarian Universalist Church in Germantown.

LOCATION: MEMPHIS IS LOCATED EAST OF THE MISSISSIPPI RIVER IN SOUTHWESTERN TENNESSEE.

GAY/LESBIAN FRIENDLY BUSINESSES: 20

GAY/LESBIAN BARS, RESTAURANTS: 11

GAY/LESBIAN ORGANIZATIONS: 16

GAY/LESBIAN RELIGIOUS ORGANIZATIONS, CHURCHES, ETC.: 4

GAY/LESBIAN BOOKSTORES: 1

GAY/LESBIAN PUBLICATIONS: 2

COMPANIES THAT PROHIBIT DISCRIMINATION:

INFORMATION NUMBER: 901-728-4297 MEMPHIS GAY AND LESBIAN COMMUNITY CENTER

TOTAL CRIMES: 62,150

VIOLENT = (MURDER = 198, RAPE = 725, ROBBERY = 5,366, ASSAULT = 3,824)

PROPERTY = (BURGLARY = 15,314, LARCENY = 23,434, MOTOR VEHICLE THEFT = ARSON = 585)

Things To Do:

Graceland, home of the late Elvis Presley is located in Memphis. There is a wide variety of recreational areas including lakes that are available for boating and year-round fishing. Hunting is very popular as well. as horseback riding, hayrides, and hidden trails. Other points of interest include: (1) Graceland, (2) Sun Studios, (3) Beale Street, (4) Memphis Pink Palace Museum and Planetarium, (5) Victorian Village, (6) Mud Island, (7) Libertyland, (8) Adventure River Water Park, (9) Memphis Belle, (10) Memphis Botanic Garden, (11) Memphis Zoo & Aquarium, (12) Dixon Gallery and Gardens, (13) Memphis Brooks Museum of Art, (14) Lichterman Nature Center, (15) T.O. Fuller State Park, (16) River Cruises, (17) Meeman-Shelby Forest State Recreation Park, (18) Playhouse on the Square, (19) Circuit Playhouse. ANNUAL EVENTS: (1) Memphis in May International Festival, (2) Beale Street Music Festival, (3) Elvis Presley International Tribute Week, (4) Memphis Music Festival, (5) Mud Island Folk Festival, (6) Mid-South Fair and Exposition. SEASONAL EVENTS: (1) Outdoor concerts, (2) Theatre Memphis.

POPULATION: 610,275 PERSONS—W = 268,600, B = 334,737, AI/E/A = 960, C = 1,275, F = 343, M = 1,812, PR = 390

POPULATION GROWTH: -5.6%

AGE OF POPULATION: (21-24) = 6.5%, (25-34) = 17.9%, (35-44) = 14.2%, (45-54) = 9.0%, (55-64) = 8.4%, (65-74) = 7.1%, (75 AND OVER) = 5.1%

HOUSING COST: OWNING = $55,700   RENTAL = $373

COMMUNITY HOSPITALS: 9 = 4,868 BEDS

CLIMATE: JAN—AVG. (39.7 DEGREES), JULY—AVG. (82.6 DEGREES), ANNUAL PRECIPITATION (52.10 INCHES)

PER CAPITA INCOME: $11,682

UNEMPLOYMENT RATE: 5.9%

JOB GROWTH SINCE 1980: -.4%

COST OF LIVING: 97.7

EDUCATION: UNIVERSITY OF MEMPHIS, UNIVERSITY OF TENNESSEE AT MEMPHIS

NASHVILLE

Gay Civil Rights: None

What the Locals Say . . .

Nashville is a semi-open community with a large gay and lesbian population, some gays and lesbians are very out, although many are still closeted. The gay and lesbian community is very organized and very vocal. The mayor is fairly friendly to gays and lesbians and recently appointed an open lesbian to the Human Rights Commission. The best places to live for gays and lesbians in Nashville is East Nashville (Homo Heights) or Lockland Springs/Edgeville and the West End/Vanderbilt University. "The Pink Triangle" at the Chute Complex is the gay lesbian bookstore. There are plenty of activities like the Sport and Fitness Network that sponsors an intramural volleyball league and is expanding to have a golf and tennis league. Nashville also has a roller skating group, a bowling and softball league and a gay cable network. There are several women's discussion groups, a women's spirituality group, gay circle (a men's discussion group), youth groups, and a partners network for couples. Pride Week is a 10 day long celebration with activities including: a rally, a parade, couples events, African-American events, film festival, worship service and a ball. "The Chute," "Connections," "Silver Stirrup," and "World's End," are 70% male and 30% female. "Roxy," and "Victor Victoria's," draws a predominately male crowd. Bars predominately women are "Ralph's," and "Chez Collette." The health care community is very supportive of HIV+ and AIDS patients. Nashville Cares is an AIDS organization that is staffed by 20+ full time staff. The hospitals are very supportive. Nashville has two gay and lesbian publications the *Xenogeny* and the

Query, a statewide paper. Both are published weekly. The MCC, Stonewall Mission and Day Spring Churches are all open and affirming to gays and lesbians.

LOCATION: NASHVILLE IS LOCATED IN CENTRAL TENNESSEE.

GAY/LESBIAN FRIENDLY BUSINESSES: 12

GAY/LESBIAN BARS, RESTAURANTS: 14

GAY/LESBIAN ORGANIZATIONS: 20

GAY/LESBIAN RELIGIOUS ORGANIZATIONS, CHURCHES, ETC.: 4

GAY/LESBIAN BOOKSTORES: 1

GAY/LESBIAN PUBLICATIONS: 2

COMPANIES THAT PROHIBIT DISCRIMINATION: N/A

INFORMATION NUMBER: 615-297-0008 GAY LESBIAN CENTER

TOTAL CRIMES: 55,500

VIOLENT = (MURDER = 87, RAPE = 577, ROBBERY = 2,709, ASSAULT = 5,791)

PROPERTY = (BURGLARY = 9,149, LARCENY = 32,456, MOTOR VEHICLE THEFT = 4,731, ARSON = N/A)

Things to Do!!!

Nashville is the capital of Country Music. Nashville also has an excellent park system with 6,600 acres of land set aside for parks. Activities include horseback riding, hiking, golf, polo, swimming, skating and sailing. Nearby lakes are suitable for boating, fishing and water sports. Specific points of interest include: (1) State Capital, (2) Tennessee State Museum, (3) The Parthenon, (4) The Hermitage, (5) Belle Meade, (6) Travellers'' Rest Historic House, (7) Belmont Mansion, (8) Museum of Tobacco Art & History, (9) Country Music Hall of Fame & Museum, (10) Opryland, (11) Country Music Wax Museum and Shopping Mall, (12) Minnie Pearl's Museum, (13) Music Valley Wax Museum of the Stars, (14) Music Village USA, (15) Car Collection Hall of Fame, (16) Sam Davis Home, (17) J. Percy Priest Lake, (18) Old Hickory Lake, (19) Cheatham Lake, Lock and Dam, (20) Radnor Lake State Natural Area, (21) Grand Ole Opry. ANNUAL EVENTS: (1) Iroquois Steeplechase, (2) Music festivals, (3) Longhorn Rodeo, (4) Tennessee State Fair, (5) Nashville's Country Holidays. SEASONAL EVENTS: Nashville Motor Raceway.

POPULATION: 495,012 PERSONS—W = 360,284, B = 118,627, AI/E/A = 1,130, C = 924, F = 419, M = 2,093, PR = 510

POPULATION GROWTH: + 8.6%

AGE OF POPULATION: (21-24) = 6.8%, (25-34) = 20.7%, (35-44) = 15.5%, (45-54) = 9.7%, (55-64) = 8.1%, (65-74) = 6.5%, (75 AND OVER) = 4.9%

HOUSING COST: OWNING = $74,400   RENTAL = $432

COMMUNITY HOSPITALS: 9 = 3,301 BEDS

CLIMATE: JAN—AVG. (36.2 DEGREES), JULY—AVG. (79.3 DEGREES), ANNUAL PRECIPITATION (47.30 INCHES)

PER CAPITA INCOME: $14,490

UNEMPLOYMENT RATE: 4.7%

JOB GROWTH SINCE 1980: + 15.6%

COST OF LIVING: 91.4

EDUCATION: VANDERBILT UNIVERSITY, MIDDLE TENNESSEE STATE UNIVERSITY, TENNESSEE STATE UNIVERSITY

TEXAS

STATE LAWS REGARDING HOMOSEXUALITY:

Although it is on the books, through legal ramifications, Texas sodomy law cannot be enforced anywhere in the state. An appellate court ruled the sodomy law was unconstitutional and applies to the entire state.

CITIES: (60,000 AND UP)

▼AUSTIN

Gay Civil Rights: Bans discrimination based on sexual orientation in public and private employment, public accommodations, housing, credit and union practices.

What the Locals Say . . .

The city of Austin is very liberal. Crimes directed toward homosexuals are rare. The media is known for its fairness; and, in fact, runs engagement announcements of gay and lesbians couples along with heterosexual announcements. Since Austin is so popular, there is a housing shortage problem. Recently the domestic partnership register to qualify for health benefits was repealed. The religious right convinced the City of Austin that it would cost the city more to allow gays and lesbians to register as domestic partners since they would receive health benefits. Although individuals can still register as domestic partners, there are no benefits. There is not a predominately gay or lesbian neighborhood or part of town. Everyone and everything is scattered throughout town. The scenery in Austin is beautiful with plenty of outdoor activities for gays and lesbians. There is currently a campaign under way to get a community center. Austin holds marches, walks, dinners, and festivals as fundraising events and political statements. Many sporting activities are offered through the churches. Hippy Hollow is a nude beach on the shores of Lake Travis that is wonderful and always crowded with gays and lesbians. As a general rule, straights are in the front of the park, near the entrance, gays tend to be in the area farther along the shore. As far as the bar scene goes, everything is available. "Oil Can Harry's" leans toward the yuppie crowd, both gay and straight. "5th Street Station" is a popular women's country and western bar. The health care atmosphere in Austin is very supportive of those infected with HIV and AIDS. *The Triangle* is a weekly newspaper for gays and lesbians. *The Chronicle* is very open to gays and often has articles about gays and lesbians. The MCC has a big congregation of gays and lesbians. There are several other churches in the area that are very welcoming.

LOCATION: AUSTIN IS LOCATED NEAR THE GEOGRAPHIC CENTER OF TEXAS ALONG THE COLORADO RIVER.

GAY/LESBIAN FRIENDLY BUSINESSES: 150

GAY/LESBIAN BARS, RESTAURANTS: 13

GAY/LESBIAN ORGANIZATIONS: 14

GAY/LESBIAN RELIGIOUS ORGANIZATIONS, CHURCHES, ETC.: 5

GAY/LESBIAN BOOKSTORES: 4

GAY/LESBIAN PUBLICATIONS: 3

COMPANIES THAT PROHIBIT DISCRIMINATION: SEE GAY CIVIL RIGHTS

INFORMATION NUMBER: 512-329-9922 HOTLINE

TOTAL CRIMES: 51,468

VIOLENT = (MURDER = 37, RAPE = 271, ROBBERY = 1,555, ASSAULT = 1,148)

PROPERTY = (BURGLARY = 8,453, LARCENY = 35,647, MOTOR VEHICLE THEFT = 4,357, ARSON = 610)

Things to Do!!!

Fishing, sailing, boating, swimming and scuba diving are available at Lake Travis, approximately one hour from Austin. There are numerous public and private golf courses and tennis courts in the capital city. Other places to enjoy include: (1) State Capitol, (2) Governors Mansion, (3) Laguna Gloria Art Museum, (4) O. Henry Home and Museum, (5) Elizabeth New Museum, (6) McKinney Falls State Park, (7) Highland Lakes, (8) Zilker Park, (9) Inner Space Cavern. ANNUAL EVENTS: (1) Livestock Show, (2) Highland Lakes Bluebonnet Trail, (3) Legends of Golf, (4) Laguna Gloria Fiesta, (5) Austin Aqua Festival, (6) Highland Lakes Arts and Crafts Trail. SEASONAL EVENTS: (1) Zilker Park Hillside Theater.

POPULATION:492,329 PERSONS—W = 328,542, B = 57,868, AI/E/A = 1,756, C = 4,174, F = 790, M = 93,323, PR = 1,425

POPULATION GROWTH: + 42.3%

AGE OF POPULATION: (21-24) = 10.1%, (25-34) = 22.7%, (35-44) = 15.6%, (45-54) = 7.9%, (55-64) = 5.6%, (65-74) = 4.3%, (75 AND OVER) = 3.2%

HOUSING COST: OWNING = $72,600   RENTAL = $410

COMMUNITY HOSPITALS: 5 = 1,392 BEDS

CLIMATE: JAN—AVG. (48.8 DEGREES), JULY—AVG. (84.5 DEGREES), ANNUAL PRECIPITATION (31.88 INCHES)

PER CAPITA INCOME: $14,295

UNEMPLOYMENT RATE: 5.0%

JOB GROWTH SINCE 1980: + 43.9%

COST OF LIVING: N/A

EDUCATION: ST EDWARDS UNIVERSITY, UNIVERSITY OF TEXAS AT AUSTIN, SOUTHWEST TEXAS STATE UNIVERSITY

CORPUS CHRISTI

Gay Civil Rights: None

What the Locals Say . . .

The gay community in Corpus Christi is, for the most part, closeted. Since Corpus is a military town, a large part of the gay community is military. The President's "Don't Ask, Don't Tell Policy" fits well in Corpus Christi. The local government is not supportive of the gay community in general, but will help with AIDS events. This is not a city where you would feel comfortable walking down the street holding your lover's hand. People who live in Corpus Christi call it the biggest small town in America. It's also known as the "closet" of Texas. There is a gay beach down toward Padre Island. A group called, Gays Getting Together, meets weekly and has movie nights and other social activities. There is a gay softball team and a bowling league called, The Gutter League. There's a group called the, Texas Riviera Empire, and there is also a chapter of the Imperial Court in Corpus. The Loving Spoonful, an organization formed to help AIDS victims, feeds lunch and some dinners to PWA's. There is the Coastal Bend AIDS Foundation and Passage House is the AIDS Hospice in the area. In general, the gay community is not very well organized in Corpus Christi as of yet. The "Hidden Door" is a cruise bar; "Numbers" and "Ubu" are both mixed dance bars; "Club Unity" is 90% women but men are welcome and do go there. There are no local gay/lesbian publications, but the papers from San Antonio cover the area. The MCC Corpus Christi is very active and sponsors social events such as bonfires.

LOCATION: CORPUS CHRISTI IS LOCATED IN THE SOUTHERN PART OF TEXAS ON THE GULF OF MEXICO.

GAY/LESBIAN FRIENDLY BUSINESSES: 10

GAY/LESBIAN BARS, RESTAURANTS: 7

GAY/LESBIAN ORGANIZATIONS: 2

GAY/LESBIAN RELIGIOUS ORGANIZATIONS, CHURCHES, ETC.: 1

GAY/LESBIAN BOOKSTORES: 0

GAY/LESBIAN PUBLICATIONS: 0

COMPANIES THAT PROHIBIT DISCRIMINATION: N/A

INFORMATION NUMBER: 512-851-1178, CLUB UNITY

TOTAL CRIMES: 27,416

VIOLENT = (MURDER = 34, RAPE = 194, ROBBERY = 509, ASSAULT = 1,488)

PROPERTY = (BURGLARY = 4,600, LARCENY = 18,919, MOTOR VEHICLE THEFT = 1,672, ARSON = 214)

Things to Do!!!

The beaches are the center of recreational activities. Sail boarding is popular because of the constant breeze. Other activities and places to visit include; (1) Fishing, (2) Padre Island and Mustang Island, (3) Corpus Christi Museum, (4) Art Museum of South Texas, (5) Museum of Oriental Cultures, (6) Sidbury House, (7) US Naval Air Station. ANNUAL EVENTS: (1) Buccaneer Days, (2) Texas Jazz Festival, (3) Summer Bayfront Concerts, (4) Bayfest, (5) Harbor Lights Celebration.

POPULATION: 266,412 PERSONS—W = 196,019, B = 12,347, AI/E/A = 1,112, C = 250, F = 1,034, M = 118,713, PR = 483

POPULATION GROWTH: + 14.8%

AGE OF POPULATION: (21-24) = 5.5%, (25-34) = 17.7%, (35-44) = 15.0%, (45-54) = 9.2%, (55-64) = 7.9%, (65-74) = 6.1%, (75 AND OVER) = 4.0%

PER CAPITA INCOME: $11,755

HOUSING COST: OWNING = $56,500   RENTAL = $373

COMMUNITY HOSPITALS: 8 = 1,406 BEDS

CLIMATE: JAN—AVG. (55.1 DEGREES), JULY—AVG. (84.1 DEGREES), ANNUAL PRECIPITATION (30.13 INCHES)

PER CAPITA INCOME: $11,755

UNEMPLOYMENT RATE: 7.6%

JOB GROWTH SINCE 1980: + 11.7%

COST OF LIVING: 94.6

EDUCATION: CORPUS CHRISTI STATE UNIVERSITY

DALLAS

Gay Civil Rights: Bans discrimination based on sexual orientation in public employment.

What the Locals Say . . .

Dallas has a very strong gay and lesbian community and numerous gay and lesbian organizations, although the political climate in Dallas is very conservative. The gay and lesbian community focuses around the Oak Lawn area of Dallas. Oak Lawn is about a 5 square mile area with expensive housing and slums. The 3900-4000 block of Cedar Springs is lined with gay and lesbian coffee shops, bars, bookstores and shops. Riverschon Park is pretty much considered a gay park. Residents of Dallas like to say that anything you could want to do, you can do in Dallas. Sports activities include gay and lesbian softball leagues, bowling leagues, volleyball leagues, and a skydiving and parachuting club. There is a pilots club, a gardening club, under 25 club, over and under 30 club, prime time club which is not exclusively, though primarily, a club for men 50 and over. Sprouts is a newly formed support group for lesbians that are just coming out. There are a variety of other support groups as well. Dallas/Ft. Worth Gay & Lesbian Alliance is the only alliance in the country to have a fully functional credit union with the only gay and lesbian identified Master Card. The Dallas/Ft. Worth Gay & Lesbian Alliance, Metroplex Republicans, and Lesbian & Gay Political Coalition are the most active political groups in the area. "Village Station," the largest bar in the area, draws a mixed crowd, "Sue Ellen's is a lesbian dance bar. Both of these bars are located on Cedar Springs. "JR's " and "Mobys Dick's" are mixed bars. "The Brick" is mainly a Levi leather bar, while "TMC" is mainly a cruise bar. The relationship between the health care community and the gay and lesbian community is pretty good, and there are resources for individuals who can't afford health care. *The Dallas Voice* is a weekly publication that serves the Dallas Metroplex. The Cathedral of Hope (an MCC church) is one of the largest and fastest growing churches in the country. Grace Fellowship and Oaklawn Church of Religious Science have large gay and lesbian congregations. There are several other churches which are open to gays and lesbians.

LOCATION: DALLAS IS LOCATED IN NORTH TEXAS.

GAY/LESBIAN FRIENDLY BUSINESSES: 85

GAY/LESBIAN BARS, RESTAURANTS: 27

GAY/LESBIAN ORGANIZATIONS: 48

GAY/LESBIAN RELIGIOUS ORGANIZATIONS, CHURCHES, ETC.: 9

GAY/LESBIAN BOOKSTORES: 2

GAY/LESBIAN PUBLICATIONS: 1

COMPANIES THAT PROHIBIT DISCRIMINATION: SEE GAY CIVIL RIGHTS

INFORMATION NUMBER: 214-528-4233 GAY AND LESBIAN COMMUNITY CENTER

TOTAL CRIMES: 110,799

VIOLENT = (MURDER = 317, RAPE = 1,000, ROBBERY = 7,420, ASSAULT = 9,439)

PROPERTY = (BURGLARY = 20,975, LARCENY = 54,183, MOTOR VEHICLE THEFT = 17,465, ARSON = 1,325)

Things to Do!!!

Dallas has 16,600 acres of lakes. Swimming, fishing, water skiing, and boating activities are popular. Other places of interest include; (1) State Fair Park-Age of Steam Railroad Museum, The Cotton Bowl, Dallas Museum of Natural History, Dallas Aquarium, Music Hall, Dallas Civic Garden Center, The Science Place, (2) Dallas Museum of Art, (3) Telephone Pioneer Museum of Texas, (4) Dallas market Center Complex, (5) Old City Park, (6) Dallas Theater Center, (7) Biblical Arts Center, (8) John F. Kennedy Memorial Plaza, (9)

Kennedy Historical Exhibit, (10) Dallas Zoo, (11) White Rock Lake Park, (12) Grapevine Lake, (13) Six Flags Over Texas, (14) Wet 'n Wild. ANNUAL EVENTS: (1) Mobil Cotton Bowl Classic, (2) Boat Show, (3) Virginia Slims Tennis Tournament, (4) Scarborough Fair Renaissance Festival, (5) Byron Nelson Golf Classic. SEASONAL EVENTS: (1) Summer Musicals, (2) Dallas Opera, (3) Mesquite Championship Rodeo, (4) Dallas Symphony Orchestra, (5) Professional Sports: Football - Cowboys, Basketball - Mavericks, Baseball - Rangers, Soccer - Sidekicks.

POPULATION: 1,022,497 PERSONS—W = 556,760, B = 296,994, AI/E/A = 4,792, C = 4,105, F = 1,474, M = 185,096, PR = 1,497

POPULATION GROWTH: + 13.0%

AGE OF POPULATION: (21-24) = 7.5%, (25-34) = 22.4%, (35-44) = 14.9%, (45-54) = 9.1%, (55-64) = 7.1%, (65-74) = 5.6%, (75 AND OVER) = 4.1%

HOUSING COST: OWNING = $78,800   RENTAL = $426

COMMUNITY HOSPITALS: 22 = 5,555 BEDS

CLIMATE: JAN—AVG. (44.6 DEGREES), JULY—AVG. (85.9 DEGREES), ANNUAL PRECIPITATION (36.08 INCHES)

PER CAPITA INCOME: $16,300

UNEMPLOYMENT RATE: 6.9%

JOB GROWTH SINCE 1980: + 14.8%

COST OF LIVING: 102.0

EDUCATION: UNIVERSITY OF DALLAS, SOUTHERN METHODIST UNIVERSITY, UNIVERSITY OF TEXAS AT DALLAS

▼HOUSTON

Gay Civil Rights: Bans discrimination based on sexual orientation in public employment.

What the Locals Say . . .

The Gay and Lesbian community of Houston is partially closeted and partially open. Due to the recent notoriety of the Houston gay bashings, some homosexuals are keeping a lower profile. The mayor of Houston has a great deal of power and is cautiously supportive of the gay and lesbian community. Most individuals do not feel comfortable being openly affectionate with their partner in public. Montrose is the most heavily gay and lesbian populated area. There are gay & lesbian businesses, bars, restaurants, as well as a residential area in Montrose. The Heights is a quieter residential neighborhood, with a few restaurants. Houston has a lot of support groups, including AIDS support groups, billiards club, cycling club, tennis club, divers club, wrestling club, and women's and mixed bowling leagues. There's also a volleyball club, softball club, roller blade club, gay rodeo, AIDS Equity League, and Gay & Lesbian Political Caucus. Houston has a radio show called "After Hours" on KTFT. The Gay Pride Celebration consists of a parade and various entertainment events. The bar scene is for the most part segregated between men and women. Some of the predominately gay male bars are: "Pacific Street," "Montrose Mining Company," "JR's," "Heaven," and "Mary's." Some of the predominately lesbian bars are located in one complex called "The Ranch"- (Ms. B's, The Ranch, Ecstasy). "Ms. B's" is quiet, "The Ranch" is country and western, and "Ecstasy" is disco. There is a very strong support system for those with AIDS in the Houston area. The County Health System can help pay for some expenses. Houston has two local gay and lesbian newspapers one is called the *Houston Voice*, and is published weekly, and the other is called *The Texas Triangle*, and is published two times a month. There are a number of churches that are open to gays and lesbians including: Grace Lutheran Church, Community Gospel Church, MCCR.

LOCATION: HOUSTON IS LOCATED IN SOUTHEASTERN TEXAS, 120 MILES INLAND FROM THE GULF OF MEXICO.

GAY/LESBIAN FRIENDLY BUSINESSES: 400

GAY/LESBIAN BARS, RESTAURANTS: 29

GAY/LESBIAN ORGANIZATIONS: 52

GAY/LESBIAN RELIGIOUS ORGANIZATIONS, CHURCHES, ETC.: 9

GAY/LESBIAN BOOKSTORES: 2

GAY/LESBIAN PUBLICATIONS: 2

COMPANIES THAT PROHIBIT DISCRIMINATION: SEE GAY CIVIL RIGHTS

INFORMATION NUMBER: 713-529-3211 GAY AND LESBIAN SWITCHBOARD

TOTAL CRIMES: 119,214 +

VIOLENT = (MURDER = 446, RAPE = 1,109, ROBBERY = N/A, ASSAULT = N/A)

PROPERTY = (BURGLARY = 27,022, LARCENY = 61,569, MOTOR VEHICLE THEFT = 27,519, ARSON = 1,549)

Things to Do!!!

Boating and sailing are popular, as well as the miles of hiking and biking trails. Other places of interest include; (1) Bayou Bend Collection, (2) Museum of Fine Arts, (3) Contemporary Arts Museum, (4) George R. Brown Convention Center, (5) Houston Zoological Gardens, (6) Houston Arboretum and Nature Center, (7) Armand Bayou Nature Center, (8) Harris County Heritage Tours, (9) Alley Theatre, (10) The Houston Symphony, (11) The Houston Ballet, (12) Houston Grand Opera, (13) Theater Under The Stars, (14) Rothko Chapel, (15) NASA Lyndon B. Johnson Space Center, (16) Astrodome, (17) The Port of Houston, (18) San Jacinto Battleground, (19) Historical Parks. ANNUAL EVENTS: (1)

Houston Livestock Show Parade and Rodeo, (2) Houston Azalea Trail, (3) Clear lake Lunar Rendezvous Festival, (4) Houston Anniversary Celebration, (5) Texas Renaissance Festival, (6) Greek Festival, (7) Christmas Boat Lane, (8) World of Christmas. SEASONAL EVENTS: (1) Summer Concerts. (2) Professional Sports: Baseball-Astros, Basketball-Rockets, Football - Oilers.

POPULATION: 1,690,180 PERSONS—W = 859,069, B = 457,990, AI/E/A = 4,126, C = 17,317, F = 5,566, M = 358,503, PR = 4,383

POPULATION GROWTH: + 6.0%

AGE OF POPULATION: (21-24) = 7.2%, (25-34) = 20.8%, (35-44) = 15.4%, (45-54) = 9.5%, (55-64) = 7.3%, (65-74) = 5.0%, (75 AND OVER) = 3.2%

HOUSING COST: OWNING = $58,000   RENTAL = $390

COMMUNITY HOSPITALS: 34 = 10,253 BEDS

CLIMATE: JAN—AVG. (52.2 DEGREES), JULY—AVG. (83.5 DEGREES), ANNUAL PRECIPITATION (50.83 INCHES)

PER CAPITA INCOME: $14,261

UNEMPLOYMENT RATE: 6.1%

JOB GROWTH SINCE 1980: + .1%

COST OF LIVING: 96.3

EDUCATION: UNIVERSITY OF HOUSTON, RICE UNIVERSITY, TEXAS SOUTHERN UNIVERSITY

SAN ANTONIO

Gay Civil Rights: None

What the Locals Say . . .

San Antonio is a real split community, a strong indication of that fact is there are 17 school districts and 5 military bases. There is not a core to organize from, although there is a very large and active gay and lesbian community. "Alamo Heights" is a great place for gays and les-bians to live, although it expensive. Jefferson, Monte Vista and the King William's District areas are very popular places to live if you are gay or lesbian. There are numerous organizations in San Antonio's gay and lesbian community. "Eighth Street Bar and Restaurant" is a popu-lar spot. Some of the more popular social groups are: Alamo Couples—for gay and lesbian couples, Girlfriends—for single les-bians, Lemosa—lesbian moms, Old Lesbians Organizing for Change, Texas Gay Rodeo Association and San Antonio Gay/Lesbian/Bisexual Veterans. Some of the most popular support groups are Gay Men, Lesbians & Their Families, Heart to Heart, PFLAG, and Disabled and Gay Support Group. Colors Introductory Services is a dating service. Political Organizations include Political Action Caucus, Esperanza

Peace & Justice Center, San Antonio Lesbian Gay Assembly (SALGA), Texas Human Rights Foundation Hotline for Legal Assistance related to sexual orientation or HIV Status and San Antonio Lambda Student Alliance (SALSA). Textures Women's Books is a feminist bookstore. Some of the most popular bars in San Antonio include: "The Night Owl," "The Crew," "Nexus II," "BB'S Pub In the Yard," and many others. *The San Antonio Marquise, Woman's Space* and *San Antonio NOW Times* are gay and lesbian publications in San Antonio. There are several AIDS organizations including: The Alamo Area Resource Center (HIV+ services), Blue Light Candle AIDS, (an awareness and fund raising organization),The San Antonio AIDS Foundation Hospice, and the San Antonio Resource Center. The MCC, Church of Today, Community Unitarians Universalist Church and the River City Living Church all welcome gays and lesbians. The Catholic group Dignity, Reformed Congregation of the Goddess, Secular Humanist Association of San Antonio are open to gays and lesbians and meet regularly.

LOCATION: SAN ANTONIO IS LOCATED IN SOUTH CENTRAL TEXAS ABOUT 150 MILES NORTH OF GULF OF MEXICO.

GAY/LESBIAN FRIENDLY BUSINESSES: 50

GAY/LESBIAN BARS, RESTAURANTS: 21

GAY/LESBIAN ORGANIZATIONS: 50

GAY/LESBIAN RELIGIOUS ORGANIZATIONS, CHURCHES, ETC.: 5

GAY/LESBIAN BOOKSTORES: 2

GAY/LESBIAN PUBLICATIONS: 3

COMPANIES THAT PROHIBIT DISCRIMINATION: SEE GAY CIVIL RIGHTS

INFORMATION NUMBER: 210-733-7300 LISA

TOTAL CRIMES: 97,671

VIOLENT = (MURDER = 220, RAPE = 553, ROBBERY = 2,979, ASSAULT = 2,973)

PROPERTY = (BURGLARY = 17,866, LARCENY = 61,284, MOTOR VEHICLE THEFT = 11,976, ARSON = 958)

Things to Do!!!

The mild climate permits outdoor activities 12 months a year. The River Walk provides a unique atmosphere for dining and shopping. Places of special interest include; (1) The Alamo, (2) Hemisphere Plaza, (3) Arneson River Theatre, (4) Hertzburg Circus Collection, (5) Paseo del Rio, (6) Market Square, (7) Vietnam Veterans Memorial, (8) San Antonio Missions National Historical Park, (9) Tower of the Americas, (10) Institute of Texas Cultures, (11) San Antonio Museum of Art, (12) Marion Koogler McNay Art Museum, (13) Southwest Craft Center, (14) Brackenridge Park, (15) Buckhorn Hall of Horns and Hall of Texas History, (16) San Antonio Botanical Gardens, (17) Fort Sam Houston Museum and Landmark, (18) Sea World, (19)

Water Park USA, (20) Natural Bridge Caverns, (21) Cascade Caverns Park, (22) Professional Sports: Basketball-Spurs. ANNUAL EVENTS: (1) Great Country River Festival, (2) Livestock Exposition and Rodeo, (3) Texas Independence Day and Flag Celebration, (4) Fiesta San Antonio, (5) Alamo Memorial Service, (6) Boerne Berges Fest, (7) Texas Folk life Festival, (8) Fiestas Navidenas, (9) Las Posadas. SEASONAL EVENTS: (1) Summer Festival, (2) San Antonio Symphony.

POPULATION: 966,437 PERSONS—W = 676,082, B = 65,884, AI/E/A = 3,303, C = 2,094, F = 1,857, M = 478,409, PR = 4,749

POPULATION GROWTH: + 23.0%

AGE OF POPULATION: (21-24) = 6.7%, (25-34) = 18.0%, (35-44) = 14.0%, (45-54) = 8.9%, (55-64) = 7.6%, (65-74) = 6.3%, (75 AND OVER) = 4.2%

HOUSING COST: OWNING = $49,700 RENTAL = $369

COMMUNITY HOSPITALS: 15 = 4,086 BEDS

CLIMATE: JAN—AVG. (49.3 DEGREES), JULY—AVG. (85.0 DEGREES), ANNUAL PRECIPITATION (30.98 INCHES)

PER CAPITA INCOME: $10,884

UNEMPLOYMENT RATE: 7.1%

JOB GROWTH SINCE 1980: + 30.6%

COST OF LIVING: 95.1

EDUCATION: UNIVERSITY OF TEXAS AT SAN ANTONIO, TRINITY UNIVERSITY, INCARNATE WORD COLLEGE

UTAH

STATE LAWS REGARDING HOMOSEXUALITY:

Heterosexual and homosexual sodomy is illegal and carries a maximum sentence of six months in prison. In 1982, the Republican party of that state, adopted a platform that homosexuals should be denied civil, political, social, and economic rights. The state also bans the purchase of school textbooks that portray homosexuality in a positive light.

CITIES: (60,000 AND UP)

SALT LAKE CITY

Gay Civil Rights: None

What the Locals Say . . .

Salt Lake is a very conservative and very Republican part of the country. There is a large population of gays and lesbians in the city and they are mostly middle-of-the-road; not open but not completely closed either. The gays living in Salt Lake are for the most part not flamboyant. The city is the bedrock in the country for the Morman religion; and, while the Mormons don't agree with the gay lifestyle, gays are pretty much tolerated and there aren't many hate crimes against them. The Avenue District is more gay-friendly and in the ninth and ninth area there are more gays. Utah, especially Salt Lake City, will surprise, possibly even astound people from other areas with its wide range of organizations, services, activities and more. In Salt Lake, there is the privately supported Stonewall Center, a 4800 square foot community center with a library that contains nearly 3000 books (all by, about and for gay/lesbian/bi/transgendered people) plus videos, audio tapes and an archive of clippings, etc. The Stonewall Center sponsors bowling, softball, Women's Circle, Men's Lunch, Gay Pride Day and many other activities and groups. It also maintains a gay info line voice mail (801-297-2555), and all in all, it's just a great resource center. Some other groups in the Salt Lake City area include the Outdoor Club which offers hiking and biking, the Mountain Cruisers, A.A. groups for gays, Gay and Lesbian Community Counsel of Utah, Gay and Lesbian Utah Democrats, Utah Gay Rodeo Association, Utah AIDS Foundation, Utahans Together Against Hate, Wasatch Leather Motorcycle Club, Thursday Womyn's Group, and the AIDS Project. The University of Utah has a Lesbian & Gay Student Union. The Utah Gay & Lesbian Business & Professional Alliance publishes a resource directory listing businesses, organizations, professionals and services available in Utah and the Rocky Mountain area. "The Deer Hunter" is a bar mostly for men; "Bricks" is a mixed dance bar; "The Sun" is also a mixed dance bar; "The Paper Moon" is a bar which is mostly for women but some men do go there.

"The Coffee Garden" is a gay-owned and gay-friendly coffee shop. And, the "Grounds For Coffee" and "The Salt Lake Roasting Co." are both coffee shops which are gay-friendly. "Cafe Haven" is a bookstore/coffee shop combination. "A Woman's Place," is a lesbian friendly bookstore, as is the "Golden Braid Bookstore." Some local monthly publications are *Pillar Of The Gay Community, The Lambreth,* and *Womyn's Community News.* The Sacred Light Of Christ MCC, Church Of Religious Science, Wasatch Affirmation, and Restoration Church Of Jesus Christ all serve the Salt Lake City community and are gay-friendly.

LOCATION: SALT LAKE CITY IS LOCATED IN NORTH CENTRAL UTAH.

GAY/LESBIAN FRIENDLY BUSINESSES: 20+

GAY/LESBIAN BARS AND RESTAURANTS: 8

GAY/LESBIAN ORGANIZATIONS: 20+

GAY/LESBIAN RELIGIOUS ORGANIZATIONS, CHURCHES, ETC.: 1

GAY/LESBIAN BOOKSTORES: 3

GAY/LESBIAN PUBLICATIONS: 3

INFORMATION NUMBER: 801-539-8800, UTAH STONEWALL CENTER

COMPANIES THAT PROHIBIT DISCRIMINATION: SEE COUNTY GAY CIVIL RIGHTS

TOTAL CRIMES: 18,453

VIOLENT = (MURDER = 19 RAPE = 204, ROBBERY = 498, ASSAULT = 681)

PROPERTY = (BURGLARY = 2,823, LARCENY = 12,831, MOTOR VEHICLE THEFT = 1,397, ARSON = 80)

Things to Do!!!

Headquarters for the Mormons and the famous Mormon Tabernacle Choir are in Salt Lake City. The major recreational attraction is skiing. Swimming and boating are available in the Great Salt Lake, which is two times as salty as any ocean. Specific points of interest include: (1) Temple Square, (2) Brigham Young Monument, (3) Pioneer Memorial Museum, (4) Governors Mansion, (5) Trolley Square, (6) Arrow Press Square, (7) Pioneer Memorial Museum, (8) Fort Douglas Military Museum, (9) Symphony Hall, (10) Salt Lake Art Center, (11) Utah Opera Company, (12) State Capital, (13) Liberty Park, (14) Pioneer Trail State Park, (15) Hogle Zoological Garden, (16) Raging Water, (17) Lagoon Amusement Park, (18) Pioneer Village and Water Park, (19) 49th Street Galleria, (20) Skiing-Alta, Brighton, Deer Valley, Park City, Park West, Snowbird, Solitude Resort, (21) Wasatch-Cache National Forest, (22) River Trips, (23) Professional Sports: Basketball-Jazz, Hockey-Golden Eagles. ANNUAL EVENTS: (1) Pageant of the Arts, (2) Utah Arts Festival, (3) Days of "47" Celebration, (4) Utah State Fair, (5) Temple Square Christmas.

POPULATION: 165,835 -PERSONS—W = 139,177, B = 2,752, AI/E/A = 2,541, C = 1,641, F = 198, M = 10,848, PR = 13,482

POPULATION GROWTH: + 1.7%

AGE OF POPULATION: (21-24) = 7.7%, (25-34) = 19.7%, (35-44) = 13.9%, (45-54) = 7.4%, (55-64) = 6.8%, (65-74) = 7.4%, (75 AND OVER) = 7.1%

HOUSING COST: OWNING = $67,200   RENTAL = $333

COMMUNITY HOSPITALS: 6 = 1,586 BEDS

CLIMATE: JAN—AVG. (27.9 DEGREES), JULY—AVG. (77.9 DEGREES), ANNUAL PRECIPITATION (16.18 INCHES)

PER CAPITA INCOME: $13,482

UNEMPLOYMENT RATE: + 5.0%

JOB GROWTH SINCE 1980: + .1%

COST OF LIVING: N/A

EDUCATION: BRIGHAM YOUNG UNIVERSITY, UNIVERSITY OF UTAH AND WEBER STATE COLLEGE

COUNTIES:

SALT LAKE COUNTY

Gay Civil Rights: Bans discrimination based on sexual orientation in public employment.

Towns and Cities included in Salt Lake County:

Alta
Bluffdale
Buena Vista
Cottonwood Heights
Dalton
Draper
East Milcreek
Fort Douglas
Garfield
Granger
Herriman
Magna
Midvale
Mount Alpine
Mt. Olympus
Nash
North Salt Lake City

Roper
Salt Lake City
Sandy
South Jordan
South Salt Lake
Sugar House
Taylorsville
Twin Peaks
White City

VERMONT

STATE LAWS REGARDING HOMOSEXUALITY:

Vermont repealed its sodomy laws. In 1992, a law was passed that banned discrimination on the basis of sexual orientation in housing, employment, public accommodations, and insurance. Vermont includes crimes based on sexual orientation as hate crimes. In 1993, the Vermont State Supreme Court ruled that a lesbian could adopt her partner's children, allowing them to share parental rights.

TOWNS: (5,000—60,000)

▼BURLINGTON

Gay Civil Rights: Bans discrimination based on sexual orientation in public and private employment and public accommodations.

What the Locals Say . . .

Burlington is a pretty nice place to live and has a fairly open gay and lesbian community. The city overall is very lesbian friendly. Although there are some gay bashings, it is rare. A Social & Support Group For Men Over 40, Senior Action In a Gay Environment (SAGE), Vermont Gay Social Alternative, and Vermont Lesbian and Gay Parents are some of the social groups in Burlington. The Gay Lesbian Bisexual Alliance at University of Vermont is located in Burlington. "Outright Vermont" is a youth group, and Vermont Coalition for Lesbian and Gay Rights is a group that sponsored a three part television series on legislative issues in the gay and lesbian community. The Gay Pride Celebration's 10th Anniversary had about 1,000 in attendance. The Celebration included entertainment, a rally, speakers, a march, dancing, etc.. The "131 Pearl" is the local gay and lesbian bar. Once a month they sponsor a buffet and dance which brings out older women in the community. "Mansfield Bucks" is a fraternity for leather and Levi. The Burlington Women's Council is an advocacy, resource, referral organization in Burlington. The Vermont Women's Health Clinic is very good. *Out in the Mountains* is a monthly gay and lesbian publication. The Unitarian Church is open to gays and lesbians. The Catholic gay and lesbian group Dignity meets regularly.

LOCATION: BURLINGTON SITS ATOP A HILL OVERLOOKING LAKE CHAMPLAIN IN WESTERN VERMONT.
GAY/LESBIAN FRIENDLY BUSINESSES: 7
GAY/LESBIAN BARS, RESTAURANTS: 1
GAY/LESBIAN ORGANIZATIONS: 6

GAY/LESBIAN RELIGIOUS ORGANIZATIONS, CHURCHES, ETC.: 3
GAY/LESBIAN BOOKSTORES: 0
GAY/LESBIAN PUBLICATIONS: 1
COMPANIES THAT PROHIBIT DISCRIMINATION: SEE STATE LAWS & GAY CIVIL RIGHTS
INFORMATION NUMBER: 802-865-7200 BURLINGTON WOMEN'S COUNCIL
TOTAL CRIMES: 3,051
VIOLENT = (MURDER = 1, RAPE = 26, ROBBERY = 9, ASSAULT = 34)
PROPERTY = (BURGLARY = 620, LARCENY = 2,269, MOTOR VEHICLE THEFT = 92, ARSON = N/A)

Things to Do!!!

(1) Discovery Museum, (2) Ethan Allen Homestead, (3) Burlington Ferry, (4) Green Mtn. Audubon Nature Center, (5) Ethan Allen Park, (6) Battery Park, (7) Burlington Ferry, (8) University of Vermont-Robert Hull Fleming Museum, Billings Center. SEASONAL EVENTS: (1) St. Michael's Playhouse, (2) Vermont Mozart Festival.

POPULATION: 38,569 PERSONS—W = 37,876, B = 390, AI/E/A = 123, C = 140, F = 38, M = 79, PR = 77

POPULATION GROWTH: + 2.3%

AGE OF POPULATION: (21-24) = 14.9%, (25-34) = 17.7%, (35-44) = 11.8%, (45-54) = 7.0%, (55-64) = 6.2%, (65-74) = 5.3%, (75 AND OVER) = 5.2%

HOUSING COST: OWNING = $113,500   RENTAL = $493

COMMUNITY HOSPITALS: 1 = 492 BEDS

CLIMATE: JAN—AVG. (16.3 DEGREES), JULY—AVG. (70.5 DEGREES), ANNUAL PRECIPITATION (34.47 INCHES)

PER CAPITA INCOME: $13,918

UNEMPLOYMENT RATE: 4.5%

JOB GROWTH SINCE 1980: + 20.0%

COST OF LIVING: N/A

EDUCATION: UNIVERSITY OF VERMONT, ST. MICHAELS COLLEGE

VIRGINIA

STATE LAWS REGARDING HOMOSEXUALITY:

Heterosexual and homosexual sodomy are felonies that carries a maximum sentence of five years.

CITIES: (60,000 AND UP)

▼ALEXANDRIA

Gay Civil Rights: Bans discrimination based on sexual orientation in public and private employment, public accommodations, education, housing, credit.

What the Locals Say . . .

Alexandria is headquarters for the National Association of Gay Pilots organization. The Virginia Partisan Gay and Lesbian Democratic Club and Gay and Lesbian Alliance Against Defamation are the political groups in Alexandria. Vocal Corps is a group that focuses on fluency communication problems. Bread and Roses is a women's chorus that sings women's music. The Northern Virginia AIDS Ministry (NOVAM) offers AIDS education and services. *Malchus* is a monthly gay and lesbian christian journal. Affirmation and Ave Maria and are religious organizations in Alexandria

LOCATION: ALEXANDRIA IS LOCATED SOUTH WASHINGTON D.C. IN NORTH EASTERN VIRGINIA.

GAY/LESBIAN FRIENDLY BUSINESSES: 1

GAY/LESBIAN BARS, RESTAURANTS: 1

GAY/LESBIAN ORGANIZATIONS: 2

GAY/LESBIAN RELIGIOUS ORGANIZATIONS, CHURCHES, ETC.: 1

GAY/LESBIAN BOOKSTORES:

GAY/LESBIAN PUBLICATIONS: 1

COMPANIES THAT PROHIBIT DISCRIMINATION: N/A

INFORMATION NUMBER: 703-684-0444

TOTAL CRIMES: 8,355

VIOLENT = (MURDER = 9, RAPE = 33, ROBBERY = 376, ASSAULT = 334)

PROPERTY = (BURGLARY = 921, LARCENY = 5,682, MOTOR VEHICLE THEFT = 969, ARSON = 31)

Things to Do!!!

Alexandria played an important role in the history of the United States. There are several historic sites to enjoy. Specific points of interest include: (1) George Washington Masonic and Historic Site, (2) Fort Ward Museum and Historic Site, (3) Mount Vernon, (4) Ramsay House, (5) Lafayette House, (6) Boyhood home of Robert E. Lee, (7) Alexandria Black History Resource Center, (8) Torpedo Factory Arts Center, (9) Pohick Bay Regional Park. ANNUAL EVENTS: (1) George Washington Birthday Celebration, (2) House Tours, (3) Red Cross Waterfront Festival, (4) Virginia Scottish Games, (5) Christmas Walk.

POPULATION: 113,134 PERSONS—W = 76,789, B = 24,339, AI/E/A = 333, C = 629, F = 740, M = 1,215, PR = 778

POPULATION GROWTH: + 9.6%

AGE OF POPULATION: (21-24) = 8.5%, (25-34) = 27.0%, (35-44) = 18.3%, (45-54) = 10.6%, (55-64) = 7.1%, (65-74) = 5.8%, (75 AND OVER) = 4.5%

HOUSING COST: OWNING = $228,600   RENTAL = $701

COMMUNITY HOSPITALS: 3 = 662 BEDS

CLIMATE: JAN—AVG. (34.6 DEGREES), JULY—AVG. (80.0 DEGREES), ANNUAL PRECIPITATION (38.63 INCHES)

PER CAPITA INCOME: $25,509

UNEMPLOYMENT RATE: 4.6%

JOB GROWTH SINCE 1980: + 16.8%

COST OF LIVING: N/A

EDUCATION: NONE

NORFOLK

Gay Civil Rights: None

What the Locals Say . . .

Norfolk is a transient area because of the big military presence. The gay and lesbian community is a mixture of those who are very out and open and those who are closeted. The political climate is like the military's "Don't Ask, Don't Tell Policy." Old Dominion, Virginia Wesley and Tide Water Community College are in Norfolk and tend to give the area a more liberal flair. There is a high concentration of gays and lesbians in the Ghant Neighborhood. Ghant is the oldest neighborhood in Norfolk and has apartments and single family dwellings and duplexes. Sport groups in Norfolk include the Mid Atlantic Bowling, Volleyball and Softball Leagues, the Frontrunners group and the Lambda Wheelers cyclist group. Hampton Roads Gay and Lesbian Coalition sponsors "Breaking The Ice" which is held in February and includes lectures, workshops, speakers, dancing and movies. Hampton Roads also sponsors a Pride Picnic. In October, Hampton Roads sponsors the Gay and Lesbian Film Festival. Support groups in

Norfolk include the Alternative Lifestyles Support Organization and the Single Lesbian Support Network. Social groups include The Mandamus Society, Lesbian and Gay Latin American Society. Virginians for Justice is an active political group in Norfolk. ODU Gay & Lesbian Student Union is an organization on the Old Dominion University Campus. "Phoenix Rising" is the largest bookstore in Virginia. "Outright Books" is a bookstore which also houses a hairstylist, TACT, All God's Children Church, and AIDS Walk For Life. "Bad Habit" is a predominately lesbian bookstore. There are several bars in Norfolk, "The Other Side" is a country western mixed bar, "Late Show," "Charlotte Webb" and "Nutty Buddy's" are mixed dance bars. The "Hershee Bar" and "Ms. P's" are lesbian bars. TACT is the Tidewater AIDS Care Taskforce. *Out N About* and *Our Own* are monthly gay and lesbian publications in Norfolk. The New Life MCC, Unitarian Universalist for Lesbian and Gay Concerns, All Gods Children Community Church and the group Dignity welcome gays and lesbians to their congregations.

LOCATION: NORFOLK IS LOCATED ON THE ATLANTIC COAST AND ALONG THE JAMES AND YORK RIVERS IN SOUTHEASTERN VIRGINIA IN THE AREA KNOWN AS THE TIDEWATER.

GAY/LESBIAN FRIENDLY BUSINESSES: 8

GAY/LESBIAN BARS AND RESTAURANTS: 9

GAY/LESBIAN ORGANIZATIONS: 12

GAY/LESBIAN RELIGIOUS ORGANIZATIONS, CHURCHES, ETC.: 4

GAY/LESBIAN BOOKSTORES: 3

GAY/LESBIAN PUBLICATIONS: 2

COMPANIES THAT PROHIBIT DISCRIMINATION: N/A

INFORMATION NUMBER: 804-622-4297, GAY INFORMATION LINE

TOTAL CRIMES: 22,209

VIOLENT = (MURDER = 62, RAPE = 204, ROBBERY = 1,428, ASSAULT = 1,075)

PROPERTY = (BURGLARY = 3,732, LARCENY = 13,535, MOTOR VEHICLE THEFT = 2,193, ARSON = 135)

Things to Do!!!

Boating and fishing of all kinds are popular in the Atlantic Ocean, Chesapeake Bay, and various lakes and rivers. Within easy distance, scuba diving in the Atlantic for sunken treasure is very popular. Other sites to see and things to do include: (1) Hunter House Victorian Museum, (2) General Douglas MacArthur Memorial, (3) Virginia Zoological Park, (4) The Water slide, (5) The Chrysler Museum, (6) Hermitage Foundation Museum, (7) Nauticus, The National Maritime Center, (8) Norfolk Botanical Garden, (9) Norfolk Naval Base and Norfolk Naval Air Station. ANNUAL EVENTS: (1)

International Azalea Festival, (2) British & Irish Festival, (3) Harborfest. SEASONAL EVENTS: (1) Virginia Symphony, (2) Virginia Opera, (3) Virginia Stage Company, Wells Theatre.

POPULATION: 253,768 PERSONS—W = 148,228, B = 102,012, AI/E/A = 1,165, C = 626, F = 4,450, M = 2,208, PR = 2,278

POPULATION GROWTH: - 4.9%

AGE OF POPULATION: (21-24) = 12.7%, (25-34) = 19.9%, (35-44) = 11.8%, (45-54) = 6.6%, (55-64) = 6.5%, (65-74) = 6.4%, (75 AND OVER) = 4.1%

HOUSING COST: OWNING = $74,500   RENTAL = $438

COMMUNITY HOSPITALS: 5 = 1,471 BEDS

CLIMATE: JAN—AVG. (39.91 DEGREES), JULY—AVG. (78.2 DEGREES), ANNUAL PRECIPITATION (44.64 INCHES)

PER CAPITA INCOME: $11,643

UNEMPLOYMENT RATE: 6.4%

JOB GROWTH SINCE 1980: + 3.6%

COST OF LIVING: N/A

EDUCATION: NORFOLK STATE, COLLEGE OF WILLIAM AND MARY, OLD DOMINION UNIVERSITY, TIDEWATER COMMUNITY COLLEGE

COUNTIES:

ARLINGTON COUNTY

Gay Civil Rights: Bans discrimination based on sexual orientation in public employment.

Towns and Cities included in Arlington County:

Arlington

WASHINGTON

STATE LAWS REGARDING HOMOSEXUALITY:

In 1976, a law went into effect that stated sexual acts between consenting adults were legal.

CITIES: (60,000 AND UP)

▼SEATTLE

Gay Civil Rights: Bans discrimination based on sexual orientation in public and private employment, public accommodations, housing, credit and union practices.

What the Locals Say . . .

The Seattle City government is very open and very liberal. There is a Lesbian serving on the city council and there are many known gay/lesbian attorneys practicing in the area. There is a large gay population living in the Seattle area. It is described by some of the locals as a very "Out and Vibrant community." The city now has a domestic partnership law on the books which at this point is only a registry and is mostly symbolic, but it is viewed as a first step toward recognizing same sex partners legally. The police chief marched in the last Gay Pride Parade. The Police Department has a Hate Crimes Division which includes crimes based on sexual orientation. A lot of gays live in Wallingford and Capitol Hill. You won't want for things to do in Seattle; there's literally an explosion of organizations, activities, and services in the area. There are sports organizations like Team Seattle, the Gay Rodeo Association, Emerald City Softball Association, Olympic Yacht Club, and Ski Buddies. Seattle abounds with social and support organizations like The Seattle Men's Chorus, Pacific Northwest Veterans Association, PFLAG, Coming of Age, Girth and Mirth Seattle, Northwest Bears, Northwest Rainbow Alliance of the Deaf, Outerlimits, Triangle Club, Gay & Lesbian Youth Association of Seattle, Youth Rap Group, Tacky Tourist Clubs of America, Lavender Panthers, and the Lesbian Resource Center just to mention a few. Political groups in the area include the Harvey Muggy Lesbian and Gay Democrats, Radical Women, Stonewall Committee for Lesbian/Gay Rights, Women's Action Coalition, and Privacy Fund. Health care for gays and lesbians is excellent. The Lesbian staffed Lesbian Health Clinic is open every 2nd and 4th Monday of the month. There's also The Lesbian Cancer Project. AIDS/HIV resources are plentiful. Among them are: ACT-UP/Seattle, Heart to Art, AIDS Prevention Project, Northwest AIDS Foundation, Fremont Public Association, Chicken Soup Brigade, and Bailey-Boushay Hospice. Lesbian/Bisexual/Gay bookstores in the area are: "Beyond the Closet Bookstore" and "Bailey/Coy Books." There are more than 35 bars and restaurants in the Seattle area. "The Timberline" is a great county/western mixed dance bar. "The Encore" is a mixed restaurant/bar. A couple of men's bars are: "Neighbors Restaurant and Lounge" and "R Place." The "Easy" and the "Wildrose Tavern & Restaurant" are both for women. Shop around - these are just a drop in the bucket. *The Greater Seattle Business Association Directory* lists between five and six hundred gay-friendly businesses. *The Seattle Gay News* comes out weekly as does *TWIST Weekly* which covers the whole state. The Lesbian Resource Center publishes a monthly newsletter called *"LRC Community News."* There's a couple of MCC churches; an Affirmations/United Methodist; a Congregation Tivah Chadasah; the Evangelicals Concerned; a Grace Gospel Church etc. Many different denominations are gay-friendly.

LOCATION: SEATTLE IS LOCATED AROUND PUGET SOUND IN NORTHWEST WASHINGTON. IT IS SURROUNDED BY THE CASCADE RANGE TO THE EAST AND THE OLYMPIC MOUNTAINS TO THE WEST.

GAY/LESBIAN FRIENDLY BUSINESSES: 500+

GAY/LESBIAN BARS, RESTAURANTS: 35

GAY/LESBIAN ORGANIZATIONS: 60

GAY/LESBIAN RELIGIOUS ORGANIZATIONS, CHURCHES, ETC.: 10

GAY/LESBIAN BOOKSTORES: 5

GAY/LESBIAN PUBLICATIONS: 5

COMPANIES THAT PROHIBIT DISCRIMINATION: SEE GAY CIVIL RIGHTS

INFORMATION NUMBER: 206-322-3953 THE LESBIAN RESOURCE CENTER OR 206-324-4297 SEATTLE GAY NEWS.

TOTAL CRIMES: 62,679

VIOLENT = (MURDER = 67, RAPE = 356, ROBBERY = 2,670, ASSAULT = 4,344)

PROPERTY = (BURGLARY = 9,247, LARCENY = 39,176, MOTOR VEHICLE THEFT = 6,819, ARSON = 320)

Things to Do!!!

The mild climate and natural surroundings give outdoor enthusiasts ample opportunities to use the beach areas for picnic areas, fishing, boating, and scuba. Other points of interest include: (1) Downtown Area-Space Needle, Monorail, Seattle Center Opera House, Playhouse, Arena and Coliseum,Fun Forest Amusement Park, International Fountain, Pacific Science Center, (2) Pikes Peak Market, (3) International District, (4) Charles and Emma Frye Art Museum, (5) Nordic Heritage Museum, (6) Museum of History & Industry, (7) Freeway Park, (8) Seattle Aquarium, (9) The Kingdome, (19) Lake Union, (20) Smith Cove, (21) Washington Park Arboretum, (22) Mount Baker-Snoqualmie National Forest, (23) Alki Beach, (24) Klondike Gold Rush National Historical Park, (25) Lake Washington Floating Bridge, (26) Seward Park, (27) Professional Sports: Football-Seahawks, Baseball-Mariners, Basketball- Supersonics. ANNUAL

EVENTS: (1) Pacific Northwest Arts & Crafts, (2) Seattle Seafair, (3) A Contemporary Theatre.

POPULATION: 519,598 PERSONS—W = 388,858, B = 51,948, AI/E/A = 7,326, C = 15,084, F = 14,689, M = 9,508, PR = 971

POPULATION GROWTH: +5.2%

AGE OF POPULATION: (21-24) = 7.6%, (25-34) = 21.7%, (35-44) = 18.1%, (45-54) = 9.2%, (55-64) = 7.4%, (65-74) = 8.1%, (75 AND OVER) = 7.1%

HOUSING COST: OWNING = $137,900   RENTAL = $463

COMMUNITY HOSPITALS: 11 = 3,046 BEDS

CLIMATE: JAN—AVG. (40.1 DEGREES), JULY—AVG. (65.2 DEGREES), ANNUAL PRECIPITATION (37.19 INCHES)

PER CAPITA INCOME: $18,308

JOB GROWTH SINCE 1980: + 11.4%

UNEMPLOYMENT RATE: 5.1%

COST OF LIVING: N/A

EDUCATION: SEATTLE UNIVERSITY, UNIVERSITY OF WASHINGTON

TOWNS: (5,000—60,000)

▼OLYMPIA

Gay Civil Rights: Bans discrimination based on sexual orientation in public employment.

What the Locals Say . . .

The lesbian community in Olympia is quite open, but the gay men's community is not as open. Olympia is unique in that it is a small town with a college and State Capitol sharing the area. Olympia has Evergreen State College which helps make the city an interesting crossing ground for liberals and conservatives. The gay and lesbian neighborhoods tend to be on the Westside and the downtown areas. Westside has older homes and the downtown area has apartments. The Evergreen Queer Alliance is a political/social group that organizes rallies or participates in other rallies. They sponsor a big Valentine Dance. The Alliance also sponsors events for National Coming Out Day, Women's Day and Labor Day. There are several Queer Punk Bands in Olympia. The Lesbian Fun Society has regular events, and the Stonewall Youth Group has special events. Olympia has women's rugby and a Gay Men's Social Network. The Olympia Film Society is an avant garde theatre. The Northwest International Gay and Lesbian Film Festival is held in Olympia. The "KLA" is a mixed dance bar. "King Solomon's Reef" is a gay restaurant, "Giant Cafe" is a mixed coffeehouse. The Olympia AIDS Task Force offers support, housing, education, and emergency financial grants, etc. *Sound Out* is a monthly gay and lesbian publication that focuses on news and social events. There are four churches that are open and affirming to gays and lesbians: St. John Episcopal Church, United Methodist, United Universalist and Eternal Light MCC.

LOCATION: OLYMPIA IS LOCATED ON THE ELLIOTT BAY, NESTLED BETWEEN PUGET SOUND AND LAKE WASHINGTON.

GAY/LESBIAN FRIENDLY BUSINESSES: 10

GAY/LESBIAN BARS, RESTAURANTS: 3

GAY/LESBIAN ORGANIZATIONS: 3

GAY/LESBIAN RELIGIOUS ORGANIZATIONS, CHURCHES, ETC.: 4

GAY/LESBIAN BOOKSTORES: 0

GAY/LESBIAN PUBLICATIONS: 2

COMPANIES THAT PROHIBIT DISCRIMINATION: SEE GAY CIVIL RIGHTS

INFORMATION NUMBER: 206-866-6000 EXTENSION 6544, EVERGREEN QUEER ALLIANCE

TOTAL CRIMES: 2,924

VIOLENT = (MURDER = 0, RAPE = 33, ROBBERY = 37, ASSAULT = 60)

PROPERTY = (BURGLARY = 313, LARCENY = 2,342, MOTOR VEHICLE THEFT = 139, ARSON = 8)

Things to Do!!!

(1) Capitol Group - Temple of Justice, Library Building, Legislative Building, Capitol Grounds, (2) State Capitol Museum, (3) Millersylvania State Park, (4) Priest Point Park, (5) Capitol Lake, (6) Olympic National Forest, (7) Tumwater Falls Park. ANNUAL EVENTS: (1) Wooden Boat Festival, (2) Capital City Marathon, (3) Super Saturday, (4) Lakefair, (5) Thurston County Fair (6) Harbor Day Festival & Tug Boat Races.

POPULATION: 36,787 PERSONS—W = 31,146, B = 420, AI/E/A = 404, C = 184, F = 198, M = 436, PR = 108

POPULATION GROWTH: + 34.0%

AGE OF POPULATION: (21-24) = 6.4%, (25-34) = 17.0%, (35-44) = 17.5%, (45-54) = 10.3%, (55-64) = 7.6%, (65-74) = 7.9%, (75 AND OVER) = 6.7%

HOUSING COST: OWNING = $77,800   RENTAL = $456

COMMUNITY HOSPITALS: 2 = 500 BEDS

CLIMATE: JAN—AVG. (38.0 DEGREES), JULY—AVG. (62.9 DEGREES), ANNUAL PRECIPITATION (50.59 INCHES)

PER CAPITA INCOME: $15,502

UNEMPLOYMENT RATE: 6.0%

JOB GROWTH SINCE 1980: + 31.6%

COST OF LIVING: 104.9
EDUCATION: EVERGREEN STATE COLLEGE

COUNTIES:
CLALLAM COUNTY

Gay Civil Rights: Bans discrimination based on sexual orientation in public employment.

Towns and Cities included in Clallam County:

Forks
Port Angeles
Sequim

KING COUNTY

Gay Civil Rights: Bans discrimination based on sexual orientation in housing and credit.

Towns and Cities included in King County:

Algona
Auburn
Bellevue
Black Diamond
Bothell
Carnation
Clyde Hill
Des Moines
Enumclaw
Federal Way
Issaquah
Kent
Kent
Kirkland
Lake Forest Park
Medina
Mercer Island
Normandy Park
Pacific
Redmond
Renton
Seatac

Seattle
Snoqualmie
Tukwila
Yarrow Point

WEST VIRGINIA

STATE LAWS REGARDING HOMOSEXUALITY:

In 1976, West Virginia repealed sodomy laws.

CITIES: (60,000 AND UP)

▼MORGANTOWN

Gay Civil Rights: Bans discrimination based on sexual orientation in public employment.

What the Locals Say . . .

Morgantown is the most culturally diverse place in the state. The city is located about an hour south of Pittsburgh. The gay and lesbian community is discreet, although fairly open. Morgantown is a college town and a small town and is a good place for gays and lesbians to live. A lot of gays and lesbians live in Morgantown but go to Pittsburgh to participate in clubs and such. "Maxwell's" is a gay-friendly restaurant. The West Virginia University Bisexual, Gay and Lesbian Mountaineers (BiGLM) is the largest organization. It is composed of students, faculty, staff and members of the community. BiGLM provides social support, and educational counseling programs for the gay and lesbian community. In October, BiGLM hosts Gay Pride Week and they bring in Nationally known speakers and performers. Womym for Womyn Potluck is a community wide social group. Equal Not Special is a political action committee. "Class Act" is the local gay and lesbian bar. The BiGLM publishes a monthly newsletter.

LOCATION: MORGANTOWN IS LOCATED IN NORTHERN WEST VIRGINIA.

GAY/LESBIAN FRIENDLY BUSINESSES: SEE PITTSBURGH

GAY/LESBIAN BARS AND RESTAURANTS: SEE PITTSBURGH

GAY/LESBIAN ORGANIZATIONS: SEE PITTSBURGH

GAY/LESBIAN RELIGIOUS ORGANIZATIONS, CHURCHES, ETC.: SEE PITTSBURGH

GAY/LESBIAN BOOKSTORES: SEE PITTSBURGH

GAY/LESBIAN PUBLICATIONS: SEE PITTSBURGH

COMPANIES THAT PROHIBIT DISCRIMINATION: N/A

INFORMATION NUMBER: 304-292-4292 GAY AND LESBIAN HELPLINE

TOTAL CRIMES: 1,362

VIOLENT = (MURDER = 0 , RAPE = 24, ROBBERY = 13, ASSAULT = 59)

PROPERTY = (BURGLARY = 208, LARCENY THEFT = 1,008 MOTOR VEHICLE THEFT = 50, ARSON = 7)

Things to Do!!!

(1) Coopers Rock State Forest, (2) Whitewater Rafting.

POPULATION: 26,679 PERSONS—W = 23,796 , B = 901, AI/E/A = 35, C = 339, F = 42 , M = 65, PR = 26

POPULATION GROWTH:- 3.4%

AGE OF POPULATION: (21-24) = 16.0%, (25-34) = 12.3%, (35-44) = 9.5 %, (45-54) = 5.8%, (55-64) = 5.8%, (65-74) = 6.5%, (75 AND OVER) = 5.0%

HOUSING COST: OWNING = $69,500   RENTAL = $355

COMMUNITY HOSPITALS: 2 = 542 BEDS

CLIMATE: JAN—AVG. (29.0 DEGREES), JULY—AVG. (72.9 DEGREES), ANNUAL PRECIPITATION (41.21 INCHES)

PER CAPITA INCOME: $10,533

UNEMPLOYMENT RATE: 5.0%

JOB GROWTH SINCE 1980: - 2.1%

COST OF LIVING: N/A

EDUCATION: WEST VIRGINIA UNIVERSITY

WISCONSIN

STATE LAWS REGARDING HOMOSEXUALITY:

In 1982, Wisconsin became the first state to adopt a gay rights bill, and in 1983, Wisconsin repealed its sodomy laws. Additionally in 1983, the age of consent was set at eighteen years of age. The state also includes crimes based on sexual orientation as hate crimes.

CITIES: (60,000 AND UP)

▼MADISON

Gay Civil Rights: Bans discrimination based on sexual orientation in public and private employment, housing, credit and union practices.

What the Locals Say . . .

Wisconsin was the first state in the country to pass a gay rights law. The city of Madison has a gay ordinance as well. The gay and lesbian population is estimated to be between 20-40,000. Even with legal protection, the community is somewhat closed. Although, Madison did have the first openly lesbian assembly person run for office and win. Gays and lesbians live throughout Madison, but there is a high number of family members in the "near east side" sometimes called the Lavender Neighborhood. This area is close to a lake, and has classy homes (about 70-80 years old), huge trees, and parks. Gays and straights, young and old live here. Politics in this area of town tend to be to the left. There are numerous coffeeshops along State Street, the strip that runs between the State Capitol and the University. The lesbian and gay sport groups are bowling, soccer, and volleyball teams. "The United" offers various support groups, peer counseling, youth groups, a local resource guidebook, and is located across from the Capitol. Madison is the site for "Action Wisconsin"; the state headquarters for gay, lesbian, transgender, and bisexual individuals. There is a gay/lesbian/feminist bookstore named "Room of One's Own." Madison also has a gay fathers group and a lesbian parenting network. "Apple Island" is an active women's space that offers dances, women entertainers (comedians and singers), and is alcohol and tobacco free. Kissing Girls Production is a lesbian theatre group. Lizards is an older lesbian organization, 10 cent society is a University of Wisconsin at Madison gay and lesbian organization. GLEE is the Gay and Lesbian Educational Employees. The "New Bar" caters to a younger crowd and is a dance bar, "Rods" is a leather bar, "The Shamrock" is a gay, straight mix, "Greenbush" serves food and has a gay and straight crowd. "Alleghre" and "Geraldine's" are mixed bars. There isn't a specific lesbian bar. The Blue Bus STD Clinic at University Health Service is an excellent resource for health needs. Madison AIDS

Support Network is well operated and well organized and is available for HIV and AIDS patients, family, friends, and partners. *The Wisconsin Light* is a statewide publication out of Milwaukee every two weeks. *In Step* is a statewide gay and lesbian magazine that is published twice a month. The following churches and groups are open to gays and lesbians: Integrity/Dignity, Affirmations, Lutheran Memorial Gay and Lesbian Fellowship, Madison Area Pagan Alliance and Reformed Congregation of the Congress.

LOCATION: MADISON IS LOCATED BETWEEN LAKE MENDOTA AND LAKE MONONA.

GAY/LESBIAN FRIENDLY BUSINESSES: 8

GAY/LESBIAN BARS, RESTAURANTS: 3

GAY/LESBIAN ORGANIZATIONS: 17

GAY/LESBIAN RELIGIOUS ORGANIZATIONS, CHURCHES, ETC.: 2

GAY/LESBIAN BOOKSTORES: 1

GAY/LESBIAN PUBLICATIONS: 3

COMPANIES THAT PROHIBIT DISCRIMINATION: SEE STATE LAWS AND GAY CIVIL RIGHTS

INFORMATION NUMBER: 608-255-8582 THE UNITED

TOTAL CRIMES: 10,616

VIOLENT = (MURDER = 2, RAPE = 99, ROBBERY = 316, ASSAULT = 214)

PROPERTY = (BURGLARY = 1,606, LARCENY = 7,466, MOTOR VEHICLE THEFT = 913, ARSON = 56)

Things to Do!!!

Madison is a recreational, cultural and manufacturing center. Specific points of interest include: (1) State Capital, (2) State Historic Museum, (3) Frank Lloyd Wright Architecture, (4) Madison Art Center, (5) Henry Villas Park Zoo, (6) Olbrich Botanical Gardens, (7) USDA Forest Products Laboratory, (8) Lake Kegonsa State Park, (9) Dane County Farmers Market. ANNUAL: (1) Paddle and Portage Canoe Race, (2) Art Fair on the Square, (3) Dane County Fair. SEASONAL EVENTS: (1) Concepts on the Square.

POPULATION: 195,161 PERSONS—W = 173,504, B = 8,109, AI/E/A = 752, C = 2,581, F = 292, M = 1,839, PR = 456

POPULATION GROWTH: + 14.4%

AGE OF POPULATION: (21-24) = 12.0%, (25-34) = 20.4%, (35-44) = 15.4%, (45-54) = 8.1%, (55-64) = 6.2%, (65-74) = 5.1%, (75 AND OVER) = 4.2%

HOUSING COST: OWNING = $75,200   RENTAL = $472

COMMUNITY HOSPITALS: 3 = 1,346 BEDS

CLIMATE: JAN—AVG. (16.0 DEGREES), JULY—AVG. (71.0 DEGREES), ANNUAL PRECIPITATION (30.88 INCHES)

PER CAPITA INCOME: $15,143
UNEMPLOYMENT RATE: 2.9%
JOB GROWTH SINCE 1980: + 17.7%
COST OF LIVING: N/A
EDUCATION: UNIVERSITY OF WISCONSIN AT MADISON, EDGEWOOD
COLLEGE

▼MILWAUKEE

Gay Civil Rights: Bans discrimination based on sexual orientation in public employment.

What the Locals Say . . .

The gay and lesbian community is both closeted and open. Politically the community is very healthy. Some people who live in Milwaukee are extremely closeted, while newcomers to the area tend to be more open. Wisconsin was the 1st state to have gay rights protection. The people of Wisconsin aren't generally the touchy/feely type out in public, and this unspoken rule applies to gays and lesbians as well. Although, nobody would say anything if you held hands. The relationship between lesbians and gay men is very segregated. The east side—(northeast of downtown) is the best place to live when you first move to Milwaukee. The area is very positive. Milwaukee is so diverse it is best to live there for awhile before determining where you want to move to stay. There are many neighborhoods, some are integrated and some are not. West of the River is a large lesbian community. The Sherman Park area is growing and is experiencing an explosion of people. The Bay View area is a good neighborhood for gays and lesbians to live. There really isn't any gay community in the suburbs. Milwaukee has something to do for just about everyone. There is a men's and women's baseball league. It is said to be home to be the gay bowling capital of the world. There are also numerous support groups. Milwaukee seems to have more than its share of small groups that get together regularly for dinner and cards, etc. There are literally hundreds and hundreds of groups. There is an annual pride festival with a march and other activities that attracted 17-18,000 participants in 1994. The majority of the bars are south of the downtown area. The following bars are predominately gay men's: "La Cage" is a dance bar, "Triangle" caters to a younger crowd, "Boot camp" is a leather Levi bar, "This Is It" caters to an older crowd, and "M & M's" caters to a yuppie crowd. The predominately lesbian bars are "Fannies" which is the largest, and "Station II." The health care system is wonderful if you can access it. The Brady East STD clinic is great. The Milwaukee area is a leader in health care. There are two newspapers for the gay and lesbian community. *Wisconsin in Step* is a statewide publication that comes out every other week, and *Wisconsin Light* is a local publication that comes out every other week. There is a strong religious community in Milwaukee. The following churches are very open to gay and lesbians: Lutheran Churches, Episcopalians, an Anglican Church, UCC, and The Sanctuary, a small MCC that is not really off the ground yet.

LOCATION: MILWAUKEE IS LOCATED IN SOUTHEASTERN WISCONSIN ON THE WESTERN SHORE OF LAKE MICHIGAN.

GAY/LESBIAN FRIENDLY BUSINESSES: 8

GAY/LESBIAN BARS, RESTAURANTS: 26

GAY/LESBIAN ORGANIZATIONS: 36

GAY/LESBIAN RELIGIOUS ORGANIZATIONS, CHURCHES, ETC.: 4

GAY/LESBIAN BOOKSTORES: 1

GAY/LESBIAN PUBLICATIONS: 2

COMPANIES THAT PROHIBIT DISCRIMINATION: SEE STATE LAWS AND GAY CIVIL RIGHTS

INFORMATION NUMBER: GAY INFORMATION SERVICES 414-444-7331

TOTAL CRIMES: 50,944

VIOLENT = (MURDER = 157, RAPE = 424, ROBBERY = 4,022, ASSAULT = 1,411)

PROPERTY = (BURGLARY = 8,250, LARCENY = 25,553, MOTOR VEHICLE THEFT = 10,615, ARSON = 512)

Things to Do!!!

In the summer, the beaches are suitable for swimming, boating, water sports, and fishing. In the winter, ice skating on ponds, trails for cross country skiing, toboggan slides and indoor ice skating are popular. Other points of interest include: (1) The Lakefront Area, War Memorial Center, Milwaukee Art Museum, Villa Terrace Decorative Art Museum, Charles Allis Art Museum, Bradford Beach, (2) Downtown Area—Pabst Theatre, Performing Arts Theatre, Milwaukee County Historical Center, Old World Third Street, Milwaukee Public Museum, Court of Honor, Discovery World, (3) Milwaukee County Zoo, (4) Mitchell Park Horticulture Conservatory, (5) Miller Brewing Company, (6) Schlitz Audubon Center, (7) Whitnall Park, (8) Professional Sports: Baseball-Brewers, Basketball-Bucks, Football-Green Bay Packers, Hockey- Admirals, Soccer-Wave. ANNUAL EVENTS: (1) Summerfest, (2) Great Circus Parade, (3) Ethnic Festivals, (4) Wisconsin State Fair, (5) Holiday Folk Fair.

POPULATION: 617,043 PERSONS—W = 398,033, B = 191,255, AI/E/A = 5,858, C = 1,416, F = 729, M = 20,988, PR = 14,028

POPULATION GROWTH: - 3.0%

AGE OF POPULATION: (21-24) = 7.1%, (25-34) = 19.0%, (35-44) = 13.4%, (45-54) = 7.9%, (55-64) = 7.7%, (65-74) = 6.8%, (75 AND OVER) = 5.6%

HOUSING COST: OWNING = $53,500   RENTAL = $418

Community Hospitals: 13 = 3,721 beds

Climate: Jan—avg. (19.9 degrees), July—avg. (73.6 degrees), Annual Precipitation (31.11 inches)

Per Capita Income: $11,106

Unemployment Rate: 5.7%

Job Growth Since 1980: - 1.7%

Cost of Living: 107.1

Education: University of Wisconsin at Milwaukee, Marquette

COUNTIES:

DANE COUNTY

Gay Civil Rights: Bans discrimination based on sexual orientation in public employment.

Towns and Cities included in Dane County:

Belleville
Black Earth
Cross Plains
Dane
DeForest
Fitchburg
Madison
Madison Township
Maple Bluff
Mazomanie
McFarland
Middleton
Monona
Mount Horeb
Oregon
Shorewood Hills
Stoughton
Sun Prairie
Verona
Waunakee

WYOMING

STATE LAWS REGARDING HOMOSEXUALITY:

In 1977, consenting homosexual relations between adults were legalized.

TOWNS: (5,000—60,000)

LARAMIE

Gay Civil Rights: None

What the Locals Say . . .

Laramie is pretty closeted. There really isn't a neighborhood or area that has a lot of gays and lesbians. Laramie does have a gay and lesbian casino night, Valentine dance, spring picnic, summer camp-out called Rendezvous, a Thanksgiving Dinner the Sunday before Thanksgiving. On National Coming Out Day, there are a variety of activities including guest speakers and dances. Wyoming does not have any gay bars because the population could not support one. The closest gay bar is in Fort Collins, Colorado, a 45 minute drive. Ft. Collins also offers the Ft. Collins Gay & Lesbian Support Group and the Lambda Community Center and a MCC Family in Christ Church. Cheyenne is about 1 hour 15 minutes away and offers the Cheyenne Gay Men's Support Group and Southeast Wyoming AIDS Project. The University of Wyoming has the LGBTA. One of the most popular activities for gays and lesbians in Laramie is private parties. Some family members will call the hot line from time to time and tell them of upcoming parties so they can invite newcomers. The newsletter is called the *United Voice.* The health care rapport between the gay and lesbian community is good. ACAP (Albany County AIDS Project) is located in Laramie.

LOCATION: LARAMIE IS LOCATED IN SOUTHEASTERN WYOMING.

GAY/LESBIAN FRIENDLY BUSINESSES: 5

GAY/LESBIAN BARS AND RESTAURANTS: 0

GAY/LESBIAN ORGANIZATIONS: 2

GAY/LESBIAN RELIGIOUS ORGANIZATIONS, CHURCHES, ETC.: 0

GAY/LESBIAN BOOKSTORES: 0

GAY/LESBIAN PUBLICATIONS: 1

COMPANIES THAT PROHIBIT DISCRIMINATION: N/A

INFORMATION NUMBER: 307-632-5362 UNITED GAYS AND LESBIANS OF WYOMING

TOTAL CRIMES: 1,034

VIOLENT = (MURDER = 1, RAPE = 5, ROBBERY = 6, ASSAULT = 66)

PROPERTY = (BURGLARY = 90, LARCENY = 828, MOTOR VEHICLE THEFT = 38 ARSON = N/A)

Things to Do!!!

(1) Laramie Plains Museum, (2) Lincoln Monument, (3) Wyoming/Colorado Railroad, (4) Wyoming Territorial Park, (5) Medicine Bow National Forest, (6) Snowy Range Ski Area.

POPULATION: 28,868 PERSONS—W = 24,857, B = 245, AI/E/A = 201, C = 233, F = 25 , M = 1,157 , PR = 20

POPULATION GROWTH: + 10.1%%

AGE OF POPULATION: (21-24) = 14.4 %, (25-34) = 18.0 %, (35-44) = 13.2 %, (45-54) = 7.2%, (55-64) = 5.2%, (65-74) = 4.2%, (75 AND OVER) = 3.3%

HOUSING COST: OWNING = $66,900   RENTAL = $343

COMMUNITY HOSPITALS: 1 = 110 BEDS

CLIMATE: JAN—AVG. (20.0 DEGREES), JULY—AVG. (64.1 DEGREES), ANNUAL PRECIPITATION (10.88 INCHES)

PER CAPITA INCOME: $11,652

UNEMPLOYMENT RATE: 3.1%

JOB GROWTH SINCE 1980: + 17.8%

COST OF LIVING: N/A

EDUCATION: UNIVERSITY OF WYOMING

Appendices

United States Sodomy Law

Alaska	California
Colorado	Connecticut
Delaware	Hawaii
Illinois	Iowa
Indiana	Kentucky
Maine	Nebraska
Nevada	New Hampshire
New Jersey	New Mexico
New York	North Dakota
Ohio	Oregon
Pennsylvania	South Dakota
Tennessee	Texas
Vermont	Washington
Washington, D.C.	Wisconsin
West Virginia	Wyoming

United States Sodomy Law

STATES WHERE HETEROSEXUAL AND HOMOSEXUAL SODOMY IS ILLEGAL

Alabama	Arizona
Florida	Georgia
Idaho	Louisiana
Massachusetts	Michigan
Minnesota	Mississippi
North Carolina	Oklahoma
Rhode Island	South Carolina
Virginia	Utah

United States Sodomy Law

STATES WHERE HOMOSEXUAL SODOMY IS ILLEGAL

Arkansas	Kansas
Maryland	Missouri
Montana	

United States Sodomy Law Map

MAP COURTESY OF NATIONAL GAY & LESBIAN TASK FORCE
UPDATED JANUARY 1994

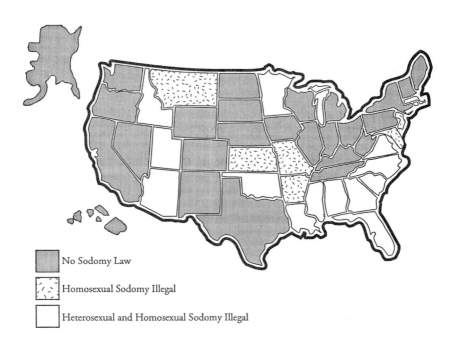

No Sodomy Law

Homosexual Sodomy Illegal

Heterosexual and Homosexual Sodomy Illegal

Domestic Partners Benefits List

JULY 1994

Benefits include medical and health insurance coverage for the domestic partners of company/agency/municipal employees, unless otherwise note. The definitions of domestic partner vary slightly, generally requiring a statement or affidavit by two adults affirming that they are in a committed partnership, are each other's sole domestic partner, share the common necessities of life, and are responsible for each other's welfare.

I. Private sector

Adobe Systems: Sunnyvale, CA; Computer software

Ask/Ingres; San Mateo, CA; Computer software

Apple Computer; Cupertino, CA; Computers/Computer software

Autodesk, Inc.; Sausalito, CA; Computer software

Banyan Systems; Westboro, MA; Computer software

Bay Area Rapid Transit; San Francisco, CA; Transportation

Bell-Northern Research; Canada; Telecommunications

Ben & Jerry's Homemade Inc.; Waterbury, VT; Consumer Goods

Berkeley Unified School District; Berkeley, CA; Public Schools

Beth Israel Medical Center; New York, NY; Hospital

Borland International; Scouts Valley, CA; Computer software

Boston Children's Hospital; Boston, MA; Hospital

The Boston Globe; Boston, MA; Publishing

Blue Cross and Blue Shield of Massachusetts; Boston, MA; Insurance

Cadence; San Jose, CA; Computer software

California Pacific Medical Center; San Francisco, CA; Hospital

Chiron Corp.; Emeryville, CA; Biotech

Consumer United Insurance Co.; Washington,DC; Insurance

DEC-Belgium; Computers/computer software

Fannie Mae; Washington, DC; Financial

Fred Hutchinson Cancer Research Center; Seattle,WA; Hospital

Frame Technology; Boston, MA; Computer software

Gardner's Supply Co.; Burlington, VT

Domestic Partners Benefits List

JULY 1994 (continued)

Genetech Corporation; South San Francisco, CA; Pharmaceuticals
Golston and Storrs; Boston, MA; Law
Group Health Cooperative; Seattle, WA; Hospital
Home Box Office; New York, NY; Entertainment
Interleaf; Boston, MA; Computer software
International Data Group; Framington, MA; Publishing
kaiser Permanente; Oakland, CA; Hospitals
Levi Strauss Corporation; San Francisco, CA; Clothing manufacturing
Lotus Development Corporation; Cambridge, MA; Computer software
MCA/Universal; Hollywood, CA; Entertainment
Microsoft, Inc.; Seattle, WA;Computer software
Milbank, Tweed, Hadley, & McCloy; New York, NY; Law
Mintz, Levin, Ferris; Boston, MA; Law
Montefiore Medical Center; New York,NY; Hospital
NeXt Computer; Redwood City, CA; Computer software
Northern Telecom; Telecommunications
Oracle Corporation; Redwood City, CA; Computer software
Orrick, Herrington and Sutcliffe; San Francisco, CA; Law
Quark, Inc.; Boulder, CO; Computer software
Para Transit Inc.; Sacramento, CA
Seattle Mental Health Institute; Seattle, WA; Healthcare
Seattle Times; Seattle, WA; Publishing
The Segal Company; Boston, MA; Benefits consulting
Shiff, Harden and Waite; Chicago, IL; Law
Silicon Graphics Inc.; Mountainview, CA; Computer software
Sun Microsystems; Milpitas, CA; Computers/Computer software
SuperMac Technologies, Sunnyvale, CA; Computer software
Starbucks Coffee; Seattle, WA; Consumer goods
Sybase Inc.,Berkeley, CA; Computer software
Thinking Machines Company; Cambridge, MA; Computer software
Time, Inc.; New York, NY; Publishing

Domestic Partners Benefits List

JULY 1994 (continued)

Village Voice, New York, NY; Publishing
Warner Brothers Pictures; Hollywood, CA; Entertainment
Ziff Davis; New York, NY; Publishing

II. MUNICIPALITIES

Alameda County, CA	Delaware, NJ	Oak Park, IL
Ann Arbor, MI	East Lansing, MI	Oakland, CA
Baltimore, MD	Hartford, CT	Rochester, NY
Berkeley, CA	Henepin County, MN	Sacramento, CA
Boston, MA	Ithaca, NY	Santa Cruz, CA
Brookline, MA	King County, WA	San Francisco, CA
Burlington, VT	Los Angeles, CA	Seattle, WA
Cambridge, MA	Madison, WI	Takoma Park, MD
Chicago,IL	Marin County, CA	State of Vermont
Dane County, WI	Minneapolis, MN	Washington, DC
West Hollywood, CA		

III. Educational Institutions

Albert Einstein College of Medicine	Stanford University; Palo Alto, CA
American University; Washington, DC	Swarthmore College; Swarthmore, PA
Clark University; Worcester, MA	University of Chicago; Chicago, IL
Colby College; Waterville, ME	University of Colorado; Boulder, CO
Columbia University; New York, NY	University of Iowa; Iowa City, IA
Cornell University; Ithaca, NY	Univ. of Minnesota; Minneapolis, MN
Massachusetts Institute of Technology;	University of Pennsylvania;
Cambridge, MA	Philadelphia, PA
Middlebury College; Middlebury, VT	Wellesely College; Burlington, VT
Pitzer College; Claremont, CA	Williams College; Williamstown, MA
Pomona College; Pomona, CA	Yale University; New Haven, CN
Simmon College; Boston, MA	University of Wisconsin; Madison, WI
Smith College; Northampton, MA	

Domestic Partners Benefits List

IV. Non-Profit Organizations

American Civil Liberties Union; San Francisco, CA
American Friends Services Committee
American Psychological Association, Washington, DC
Episcopal Church of Newark, Newark, NJ
Greenpeace International; Washington, DC
Human Rights Campaign Fund, Washington, DC
KQED Radio, San Francisco, CA
Lambda Legal Defense & Education Fund; New York, NY
Los Angeles Philharmonic; Los Angeles, CA
Minnesota Communications Group/Minnesota Public Radio; St. Paul, MN
Museum of Modern Art; New York, NY
National Gay & Lesbian Task Force Policy Institute; Washington, DC
National Organization for Women; Washington, DC
National Public Radio; Washington, DC
Planned Parenthood Association; New York, NY
Union of American Hebrew Congregations; Washington, DC
WGBH; Boston, MA

National Bulletin Boards

NAME	STATE	PHONE #	BAUD RATE	COMMENTS
Ten Forward	AB	403 424-3258	9600	
The Beast	AB	403 433-3787	14.4	leather
Visions	AB	403 791-0372	9600	
Ban-Aids	AL	205 264-8090	14.4	
Southern Stallion	AL	205 322-3816	16.8	
DataLynx	AL	205 328-7688	2400	
Infinite Diversity	AL	205 554-1687		
Glee Club	AL	205 758-6367	2400	
Civic Forum	AL	205 880-1979		
Byte Me!	AL	205 979-2983	14.4	
Fire! & Ice Hotel	AZ	602 246-1317	14.4	
2SF	AZ	602 252-6194		
Cloud 9	AZ	602 254-9682	14.4	
Taz's Temple	AZ	602 265-6976	14.4	
Planet X	AZ	602 279-3060	14.4	$
Realm - Black Stallion	AZ	602 371-3457	Gay areas	
Grotto	AZ	602 437-9100	14.4	
Nick's Place	AZ	602 789-1100	14.4	
Lavander Ranch	AZ	602 804-1767	14.4	Lesbian / Females Only
Desert Connection	AZ	602 827-9465	2400	
Firestarter	AZ	602 970-4626	19.2	
Petting Zoo	AZ	602 992-0019	2400	
Dykes Express	BC	604 263-1989	2400	
The Gay Exchange	BC	604 540-7071	19.2	
Bi-Choice	BC	604 540-0618	14.4	
Lambada Speaks	BC	604 681-3667	14.4	
PC Workshop	BC	604 682-0914	14.4	
Kitsilano	BC	604 683-0421	14.4	
684-Play	BC	604 684-7529	14.4	$
Access 1	BC	604 736-7850	9600	$
Neon Sky	CA	209 237-8219	2400	
Mindquest	CA	209 549-2711		
Death Vally Free Priz.	CA	209 551-8329	14.4	
Just Another BBS	CA	209 579-2949		
GLADD LA	CA	213 658-6516	2400	
Luv Conection	CA	213 663-6886	2400	$
DAIMP	CA	213 825-3736		
Starchat	CA	213 849-4048	2400	$

National Bulletin Boards (continued)

NAME	STATE	PHONE #	BAUD RATE	COMMENTS
Online BBS	CA	213 876-8589	14.4	$
Hankie Express	CA	213 899-7981		
Board With No Name	CA	310 274-9544	2400	
Delos	CA	310 274-0585	14.4	$
Thor's International	CA	310 289-0345	2400	
Ath-Elite	CA	310 358-9222	14.4	500 number avail.
Butch's Board	CA	310 436-3299	2400	$
Video Gay	CA	310 558-4336	2400	
Route 66	CA	310 652-1066	28.8	$
Modem Boy	CA	310 659-7000	2400	$
Pacific Coast Highway	CA	310 842 8790	14.4	$ #'s for surounding area codes
ASI	CA	408 248-0675	2400	
Trex II	CA	408 294-6969	2400	inhibit error control
HTG/Outreach	CA	408 374-6608	14.4	
Santa Cruz Online	CA	408 458-2528	14.4	
Wizard's Castle	CA	408 559-7062		
The Shrine	CA	408 747-0778	9600	
MEATing Place	CA	408 926-6174	14.4	pswd=ORA
San Jose Connection	CA	408 956-8819	14.4	$
Tatertots News & Mail	CA	415 255-8340	14.4	
Trex II	CA	415 327-2194	2400	inhibit error control
Wally World	CA	415 349-6969	28.8	thousands of GIFs
Chaz	CA	415 362-2227		
Love Bytes	CA	415 383-2983		
Studs	CA	415 495-2929	14.4	$
Lambda	CA	415 572-2591	9600	$
PC Bear's Lair	CA	415 572-9626	2400	$
Paradise	CA	415 572-8263	2400	
HTG/Outreach BBS	CA	415 572-9594	14.4	$
AIDS Information	CA	415 626-1246	2400	AIDS
Keyhole	CA	415 626-9419	9600	anal,fisting, & bondage
NoName North	CA	415 661-0847	2400	$
Five Star	CA	415 703-0150	14.4	$
Eye Contact	CA	415 703-8200	2400	$
Hopper's World	CA	415 749-1254	2400	
Backdoor	CA	415 756-9587	2400	$ pwd=leather
Station House	CA	415 821-4273	2400	$ pw=gay 14.4 avail. sub.
NoName (North)	CA	415 826-9626	14.4	$
AIDS Action	CA	415 863-9718		
Bears Anonymous	CA	415 863-8921	14.4	
Fog City	CA	415 863-9697	2400	$
SF Oyster	CA	415 864-0890		
Alternatives	CA	415 922-5489		
California Connexion	CA	415 927-2739		
Balboa BBS	CA	500 488-0112	19.2	$
Big Board	CA	510 247-1056	14.4	$
Sir James	CA	510 261-6863	14.4	
Night Creature	CA	510 481-9774	14.4	

National Bulletin Boards (continued)

NAME	STATE	PHONE #	BAUD RATE	COMMENTS
Zebra Collection	CA	510 540-7228	$	
Gay Burbs	CA	510 893-4423	14.4	other area code numbers
ANDROS	CA	619 233-6253	14.4	
Hillcreast Community	CA	619 291-0544	9600	
Boy Board/Lambda Lounge	CA	619 452-2998	14.4	
Gay Lists	CA	619 484-8866	14.4	
Synchronicity	CA	619 523-1252		
HOMO	CA	707 546-9259		
MadHouse	CA	707 747 6380	12.2	req. adult access
Hiding Place	CA	707 887-0381	14.4	
Taboo Topics	CA	714 240-8480	2400	14.4 availb.
Eyes of the World	CA	714 526-6738	2400	request G/L/B access
ReSourse System	CA	714 539-3894	2400	pswd: rainbow
Waveline	CA	714 563-9421	2400	$
Heaven West	CA	714 572-8500	14.4	pswd: gay
ConnecXions	CA	714 597-1884	2400	
Heaven West	CA	714 666-2393	2400	
Pleasure Connection	CA	714 773-5326		
Ziggy's Diner	CA	714 776-4230	14.4	$ pswd: gay
West World	CA	714 828-3727	9600	
Butch's Board	CA	714 891-2667	2400	
EnigmaScape	CA	805 541-4012	14.4	
Thunder Penguin	CA	805 685-7742	9600	Comment to SysOp
New Frontiers	CA	805 724-1800	14.4	
True Colors	CA	805 823-1431		
Delos	CA	818 242-2365	2400	$
Athelete's Bench	CA	818 247-2282	2400	$ 9600 avail.
Alternate Lifestyles	CA	818 287-9285	9600	$
Mog-urs EMS	CA	818 366-1238		
Talk Channel	CA	818 506-0620	2400	$
SM Board	CA	818 508-6796	2400	$ 14.4 avail. sub.
Oracle I	CA	818 509-9681	2400	$ 14.4 avilb. sub.
Star*Games	CA	818 566-3026		
Skinner Jack's	CA	818 760-2147	9600	$
Cross Connection	CA	818 766-8887	9600	$ TV/TS Support
Stonewall West	CA	818 781-9506	9600	
Singles	CA	818 883-5065	14.4	req. dlo sp comm pkg
Stonewall	CA	818 907-1684	2400	
Joystick	CA	818 952-1311	14.4	pwd=gaynet
Starchat	CA	818 954-0790	2400	$
Secrets	CA	818 960-5260	14.4	
Oracle III	CA	818 980-6743	2400	$ pwd=gay
Lambda Online	CA	818 985-4153	2400	
X!!!	CA	818 989-3740		
Library	CA	818 999-4391	14.4	
Acropolis	CA	916 967-5817		
Leather First	CA	916 974-1262	2400	
Blue Parrot Cafe	CO	303 321-4281	2400	

National Bulletin Boards (continued)

NAME	STATE	PHONE #	BAUD RATE	COMMENTS
NixPix	CO	303 375-1263	2400	$
Leather Company	CO	303 399-4385	14.4	
Denver Exchange	CO	303 458-1227	2400	$
Lambda Cove	CO	303 832-7596	2400	$ 14.4 avail
The Network	CO	303 861-7528	14.4	$ pswd=GA Y
Male Box	CO	719 637-0532	14.4	
Lifestyles BBS	CT	203 481-4836	14.4	$
Lambdaconn II	CT	203 877-6667	28.8	$
Emerald City	CT	203 934-0026	9600	$
HRCF-NET	DC	202 639-8735	2400	Politics/Info
Cockpit	DC	202 728-0055	14.4	
QueerCom	DE	302 323-0535	14.4	
East Coast Bears	DE	302 947-1790	9600	
PC Powerstation	FL	305 383-2341	14.4	
Rainbow Connection	FL	305 388-2816	14.4	
MineShaft	FL	305 477-0558	14.4	$
Tool Shed	FL	305 748-3159	2400	$
Underground	FL	305 791-3272	2400	
Jailhouse	FL	305 944-6271	9600	
Dracula's Castle	FL	305 964-2696	9600	
Gaylink	FL	407 381-8228		
Oneline Network	FL	407 632-0334		
Alternat Network	FL	407 633-6018	14.4	
Compu Who?	FL	407 645-4833	2400	$ 14.4 avail. sub.
Compu-Link	FL	407 856-0385	2400	$
Adonis BBS	FL	407 881-8641	14.4	$
Compass Popints	FL	407 966-4709	2400	
Mercury Opus	FL	813 327-3556	2400	
Trans Action	FL	813 371-8395	14.4	TV/TS
Special Place	FL	813 372-7525		
Mistybase II	FL	813 546-1912		
Lambda Unlimited	FL	813 576-0656	14.4	
Eternal Quest	FL	904 353-9031	14.4	request g/l/b access
Experimental	FL	904 375-7555		
Charles'	FL	904 396-4931	9600	
Arcobalendo di Speranza	FL	904 432-0997	14.4	
Picture Perfect	FL	904 629-4501	14.4	Adult with gay area
Sun-Sand-Surf Resort	FL	941 486-8010	14.4	Florida List Contact pswd=gay
Dreamerz	GA	404 237-3094		
The Gay Church	GA	404 264-1202		
Trash Shack	GA	404 320-0026	14.4	
The Logic Board	GA	404 325-8476	2400	
Meet Factory	GA	404 350-0308	2400	
Southeastern Express	GA	404 361-9880		
AIDS Infoline	GA	404 377-9563		
Midnight Express	GA	404 381-5959		
Manor II	GA	404 432-8330	9600	$
No Frills BBS	GA	404 435-9608	14.4	

National Bulletin Boards (continued)

NAME	STATE	PHONE #	BAUD RATE	COMMENTS
1st United Church	GA	404 552-8336	14.4	
Our House	GA	404 881-8319	2400	
Cruise Street	GA	404 892-6971	2400	
Over the Rainbow	GA	404 962-7629	$	
Graffiti Online	GA	404 972-4999	2400	$ 14.4 avalb
The Party Line	GA	404 974-7136	2400	
Hotlanta Chatline	GA	404 992-5345	9600	
Hitchhiker	GA	404 997-7899	2400	
Reno's Tavern	HI	808 531-8581		
GQ Link	HI	808 599-4577		
Tropical Night	HI	808 623-0702	14.4	
Alternatives CBIS	IA	515 285-1190	16.8	
Modem Men	IA	515 945-6636	14.4	
Thunderbolt!	IL	312 248-0109	14.4	
After the Bars	IL	312 262-3626	2400	9600 avail. sub.,
Esmerelda's Palace	IL	312 288-4491	14.4	TV
Talamasca	IL	312 334-9092	14.4	
Cock Pit	IL	312 337-2410	2400	$ 14.4 avail.
PLeasure Palace	IL	312 384-7957	14.4	$ mixed with gay areas
10% Connection	IL	312 478-0419	9600	Lesbian with gay areas
The Zoo	IL	312 743-9791	2400	$ 14.4 avalb. sub.
I&E System Of Chicago	IL	312 751-9194	2400	pw=list, 9600 avail.
MAHIE	IL	312 772-5958	14.4	AIDS & HIV info
Orgasm	IL	312 772-0168	14.4	$ password= the best
Scandals	IL	708 356-5633	28.8	
RISQILLY !!!!!!!!!!	IL	708 495-6609	14.4	HOME of the G&L BBS LIST
RISQILLY !!!!!!!!!!	IL	708 495-6609	28.8 avail.	
Metro	IL	708 653-6467	14.4	$
Absolute Pleasure	IL	708 677-3369	14.4	$ adult with g/l sections
Hot Rocks	IL	708 690-2902	28.8	
Love Connection	IN	317 236-6740	2400	$
G.A.P.O.I.	IN	812 283-5755	14.4	
Geneva Convention	IN	812 284-1321	2400	$
Electronic Male	IN	812 333-1912	14.4	
Resource Center	IN	812 877-4342		
Land of Awes	KA	316 269-4208	2400	
Male Exchange	KA	913 649-6603	2400	14.4 avail.
Side Streets	KA	913 649-9053		
On the Town	KY	606 252-6636	9600	
Hot Tub	KY	606 441-2941	2400	
Rainbow Cafe	LA	504 340-9893	14.4	
Leather Connection	LA	504 454-0380	14.4	$
Isle of Man	LA	504 866-6716	2400	$ 14.4 avail. sub.
Toyshoppe	MA	413 747-8459	14.4	$
Bit Bucket	MA	508 892-7176	14.4	
Kangaroo Court	MA	508 970-2458	9600	
Cruise	MA	617 254-3201	2400	$
SSS	MA	617 383-2789	9600	$

National Bulletin Boards (continued)

NAME	STATE	PHONE #	BAUD RATE	COMMENTS
Block Party	MA	617 662-5445	2400	$
The Den	MA	617 662-6969	2400	$
Grooves	MB	204 475-0147	14.4	
Flying PcAt	MD	301 206-9162	14.4	
Dupont Plaza	MD	301 208-0832		
PAAINE BBS	MD	301 235-8530		
Connections	MD	301 560-1086	2400	$
Jim's Dreams	MD	301 581-1422		
Purple Haze	MD	301 661-8861	2400	$
Agora	MD	301 924-1582		
Honey Board	MD	301 933-1655	9600	
Hotline	MD	310 596-8102	14.4	$
Harbor Bytes	MD	410 360-6874	14.4	$ G&L; HI V/AIDS info
Our Place	MD	410 542-7730	2400	
Photoshop	MD	410 720-6317	14.4	
Hotline	MD	410 799-8102	14.4	$
RendezVous	MD	410 876-5029	2400	pw=oracle
Vacation Spot	MI	313 487-8239	9600	
Distant Horizons	MI	313 677-0513	14.4	
Babybear's Playden	MI	313 839-3430	14.4	req. dlo sp comm pkg
Flaming Dragon	MI	517 336-7846	14.4	
Magnolia Candlelight	MI	601 939-5622	14.4	
Sysops BBS	MI	810 333-2352	14.4	dlo appl. for gay areas
Fountains Of Pleasure	MI	810 348-7854	2400	
Midnight Sun	MI	810 540-3616	14.4	
Blue Light Special	MI	810 542-6619	14.4	
Night People	MI	810 569-1299	2400	
Minnesota Underground	MN	507 835-8001	2400	adult/leather/S&M
Top City	MN	612 225-1003	2400	
R Place	MN	612 225-8397	2400	$ 14.4 avail.
Outlines	MN	612 560-1870	9600	
Friendship Express	MN	612 566-5726	2400	$
Sound Sourse	MN	612 645-7083	14.4	
Cloud 9	MN	612 871-4885		
Green & Yellow	MN	612 879-0313	14.4	$
Carolyn's Closet	MN	612 891-1225	14.4	
Minnesota Info. Exch.	MN	612 894-1642	9600	HI V/AA/NA
The Aviary	MO	314 544-2569	14.4	
Maggie's Place	MO	314 642-7144		
Citadel	MO	314 664-6877	14.4	$ AIDS, TV/TS
Hotflash	MO	314 771-6272	2400	$ pw=gaylist
Metro	MO	314 780-2282	14.4	
Toad Hall	MO	314 965-0662		
ARC Angel Express	MO	417 864-4573	14.4	
The Lair	MO	816 356-4554	14.4	
Boardroom to Bedroom	MO	816 483-7018	14.4	
Neon Blue	MS	601 329-3247	19.2	pswd=Gay
Magnolia Candlelight	MS	601 939-5622	14.4	

National Bulletin Boards (continued)

NAME	STATE	PHONE #	BAUD RATE	COMMENTS
Kudzu Konnection	MS	601 957-1259	28.8	
Exchange BBS	NC	704 342-2333	2400	$
Split Images	NC	704 637-6541	2400	
Pink High Heels	NC	910 686-4932	$	
Quest	NC	919 288-3738	2400	
GLIE	NC	919 783-7261	2400	
Pink Triangle	NC	919 846-9443		
Christopher Street	NJ	201 328 0741	14.4	New Number
Nat'l Gay Teens Org.	NJ	201 402-9043	14.4	Ages 12 - 20 ONLY
Arbitrage	NJ	609 347-6028	14.4	spec. comm software req,
La Dolce Vita	NJ	609 722-0499	14.4	
Inferno	NJ	609 886-6818	9600	
Amazon's	NJ	609 933-1721	14.4	
The Underground	NJ	908 262-9666	2400	
Isle-Net	NJ	908 495-6996	2400	$
Best Buy	NJ	908 634-5117	$	
Backroom II	NJ	908 758-1122	2400	NJ LIST Contact - 28.8 avail.
GLEAM	NJ	908 821-1684	14.4	$
Xonk's World	NJ	908 828-5008	14.4	
gLiTcH	NJ	908 968-7883	9600	$
Visual Impact	NV	702 248-0825	28.8	
Art Gallery South	NV	702 255 8241	28.8	
Transitions	NV	702 366-9633	2400	
Spirit Knife	NV	702 656-7654	14.4	
Sisters, Fam, & Frnds	NV	702 891-8532	14.4	request g/l/b access
Magic Flute	NV	702 891-8532	9600	
Virtual Exchange	NY	212 267-5030	14.4	$
Communication Special	NY	212 645-8756	14.4	
Bears Cave	NY	212 677-7426	2400	
Male Stop	NY	212 721-4180	2400	$
Village	NY	212 780-9653	14.4	$
Male Forum	NY	516 689-0286	28.8	$ 212 ac number aval.
Grafix	NY	516 689-2853	9600	$ adult with G/L subsection
Pride	NY	516 785-6080	14.4	
Utopian	NY	516 842-7518	2400	$
Gay '90s	NY	516 867-1671	14.4	
Special Friends	NY	607 724-8533	2400	$
Pier	NY	716 253 3583	14.4	28.8 avail.
Multicom 4	(Rochester) NY	716 473-4070	2400	
Multicom 4	(Buffalo) NY	716 633-1111	2400	
Info Society	NY	716 684-8307		
Rendezvous	NY	716 773-6224	2400	$
Channel 33	NY	718 279-1585	28.8	$
Wall-2	NY	718 335-8784	14.4	
New York Online	NY	718 596-5881	14.4	$
Night Stick	NY	718 898-9195	14.4	$ Leather, Uniforms, Bears
The Backroom	NY	718 951-8256	2400	$ 14.4 at 718-951-8445

National Bulletin Boards (continued)

NAME	STATE	PHONE #	BAUD RATE	COMMENTS
Flatline	NY	914 565-9030	14.4	
Lotu!	NY	914 961-0399		
Free-Net	OH	216 368-3888	2400	
Bill & Bob's Place	OH	216 741-5888	2400	$
Insomniac	OH	216 940-2722	14.4	
Connecting Point	OH	419 255-4350	2400	
Pleasure Dome	OH	419 829-6129	14.4	
The Levee	OH	513 222-6107	9600	
G/L/B Dayton	OH	513 461-6000	14.4	
C G A L	OH	513 867-0998	14.4	$
Carol's Closet	OH	614 389-1719	14.4	TV/TS
Gay Male Connection	OH	614 529-8112	14.4	
Warden Diamond	OK	405 677-5278		
Gayblade	OK	405 949-2090	16.8	
Other Side of Mirror	OK	918 838-7755	21.6	$
Dungeon	ON	416 926-8734	2400	
Kaikatsu na Sakaba	ON	416 968-1174	28.8	$
Pigpen	ON	613 723-3143	14.4	
King's Knight	ON	613 728-4122	14.4	$
Menage	ON	613 728-0411	14.4	
Gay Blade	ON	905 882-4800	14.4	$
Connection	ON	905 889-2563	14.4	$
Hot Pockets	OR	503 232-2803	2400	$
Illuminations	OR	503 285-6632	28.8	
1st Choice Comm. I	OR	503 291-9815	14.4	
Gay Net	OR	503 295-0877	14.4	
Club Eugene	OR	503 345-7988	14.4	AIDS/reqst. G/L access
Diplomat	OR	503 659-5712	14.4	
Worldsys	OR	503 661-3578		
Gase Support	OR	503 786-0355	14.4	
The Keystone	PA	215 242-3716	14.4	
Lambda Connection	PA	215 336-4361		
Afro_American BBS	PA	215 844-8145	2400	
Dru Com	PA	215 855-3809		
The Door	PA	610 372-0177	19.2	$ pw=hunks
Club Philadelphia	PA	610 626-7398	9600	
Locker Room	PA	610 691-0491	14.4	
Bill & Rob's Place	PA	610 940-0284	14.4	
Stonewall's Haven	PA	717 843-2361	9600	
QG-Alpha	QC	418 651-8528	14.4	French Language
Le Grand Souk	QC	514 253-6963		
L'Entre Nous	QC	514 478-4863	2400	
Mike O's	QC	514 528-8878		
S-TEK	QC	514 597-2409	14.4	$
Le Bec Du Bonheur	QC	514 831-8571	14.4	French Language
Big Dogs	SC	803 769-6131	14.4	
Capital Connection	SC	803 926-9810	14.4	$ mail in reg. form
Starfire Couriers	SK	306 359-1423	14.4	

National Bulletin Boards (continued)

NAME	STATE	PHONE #	BAUD RATE	COMMENTS
Southern Nights	TN	615 367-6755	14.4	
Personals	TN	901 274-6713	14.4	
Riverside	TN	901 373-5348	9600	
Gay Fido	TN	901 377-8280		
Second Wind	TN	901 382-9466		
Two's Company	TN	901 680-9250	2400	
Lambda World (GSN)	TX	210 646-7061	14.4	message based system
First Time	TX	214 231-5250	Ft Worth # avail.	
Dallas Mandate	TX	214 528-1816		
Your Place or Mine	TX	214 602-1070		
Dallas Chat Line	TX	214 954-6900	2400	
Dallas Alt Lifestyles	TX	214 954-6969	2400	
D&D Computer	TX	409 899-4573		
BetterDays&BetterLayz	TX	512 250-0848		
Private Pleasures	TX	512 339-6268	14.4	$ cmnt sysop for G/L/B access
Nudie Bar	TX	512 396-7254		
Austin Party Board	TX	512 442-1116		
Arda	TX	512 443-6844		
Health Link BBS	TX	512 444-9908		
Club Orion	TX	512 447-1860		
Alpha Complex	TX	512 478-3332		
Turnabout	TX	512 525-0583	2400	
Tangled Triangle	TX	512 835-4848	14.4	
Water Closet	TX	512 836-8071		
Austin City Limits	TX	512 836-8287		
Lambda Link	TX	512 873-8299	9600	
C.D.S. BBS	TX	512 887-0787	14.4	$
Hotlines	TX	512 918-1238	14.4	
HAL	TX	713 530-7500	2400	
Bear's Den	TX	713 550-9243	14.4	
Pink Triangle	TX	713 779-2434	2400	
Isle Of Lucy	TX	713 868-3140	2400	
Private Line	TX	713 933-0499	14.4	
PIC of MID Town	TX	713 961-5817	9600	
PC Datalink	TX	806 655-7918		
Momentary Lapse	TX	806 762-2902		
National Gay DB	TX	817 277-5403		
Diamond's Mine	TX	817 322-5488	mixed	
Stallions Coral	TX	817 545-7317	9600	
Starbase Lamda	TX	817 577-3618		
White House	TX	817 696-0791		
Park!	TX	817 752-1939		
Other Side	TX	817 847-7749	2400	$
Vital Signs	UT	801 255-8909	14.4	
Expresso Yourself	UT	801 486-6397	16.8	reqst G/L/B access
Meat Market	UT	801 487-5245		
Magic Carpet	UT	801 565-1216	9600	$ pswd=GA Y
Hot Bauds	UT	801 964-9560	9600	$

National Bulletin Boards (continued)

Name	State	Phone #	Baud Rate	Comments
Fergussi	VA	703 271=4080	14.4	$ $
Bear Com	VA	703 525-5136	2400	$
The Male Image	VA	703 556-9472	14.4	Scott Day's Color Boys
GLIB	VA	703 578-4542	14.4	$
Interlace	VA	703 893-0470	2400	$
Pleasure Dome	VA	804 490-5878		
Imperial	VA	804 740-3093	14.4	
Reality, Ink.	VA	804 750-1776	14.4	
The Room Next Door	WA	206 223-8763	14.4	$
Spectrum	WA	206 271-9552	14.4	
STAGE	WA	206 286-8047	2400	$ 14.4 avail.
Man Hole	WA	206 322-2246	14.4	
S&M Exchange	WA	206 325-4191	9600	$ Bondage, Kink, Leather, S&M
Pink Triangle	WA	206 340-8531	14.4	
Paradise Lost	WA	206 365-7435	2400	
Beyond The Grave	WA	206 433-7652	14.4	request gay access
Imagination Station	WA	206 440-9212	14.4	
28 Barbary Lane	WA	206 525-2828	2400	$ 14.4 avail.
Puget Sound	WA	206 743-0162	14.4	$
Paul's Waka Waka	WA	206 783-7979	28.8	Chubbies,Chasers & Bears
Pride Line	WA	206 788-2230	14.4	
Bubba's	WA	206 854-0896	2400	
Emerald Onramp	WA	206 860-9766	14.4	
Rendezous	WA	206 860-1557	14.4	
Two Babes	WA	206 885-4236	14.4	$ 100's of Lesbian GIFs
The Mall	WA	206 935-6255	2400	$
Hidden Desires	WA	509 457-6663		
Spawning Grounds	WA	509 965-9562		
Powerline	WI	414 276-9574		
Crossroads	WI	414 282-0494	2400	$ pswd=gay
GLINN Multi-Board	WI	414 289-0145	2400-14.4 avail.	
Back Door	WI	414 744-6969	28.8	$
Starcomm	WI	414 873-6969	9600	
Party Board	WI	608 258-9555	2400	$

International Bulletin Boards

BBS Name	Ctry Cd	Phone #	Baud Rate	Country/Notes
Bi Link Netherlands	+31	104766313	28.8	Netherlands (bisexual)
Gay Palace	+31	104423725	14.4	Netherlands
Fantastico	+31	1883247650	2400	Netherlands -Dutch Only
The Darkside	+31	206969263	14.4	Netherlands
Gay Private	+31	206147671	14.4	Netherlands
HIV+BBS in Holland	+31	206647461	14.4	main AIDS info bbs
Male & Male Gay	+31	206693616	14.4	Netherlands
Apollo people	+31	250719774	14.4	Netherlands - not nice
Lambda Line Int.	+31	592 056895	14.4	Netherlands
gay-biseks CRUISING	+31	703450380	14.4	Netherlands
Gaypix	+31	889450289	14.4	Netherlands
GayPar	+32	26753117	19.2	Belgium
Gay Impact - Paris	+33	145227018	28.8	France
Datafobi Act Up BBS	+358	0257969	2400	Finland
Slurps	+358	01352121	2400	Finland
Western Salon	+43	5224-56168	14.4	Austria
Queery Box	+43	732 314877	14.4	Austria
Chapps	+44	131 539 1132	14.4	United Kingdom
Lambda Edinburgh	+44	131 556 6316	2400	United Kingdom
Hawks Castle	+44	1344411 621	16.8	United Kingdom
Ground Zero	+44	1376511 581	9600	United Kingdom
Forum	+44	1482466 312		United Kingdom
Min of Software	+44	1522210 151		United Kingdom
Boysville	+44	116 255 9171	14.4	United Kingdom
Mr Magic	+44	1638743 655	14.4	United Kingdom
Mininet 3	+44	1642672 813		United Kingdom
Ooh !	+44	181 395 3108	19.2	United Kingdom
Rainbow's End	+44	181 459 3440	9600	United Kingdom
Pos+Net	+44	181 695 6113	14.4	United Kingdom
Pink Triangle	+44	181 963 1411	14.4	United Kingdom
Cloud Nine	+44	181 806 7802	2400	United Kingdom
Ready Room	+44	192253644	14.4	United Kingdom
Phantasmagoria	+44	1933402224	14.4	United Kingdom
Nigth Owls	+46	13-143828	14.4	Sweden
Gay Telegraph	+46	8326152	2400	Sweden - 14.4 avail.
SGBB	+49	406907117	14.4	Germany

International Bulletin Boards (continued)

BBS Name	Ctry Cd	Phone #	Baud Rate	Country/Notes
Aigytos BBS	+49	511-713986	14.4	Germany
GayLife BBS	+49	6074-5113	14.4	Germany
Devil's Gay Land	+49	711-339079	14.4	Germany
Pink PANTHER	+49	821-586850	14.4	Germany
Wupperbote BBS	+49	202-450353	14.4	Germany
Trabbi's Paradise	+49	202-4781434	14.4	Germany
GAY-BOX Niederberg	+49	2053-41282	14.4	Germany
Omega	+49	208-762546	14.4	Germany
C-Sphinx	+49	211-318807	14.4	Germany
Derendorfer	+49	211-445721	14.4	Germany
GayWorld-GERMANY	+49	211-5580425	14.4	Germany
GAYCOMM Port 1	+49	2161-601635	14.4	Germany
Nightman	+49	2203-294327	14.4	Germany
Die Baerenhoele	+49	221-708519	9600	Germany
GAYLINE -cologne-	+49	221-737134	14.4	Germany
BlueBocs	+49	231-72617261	14.4	Germany
Male Box	+49	5126-81116		Germany
Message Box	+49	2351-62466	14.4	Germany
Creative Brains	+49	2352-23234	14.4	Germany
Wharft	+49	241-523772	14.4	Germany
Pink Harmony	+49	241-604398	14.4	Germany
Gay Box - Bremen	+49	421-6168191		Germany
Mac's Box	+49	2434-6768	14.4	Germany
TMB	+49	30-75357443	14.4	Germany
HIVNETBerlin	+49	30-8618673	14.4	Germany
TERRA BBS	+49	30-8210307	14.4	Germany
Boybox Dresden	+49	351-4940804	14.4	Germany
Words	+49	40-28052015	14.4	Germany
CMS GAY	+49	5221-67127	14.4	Germany
MICOS I	+49	5222-16687	14.4	Germany
Amiga Venture	+49	5265-7515	14.4	Germany
Dao-Lin-H'ay	+49	5281-79372	14.4	Germany
Gay Box	+49	531-72054	14.4	Germany
Goliath Box	+49	5453-80077	14.4	Germany
SAVOY	+49	5624-8011	14.4	Germany
Rainer's MB	+49	5722-3848	14.4	Germany
COM Mailsystem	+49	6104-65547	14.4	Germany
Splash	+49	611-503571	14.4	Germany

International Bulletin Boards (continued)

BBS Name	Ctry Cd	Phone #	Baud Rate	Country/Notes
UranusBBS	+49	6131-384590	14.4	Germany
BmU	+49	6187-27166	14.4	Germany
Gay Power BBS	+49	69-2979530	14.4	Germany
NICE BITS BBS	+49	69-4960751	14.4	Germany
Pegasus BBS	+49	69-519804	14.4	Germany
NAFETS	+49	69-835841	14.4	Germany
Young Gay	+49	711 6076178	14.4	Germany
Viviane	+49	711-9924566	14.4	Germany
Infopool Stuttgart	+49	7152-56330	14.4	Germany
The Filing Dutchman	+49	7248-8711	14.4	Germany
Beatit	+49	8251-999991	14.4	Germany
Kuschelbox	+49	8441-81908	14.4	Germany
SemmyGro	+49	89-3545419	14.4	Germany
Bavaria	+49	89-405722	14.4	Germany
KNUSPER-BOX 2	+49	89-4481795	14.4	Germany
Pink Cadillac	+49	89-6257611	14.4	Germany
Tadzio	+49	89-657447	14.4	Germany
OASE	+49	89-6883262	14.4	Germany
Diver-Mailsystem	+49	89-6920837	14.4	Germany
Manbox	+49	9129-9621	14.4	Germany
Manni's Mailbox	+49	9372-8351	14.4	Germany
Panik BBS	+49	941-379607	14.4	Germany
Schatz-Truhe	+49	941-993961	14.4	Germany
PinkBoard	+61	23316370	14.4	Australia
Wsateland	+61	38598977	9600	Australia
Axiom	+61	35094417	9600	Australia
Big Ted's	+61	34172440	14.4	$ Australia
Bridge	+61	3686-6107	14.4	Australia
Where Life Begins	+61	37954900	9600	Australia
Millenium 2 areas	+61	62825199	14.4	Australia - ask for gay
Far Northern News	+61	70331553	9600	Australia
Atom	+61	78121249	9600	Australia
Forgottem Realms	+61	72883680	9600	Australia
Soft-Tech	+61	78691131	9600	Australia
Edge of Reality	+61	78861886	9600	Australia
Pleasure Dome	+61	75787652	9600	Australia
Sideways Board	+64	4384-2323	14.4	$ New Zealand

International Bulletin Boards (continued)

BBS Name	Ctry Cd	Phone #	Baud Rate	Country/Notes
Meetboard	+64	4384-3914 14.4		$ New Zealand
Portunus' Little CBCS	+64	9372-5454	2400	New Zealand
BorderLine	+64	9376-2901	2400	New Zealand
GayBos	+64	9817-7364	2400	New Zealand
Sexy MF	+64	9528-9880	2400	New Zealand

$ = Pay System
AIDS = AIDS information (May or may not be gay)
TV/TS - has a separate sections for TV/TS or is mainly TV/TS
pw= password if needed

As of Jan. 92 we no longer list 300 baud or part time BBS's
As of Jan. 95 we no longer list 1200 baud systems

To add, delete or update the list, we need the following information:

BBS Name
Phone Number & Area Code & Country & State or Province
Top Baud Rate
Do They Charge?
Any special notes.

PLEASE send as much information as possible to:

THE LIST message area on RISQILLY BBS in Chicagoland, (708-495-6609) or leave a note to the Sysop there.

(Guest access available and North American LIST database online) or Sysop at Logoff on BACKROOM II, Rumson, NJ, (908-758-1122)

(Guest logon as   1st name LIST   last name GUEST, password: visitor) or to the sysop SUN, SAND, and SURF BBS in Venice, FL, (914-486-8010)
(Guest logon as GUEST, password: visitor) (list file password = GAY)

International Bulletin Boards (continued)

WARNING:

Bulletin board systems go up and down constantly, so the information contained in this list may already be obsolete the day after it is released. Remember to monitor your modem phone calls to new numbers and don't just keep re-dialing the same number over and over. Be courteous when visiting someone's home via modem.

If you get a phone number that is no longer in service or is answered by someone (voice), please apologize and tell us as soon as possible so we may make the changes as soon as possible.

The Copy of **THE LIST** on Risqilly is updated daily.

THE GAY & LESBIAN BBS LIST - June 1995
Published monthly by Risqilly BBS 708-495-6609   Chicagoland * 1985 - 1995
10 years serving the Gay & Lesbian Community
Copyright (c) 1995 - All Rights Reserved

This list may be copied, but only in it's original and complete form.

Companies that Don't Discriminate

Participating Fortune 1000 Companies that offer significant domestic partner benefits for the same-sex partners of their employees, including medical and dental coverage, child care benefits, family/personal/sick leave (partner care), and bereavement leave:

APPLE COMPUTER INC
LEVI STRAUSS ASSOCIATES INC
MICROSOFT CORPORATION
SILICON GRAPHICS INC
VIACOM INC

Participating Fortune 1000 Companies that have a non-discrimination policy that includes sexual orientation:

3M
ADVANCED MICRO DEVICES INC
AETNA LIFE & CASUALTY CO
APPLE COMPUTER INC
BANK OF AMERICA
BANK OF BOSTON CORP
BANKERS TRUST COMPANY
BAY VIEW CAPITAL CORP
CALIFORNIA FEDERAL BANK
CBS, INC
CIGNA CORPORATION
COMDISCO
COMMONWEALTH EDISON
CORESTATES FINANCIAL CORP
DAYTON HUDSON CORP
DOW CHEMICAL CO
DUN & BRADSTREET CORP
EL DU PONT DE NEMOURS & CO
EASTMAN KODAK CO
FANNIE MAE
FIRST BANK SYSTEM
FORT HOWARD CORP

Companies that Don't Discriminate (continued)

GANNETT CO INC
GENERAL MOTORS CORP
H B FULLER CO
HARLEY DAVIDSON INC
HERMAN MILLER INC
IBM
J E SEAGRAM CORP
LEVI STRAUSS ASSOCIATES INC
MARRIOTT CORP
MASSMUTUAL LIFE INSURANCE
MCCAW CELLULAR COMMUNICATIONS
MICROSOFT CORP
NEW YORK LIFE
NEW YORK TIMES CO
NORTHERN TRUST COMPANY
PACIFIC GAS & ELECTRIC
PARAMOUNT COMMUNICATIONS,INC
PENN MUTUAL LIFE INSURANCE CO.
PINNACLE WEST CAPITAL CORPORATION
PITNEY BOWES INC
POLAROID CORP
PUBLIC SERVICE ELECTRIC & GAS
RJR NABISCO HOLDINGS CORP
SAN FRANCISCO FEDERAL
SILICON GRAPHICS INC
SOUTHWESTERN BELL CORPORATION
SPRINT COMMUNICATIONS
ST. PAUL COMPANIES
SUNTRUST BANKS
SUPERMARKET GENERAL CORPORATION
TEACHERS INSURANCE & ANN ASSO OF
THE PROCTER & GAMBLE CO.
THE PRUDENTIAL INSURANCE COMPANY
TIMES MIRROR CO
U.S. BANCORP
U.S. WEST, INC.

Companies that Don't
Discriminate (continued)

UJB FINANCIAL CORPORATION
UNUM LIFE INSURANCE COMPANY VIACOM
WACHOVIA CORPORATION
WALT DISNEY COMPANY
WASHINGTON MUTUAL SAVINGS BANK
WELL FARGO & CO.

Courtesy of National Gay & Lesbian Task Force
October 15, 1993

The following Governmental Agencies have employment policies that bar discrimination:
▼The Federal Bureau of Investigation
▼The Department of the Interior
▼The White House
▼The Department of Housing and Urban Development
▼The Department of Transportation
▼The Office of Personnel Management
▼The State Department

Bibliography

Alyson Publications. (1994-1995). The Alyson Almanac. (3rd Ed.). Boston, MA: Author.

American Chamber of Commerce Research Association. (1994). Cost of Living Index. Third Quarter.

Green, Frances (Ed.). (1994). Gay Yellow Pages: The National Edition. New York, New York: Renaissance House.

National Gay and Lesbian Task Force Policy Institute (Eds.). (1994). Lesbian, Gay and Bisexual Civil Rights In The United States. Washington, DC: National Gay and Lesbian Task Force.

National Gay and Lesbian Task Force Policy Institute (Eds.). (1994). The Right To Privacy In The United States (Sodomy Map). Washington, DC: National Gay and Lesbian Task Force.

National Gay and Lesbian Task Force Policy Institute (Eds.). (1993). Fortune 1000 Survey. Washington DC: National Gay and Lesbian Task Force.

National Gay and Lesbian Task Force Policy Institute (Eds.). (1994). Domestic Partner Benefits List. Washington DC: National Gay and Lesbian Task Force.

National Gay and Lesbian Task Force Policy Institute (Eds.). (1994). Private Companies With EEO Protection. Washington DC: National Gay and Lesbian Task Force.

National Lesbian and Gay Journalists Association (Eds.). (1995) Employers/Unions With Domestic Partner Medical Benefits. Eureka, California.

Travel Publications, Inc. (Eds.). (1995). Mobil 1995 Travel Guide (Vols. Mid-Atlantic, California and the West, Great Lakes, Northwest and the Great Plains, Southeast, Southwest and South Central, Northeast). New York, New York, Fodor's.

United States Bureau of the Census, County and City Data Book: (1994). Washington, DC: United States Government Printing Office, 1994.

United States Department of Justice. (1993). Federal Bureau of Investigations Crime In The United States. Washington DC: United States Government Printing Office.

NEW CITIES, TOWNS, OR COMMUNITIES

Are you living in a place or do you know of a place or places that should be included in the next revision of this book? If so, please fill out the form below and send to the address noted at the bottom of the page.

CITY & STATE CONTACT #	CONTACT ORGANIZATION

Send To:

RELOCATION STATION
1725 B. MADISON AVENUE
SUITE #774
MEMPHIS, TN 38104

OR

E-MAIL US AT

AOL = GRPL2MOVE OR

COMPUSERVE = 102164,2115

Great Gay & Lesbian Places to Live
"The Official Guide"

PLEASE SUPPORT YOUR LOCAL BOOKSTORE

THIS BOOK SHOULD BE AVAILABLE AT YOUR NEAREST GAY OR FEMINIST BOOKSTORE, AND IT WILL PROBABLY BE AVAILABLE AT OTHER BOOKSTORES AS WELL. IF YOU CAN'T GET THIS BOOK LOCALLY, ORDER BY MAIL USING THIS FORM.

• •

ENCLOSED IS $16.95 FOR THE BOOK, GREAT GAY & LESBIAN PLACES TO LIVE.. (ADD $1.00 POSTAGE WHEN ORDERING JUST ONE BOOK. IF YOU ORDER TWO OR MORE, WE'LL PAY THE POSTAGE.)

NAME: _____

ADDRESS:_____

CITY:_____ STATE: _____ ZIP: _____

• •

RELOCATION STATION
1725 B. MADISON AVENUE, SUITE 774
MEMPHIS, TENNESSEE 38104